THE NEW ROBBER BARONS

How Bankers Created an International Oligarchy

JANET M. TAVAKOLI

Lyons McNamara LLC

Revised edition with appendices and index, 2026.

Published by Lyons McNamara LLC, Chicago, Illinois.

Tavakoli, Janet M.
The New Robber Barons: How Bankers Created an International Oligarchy / Janet M. Tavakoli

ISBN-10: 0985159030
ISBN-13: 978-0-9851590-3-0 (Paperback Edition)

Books by Janet Tavakoli

NONFICTION

Risk

Decisions: Life and Death on Wall Street

Unveiled Threat: A Personal Experience of Fundamentalist Islam and the Roots of Terrorism

The New Robber Barons

Dear Mr. Buffett: What an Investor Learns 1,269 Miles from Wall Street

Structured Finance and Collateralized Debt Obligations

Credit Derivatives and Securitization (3rd Edition)

Finance Classics

Fifty Years in Wall Street
Parts One and Two
By Henry Clews.
Foreword by Janet Tavakoli.

The Wall Street Point of View
By Henry Clews.
Foreword and Annotations by Janet Tavakoli.

Twenty Years of Inside Life in Wall Street
or
Revelations of the Personal Experience of a Speculator
(Annotated)
By William Worthington Fowler.
Foreword and Annotations by Janet Tavakoli.

FICTION

Financial Fiction by Janet Tavakoli

Archangels: Rise of the Jesuits
"Conspiracies within conspiracies, a fast-paced thriller"
—*Publishers Weekly*

Janet Tavakoli writing as Michael K. Clancy

Zombie Apocalypse:
Three Complete Novels (The Origin / WILDFIRE / Ghost Territory)

Zombie Apocalypse: The Origin

Zombie Apocalypse 2: WILDFIRE

Zombie Apocalypse 3: Ghost Territory

Zombie Apocalypse 4: Rise of the Dead

Acknowledgments

I would like to thank the many people who offered comments, encouragement, and suggestions. In particular, I thank Libby Fischer Hellmann. Without her generous encouragement and advice, this compilation would never have been completed.

Many of these articles, particularly the later ones, first appeared online, and several were featured prominently on the front page of the *Huffington Post*. Arianna Huffington and the professional staff at the *Huffington Post* handled every question and request at the speed of light. I am also grateful to "Tyler Durden" at ZeroHedge.com, Barry Ritholtz at The Big Picture, Henry Blodget and the team at Business Insider, Karl Denninger at Market-Ticker.org, the team at FT Alphaville, the blog at the *Wall Street Journal*, the team at the *New York Times*' DealBook, Michael Shedlock, Andrew Tobias at Money and Other Subjects (andrewtobias.com), Robert Wenzel, Ron at Wall Street Pit Group, "Arthur Cutten" at Jesse's Café Américain, Steve Megremis (dailybail.com), and many others. They honored my work by sharing their web real estate to feature, excerpt, quote, or comment on it.

I would also like to thank Nancie Poulos, Arturo Cifuentes, Hilary Till, Pamela van Giessen, William J. Mikus, David Pelleg, Edward Stone, Jim Rogers, J. Allan Meyer, and Rita Ilse Guhrauer, as well as the many people who did not wish to be named but who served as sounding boards.

The opinions and theories in this book do not necessarily represent those of the people I have thanked. I alone am responsible for any errors, statements, interpretations, or conclusions.

Contents

Books by Janet Tavakoli iii

Acknowledgments v

Preface 17

CHAPTER 1 Bailouts for the Oligarchs 21

Proposed Alternative to the Various Versions of the Paulson Plan 21

The Emergency Economic Stabilization Act of 2008 21

More Phony Accounting 22

Warren Buffett Urged Mark-to-Market Accounting 22

Treasury Secretary Henry Paulson Was a Section 8 23

Selling Democracy On the Cheap 23

Ponzi Schemes and Stress Tests 25

Wall Street and Washington Hope You Are Gullible: Disappoint Them 28

Bankers Get Bonuses, the USA Gets the Great Recession 28

Global Ponzi Scheme 29

More Bonuses for Bankers, a Deeper Recession for the USA 29

Reform Starts with the President and Congress 30

2012: Voters Nix Incumbents, Demand Financial Reform and Fed Fraud Audit 31

CHAPTER 2 Goldman Sachs: "God's Work" 33

Jamie Dimon and Warren Buffett Were Warned AIG Had Serious Trouble One Year Before the September 2008 Crisis (and Goldman Sachs Knew Too) 33

Goldman Knew (or Should Have Known) the Consequences 35

Details of AIG's Trades Were Kept Secret Even by the SEC 36

Goldman Sachs Worried About Billions in Crippling Losses 37

Wall Street's Advice to Joran van der Sloot (satire) 37

Free Copies for the Grand Jury 39

AIG Paying Out Millions in Bonuses 40

Did AIG Insure Dodgy Mortgage Products for Goldman Sachs? 41

AIG Bubble: Irrational Exuberance 42

Goldman's Lies of Omission 43

Goldman Abhors Conflicts of Interest (for Others) 47

Goldman's Conflicts of Interest 48

David Viniar and Ralph Cioffi 49

Goldman's Undisclosed Role in AIG's Distress....49
Backdoor Bailout for Goldman Sachs....52
Goldman's Turn to Apologize....53
AIG Continued to Write Risky CDO Protection After 2005 [Lewis and TIME are Incorrect.]....53
Goldman CEO Lloyd Blankfein to Treasury Secretary Hank Paulson: "OK, Now What?" (Humor)....55
Goldman Sachs: Bullies on the Block....55
Money Cartel's Yes Men....56
Investigating a Criminal Cover-Up....58
Dodd-Frank Reform Failure: "Customer Transactions" Were Behind the Meltdown....59

CHAPTER 3 Caveat Emptor....61
Bank of America Says Merrill's Huge Hit was in December (Not November)?....61
Merrill's Murder/Suicide....63
Ken Lewis Must Go....64
Bank of America's Shareholders Should Reject Bonus Plans....64
JPMorgan's Losses From Indecent Exposure....68
Financial Reform Failure....68
"Scared Sh*tless"....68
Ramp up Risk and Cross Your Fingers....69
Jamie Dimon and Robert Rubin: Evasive on "Fraud as a Business Model"....70
Jamie Dimon's Evasion....71
Robert Rubin Dodges Responsibility....72
The Biggest Headache for Investors in Groupon and Facebook....73
Impermanent Value....74
Mark Zuckerberg's Value Problem: "My" Facebook Profile Was a Fraud,So Was "Warren Buffett's"....75
The Antisocial Network....76
Investors Should Take Note of Phony "Users"....77
Reasonable Questions....77
The "Social Network" Broke the Social Contract....77

CHAPTER 4 Gold and Silver....79
Washington Must Ban U.S. Credit Derivatives as Traders Demand Gold....79
Speculators Want U.S. CDS Payoffs in Gold....80
Global Disaster in the Making....80
Washington Must Ban U.S. Credit Derivatives: Games and Gold (Part 2)....81
Gold is Collateral on the London CME....81
Sovereign Credit Default Swap Contracts: Tower of Babble....82

Regulators "Can't Find" Evidence of Market Manipulation 82
Time for Reform is Overdue 83
How to Corner the Gold Market 83
Gold Game Changer: J.P. Morgan Accepts Bullion as Money 87
Abolish Credit Default Swaps on Sovereign Debt 88
Destruction of the Volcker Bubble Deflator 88
Trifecta of Absent Financial Regulation: CDS, Currencies, Commodities 89
Today's Silver Scandal 89
Back to the Future 90
Price Manipulation: Look for Motive 91
The Silver Arbitrageurs 91
The Silver Foxes 92
Silver Price War 93
Absent Regulation 93

CHAPTER 5 Criminal Behavior 95
Madoff Deserves Lots of Company 95
A Giant Ponzi Scheme 95
SEC Strategy 96
Complicated and Cryptic 96
Bonuses 96
Premise of *Fortune* Cover Story is Incorrect 96
Investment Fund Managers: Nine Warning Signs 97
These nine warning signs alarm the savviest money managers in the world: 97
Wall Street's Fraud and Solutions for Systemic Peril 99
Delusional Complacency 100
Existing Solutions to Halt Growing Systemic Risk 101
Banging the U.S. Stock Market 103
IKB's CEO Found Guilty of Market Manipulation
Some U.S. Bank CEOs Should Also Face Charges 105

CHAPTER 6 Pundits and Junk Science 107
Reporting v. PR: Meredith Whitney and AIG 107
Taleb Kills $20 Billion Mythical Swan 110
The Market Can Stay Irrational
Longer Than You Can Stay Solvent (or Patient) 111
Taleb's Stranded Swan? 112
Winners' Swan Dive 113
Gasparino's Glass Jaw Was CNBC's Draw 115
Footwork Needs Work 116
Gasparino Can't Take a Punch 116
Where Were Drama Pundits When It Mattered? 117
Meredith Whitney's Unreported Death Threats
(See also: "Reporting v. PR") 117

Nassim Nicholas Taleb's Backfiring Blunderbuss (See "Taleb Kills $20 Billion Mythical Swan" and "Taleb's Stranded Swan?") ... 118
Gasparino's Shadow Boxing (See also: Gasparino's Glass Jaw Was CNBC's Draw) ... 119
Serious Issues For Serious People ... 120
Michael Lewis: Junior Salesgirlieman ... 121
Michael Lewis is Wrong Again: It was Fraud ... 123
Wealthy Patriots Wage Class War ... 123
Fraud "Blind Spot" ... 124
Audience Calls for Integrity ... 125
"Countrywide Broke the Law. Homeowners Did Not." ... 125
CCGA and Academia Need to Get Their Crimes Straight ... 126
Class Warfare ... 127

CHAPTER 7 Politicians' Inaction ... 129
President Obama's Right to Free Speech ... 129
Washington's Bipartisan Betrayal: The 2015 Global Financial Crisis ... 131

CHAPTER 8 Rating Agencies ... 135
Revoke Rating Agencies' NRSRO Designation for Structured Products ... 135
Ackman Versus Wall Street's Ponzi Scheme ... 136
"Friends in High Places" ... 136
Bankers Get Bonuses, USA Gets the Great Recession ... 138
Tavakoli Structured Finance Revokes Credit Rating Agencies' NRSRO Designation: Issues and Solutions for Restoring Credibility to the Credit Rating Agencies and Rehabilitating the Alternative Banking System ... 139
I. REVOCATION OF THE NRSRO DESIGNATION ... 139
A. Rating Agencies' Role in the Financial Collapse: The Sovereign Effect ... 141
B. Rating Agencies' Current Practice Is Junk Science ... 144
II. NOT MERE OPINIONS: PART OF REGULATORY AND MARKET FRAMEWORK ... 145
A. Ratings Cartel: Moody's, S&P, and Fitch ... 146
III. RATING AGENCIES LACK REASONABLE STANDARDS: DODD-FRANK'S MISSES ... 147
A. Rating Scales Are Self-Defined: Benchmarks and Methodologies Change Arbitrarily ... 148
B. Rating Agencies' Excuses for Heterogeneous, Multi-year Failures ... 150
IV. MISRATING COMMERCIAL FINANCIAL SERVICES' SECURITIZATIONS 1995-1998 ... 151
A. Underwriter Hired Analysts Who Rated the Deals ... 152

B. Rating Agencies Relied on Biased Proxy Data and Ignored Statistical Principles 152
C. Rating Agencies Ignored Statistical Principles and Red Flags for Three Years 153
D. Rating Agencies Ignored an Audit and "A Classic Situation for Fraud" 153
V. CONSTANT PROPORTION DEBT OBLIGATION SCANDAL 2006-2008: LEVERAGED CREDIT BETS 155
A. CPDOs: Phony "AAA" Ratings for New Structured Credit Products 155
B. Moody's Is Exposed Having Changed CPDO Rating Methodology 156
C. Moody's: Both Methodology and Integrity Were Questionable 157
D. CPDO Investors Lost Most of Their Principal on New "Aaa" Rated Products 157
E. Standard & Poor's Also Claimed a Model Error and Defended Its Unsound Methodology 157
VI. RATING AGENCIES' ROLE IN THE FINANCIAL MELTDOWN 158
A. Misrated From the Start: RMBSs, CDOs, CDO-Squared 159
B. Credit Derivatives: Documentation Risk Not Captured By Ratings 160
C. 2006 Onward: Tail End of a Ponzi Scheme 161
D. Raters' Role in Violation of Securities Laws: "Investment Grade Rated" Was Junk 162
E. Merrill Lynch's Example of Ponzi Finance 163
F. Merrill Lynch: Signs of A Classic Control Fraud 165
G. Monoline Insurers 166
H. Rating Agencies' Misrepresentations Throughout 2007 and Beyond 167
VII. SOVEREIGN RATINGS 168
A. Sovereign Rating Example: Iceland's "Aaa" 169
B. United States: "AAA" in Label Only 170
VIII. RESTORING CREDIBILITY: WHAT REGULATORS MISSED AND WHAT THEY GOT RIGHT 173
A. Create Objective Benchmarks and Rating Scale: Revoke the Raters' Ability to Legislate 173
B. Solution: Eliminate "Mezzanine AAA" Tranches and "Super Senior" Tranches 174
C. Focus Is On Wrong Metrics with Uninformed Guesses as Model Inputs 175
D. Rating Agencies Must Review Evidence of Underwriters' Due Diligence 177
E. Rating Accuracy Should Be the Only Measurement of Success 179
F. Conflicts of Interest: Chinese Wall Is Needed 180
G. Conflicts of Interest: Joint Ventures 181
H. Conflicts of Interest: Banks and Rated Entities Hiring Raters' Employees 181
I. Mistaken Idea: Rating Agencies Design Securities 182
J. A Mistaken Idea On Fees, and the Real Fee Issue 182
K. Ban Credit Derivatives and Total Return Swaps in Rated Structured Financial Products 183

L. Other Derivatives in Rated Structured Financial Products....184
M. "Managed" Deals....184
N. An Observation: "Agencies" are Companies; Shareholders Cannot Govern Rating Agencies....185
O. Thwarting Dodd-Frank: Risk Retention and "Conflict of Interest" Transactions....186
IX. CONCLUSION....187

CHAPTER 9 Fannie Mae and Freddie Mac 191
"Fraud As a Business Model"....191

CHAPTER 10 Warren Buffett's Twist: "Please, sir, I want some more." 195
Warren Buffett's Wall Street War....195
Warren Buffett, Stop Using My Credit Card!....197
Warren Buffett and Charlie Munger: Winning the Class War....200
Warren Buffett Jumped the Squid....200
Charlie Munger's War....201
Buffettgate: An Unenforced Policy Isn't a Policy....202
Berkshire Hathaway's Cover Story....203
Warren Buffett and the Boys of Wall Street....204
A Question of Character....204
"What Motivates You?"....205
Buffett's Gentle Treatment by the Financial Press....206
If It Isn't "Unlawful," Why Did Buffett Give the SEC "Very Damning Evidence?"....207

CHAPTER 11 The "Regulators" 209
Inside the Wall Street Journal's Future of Finance Initiative....209
Treasury Cover-Up of Goldman's Role in AIG Crisis....211
Timothy Geithner, I Call Your Bluff....214
Show Bernanke and Geithner the Door....216
Congress Exposes Profiteering in AIG's Deals: Delay Enabled Cover-Up....219
Plenty of Time to Renegotiate AIG's Contracts....219
Details That Could Anger the Public....219
Profiteering and Track-Covering: Possible Reasons for Redaction....221
Congress's FCIC Nearly Nailed Former Citigroup Executives to the Wall—Then Blew It....222
President Obama: Bring Back William Black....224
Failed Regulators Are Still in Charge....224

CHAPTER 12 Media Circus 227
ProPublica's (and *NY Times'*) "Untold" Magnetar Story Creates Excuses for Wall Street and Washington....227

Classic and Massive Ponzi Scheme 228
Washington Ignored Pre-Crisis Media Reports 228
Tavakoli's Top Ten Business Books (satire) 230
2011: The Year *60 Minutes* Misled Americans About Municipal Bonds 231
A "Performance" 232
A Wild Guess 233
Genuine Research via Bloomberg 233
A Stellar Performance 234
CNBC Schools 60 Minutes 234

CHAPTER 13 The Eurozone 235
Wall Street's Advice to the IMF: Control Your Alleged Rapists! (satire) 235
Jeopardizing Our Health 235
Targets Can Shoot Back 235
The IMF Can't Even Negotiate "Consensual Sex" 236
Remember Whom You're Supposed to Be Screwing 236
Euro Endgame 237
Euro: Super Deutsche Mark with a French Accent 238
Deep Discounts: If PIIGS Owe You Money, You're in Trouble 239
Endgame for the Euro 240
"Standard" Credit Default Swaps on Greece Are a Sham and It's Not a Surprise 240
First Step in a CDS: Protect Yourself from the ISDA Cartel 241
Language Arbitrage: You're Not a Sucker, You're a Customer 242

CHAPTER 14 MF Global Implodes 243
Credit Derivatives and Leverage Sank MF Global 243
MF Global Admitted "Diverting" Money from Segregated Accounts 243
Liar's Poker 244
More Liar's Poker 244
Rogue Trader and Questionable Risk Management 244
CFTC's Unprecedented Failure to Move Customers' Assets Before FCM's Bankruptcy 244
MF Global Revelations Keep Getting Worse 246
Implausible Denial and an Ugly Surprise 247
"Repo-to-Maturity" is a "Total Return Swap-to-Maturity," A Type of Credit Derivative 248
Probable Shortfalls Throughout 2011 250
Regulators Waive Required Tests for Jon Corzine 250
Jon Corzine to Credit Derivatives Head: Next Time "Double Up" (See note below) 251
MF Global Becomes a Primary Dealer Unregulated by the Fed: How Did That Happen? 252
MF Global Stalled and Wrote Rubber Checks 252

Tip-Offs for Some Customers? 253
CFTC's Gary Gensler Didn't Act 253
MF Global Debacle Damages a Key Global Market 254
Is Crony Capitalism Wrong? 254
Apparent Damage Control: That's How They Roll 256
Breach of Then Treasury Secretary Paulson's
Duty as a Public Steward 257
Corzine Dodges the Fraud Question 258
Corzine Knew or Should Have Known About an Alleged Federal Crime 259
"Finding" Money Doesn't Excuse Fraud 259
Never Allowable to Filch Customers' Funds 260
At Issue is Massive Fraud 260
Rehypothecation Is An Old Story: MF Global's Story Is a Different
Story of Filched Funds 261
Lies, Cover-ups, and Rubber Checks While Corzine Headed MF Global .262
Filched Funds 262
Another Potential Crime: Did MF Global
Misrepresent Source of Funds to the Fed? 263
CME Head Terry Duffy: Under Corzine, Inaccurate Report Kept
Regulators in the Dark 264
Allowable Rehypothecation: Problematic, But
A Different Problem Than MF Global's 265
Honest People Don't Look for Malicious Loopholes 266
Congresswoman Marcy Kaptur Confronts
MF Global and Wall Street 267
A Few Good Men and Women 268
Representative Hayworth:
"Goldman Sachs former partners... respect you greatly." 268
Representative Huizenga: "Thousands feel cheated" 269
Are the Congressmen From New Jersey Going Easy on Corzine? 269
Representative Kaptur on MF Global:
"I believe most of us would call that theft." 270
A Rigged Financial System and Another Former Goldman Sachs CEO ...270

CHAPTER 15 Banana Republic 273
Anchored Under Water 273
Stranguflation: Deflation and Inflation
Where It Hurts America Most 274
Jobless "Recovery" 274
Deflation Plus "Staple" Inflation 275
How to Thwart the Assassins of the American Dream 276
Banks (not Fannie and Freddie) Crippled the Housing Market 277
Hide Billions of Losses, Take Bailouts, Collect Billions, Skip Jail 279
Banks Stall the Recovery and Prolong the Great Recession 279
Voters Must Demand the Solution 280
Third World America: "Fast Tracking to Anarchy" 280

Spiraling Out of Control: Open Season on Cops 281
Media Strafing 283
Mug Mile 283
Buy Back America 284
In Third World America, You Can't Buy a Ream of Paper on Minimum Wage 286
Sanders: The U.S. Is a Banana Republic 287
Deflation and Inflation: Where It Hurts You Most 287
Third World America 2011: Forget "Fast Tracking to Anarchy" We've Arrived 288
The Spring of Anarchy: "A City At War With Itself" 288
Police Superintendent has to Stop Lying to Citizens* 289
Memorial Day Mobs: Boston, Nashville, Long Island, Miami, Rochester, and Charlotte 290
And Stop Lying to My Friends 290
It's Not a Race War; It's a Class War 291
U.S. Downward Mobility 291
Elected Citizen-on-Taxpayer Financial Crime 292
Ongoing Mugging by Wall Street Banks 293
We Need the Mother of All Reforms 294
The Middle Class is Drowning in Debt and Choking on Lies 295
Ground Zero for America's Debt Crisis 297
Chicago Police Superintendent McCarthy's Cheap Shot: "Government Sponsored Racism" 298
Endnote: Transcript of Chicago Police Superintendent Garry McCarthy addressing the Congregation at St. Sabina's Church in Chicago, Illinois on June 5, 2011 (from above video): 299
Why Some Housing Prices Are Still Falling and Subprime Loans Are Still Sliding 303
Mortgage Loans with Less than Zero Value 304
Triple Tragedy: Meltdown, Spreading Contagion, and Crime 304
"Countrywide Broke the Law" 305
Fed's August 2007 Back Door Bail Out of Countrywide 305
BofA, Wells Fargo, U.S. Bank, Deutsche Bank, and JPMorgan Cut and Run 306
Investing: Bad News, Good News, and What's Next 306
The Bad News Isn't Going Away 307
Good News (for Now) 307
What Happens Next? 308

CHAPTER 16 China: Our Debt, Her Debt 311
China Defaults, Currency Basket Threatens Dollar 311
Clear and Present Danger 312
Chanos Crash: Timing China's Financial Meltdown 316
Bailouts, Railroading, Cover-ups, and the Chinese "Miracle" 317
Tens of Millions of Mate-less Men 317

China's Housing Price Crash....318
China's Debt and Coming Hard Landing....319
When Will Strain Lead to a Crash? 320
Chanos ("China Chaos") Derivatives....321
China 2012: The Year of the Bull (Rogers) or the Bear (Chanos)?....321
Jim Rogers: China Bull 322
China's Big Picture 322
Trouble is Opportunity....323
Long Term Outlook: Speaking the Language 324
Explosive Demand 324
Rogers' Bull Trades....325
Jim Chanos: China Bear....325
Debt and China's Housing Price Crash 326
The Wukan Rebellion 327
Slowdowns, Growth, and Savings 328
A Bull and a Bear in the China Shop 329

APPENDICES 331
APPENDIX I 331
APPENDIX II. 332
APPENDIX III....333
APPENDIX IV. 334
APPENDIX V....335
APPENDIX VI. 336
APPENDIX VII. 338
APPENDIX VIII....339
APPENDIX IX. 340
APPENDIX X....341
APPENDIX XI. 342
APPENDIX XII. 343

About the Author....344

ENDNOTES....345

INDEX....369

Preface

In September 2008, the largest credit bubble in world history nearly brought down the global financial markets. Years of cheap Federal Reserve funds fueled a sprawling Ponzi scheme of corrupt lending practices. Loans were financed through fraud-based securitizations. Fake investment-grade ratings and undisclosed material problems with the collateral lured unwary investors. Malicious financial engineering artificially propped up prices for years. When the game finally fell apart, the market panicked, and fear drove sales of good and bad assets alike at fire-sale prices.

Financiers, including the heads of banks and investment banks, famous investors, and captains of industry, feared the collapse of the global economic system. Taxpayer-funded bailouts averted disaster. Financiers benefited, and continue to benefit, from bailouts without consequences: trillions of dollars in direct cash injections, credit lines, and government guarantees, along with an unprecedented stretch of suppressed interest rates that let banks borrow at almost no cost.

This history-making bailout imposed no penalties on the chief culprits of the collapse. Instead, the malefactors were allowed to engineer the bailout themselves, and it rewarded them richly with benefits unimaginable before the crisis. All of this came at the expense of deceived taxpayers, who still provide cheap funding to unrepentant and unreformed banks. Lavish lobbying and campaign contributions ensure loyal support in Washington, D.C. Too Big to Fail has become Too Influential to Control.

My previous book, *Dear Mr. Buffett: What an Investor Learns 1,269 Miles from Wall Street*, was rushed to press in September 2008. It appeared shortly after Fannie Mae and Freddie Mac were placed into conservatorship, immediately after Lehman Brothers and AIG imploded, and just before Warren Buffett struck his deal to invest in Goldman Sachs on far better terms than U.S. taxpayers received for their TARP money. In it, I warned about the forming bubble, explained the events leading up to the crisis, and showed how the world could have avoided this ongoing disaster.

My earlier book, *Structured Finance and Collateralized Debt Obligations* (2nd edition), illuminated the complex and opaque securitizations that enabled fraudulent lending in the United States. For some readers, the book inspired the big short. For others, it was the black-magic playbook. Securitization "professionals" at banks and investment banks drove the money train from debtors to unwary investors, while law firms, investment banks, CDO "managers," hedge fund "managers," and rating agencies pocketed unprecedented fees along the way.

Wall Street made a mockery of Sarbanes-Oxley, which went unenforced: executives who signed off on materially misleading financial statements were excused rather than indicted. Members of Congress who were supposed to investigate instead acted as apologists. Nothing was fixed, and disasters recur like clockwork.

MF Global's bankruptcy on October 31, 2011, delivered a hard punch to the gut of the global futures market. Farmers and manufacturers who rely on futures to hedge price risk feel profoundly betrayed, and their confidence in the market has been irrevocably shaken. Customers whose money was supposedly held in segregated accounts discovered it had been used to fund risky bets made by the firm's chief.

That chief was the unindicted Jon Corzine: MF Global's CEO, former head of Goldman Sachs, former Governor of New Jersey, former U.S. Senator from New Jersey, and a top campaign-finance bundler for President Obama.

MF Global's customers were robbed twice. First, the firm diverted money from "segregated" customer accounts in a futile attempt to stave off disaster in its own proprietary trades while it tried to sell assets and part of the company. Then the bankruptcy was structured to serve powerful creditors, including JPMorgan Chase, one of the beneficiaries of the taxpayer-funded rescue of the global financial system in 2008.

Meanwhile, investors earn next to nothing on "risk-free" U.S. government obligations because interest rates are held down. Fixed income from bonds stagnates at low levels while the prices of everything people need to survive soar. Investors are pushed into the stock market in the hope of riding the expanding bubble. The U.S. economy is in the grip of stranguflation.

The New Robber Barons is a compilation of selected articles written between September 2008 and 2012, ending a few months after MF Global's implosion. It is a selective chronicle of how the New Robber Barons prospered, and continue to prosper, at the expense of those without government connections.

Most of the articles written after 2010 first appeared online in the *Huffington Post*, although I retain the copyright. This book organizes them by topic to make it easier to see how interested parties exploited the financial crisis and how they continue to exploit it. The original commentaries are unrevised so that readers can follow my thinking in real time. Some background is repeated across commentaries because each was written to stand alone as events unfolded.

"In truth, avarice is seldom capable of adopting any broad view, and there seems to be but one power that can prevent its invading both public and private rights. I fear that nothing but the strong arm of the law will be found satisfactorily effective."

—Henry Clews 1836-1923

CHAPTER 1 Bailouts for the Oligarchs

Proposed Alternative to the Various Versions of the Paulson Plan

The Emergency Economic Stabilization Act of 2008
September 25, 2008 (Updated Oct 2008)

In a letter to the *Financial Times* on September 29, 2008, I wrote: "Rather than adopt any form of the Paulson plan, which uses billions of US taxpayer dollars and forces risk and potential losses on taxpayers—rather than those who enjoyed the gains—I advocate an alternative."[1]

The Treasury's plan was a variation of the Paulson Plan. It used hundreds of billions of taxpayer dollars (trillions when one included guarantees and other supports including near zero cost funding from the Fed) and forced risk and potential losses on taxpayers—instead of having those who enjoyed the gains take the consequences. I advocated a viable alternative.

In September 2008, there was no longer time to break up the banks all at once and no time for unwinding AIG. But a temporary backstop was possible, along with a restructuring in which either 1) creditors agree to discount debt in exchange for warrants (for potentially viable enterprises) or 2) creditors agree to transform (possibly discounted) debt into new equity—a new capital structure in which former shareholders are wiped out.

Instead of TARP, handing out money to cover banks' losses, we could have forced creditors to accept a restructuring plan. This is what was done during the Great Depression. Creditors, i.e., debt holders including credit default swap counterparties, would have been compelled to accept a restructuring plan. That required partial forgiveness of debt in many cases and/or a debt for equity swap.

The government's bailout plan destroyed capitalism. In a capitalist system, those who stood to gain—and already made off with large gains—would have to bear the risk. The bailouts represented a corruption of capitalism. Crony capitalism violates the spirit of democracy established by the Founding Fathers of the republic known as the United States.

More Phony Accounting

During the crisis, no one trusted the value of the assets. Today, asset valuations are highly suspect, because we changed accounting rules to accommodate cash-strapped banks in April 2009.

The proposed Act released on September 28, 2008 extended the SEC's authority to suspend mark-to-market accounting (FAS 157) when it is "in the public interest and protects investors." The SEC's proposed Act buried problems and prolonged price uncertainty to serve the interests of systemically dangerous banks. That particular bill did not pass, but in April 2009, the accounting rules were changed anyway.

It was a huge mistake. FASB board members supported mark-to-market accounting in September 2008, and supported mark-to-market in general, especially in illiquid markets. The SEC should have, too, but its September 2008 proposal exposed how captured it was.

Accounting changes promoted hold-to-maturity pricing for credit derivatives trading books and portfolios of residential mortgage backed securities and collateralized debt obligations, among other troubled assets. The danger was, and is, that Federal portfolio managers can claim they are making money on carry trades while the assets are declining in value due to defaults or permanent value destruction of collateral. This situation can continue for a long time to create the false appearance of profitability. In other words, U.S. taxpayers can be told they are making money, when in reality they are losing money. I would rather know the market price, even if the news is bad news.

Bloomberg Magazine later reported that the money we were told we made on AIG only appeared that way through some fiddling. Bloomberg didn't even include the billions of taxpayer dollars paid to Goldman, Merrill, and other AIG counterparties whose CDOs should have been investigated instead of forking over protection payments.

Warren Buffett Urged Mark-to-Market Accounting

Warren Buffett came out strongly in favor of mark-to-market accounting in an interview with Charlie Rose on October 1, 2008, and in another interview with *CNNmoney* on October 2, 2008. He proposed another viable alternative to the bills floating in Congress.

Buffett proposed to allow private equity investors to put up 20%. The U.S. Treasury would put up 80% with the following terms: the Treasury gets paid back first, receives interest on its investment, and gets a share of the profits. This would ensure market pricing and allow the banks to delever, while the Treasury—the only source of a large enough balance sheet—levered up with the protection of a 20% cushion and mark-to-market pricing. The government ignored Buffett's proposal.

Treasury Secretary Henry Paulson Was a Section 8

All of this spells dark times for the future of the republic. On September 20, 2008, at the height of the crisis, Henry Paulson, former CEO of Goldman Sachs, and then the 74th U.S. Secretary of the Treasury, did not merely request immunity for actions he was about to take. In his original draft proposal of the Bailout Plan, he requested imperial powers:

> Sec. 8. Review.
>
> Decisions by the Secretary pursuant to the authority of this Act are non-reviewable and committed to agency discretion, and may not be reviewed by any court of law or any administrative agency.

Paulson was not an elected official, yet he requested powers that surpassed those granted to any representative of the citizens of the United States.[2]

Selling Democracy On the Cheap

September 30, 2008

Treasury Secretary Henry Paulson was unsuccessful in his first attempt to grab absolute power, but he tried again. His revised draft included this in Section 8: "Decisions by the Secretary pursuant to the authority of this Act are non-reviewable and committed to agency discretion, and may not be reviewed by any court of law or any administrative agency."

I told *Bloomberg TV* this is the most dangerous bill to come before Congress in my lifetime. "We are selling democracy on the cheap."[3]

New bailout plans include "Enron" accounting, which effectively thwarts oversight. [In April 2009, banks got their way and accounting rules were relaxed.] A lot of work has been done in the past couple of days to give Congress a bad education. If Paulson is allowed to use "hold to maturity" pricing, excessively high prices can be paid, and assets that have permanent losses can be easily covered up—just as investment banks covered up their permanent losses on securitized assets for many quarters.

In other words, if you do not use mark-to-market accounting, it is much easier to lie.

Therefore I recommend that we make it more difficult for anyone to lie to American taxpayers, and say we should adopt mark-to-market accounting. If we absolutely had to sell, what would we get for our money? We have a right to know.

It is not in the interests of U.S. citizens and taxpayers to abandon mark-to-market accounting for a proposal in which taxpayer funds are being used. If we would have to sell the assets at a loss due to downward moves in market prices, we have a right to know that. If the assets have permanent losses so that even if we hold to maturity we would have losses, we have a right to know that too. At any given time, we have a right to know what our "investment" is worth (but I am in the group that feels this "investment" should not be made and we should pursue this alternative). Congress seems to have decided that U.S. citizens cannot handle the truth.

The proposed Act released on September 28 (and voted down) extends the SEC's authority to suspend mark-to-market accounting (FAS 157) (P. 88) when it is "in the public interest and protects investors."

Do not expect a thaw in the market freeze. The proposed Act buries problems and prolongs price uncertainty. This bill did not pass, but future versions may include this provision. This is a huge mistake. FASB board members support mark-to-market accounting, *especially* in illiquid markets. The SEC should, too. This provision promotes hold-to-maturity pricing for credit derivatives trading books and CDO portfolios.

The danger is that Federal portfolio managers can claim they are making money on carry trades while the assets are declining in value due to defaults or permanent value destruction of collateral. This situation can continue for a long time to create the false appearance of profitability. In other words, U.S. taxpayers can be told they are making money on their $700 billion investment, when in reality they are losing money.

I would rather know the market price, even if the news is bad news.

Ponzi Schemes and Stress Tests

May 8, 2009

Now that we are stress testing banks that have merged with entities involved in the housing and municipal bond market debacles, we should also revisit the Ponzi scheme. But first, I'll digress to comment on how we will handle the results of the "stress test," since that is how we will claim we have solved the banks' problems. While the government will convert preferred shares to voting common shares, this is otherwise simply an accounting game.

Credit derivatives were used for this nonsense in Europe, and we have a name for it: regulatory capital arbitrage. This time the U.S. will dilute shareholder value and claim banks have new capital. Moreover, the "stress tests" are anything but that. The "stress" scenario used in the "test" is my probable base case. You'll recall in August of 2007, Ben Bernanke said subprime losses would only be $50 billion to $100 billion, and I called for more than triple that amount. It turns out I was too optimistic. I was in the right direction then, and I am in the right direction now. Our government is in the habit of telling the truth much too slowly.

We need fiscal stimulus and need to strengthen banks. I believe, however, that we should experience more pain now to gain a better future. Specifically, we should put some banks into receivership and not continue to bail out bank creditors with public money. Likewise we need to enforce controls on securitization (shadow banking) to restore credibility to this powerful tool. Until we confront the fact that global confidence in securitization was shattered by a massive Ponzi scheme, we cannot fix the securitization industry and unfreeze the capital markets. Global investors are waiting for us to clean up our own backyard.

Pundits claiming this was merely a bubble or merely a case of bad models do the industry no favors. There were no black swans or swans of any other color. There were simply Black Barts imitating the highwayman that engaged in bloodless robbery. While there was a bubble, it was inflated by a Ponzi scheme.

The *Wall Street Journal* missed a golden opportunity. It wrote that if Madoff's alleged losses exceeded $50 billion, it would "dwarf past Ponzi schemes."[4] Yet, Madoff was a piker.

The largest Ponzi scheme in the history of the capital markets is the relationship between failed mortgage lenders and investment banks that securitized the risky overpriced loans and sold these packages to other investors—a Ponzi scheme by every definition applied to Madoff. These and other related deeds led to the largest global credit meltdown in the history of the world.

Investment banks raised money from new investors to pay back old investors (mortgage lenders' dividends to shareholders and investment banking creditors of mortgage lenders which often included themselves). When mortgage lenders imploded, investment banks sped up opaque securitizations to offload worthless tranches of CDOs mixed in with others to careless so-called sophisticated investors along with naive investors. Raising money from new investors to pay back old investors, even if you are the old investor covering up losses, is a Ponzi scheme.

Bernard Madoff confessed—not the securitization "professionals" who work or worked for famous investment banks, certain CDO managers and certain hedge funds. One securitization professional gave an interview to *Reuters* in which he tried to claim that shady activity was not a Ponzi scheme since CDOs are legal.[5] But using a legal financial instrument to commit fraud is still fraud. If you pawn off product by mixing it into a CDO portfolio, and you know or should know it is worthless (or even simply misrepresented), you must disclose that fact. But that is not what happened.

Overpriced and overrated tranches of RMBS, CDOs and even CDO-squared, that on their own wouldn't get a decent bid from any knowledgeable securitization professional, were repacked to sell on to other investors. When new investors dried up, these products were held on the books as if the irresponsible ratings had meaning. This delayed the recognition of losses long enough to get through another bonus cycle.

The SEC has been silent on the dodgy securitization activities it “regulated” over the past several years. Congress and others agree, claiming there will be time to find out who is responsible later. *Bail now, scapegoat later.*

Legacy investment banks and other bailout recipients have hundreds of billions of dollars’ worth of assets in opaque accounting buckets known as Level 2 (mark-to-model) and Level 3 (mark-to-management assumptions). Good luck trying to find details. This makes the "stress tests" less meaningful than they already are.

Self-proclaimed sophisticated investors like bond insurers are responsible for their own due diligence, and they may not be able to press claims against errant banks and investment banks. But now that the taxpayer has bailed out these entities, and now that the Fed is using taxpayer money to subsidize the funding costs of the banking system, the situation has changed. The U.S. housing market has been damaged along with the municipal bond markets. The net effect is a massive crime on the U.S. economy, and taxpayers, at least, may wish some form of satisfaction in the form of greater regulation and economic claw back.

Some pundits want to claim the problem was mathematical outliers. The real problem is there were too many outright liars hiding behind the curtain of structured finance. Until we squarely face our problems, we cannot fix them. We had a financial Pearl Harbor, but investment bankers piloted many of the planes. We need to face that problem to restore confidence in the financial system. Once-over-lightly stress tests combined with regulatory capital window dressing will not solve our problem. What we need now is financial military police action combined with a financial Marshall Plan to restore our devastated financial system.

Wall Street and Washington Hope You Are Gullible: Disappoint Them

February 14, 2010

If a high-on-crack driver crashed his speeding rental car into your house and killed your spouse, you would be outraged if law enforcers took bribes and gave the driver a pass on a blood test. If the judge then merely fined the killer and ordered you to pay it, you would appeal, wondering what happened to justice. If the government then handed the crack-driver keys to a bigger rental car and presented you with the rental bill, you would certainly protest.

How is it, then, that you have remained largely silent in the face of the same sort of behavior by Wall Street and Washington? Bonus-seeking bankers careened off the right path and ran Ponzi schemes that nearly ruined our economy. Bureaucrats and elected officials bailed them out without demanding consequences. Bankers are revving their engines again.

Bankers Get Bonuses, the USA Gets the Great Recession

Taxpayers are asked to believe that over-borrowing by U.S. consumers created a global financial crisis. This myth aids and abets Wall Street. The economy was nearly destroyed because banks borrowed massively, and they borrowed many multiples more than they could afford. Wall Street pumped the Fed's cheap money through financial meth labs, and deceptive financial vehicles ran over securities laws at top speed.

More than 20% of mortgage loans—including originally sound loans—are underwater, meaning the borrower owes more than the home is worth. Official unemployment numbers hover at around 10%. If you include underemployment, it is around 18%. In depressed areas where the nation's poorest—chiefly minorities—have been hurt the most, unemployment has soared past 30%. For this destitute group, unemployment combined with underemployment exceeds 50%.[6]

As U.S. soldiers fought wars in Iraq and Afghanistan, Wall Street flattened Main Street. Our foreign wars drag on, while the U.S. battles a crippling recession at home.

Global Ponzi Scheme

Fraud by borrowers, fraud on borrowers, and speculation by people who thought home prices would rise forever have all tarnished mortgage lending. Yet this pales compared to the epidemic of predatory lending.

Predatory snipers committed financial murder as deliberately as British soldiers gave smallpox contaminated blankets to Native Americans. Honest homeowners were systematically targeted and actively misled into bad mortgage products. Loans were presented as gifts, but these Trojan horse loans hid destructive risk. "Disclosures" were acts of malice.

When Wall Street packaged these loans and sold deceptive "investments," documents did not specifically disclose that credit ratings were misleading. If you know or should know a car's gas tank will blow up, you cannot use a misleading third-party consumer report as an excuse. Yet bonus-seeking bankers used this sort of excuse to get through a few more highly-paid bonus cycles, before it all fell apart. Only the elite crowd of insiders prospered.

This was the most massive Ponzi scheme in the history of the global capital markets. U.S. taxpayers became unwilling unsophisticated investors when we bailed out the financial system. We must hold Wall Street accountable for its fraud.[7]

More Bonuses for Bankers, a Deeper Recession for the USA

Banks that contributed to our economic distress are heralded as geniuses at risk management, after taxpayers saved them from ruin. Wall Street escaped prosecution (so far), and Congress gave it a faster and more powerful car.

Paul Volcker suggested reforms, and special interest groups successfully lobbied to make them meaningless. His proposal to limit "proprietary" trading—a small step in the right direction—has been thwarted by banks claiming they engage in high risk trades on behalf of customers. Washington seems to have already forgotten that AIG nearly went bankrupt—and nearly took the entire financial system down with it—because of Wall Street's "customer" trades. Wall Street and AIG insiders grew rich on bonuses based on a myth, and taxpayers funded AIG's $180 billion bailout.

Wall Street now makes most of its "profits" from high-risk trading, and rewards risk with huge bonuses. It has unfettered access to more U.S. taxpayer money than in the history of the United States. Traditional banking suffers; it cannot generate enough revenue to "justify" massive bonuses. Bankers get billions in bonuses based on a myth, and U.S. taxpayers get a deeper recession and more risk.

Reform Starts with the President and Congress

Congress has protected Wall Street and passed on the costs to hard-working taxpayers. "Too-big-to-fail" financial institutions are too big to exist, and it is past time to break them up. They currently enjoy around $13 trillion of taxpayer-funded support, including tens of billions of FDIC debt guarantees for each of the too-big-to-fail banks and more than $2 trillion in nearly zero-cost funding from the Fed.[8]

President Obama has not yet condemned Wall Street's massive fraud, and Congress's bailout methods rewarded Wall Street's malicious mischief. The House just passed a bigger bailout bill that will give too-big-to-fail Wall Street banks access to $4 trillion the next time they crash the economy.[9]

Congress must start again from scratch, and give us real reform. Washington needs to get back in the driver's seat, and voters need to make Congress steer straight this time by calling and writing representatives and senators.

In a control fraud, only insider agents prosper. The losers are financial institutions' shareholders and debtors, investors, borrowers, and the U.S. taxpayer.

Banks covered up indefensible lending—enabled by complicit rating agencies, "creative" accounting at related mortgage lenders, crooked CDO "managers," venal hedge funds, crony accountants, and captured regulators. They parked the risk on their own balance sheets, on the balance sheets of Fannie Mae or Freddie Mac, in off-shore vehicles, or on unwary investors around the globe.

Sometimes banks "transferred" risk with credit derivatives backed by phony securities that harmed "sophisticated" insurers like AIG, Ambac, MBIA, FGIC, and ACA—all of which were either bankrupted or damaged.

2012: Voters Nix Incumbents, Demand Financial Reform and Fed Fraud Audit

July 1, 2010

The only part that needs to wait is the voting. Federal Reserve Chairman Ben S. Bernanke and then-New York Fed President Timothy Geithner told senators on April 3, 2008, that the tens of billions of dollars in "assets" the government agreed to purchase in the rescue of Bear Stearns Cos. were "investment-grade." They didn't share everything the Fed knew about the money.[10]

By using its balance sheet to protect an investment bank against failure, the Fed took on the most credit risk in its 96-year history and increased the chance that Americans would be on the hook for billions of dollars as the central bank began insuring Wall Street firms against collapse. The Fed's secrecy spurred legislation that will require government audits of the Fed bailouts and force the central bank to reveal recipients of emergency credit.

Congress's proposed financial reform bill would not have prevented the last disaster, fails to address current problems, and will not prevent the next disaster (more on this in a future post). Among other things, lawmakers are leaning to a provision to allow an audit of the Federal Reserve Bank, but this should be a thorough fraud audit, and there should be ongoing audits.

*****

"The basements of William, Wall and Broad Streets, and of Exchange Place, seemed to have been suddenly penetrated with innumerable burrows, inhabited by new and singular animals—mostly rodents—gnawing at the vast cheese of speculation."

—William Worthington Fowler 1832-1881

CHAPTER 2 Goldman Sachs: "God's Work"

Jamie Dimon and Warren Buffett Were Warned AIG Had Serious Trouble One Year Before the September 2008 Crisis (and Goldman Sachs Knew Too)

January 26, 2010

In August 2007, the *Wall Street Journal's* David Reilly called for hot news. I replied that AIG had material mark-to-market losses for the second quarter of 2007, yet it took no write-downs whatsoever for its credit default swaps on underlying mortgage related "super senior" collateralized debt obligations (CDOs).

I looked at one aggregate position of credit default swaps (CDSs) amounting to more than $19 billion.[11] The mark-to-market losses were just one part of the problem. Since too many of the assets backing the position had high risk of severe principal losses, it also had a lot of "cliff risk," as in falling off of one. AIG had a grave problem just from this position alone, and AIG had other serious problems.

Initially, I agreed to talk to Reilly on background, but I didn't want to be named or quoted. AIG vigorously denied it would ever take a write-down or a loss on the CDSs, much less one that was material to its earnings statement.

Reilly called me again asking if I were sure. I said I was positive.

He called AIG again and then me, asking for a quote this time. I didn't want to get into a fight with AIG in the "Heard on the Street" column and reminded Reilly that I only agreed to talk to him on background.

Reilly's editor called me and said that given that AIG's denial was so forceful, the paper needed me to go on the record. I know and trust this editor, so I agreed. Reilly quoted me but omitted that I said the difference was material.[12]

Even the *Wall Street Journal* hesitates to use the word "material" to describe an accounting misstatement. It guarantees a conference call with lawyers.

Before Dave Reilly wrote his article, he talked to experts, including me, for background. Then he called AIG to ask them for their thinking. AIG stood firm. Then Reilly called me again. He didn't want the Wall Street Journal to look stupid, but told me "they pay me to go out on a limb." He said he needed me to go on the record. It would make the article more forceful. I did not think that AIG would tell Reilly: You know, you have a point, maybe we should recheck our homework, but I did not anticipate arguing with AIG in the Wall Street Journal's "Heard on the Street" column. I hesitated. AIG, a large global conglomerate, has the resources to crush me like a bug. I finally agreed to go on the record." "For example, AIG wrote credit default protection on a whopping $19.2 billion "safe" investment that had exposure to subprime loans (a super-senior tranche of a CDO backed by BBB rated tranches—the lowest rating that is still investment grade—of residential mortgage-backed securities, and these were backed by a significant amount of subprime loans. By August 2007, the prices of the collateral backing the super senior had tanked.) Anyone who buys insurance knows that even if you are 'safe,' if you are in a high risk category, your cost of insurance goes up. If AIG were to pay someone to take over its insurance-like obligation, AIG would have to pay more than it had received, and AIG should have shown this as a loss.

AIG's stance seemed bizarre given that five insurance executives from AIG and Berkshire Hathaway's Gen Re Corp (even Warren Buffett cannot control every action of every employee) were under investigation (and eventually found guilty) of conspiracy to inflate AIG's reserves and mislead investors about AIG's earnings.

By June 2008, AIG recorded two back-to-back quarters of its largest losses ever. AIG took more than $20 billion in write-downs on its derivative positions through the first quarter of 2008; net losses for the fourth quarter of 2007 were $5.3 billion, and in the first quarter of 2008, AIG reported losses of $7.8 billion. In February 2008, its auditor said it found "material weakness" in AIG's accounting.[13]

I called Warren Buffett about my concerns, but stuck to the public information already in the article.[14]

I stuck my neck out and met with Jamie Dimon, CEO of JPMorgan Chase, adding that the difference was material. JPMorgan Chase's credit derivatives positions exceeded those of all other U.S. banks combined at the time. JPMorgan was not a participant in the problematic deals, and it was not a recipient of AIG's subsequent settlement payments, but stability in the credit derivatives markets was an important issue. Jamie dismissed my explanation of the looming cliff risk and said he understood CDOs. (Dimon later said he wished he had listened to me back then.) In August of 2007, he did not want to contemplate a potential implosion of AIG.

Goldman Knew (or Should Have Known) the Consequences

Unbeknownst to me at the time, in July 2007, Goldman Sachs and AIG began a prolonged battle over prices and collateral payments. In February 2008—six months after Reilly's *Wall Street Journal* article—PricewaterhouseCoopers (PWC) said it found "material weakness" in AIG's accounting. PWC was also Goldman Sachs's auditor. Goldman hedged against the possibility that AIG could go bankrupt and also extracted billions more in collateral from AIG before the crisis. By the September 2008 initial bailout, Goldman Sachs had extracted $7.5 billion in collateral from AIG against these trades.

Goldman should have been well aware of the cliff risk posed by CDOs that it hedged with AIG. Moreover, Goldman created CDOs that other banks hedged with AIG, including some hedged by French banks Calyon and Societe Generale. In fact, Goldman Sachs was a key architect of AIG's crisis.[15]

If any of the assets backing the CDOs were as bad as Goldman Sachs Alternative Mortgage Products' GSAMP Trust 2006-S3, the BBB-rated tranches (and most of the higher rated tranches) would be worth *zero* today. Goldman itself created some assets that amounted mostly to hot air, so it was in a good position to know that the CDOs AIG hedged were "backed" by too many value-destroying "assets."[16]

Details of AIG's Trades Were Kept Secret Even by the SEC

The government's 100% payout to AIG's counterparties was extraordinary under these circumstances, and the negotiations were done in secret. In September of 2008, the Fed agreed to the first AIG bailout rather than let it sink into bankruptcy. It was very much to the benefit of Goldman Sachs and the other recipients of bailout funds that the details of the CDOs and the assets backing them were kept secret. Some CDOs held up moderately well, but others looked so bad, a public view of details would have prompted an immediate investigation. There appears to be a cover-up, and even the report of the Office of the Special Inspector General for the Troubled Asset Relief Program (SIGTARP Report) did not reveal key details.[17][18] So much for Washington's so-called investigations.

> Janet Tavakoli, founder of Chicago-based Tavakoli Structured Finance Inc., a financial consulting firm, says the government squandered billions in the AIG deal. "There's no way they should have paid at par," she says. "AIG was basically bankrupt." [19]
>
> "They didn't want you to know which deals had soured the fastest," said Tavakoli, president of Tavakoli Structured Finance and a vocal critic of the AIG bailout. "The reason they didn't want to release these details is because it would have shown that some securities suffered only moderate discounts while others were worth much, much less. And that could have prompted an investigation into the deals that performed the worst." [20]

Even the SEC allowed details to be suppressed until 2018.[21]

In September 2008, a good negotiator would have insisted that the collateral already extracted from AIG by Goldman Sachs, Societe Generale and others should be recharacterized as a loan and paid back after the crisis. As for subsequent payments including those made in November 2008—if they were made at all—they would only have been made as a loan.

Goldman Sachs Worried About Billions in Crippling Losses

Public funds bailed out AIG in September 2008, and the public did not get transparency. The secrecy benefited those involved in the initial negotiations, those involved in subsequent negotiations, and the banks that received the payments.

Now that the crisis is over, this issue should be reopened, and billions in collateral should be clawed back to pay down public debt, before Goldman Sachs pays more than $16 billion in taxpayer subsidized bonuses to its employees.

Goldman's CEO Lloyd Blankfein knew that if AIG failed, Goldman's counterparties would suffer collateral damage, and if AIG failed in September 2008, Blankfein worried about billions in crippling losses for Goldman Sachs.[22] Yet, in an October 2009 *Wall Street Journal* interview, Blankfein said he didn't suspect AIG had problems producing collateral: "I never had reason to suspect....[I]t never occurred to me."[23]

Wall Street's Advice to Joran van der Sloot (satire)

June 8, 2010

Before we get to your problem areas, we'd like to congratulate you on almost having "the right stuff." You are a manipulator and an unabashed liar. You have no remorse. You are a master at twisting things to suggest your victims had it coming, and you don't think of them as human beings.

You suggest that Natalee Holloway threw herself at you when you weren't even interested. Stephany Flores "intruded" on your private life, after you escorted her to your room. She took your computer—presumably a computer that either didn't have logon password protection, or for which you gave her the password. She failed to acknowledge your greatness and recoiled in horror. How dare she? What an insult to your Weltanschauung! You couldn't allow her to roam free with that sort of judgmental attitude aimed in your direction. We appreciate your attitude and then some.[24]

Unfortunately, you are a piker and more than a little sloppy.

Extorting money in exchange for information was truly inspired, but you only collected $25 thousand of the $250 thousand you originally asked for. We are really big on extortion, and we know how to keep milking our victims. We threatened our government that the financial system would collapse, if it allowed shareholders to be wiped out and debt holders to accept debt for equity swaps. We had our government eating out of our hands, begging us to take hundreds of billions in TARP money, and hundreds of billions more in back-door bailouts and ongoing Fed subsidies.

We deflected some blame to Fannie and Freddie, even though most of the problematic subprime mortgages were fueled by money raised from our private securitizations. We got Congress to pressure Fannie and Freddie to lower their standards and buy hundreds of millions of our "AAA" rot. After our Ponzi schemes unraveled, they were forced to pick up the slack. Meanwhile, we make money hand-over-fist funded by our victims, U.S. taxpayers.

We pillaged entire neighborhoods driving millions into bankruptcy. We destroyed families and drove a few of our victims to suicide.[25] As for lack of remorse, we've even propagated what Elizabeth Warren calls the "myth of the immoral debtor."[26] We *excel* at shifting blame and kicking our victims when they're down. Fortunately for us, we devastated the finances of the least powerful people. The public outcry from our victims has been successfully muted.

This brings us to the most important part, and here's where you really screwed up. If you kill an influential customer, don't get caught in unfriendly territory. If you forget that rule, *don't confess.*

Notice how well things went for you in Aruba where your family had connections? Your friends and family sheltered you. The justice system seemed designed to protect you. The entire investigation was a farce to feed the media. It left you free to commit more crimes. In Peru, your victim's family has connections, and now the shoe is on the other foot. You don't see us vacationing in China do you? They take financial crimes seriously.

We stay in friendly territory. "Investigations" and "financial reform" are designed to feed sensational—but harmless—content to the media. They love us! We've bought most of Congress, the SEC crafts lame complaints, the entire regulatory system is captured, rating agencies are in our pocket, the FBI's budget is a joke, and the Department of Justice can't seem to remember its purpose. We cratered the economy and got the financial equivalent of a traffic ticket. This has left us free to make a mockery of traditional banking and ramp up global systemic risk. We're rolling in more cash than ever before.

You probably noticed that all of this good advice comes a bit too late to be helpful. We'd like to say it's because we have a conscience, and that you are a bigger creep than we are, except you'd see through that. The fact is we enjoy rubbing salt in wounds, and when it comes to creating havoc and misery, we just want you to know that we are better at it than you are.

Free Copies for the Grand Jury

My book on the global financial meltdown, *Dear Mr. Buffett: What an Investor Learns 1,269 Miles from Wall Street*, explains that the relationship between failed mortgage lenders and Wall Street securitization departments was a widespread interconnected Ponzi scheme, which is illegal in the United States, and names culprits: mortgage lenders, investment banks, CDO managers, credit rating agencies, monoline insurers, regulators, Congress, and more. Some were criminals, others were enablers. If the Department of Justice ever decides to prosecute, I will provide free copies for the first grand jury.

*****

AIG Paying Out Millions in Bonuses

March 14, 2009

The Wall Street Journal reported ("AIG to Pay $450 Million in Bonuses," by Liam Pleven) that AIG CEO Edward Liddy said the company had entered into the bonus agreement in early 2008 before AIG got into dire financial straits and was forced to obtain a government bailout last fall. In the fourth quarter of 2008, AIG lost $61.7 billion, but it was in trouble long before that due to AIG Financial Products Group, even if AIG did not own up to it at the time.

According to the article, "The large bulk of the [bonus] payments at issue cover the AIG Finance Products Group." Yet, this group had problems as far back as the second quarter of 2007, and AIG was in severe financial straits long before the first quarter of 2008. In my opinion the government interfered with the "sanctity" of AIG's credit derivatives contracts claiming it was in the public's interest, and as a matter of public policy, Treasury could have found a way to alter AIG's bonus agreements given the extraordinary circumstances.

In August of 2007, I challenged AIG's accounting saying they had large unreported losses. I was challenging AIG's earnings for the second quarter of 2007, and contrary to Liddy's representations in the above article, AIG had grave concerns by the first quarter of 2008.

*****

Did AIG Insure Dodgy Mortgage Products for Goldman Sachs?

March 25, 2009

AIG had a lot of cliff risk (as in falling off of one) in some of their credit derivatives linked to mortgage-backed products, and I questioned these trades in August of 2007. Goldman Sachs was a key trading partner. Some of the mortgage products coming out of Goldman Sachs Alternative Mortgage Products looked dodgy. AIG seems to have done most of its trades with Goldman during Hank Paulson's tenure as CEO at Goldman, and tough questions should be asked about the nature of the risk that AIG put on with Goldman Sachs.

According to the *Wall Street Journal* prior to AIG's September 2008 bailout, Goldman had insured $20 billion of chiefly mortgage backed products, and Goldman had already received $7.5 billion in collateral that contributed to AIG's cash problems. From the time of the bailout until the end of 2008, Goldman received another $8.1 billion in collateral from AIG for a total of $15.6 billion before the end of 2008 (the remaining exposure was said to be hedged with credit default swaps among other hedges).[27]

The key question is whether Goldman asked AIG to insure products that were as dodgy as the deal from Goldman Sachs Alternative Mortgage Products exposed by *Fortune*'s Allan Sloan in his October 16, 2007 Loeb Award winning article: "Junk Mortgages Under the Microscope."[28]

Was the lack of disclosure at the time of the bailout to save Goldman from embarrassment or is there a perfectly innocent explanation?

An explanation is due because one could argue that Hank Paulson as former Treasury Secretary (prior to that he was Goldman's CEO) was an interested man. Another interested man, Lloyd Blankfein, Goldman's current CEO, had discussions with Treasury Secretary Geithner. They denied the discussions were about AIG.

Notice I said these were interested men, not persons of interest. Yet a detailed explanation of the underlying risk that AIG insured for Goldman Sachs—and others—is in order.

AIG Bubble: Irrational Exuberance

August 28, 2009

American International Group Inc.'s equity is currently worth zero, whatever manic depressive Mr. Market may say today (today's open 52.98). It is likely to remain zero based on AIG's own analysis of its future over the next few years. In fact, its obligations to the U.S. Treasury would trade at a discount today. The only reason AIG's stock should trade above zero today is if you believe crony capitalism will fund the birth of an AIG clone—in other words if you believe AIG's future will be a rigged game.

Today's *Wall Street Journal* reported that AIG has changed its timetable for selling assets. That was to be expected, because if it sold its assets quickly, shareholders would get nothing, and the government would not get paid in full. It is also AIG's probable future scenario, albeit the losses may be mitigated.[29]

AIG's new Chief Executive Robert Benmosche "is willing to wait as long as three years to spin off stakes in two multibillion-dollar foreign units." He's waiting for a "fair" price, and he admits that if he sells too soon (or doesn't get a "fair" price), there will be losers all around.

Benmosche's own analysis shows AIG "wouldn't be able to repay the government even if it sold everything." His strategy is loss mitigation, not a return to AIG's salad days.

Even the U.S. Treasury, not known for its transparency or candor during this crisis, wrote that its AIG investment is highly speculative.

AIG seems disappointed that its Asia focused life insurance unit, American International Assurance Co. ("AIA"), might only raise a little more than $5 billion as estimated last spring, especially since AIG valued it at $20-$40 billion in February 2009. AIG is also disappointed with valuations for American Life Insurance Co ("Alico").

As Mr. Benmosche pointed out: "If the U.S. government doesn't continue to support AIG, we will fail. We have no right to use the government funding to make a profit; that is inappropriate."

If the government's new policy is to be long-term distressed private equity investors in entities like AIG, then the U.S. Treasury should get a share of the profits. The same goes for some former investment banks—now banks—with which we are long-term business partners. We support them with cheap funding and low borrowing costs due to our guarantees and ongoing liquidity support. We should ask for a large share of the profits, if any.

*****

Goldman's Lies of Omission

October 28, 2009

In my opinion, David Viniar's (CFO of Goldman Sachs) comments in the fall of 2008 were a ~~lie~~ and for that matter, Lloyd Blankfein's (CEO of Goldman Sachs) later comments to the Wall Street Journal were disingenuous.[30]

In the context of what was happening near the time of AIG's implosion, the key question was "What is going on between Goldman and AIG?" Their rhetoric surrounding this issue is a deft dodge. They may claim they didn't "technically" lie, but Goldman's business exposure to AIG posed both credit risk and reputation risk. They seem to overlook elements of the former and put insufficient value on the latter.

Goldman's exposure *was not,* as Viniar stated in September 2008, "immaterial " whatever the outcome at AIG." Given Goldman's key role in AIG's distress, a reasonable liquidator of AIG may have clawed back most of the $7.5 billion in collateral Viniar claimed as a "hedge." If AIG had gone bankrupt, the underlying CDOs would likely have plummeted further in value—as has happened in past similar market upsets—and his "hedges," even if they remained whole would not have covered the loss. In fact, after the fall of 2008, the CDOs continued to rapidly lose USD billions in value. Secondary market values as of December 2009 for similar CDO product are bid at single digit pennies on the dollar in a supposedly more stable market.[31]

Now that the crisis is over, and given the special circumstances of the crisis, and Goldman's contribution to value-destroying securitizations, it is in the public interest to claw back the money paid to Goldman Sachs. AIG did not need to settle for 100 cents on the dollar in November 2008, and in September 2008, a good negotiator would have refused to hand over more collateral, and should have clawed some back (or insisted it was a temporary loan).

In late July 2008, SCA settled with Merrill for $500 million on $3.7 B of contracts, or around 13.5%. On August 1, 2008, Ambac settled $1.4 B with Citi for $850 million, or around 60% on the dollar, but unlike SCA and AIG, Ambac wasn't on the brink of insolvency at the time. Calyon, a French bank also involved in AIG's transactions, settled similar contracts with FGIC, another bond insurer, for only ten cents on the dollar in August 2008, yet $13.9 billion of Goldman's contracts with AIG were settled for 100 cents on the dollar in November 2008 via purchases by Maiden Lane III. Ambac recently settled similar credit default swaps for ten cents on the dollar ($5 billion in contracts for around $500 million) as Ambac needed capital, and MBIA has made deeply discounted settlements.[32]

The November 17, 2009 SIGTARP report notes that Goldman refused to negotiate a settlement for AIG's contract because it would have lost money. It is time to ask Goldman to buy back these CDOs from the Fed for 100 cents on the dollar, and there is another large position still held by AIG of Goldman's Abacus CDOs that should also be considered for repurchase by Goldman Sachs, given the public's large investment in AIG.

Goldman should have plainly stated that it was owed billions in additional collateral from AIG—after already having collected billions—due to credit default swap contracts and other trading positions. Whether or not Goldman thought its credit risk was totally hedged is a separate, albeit important issue, and I'll get to that later.

Among the proximate causes of AIG's failure were previous calls for collateral made by its credit default swap trading counterparties, including Goldman Sachs. They were entitled to pressure AIG on its prices and demand more collateral; I had publicly challenged AIG's prices myself more than a year earlier. These actions gave a major push to AIG's subsequent credit downgrade, which tripped contract triggers that AIG had unwisely permitted its more clever counterparties to insert. (The credit default swap market is not standardized.) This meant AIG had to come up with collateral equal to the entire remaining amount of the credit default swap contract.

Unfortunately, AIG was essentially bankrupt at this point and it couldn't meet its obligations. The government could have stepped in and renegotiated its contracts. [Goldman's "hedges" might have disputed whether a reduced payment triggered a restructuring event, if applicable, in their contracts.] But that isn't what happened.

Absent a bailout of AIG, Goldman was vulnerable to increasing systemic risk which would have likely affected its hedge counterparties and many of its other trading counterparties. Liquidity was very tight in the fall of 2008. [In March of 2008, Alan Schwartz, then CEO of Bear Stearns, saw tens of billions of dollars of seeming liquidity disappear in hours. Schwartz publicly stated he had ample liquidity, until suddenly he did not.] In September of 2008, Goldman negotiated for additional capital with Berkshire Hathaway and paid up for it.[33] The outcomes for both AIG and Lehman were uncertain.

If AIG had gone under, the already illiquid market would have frozen. Collateral requirements for all trading would have increased (just as they did the week Bear imploded), and Goldman would have had problems collecting from many trading counterparties, if not the exact counterparties "hedging" its exposure to an AIG disaster.

It is never a given that hedges will pay off when the chips are down. A counterparty may dispute whether the contractual definition of a credit event is met, if only to buy time. Even when there is no default at issue, counterparties can try to change the rules when the market is in turmoil. In the fall of 2008, there were already anomalies in the derivatives market. For example, China refused calls for collateral on derivatives contracts in Asia, and its counterparties were forced to renegotiate. The entire market pretended this event didn't cause a cross default.[34]

Goldman was not a disinterested party in AIG's bailout. AIG's bailout—and the way the payouts were handled for its trading counterparties—hugely benefited Goldman Sachs. Goldman received a cash payment worth more than $10 billion from the U.S.

Treasury—via AIG—during a system-wide liquidity crunch. Under the circumstances, I cannot think of any scenario that would have provided a more certain and stable outcome for Goldman Sachs.

> Citigroup Inc. agreed last year to accept about 60 cents on the dollar from New York-based bond insurer Ambac Financial Group Inc. to retire protection on a $1.4 billion CDO. [Ambac said the underlying was worth about zero, and the protection payment would otherwise have been the full $1.4 billion].[35]

It is a strong statement to say that a CFO lied to the public, and in my opinion, David Viniar, Goldman's CFO, lied about Goldman's exposure to AIG while the AIG bailout was in progress in September 2008. Viniar spoke about risk management, but that is a separate issue from whether or not Goldman Sachs would have money at risk due to its direct business with AIG. Goldman Sachs would have been out billions of dollars in collateral had a bankruptcy-like settlement been negotiated with AIG, and that is material (see also the commentary above).

This is what David Viniar said during his Sept 16, 2008 earnings call:

> **David Viniar** - The Goldman Sachs Group, Inc. - EVP, CFO "Sure. Without giving exact numbers, let me just tell you how we think about this. AIG and Lehman, big important financial institution counterparties to Goldman Sachs. We did and we do a lot of business with both of them, as we do with all other major financial institutions. The way we do business with financial institutions is by having appropriate daily margin terms. That is how we are able to do the volume of business with each other that we do. And that goes for AIG, Lehman, and also Morgan Stanley, and JPMorgan, and Citi, and UBS, and Credit Suisse. That is how we manage our risk. In addition to the margin terms, we augment our risk management

> with appropriate hedging strategies. You heard at the beginning of my remarks that we believe one of the biggest challenges we have is to avoid large concentrated exposures; and we took that very much into account in managing our credit exposures to Lehman and to AIG, as well as we do with any other financial institution. **Given that, what I would tell you is given the outcome at Lehman and whatever the outcome at AIG, I would expect the direct impact of our credit exposure to both of them to be immaterial to our results." [Emphasis added.]**[36]

On September 16, *Bloomberg*'s Erik Holm and Christine Richard wrote of the dire global market consequences of an AIG failure. For example, Bank of America had just agreed to merge with Merrill Lynch & Co., which held $6 billion of super senior exposure to collateralized debt obligations hedged with an insurer. I told *Bloomberg*: "It's impossible [without more disclosure] to know which insurance company they're referring to, though if it is AIG, it may have emboldened AIG to go to the Fed." AIG's downgrade would result in another write-down for Merrill. Merrill later received a $6.3 billion bailout payment from AIG.

Goldman Abhors Conflicts of Interest (for Others)

The public wanted to know if Goldman Sachs was one of AIG's large credit derivatives counterparties, since it was involved in the bailout negotiations. In September 2008, AIG's fresh credit rating downgrade (from AA to A) triggered a clause, requiring it to provide 100% collateral for many of its CDS contracts. It meant AIG had to quickly come up with tens of billions for some of its counterparties, and it was unable to do it. It was in that context that David Viniar made his September 16 remarks and obscured the fact that Goldman was not disinterested.

Goldman's board first learned of its ongoing collateral dispute with AIG in November 2007, and Goldman bought protection against the possibility that AIG would fail (only $1.5 billion was in dispute at this early stage).[37]

In July 2008, PricewaterhouseCoopers (PWC), the auditor for both Goldman and AIG, briefed Goldman's board about Goldman's hot dispute with AIG over its portfolio value. Goldman wanted more collateral, and AIG resisted. The amounts in dispute had grown larger.

Lloyd Blankfein said AIG was "marking to make-believe."[38] Goldman's co-president, Jon Winkelried, questioned PWC about its conflict of interest. Goldman increased its hedges; it paid $150 million for credit protection on $2.5 billion of debt. It also extracted billions more in collateral from AIG.

Goldman's Conflicts of Interest

Gary Cohn, president and COO of Goldman Sachs, boasted that Goldman over-hedged its exposure to AIG and might make $50 million if AIG collapsed.[39] Yet the November 17, 2009 SIGTARP report stated Goldman would "not agree to concessions, because it would have realized a loss if it had."[40]

This suggested Goldman was under hedged and would have suffered material losses without the government bailout. The report also questioned Goldman's prices of the CDOs and even its ability to collect on its hedges on AIG bankruptcy risk if AIG had collapsed. That is splendid information, since some (or all) of those hedges may have paid out given the circumstances of the AIG bailout.[41]

Participation in the bailout negotiations gives one a chance to structure the bailout in such a way to trigger as many hedge contracts as possible and get a double whammy. Whether or not it maximized its outcome, Goldman was not disinterested.

Stephen Friedman, a Goldman Sachs board member and then also Chairman of the Board of the New York Fed, bought shares of Goldman Sachs before the public knew that Goldman Sachs would receive full payments from AIG with public funds. Things were looking up for Goldman Sachs, and Friedman was in a better position than the public to know that. The public was still in the dark.[42]

*****

David Viniar and Ralph Cioffi

David Viniar and Ralph Cioffi, formerly co-head of Bear Stearns Asset Management and now fending off a dispute with former investors, have something in common. After I publicly opposed his proposed Everquest IPO, Cioffi claimed it had little exposure to subprime, because he was "hedged." In my experience, one usually addresses a deal's gross exposure, and then talks about being hedged. As it happened, Cioffi was under hedged.[43]

Ralph Cioffi had more in common with Goldman than disclosure style. *Reuters'* Matthew Goldstein reported that in March 2007, the funds Cioffi managed became the largest single investor in one of Goldman's toxic CDOs. The funds made a $300 million investment in Timberwolf I, a $1 billion Goldman deal. It was managed by Greywolf Capital, a firm founded by former Goldman bond traders. Within two weeks of the purchase, Goldman began marking down the value of the securities it just brought to market.[44]

Goldman's Undisclosed Role in AIG's Distress

November 10, 2009

Goldman wasn't the only contributor to the systemic risk that nearly toppled the global financial markets, but it was the key contributor to the systemic risk posed by AIG's near bankruptcy. When it came to the credit derivatives American International Group, Inc. (AIG) was required to mark-to-market, Goldman was the 800-pound gorilla.

According to *Bloomberg News*, calls for billions of dollars in collateral pushed AIG to the edge of disaster. The entire financial system was imperiled, and Goldman Sachs would have been exposed to billions in devastating losses.[45]

A Goldman spokesman told me its involvement in AIG's trades was only as an "intermediary," but that isn't even close to the full story. Goldman underwrote some of the CDOs comprising the underlying risk of the protection Goldman bought from AIG. Goldman also underwrote many of the (tranches of) CDOs owned by some of AIG's other trading counterparties.[46]

Even if all of Goldman's CDOs had been pristine, it poisoned its own well by elsewhere issuing deals like GSAMP Trust 2006-S3 that—along with dodgy deals issued by other financial institutions—eroded market trust in this entire asset class and drove down prices.

By September 2008, Goldman had approximately $20 billion in transactions with AIG. Goldman was AIG's largest counterparty, and its trades made up one-third of AIG's approximately $62.1 billion. Goldman's trades totaled $23 billion as of November 2007. As of November 2008, the remaining amount was $22.1 billion of which $13.9 billion was resolved by Maiden Lane III's purchase of $62.1 billion of CDOs. AIG retained another $8.2 billion of Goldman's credit default swaps referencing multi-sector CDOs in transactions requiring market prices.[47]

Goldman's current and former officers were influential in varying degrees in AIG's bailout. Hank Paulson was then Treasury Secretary and a former CEO at the time Goldman put on its trades with AIG and underwrote deals bought by some of AIG's counterparties. Lloyd Blankfein was CEO of Goldman and was influential in the bailout discussions. Stephen Friedman, then Chairman of the NY Fed, also served on Goldman's board.

AIG's other trading partners for the CDSs requiring mark-to-market prices included French banks Societe Generale (SocGen) and Calyon, Bank of Montreal, Wachovia, Merrill Lynch, UBS, Royal Bank of Scotland, and Deutsche Bank. Societe Generale (SocGen) was AIG's next largest counterparty with $18.7 billion (as of November 2007). SocGen, Calyon, Bank of Montreal, and Wachovia bought several (tranches) of Goldman's CDOs and hedged them with AIG.

On November 27, 2007, Joe Cassano, the former head of AIG's Financial Products unit, wrote a memo about the collateral AIG owed to its counterparties. Goldman, SocGen, Calyon and others required more than $4 billion. Goldman asked AIG for $3 billion of the $4 billion required in collateral calls. By September 2008, Goldman had called $7.5 billion in collateral from AIG.

AIG lists its transactions as negative basis trades. AIG may have used the term "negative basis trade" loosely. Whether Goldman was an intermediary (stood between AIG and yet another counterparty), or whether it booked negative basis trades,

Goldman had to manage its risk in the event AIG went under. This suggests Goldman earned a net profit by purchasing—or holding its own—CDO tranches and then hedging them with AIG.

The November 2009 SIGTARP report shows that Goldman held this risk in the form of credit default swaps for which it was a protection seller and it hedged its risk with AIG. Whether the risk was held as cash or credit default swaps, the negative basis trades, profitability, and risk to Goldman Sachs still applies. As AIG's financial situation worsened, Goldman bought further protection in the event AIG collapsed.

SocGen's negative basis trades totaled $18.6 billion. For example, SocGen bought protection from AIG on two tranches of Davis Square VI, a deal Goldman underwrote. According to AIG's documentation, SocGen got its prices for marking purposes for Goldman's deals from Goldman. As of November 2007, Goldman marked down these originally "AAA-rated" tranches to 67.5%, down by almost one-third.[48]

SocGen's list includes other deals underwritten by Goldman: Altius I, Davis Square II, Davis Square IV, the previously mentioned Davis Square VI, Putnam 2002-1, Sierra Madre, and possibly more. SocGen hedged this risk by purchasing protection (in the form of credit default swaps) from AIG.

Calyon had $4.5 billion of negative basis trades with AIG. Calyon and Goldman were co-lead on at least two deals: Davis Square II and Davis Square V. According to AIG's memo, Calyon got its prices for these deals from Goldman.

Goldman's list of negative basis trades prominently featured many of Merrill's CDOs (as underlying risk), and Merrill had its own list amounting to around $9.9 billion (as of November 2007). In Sept 2008, at the time of AIG's near collapse, Bank of America had just agreed to merge with Merrill, which held $6 billion of super senior exposure to CDOs hedged with an insurer, now revealed to be AIG. Both Ken Lewis, then CEO of BofA, and Hank Paulson received tough questions about the merger, but not tough enough. Lewis later testified that Hank Paulson (then Treasury Secretary and formerly CEO of Goldman at the time of the AIG related trading activity) urged him to be silent about Merrill's troubles. Merrill later received a $6.3 billion bailout payment from AIG.[49]

Bank of Montreal had $1.6 billion in negative basis trades with AIG, and at least two Goldman transactions (Davis Square I and Putnam 2002-1) made up 6 of its 9 positions with AIG. Wachovia had 6 trades with AIG, all related to Davis Square II, a deal that Goldman underwrote.

Goldman questioned PriceWaterhouse, Goldman's and AIG's common auditor, about prices. Goldman wanted lower prices, which meant that AIG would have to produce more collateral. When AIG was downgraded in September 2008, AIG was required to put up an aggregate amount of $14.5 billion in additional collateral to equal the full difference between original prices and market prices. But "market prices" in this illiquid market were influenced by Goldman Sachs.

Goldman was right to question the prices, make calls for collateral, and protect itself. Goldman's activity was not the same as that of an arsonist buying fire insurance, but its trading activities with AIG and others were accelerants of AIG's problems.

During AIG's bailout, Goldman had influence over the decision to use public funds to pay 100 cents on the dollar for these CDOs (the underlying risk of the credit derivatives), but none of the information about the volume of Goldman's trades with AIG—or the Goldman CDOs hedged by AIG's other counterparties—was made public.

Goldman's public disclosures in September 2008 obscured its contribution to AIG's near bankruptcy and the need to bail out Goldman's trading partners in AIG related transactions. Goldman's trading activities played a starring role in the near collapse of the global markets.

Backdoor Bailout for Goldman Sachs

Before September 16, 2008, AIG tried to negotiate a settlement for forty cents on the dollar. Other insurers have negotiated even deeper discounts to settle their CDS contracts on CDOs. The SIGTARP report shows that the FRBNY's decision to pay 100 cents on the dollar to resolve $13.9 billion (part of Goldman's $22.1 billion) of credit default swaps by purchasing the underlying CDOs in Maiden Lane III was important to Goldman Sachs. "Goldman Sachs...did not agree to concessions, because it would have realized a loss if it had."

Was this a backdoor bailout? According to Pulitzer Prize winner Gretchen Morgenson:

> On the question of whether this payout was what the report describes as a "backdoor bailout" of A.I.G.'s counterparties, Mr. Barofsky concluded: "The very design of the federal assistance to A.I.G. was that tens of billions of dollars of government money was funneled inexorably and directly to A.I.G.'s counterparties." [T]his was money the banks might not otherwise have received had A.I.G. gone belly-up.[50]

Treasury Secretary Timothy Geithner, then President of FRBNY, appears in Ms. Morgenson's article with apparent Stockholm syndrome rivaled only by Patty Hearst. He seems to echo Goldman's talking points after discussions with Goldman's CFO.[51]

Goldman's Turn to Apologize

In light of the SIGTARP report, I withdraw my earlier apology to Goldman. Public commitments to AIG are currently around $182 billion. If you wonder what Goldman CEO Lloyd Blankfein meant when he said Goldman Sachs "participated in things that were clearly wrong and we have reason to regret and we apologize for them,"[52] think of Goldman's role in AIG's crisis, Goldman's bailout, and Goldman's ongoing heavy taxpayer subsidies. That way, one of you will be genuinely sorry about it.

AIG Continued to Write Risky CDO Protection After 2005 [Lewis and TIME are Incorrect.]

March 20, 2010

Several people asked me this week whether AIG wrote credit default swap protection after 2005, since Michael Lewis wrote that AIG stopped writing protection at the end of 2005. Actually, AIG wrote protection after 2005 including protection on suspect residential mortgage products. In fact, AIG continued to write protection, even after I challenged its failure to take material write downs on its "super senior" CDSs in August 2007.

One had to do analysis to know this, until Congress released details of AIG's Schedule A filing. The general public would not have had access to the necessary information, since AIG's schedule A was redacted. Matthew Goldstein filed a FOIA for the redacted Schedule A data. When that didn't work and Congress finally released the information, he summarized AIG's post-2005 activity.[53]

Some of AIG's worst performing trades occurred after 2005. Notably, Matthew Goldstein points out in his article that Goldman Sachs was the biggest single purchaser of default protection from AIG on CDOs backed by residential mortgage backed securities after 2005. Goldman "purchased CDS on 10 securities with a face value of $6.54 billion." Deutsche also bought protection on $7.4 billion of commercial real estate backed CDOs from AIG after 2005 (Max 2007-1 and Max 2008-1).

$8.2 billion of Goldman synthetic CDOs, including Abacus deals originated after 2005, were not assumed by Maiden Lane III. The risk of these credit default swaps remains AIG's—and taxpayers'—obligation.

Less obvious is a secondary effect of managers at times trading very risky post-2005 CDOs into the CDO portfolios managed for AIG.

The above does not address AIG's securities lending, other long-dated derivatives exposures, or its mortgage related investments for its insurance portfolios.

Endnote: Stephen Gandel wrote an incorrect story for *TIME*. He didn't obtain updates from the rating agencies, and he either didn't hear or didn't understand what I said, because what he wrote does not represent my position regarding AIG.

*****

Goldman CEO Lloyd Blankfein to Treasury Secretary Hank Paulson: "OK, Now What?" (Humor)

August 23, 2010

It's September 2008. Goldman and AIG are trading in the markets, and Goldman notices that AIG seems to be having very severe liquidity problems. AIG needs to renew repo agreements after investing the trades' cash in plunging mortgage collateral bought from investment banks, and asks around for various other sources of funding.

Recognizing an emergency, Blankfein whips out his cell phone and calls Hank Paulson. He gasps to the Treasury Secretary and former Goldman CEO: "AIG, one of my biggest trading partners is going under! This will cause a market meltdown! What should we do?"

Paulson, in a calm comforting voice says: "Take a deep breath and pull yourself together. I can help. First, let's make sure AIG is really going under."

There is a long pause, during which Blankfein checks the status of his credit default protection and other hedges against an AIG failure, yanks AIG's credit lines, and presses AIG with calls for collateral on credit default swap agreements on plummeting CDOs.

Blankfein's voice finally comes back on the line. He says: "OK, now what?"

Goldman Sachs: Bullies on the Block

September 13, 2010

For most Americans, the Great Recession never ended, and for many of the 14.9 million unemployed Americans, it's a 21st century Depression. Yet in December 2009, Larry Summers, director of the White House National Economic Council, told ABC news: "Today, everybody agrees that the recession is over, and the question is what the pace of the expansion is going to be."[54]

The recession was over for bailed-out banks paying billions in bonuses. Taxpayers fund Wall Street with nearly zero-cost loans, and Congress changed accounting rules in April 2009 so that Wall

Street firms could hide losses to create the illusion of "big profits," as they try to fill the gaping holes in their balance sheets.

Money Cartel's Yes Men

The money cartel is as dangerous as the Mexican drug cartel. Its weapons of choice are taxpayer subsidized funds for swarms of Washington lobbyists, "money jobs" for politically connected yes men, and lucrative positions for former regulators and the law firms that hire them. Wall Street is winning the class war, and taxpayers supplied the arms.

Wall Street's PR spin, lobbying, money train to Congress, and bullying of fact finders have kept much of the truth away from the public. Frank Rich of *The New York Times* pointed out: "What we don't know will hurt us, and quite possibly on a more devastating scale than any [Al] Qaeda attack. Americans must be told the full story of how Wall Street gamed and inflated the housing bubble, made out like bandits, and then left millions of households in ruin."[55]

In my book on the global financial meltdown, I explain the relationship between failed mortgage lenders and Wall Street's private-label tentacled securitization process. It was a widespread interconnected Ponzi scheme. The bulk of toxic mortgages were the result of Wall Street's private label securitization (loan packaging) machine. Fannie and Freddie were forced to buy hundreds of billions of "highly rated" Wall Street mortgage backed "assets," and they are now Wall Street's ongoing mortgage dumping grounds. There should be thousands of felony indictments for accounting fraud and securities fraud.

Goldman's Abacus 2007-AC1, was a CDO at issue in a U.S. Securities and Exchange Commission lawsuit against Goldman alleging failure to disclose material information to investors. Goldman settled for $550 million, of which $250 million was paid in reparations to two sophisticated foreign banks.[56] Among other issues the SEC's settlement swept under the rug was that the Abacus deal may have been used to unload other complex value-destroying CDOs Goldman created.[57]

Goldman also knew or should have known the character of the risk of $14 billion of third-party value destroying CDOs it protected with AIG. Goldman claimed it acted as an "intermediary," as opposed to say, exchanging favors in a complicated game of *you bury my bodies and I'll bury yours*. The Fed used taxpayer dollars to settle these transactions for 100 cents on the dollar, an appalling example of crony capitalism.

Moreover, Goldman had also created additional value destroying CDOs (some were backed by cash assets and credit derivatives referencing value destroying CDOs), against which other banks—including some foreign banks—bought protection from AIG. Crony capitalism bailed out Goldman's trading partners for 100 cents on the dollar, even though other bond insurers were settling deals for much less than that, and many of these deals were worthy of thorough investigations and audits.

Goldman reneged on its offer to provide me with confirmation of the fact that it hadn't bought credit default protection [for a potential default by AIG] on more than a small fraction of the full notional amount of the CDOs it hedged with AIG. Contrary to its assertions to Congress, Goldman Sachs was significantly exposed to AIG's potential failure. It had both economic and reputation risk.

"Collateral" held by Goldman in September 2008 would likely have been clawed back by a sensible liquidator, after the nature of the CDOs was known. Even if Goldman got to keep the collateral, an AIG failure posed significant economic risk, since its hedges [credit default swaps on AIG] were relatively small, and the prices of the CDOs were plummeting.

Goldman also had litigation risk on the CDOs it underwrote (Davis Square and more) and sold to foreign banks that bought protection from AIG. Taxpayer money later made that problem disappear when the Fed settled for 100 cents on the dollar. This information had been suppressed and kept from public view.

> Goldman's other big role in the CDO business that few of its competitors appreciated at the time was as an originator of CDOs that other banks invested in and that ended up being insured by AIG, a role recently highlighted by Chicago credit consultant Janet Tavakoli. Ms. Tavakoli reviewed an internal AIG document written in late 2007 listing the CDOs that AIG had insured, a document obtained earlier this year by CBS News. [CBS did not have the data to

make the connection between the CDOs and Goldman's large role as underwriter of CDOs backing its own trades and the trades of other banks.][58]

Goldman was unsuccessful in misleading me, but what chance would non-financial professionals have against Goldman's hokum? Goldman misled many members of the press, Congress, and even "investigators" (unless investigators were going along for the ride) for a very long time.

Why did Goldman Sachs try to pass itself off as merely an "intermediary?" In my opinion, it was trying to make its role sound innocuous when it was not. In its role as a structurer and underwriter of CDOs, Goldman was responsible for a high standard of thorough due diligence.

Investigating a Criminal Cover-Up

On November 17, 2009, a week after my report on Goldman's hidden role in AIG's crisis, SIGTARP released its report. Despite discussing AIG and its problematic protection on CDOs, the report did not mention Goldman's key role as underwriter (creator) of many of the CDOs, including CDOs for which foreign banks were paid billions in the AIG settlement. It appears that either the well-staffed TARP investigators knew less than I did, or they didn't understand the implication of information they had (if they had it), or there was a cover-up. In other words, the SIGTARP report contained information that was less damaging to Goldman's fairy tales than what I had already put in the public domain on November 10, 2009.

That begs the question. When Goldman called me (before my November 10 report), did Goldman already know that the SIGTARP report would not contradict its story? In other words, did it know the SIGTARP report would fail to reveal its role as creator (underwriter) of many of the value destroying CDOs? Was SIGTARP part of a cover-up?

Documents filed with the SEC had been redacted so that the names of the CDOs backing credit default swaps, the size of individual deals, the fallen prices of the CDOs, and the names of the banks tied to each deal were not revealed. Was the SEC also part of a cover-up?

I sent my concerns to staffers on the Senate Banking Committee, the Financial Crisis Inquiry Commission, and other Congressional offices that had previously contacted me for information.

SIGTARP is now partly blaming Fed secrecy, yet why has SIGTARP been so slow to connect the dots? SIGTARP is now investigating a potential criminal cover-up.[59]

Perhaps it's also time to investigate SIGTARP's process, since it reeks like three day old fish.

Dodd-Frank Reform Failure: "Customer Transactions" Were Behind the Meltdown

Goldman was responsible for huge systemic risk, even though it characterized its AIG trades as "customer transactions." It's one thing to provide emergency relief for "troubled assets," and it's quite another for Congress to delay so long in asking how these assets came to be so troubled in the first place. Congress has neither uncovered the truth nor mitigated the risk of even greater future devastation. The Dodd-Frank Bill does not provide necessary financial reform, because Wall Street lobbyists successfully tailored the language to suit bankers.

Senator Carl Levin (D. Mich.), Chairman of a senate investigative panel, issued a memo stating that Goldman "magnified the impact of toxic mortgages."[60]

> In one case, a $38 million subprime-mortgage bond created in June 2006 ended up in more than 30 debt pools and ultimately caused roughly $280 million in losses to investors by the time the bond's principal was wiped out in 2008, according to data reviewed by The Wall Street Journal.

In other words, Goldman kept repackaging, reselling or protecting (buying credit default protection on) losers. It took the wrong kind of nerve for Goldman's CEO to say he was doing "God's work,"[61] when the reality includes this brand of malicious mischief.

Jesse's Cafe Americain provides perspective to Blankfein's boast:[62]

> There will be hard times in the last days. People will love only themselves and money. They will brag and be proud, tearing others down. They will be without love, gratitude, respect, or forgiveness. They will tell lies and be out of control. They will despise what is good and betray friends. They will believe they are better than others, and will love only what pleases them. They will say they are serving God, but their actions will show they are not. 2 Timothy 3:1-5

All of the large Wall Street banks generate huge risk in foreign exchange, commodities trading, interest rate derivatives, credit derivatives and more. The Dodd-Frank Bill's so-called financial reform leaves the entire financial system at great risk from "customer transactions."

America's middle class is caught in the middle of a bi-partisan betrayal. Righting these wrongs will not be easy. Among other things, it may require an amendment to our Constitution to prevent money cartels from buying off our elected officials.

*****

CHAPTER 3 Caveat Emptor

Bank of America Says Merrill's Huge Hit was in December (Not November)?

January 26, 2009

James Mahoney, a Bank of America spokesman said: "Beginning in the second week of December, and progressively over the remainder of the month, market conditions deteriorated substantially relative to market conditions prior to the Dec. 5 shareholder meetings. So Merrill wound up making adjustments for the quarter that were far greater than anticipated at the beginning of the month [December].

These losses were driven by mark-to-market adjustments which were necessitated by changes in the credit markets, and those conditions change on a daily basis."[63]

Maybe. But BofA and Merrill will have to explain that in some detail, because shareholders will want to know why the November roiling of the markets did not cause huge mark-downs. How about some disclosure to reassure everyone? Especially since at least one investment bank already explained how November was such a horrific month that they had a surprise loss due to the credit markets. Yet, BofA says Merrill's surprise loss was in December, so let's recap November.

This did not get enough press, but in early November, Chinese banks (top tier banks like Bank of China and Industrial and Commercial Bank of China) refused to fork over billions in collateral on dollar/yen FX trades which were out of the money after the yen's October appreciation. The headlines should have read (but didn't): "Chinese Banks say: *STUFF IT*."

The Chinese banks won a game of drag race "chicken" with foreign banks. Most credit support annex agreements would say that closing out these trades would be an event of default, and then the cross default on all the trades would kick in with the same counterparty. But the credit of the Chinese banks was better than many of their counterparties, and they renegotiated contracts with the Chinese banks.

What inspired Chinese banks to play and win this game of brinkmanship? The motive may be entirely unrelated to the bath that highly-placed "retail client" Chinese have taken with investments in mini-bombs, er, I mean mini-bonds, sold to them with "AAA" ratings by U.S. investment banks. The latter is just icing on the rice cake.[64]

Hedges on exotic equity trades failed (delta "hedging") in October when Volkswagen rose, and French banks took losses, and around $50 billion of these trades would roll in December. That was obvious in November. Correlation books took huge hits. Also in November in Asia, I believe, correlation trades blew up and *Merrill Asia's correlation book may have taken huge losses*, and it was partly linked to structured (equity) products. "Correlation" trades unwound like crazy and there were large losses. Yet, Merrill says it did not take huge losses in November?

In the last three weeks (primarily last two weeks) of November, corporate leveraged loans, private equity (and related loans) and commercial real estate hit the skids.

Some of November's events triggered Goldman's surprise loss of more than $2 billion, most of which (for Goldman) occurred in the last two weeks of November reportedly from corporate leveraged loans, correlation trades, private equity and related loans and commercial real estate. But according to Merrill, its losses were in December, not November. Maybe. But as a U.S. taxpayer, I say: *Prove it.*

I would like to see a detailed explanation of how Merrill's rubber gripped the road round Dead Man's Curve during a horrific November (Goldman could take a lesson from Merrill—who knew?), and I'd like to see the breakdown of its surprise losses in December.

*****

Merrill's Murder/Suicide

February 7, 2009

Yesterday, Tom Patrick of Vernon Capital and former executive vice Chairman of Merrill Lynch (ousted from Merrill in 2003), told CNBC that Merrill Lynch committed suicide. He said that from June 2006 to March 2007 Merrill's super senior CDO positions rose from $4 billion to $60 billion and it never sold a bond.

Tom Patrick and CNBC just woke up to the problems at Patrick's former stomping grounds. *Sort of.*

As appalling as Tom Patrick's and CNBC's late-to-the-party revelations sound, it wasn't that simple and it wasn't that innocent.

As I told CNBC on October 24, 2007, Merrill suppressed key facts, hadn't hedged properly quarters earlier, failed to report losses, and had an Enronesque problem. (In January of 2007, I wrote an article for GARP saying risk professionals should bail out and short the positions.)

Tom Patrick confirmed what I had told CNBC (and many others) long ago. Merrill's risk would boomerang back on its balance sheet. There were few actual sales, just temporary transfers of risk. But that was just a part of the problem.

It is a shame that Merrill couldn't quietly commit suicide. In trying to delay its own death, it dragged others down with it.

As I explain in my new book, *Dear Mr. Buffett* (Warren Buffett will feature the book prominently at the Berkshire Hathaway Annual Meeting in May 2009), any investment banker worth their salt knew that "super senior" and "AAA" tranches and other "investment grade" tranches did not deserve those ratings, yet bond insurers, special purpose investment vehicles, and hedge funds participated in the madness adding risk and leverage to the financial community.

Investments in pension funds, mutual funds and retail investments soured. For some of these "sophisticated investors" it seemed like a suicide pact with Merrill and other culpable investment banks. But for many naïve retail investors and for prudent financiers who are watching the effects on the global financial community, Murder/Suicide seems a more apt description. Moreover, Merrill was not the only investment bank that participated in this madness.

Ken Lewis Must Go

April 24, 2009 (Ken Lewis resigned at the end of September 2009)

The key issue is whether Ken Lewis disclosed losses to shareholders in the early December meeting. He did not. Furthermore, if you look at the linked article in my analysis below, it seems James Mahoney, BofA's spokesman, was (intentionally or otherwise) part of a cover-up (see January 26 *WSJ a*rticle embedded in the link below).

In my opinion, the bottom line is—and was—that Ken Lewis must go.

Hank Paulson was hyped as one of the best and brightest, because he was a former Goldman CEO. But I would argue that he must believe his own hype if he thought that people would not immediately question the timing of the Merrill losses and Lewis's disclosure. It was extremely inappropriate for him to even opine on whether Ken Lewis should disclose the losses, much less reportedly pressure Lewis not to disclose.[65] That aside, Lewis is an adult and a highly paid CEO responsible for his decisions.

Around the end of January, I publicly challenged BofA's representation of the timing of the Merrill losses. There were large losses in Oct/November, but it seemed primarily November, and Lewis should have known this going into the December shareholder meeting. Obviously I was only working with publicly available information and experience that Ken Lewis should probably have as well. This is my analysis. You may wish to compare this with Merrill's fourth quarter release and subsequent admissions.

Bank of America's Shareholders Should Reject Bonus Plans

January 12, 2010

In July 2009, New York Attorney General Andrew Cuomo reported that, among other things, the compensation structures at most banks were "a major impetus for the subprime fiasco."

Bank of America, Merrill Lynch (now part of Bank of America), Washington Mutual (now part of JPMorgan Chase), Wells Fargo,

General Electric, JPMorgan Chase, Citigroup, Bear Stearns (now part of JPMorgan Chase), AIG, and Wachovia (now part of Wells Fargo) were participants or are now current owners of the top 20 subprime (or high interest loan) lenders during the period of the worst abuses from 2005 through 2007.[66] In addition, these financial institutions, along with Goldman Sachs and Morgan Stanley, contributed funding through credit lines or sales without which the lending would not have been possible.

Shareholders fed up with the fact that key contributors to the global credit crisis plan to pay billions of dollars' worth of cash and stock in bonuses to employees might consider following Goldman's suit. Goldman Sachs's shareholders brought separate actions against the Board of Directors for alleged breach of fiduciary duties in approving billions of dollars in bonuses.

Bank of America and its acquisitions, Countrywide and Merrill Lynch, were neck-deep in the subprime crisis. In July 2008, Bank of America acquired Countrywide, which made $97 billion in subprime or high interest loans during the peak years of 2005 through 2007.

Countrywide was renamed Bank of America Home Loans in February 2009. Separately, BofA bought Merrill Lynch, which bought First Franklin from Nat City in September 2006. First Franklin was one of the top four subprime lenders with more than $68 billion in loans from 2005 to the end of 2007. The operation was closed in March 2008.

On October 6, 2008 (three days after TARP was approved), Bank of America agreed to settle a multi-state predatory lending lawsuit against Countrywide for $8.68 billion. Bank of America received its first $25 billion TARP injection around three weeks later.

Bank of America proposes to pay billions of dollars' worth of cash and stock bonuses to its Merrill Lynch employees. Merrill Lynch claims that the fact that it lost tens of billions of dollars on so-called super senior "investments" during the crisis is proof it innocently sold risky investments to others. Don't believe it.

Here's what happened. Merrill was involved with a lot of subprime lending and packaging and knew or should have known exactly what it was doing. What is more, Merrill had other pockets of risk unrelated to subprime.

For example, in December 2006, Ownit, a California-based mortgage lender partly owned by Merrill, declared bankruptcy. Its CEO, William Dallas, stated he was paid more to originate no-income-verification loans than for loans with full documentation.[67]

Michael Blum, then Merrill Lynch's head of global asset-backed finance, sat on Ownit's board. (Blum left Merrill in mid-2008 after the securitization was cut back.) When Ownit declared bankruptcy—instead of demanding a fraud audit—Blum faxed in his resignation.

After the bankruptcy, Merrill continued packaging Ownit's loans. Following a multi-year pattern, Merrill disguised the risk. Merrill packaged Ownit's risky loans in 2007, and failed to disclose that it was Ownit's largest creditor.[68]

Within a year, the so-called "AAA" rated tranche was downgraded to a junk rating of B, meaning you are likely to lose your shirt. (A mutual fund was stuck with it.) This meant that "investment grade" tranches below the "AAA" were worthless or nearly worthless, because those investors agreed to take losses before the "AAA" investors.

Losses were not simply due to fickle market prices. There was permanent value destruction.

Merrill Lynch further disguised risk by repackaging phony "investment grade" tranches into new investments called CDOs and CDO-squared. Credit derivatives amplified the problem, because one could sell value-destroying investments more than once. This was only obvious to professionals, because some mortgages took a couple of years for payments to reset. By 2007, things were so bad that many loans were total shams and began defaulting almost immediately. This is the classic end of a Ponzi scheme.

Merrill Lynch did not sell tens of billions of uninsured so-called super-safe "super senior" CDOs, because if it had, in-the-know market players would have discounted them.

Merrill Lynch could not find enough demand from bond insurers to disguise its risk. AIG stopped insuring Merrill's CDOs before the end of 2006. Merrill insured other CDOs with other bond insurers: ACA (now bankrupt) and municipal bond insurer MBIA, which was since downgraded from AAA to junk.

Merrill's employees wanted to continue to earn high bonuses, so they did not sell them, they did not record losses, and they temporarily got away with this fiction. Merrill's accountants—like all of Wall Street's accounting firms—failed in their jobs.

At the beginning of 2007, the problem was obvious to many alert non-professionals, but the SEC still let Merrill (and other Wall Street firms) get away with it. That year, Merrill Lynch issued 30 CDOs amounting to $32 billion. Within a year, every single CDO had its "AAA" tranches downgraded to junk by one or more rating agencies.[69]

By the second quarter of 2007, Merrill's executives still told shareholders things were rosy. Yet Bear Stearns's hedge fund creditors heavily discounted similar investments and put low prices on many of them. Credit derivatives benchmarks began a death spiral. Merrill Lynch failed to take billions of dollars of losses for the second quarter of 2007, despite publicly available information that belied its accounting reports.

Bank of America struck a deal to acquire Merrill Lynch in September 2008. In January 2009, one month after the shareholder vote on the merger, BofA revealed that Merrill reported more than $15 billion in losses for the fourth quarter of 2008. Even then BofA did not come clean about the exact timing of the losses. BofA claimed the losses occurred in December. I publicly refuted the claim and said most of the losses had probably occurred in November due to trading activities unrelated to subprime or CDOs.

Bank of America kept shareholders in the dark and took another $20 billion in TARP money. The Slumbering Esquires Club (SEC) may just now file a new complaint to add the charge that Merrill failed to disclose the enormous material losses before the December 2008 shareholder vote.[70]

Bank of America continues to receive massive subsidies from the U.S. taxpayer without which its level of earnings would not be possible. BofA took $45 billion in TARP money (since repaid), has guarantees of $118 billion against bad assets, and continues to receive massive amounts of taxpayer financing subsidies in various forms.

Why should Bank of America—or any other firm involved with the debacle—hand out billions of dollars' worth of cash and stock to employees while pretending its business model and incentives aren't fatally flawed?

JPMorgan's Losses From Indecent Exposure

August 9, 2010

JPMorgan Chase's fixed-income revenue fell almost 28% to $3.6 billion in the second quarter, down from $5.5 billion in the first quarter, and down from $4.9 billion for the same period last year. JPMorgan blamed an interest rate squeeze and bad results in the credit markets and the commodities markets.

There were no details of its significant loss from unwise, gigantic, wrong-way wartime coal bets. The bank took a short position so enormous that it was oversized relative to the global coal market, and second quarter losses reportedly were in the hundreds of millions of dollars.[71]

Financial Reform Failure

Blythe Masters, managing director in charge of JPMorgan's global commodities group, spent time lobbying in Washington to dilute financial reform. By her own admission, JPMorgan's recent speculation in coal wasn't client driven; the risk was taken on JPMorgan's behalf. The Dodd-Frank Financial Reform Bill does nothing to prevent a repeat—or even a potentially worse—debacle.

The commodities division isn't the only area in which JPMorgan is vulnerable. Credit derivatives, interest rate derivatives, and currency trading are vulnerable to leveraged hidden bets. Ambitious managers strive to pump speculative earnings from zero to hero.

Instead of transparent and regulated markets, we have dark markets, hidden leverage, proprietary speculative trading, lax regulation and oversized risks.

"Scared Sh*tless"[72]

Blythe Masters told her remaining employees that competitors are "scared sh*tless" of JPMorgan's commodities division. She claimed the layoffs of 10% of front office staff are not a sign of JPMorgan "panicking" and called the risk taking in coal trading that left JPMorgan wide-open to a massive short squeeze a "rookie error."

For individual traders, JPMorgan doesn't follow the Wall Street maxim: *He who sells what isn't his'n, must buy it back or go to pris'n.* The U.S. can count on JPMorgan to continue both long and short market manipulation and take its winnings and losses from blind gambles. Shareholders, taxpayers, and consumers will foot the bill for any unpleasant global consequences.

Physical oil traders from JPMorgan's brand new RBS Sempra Commodities LLP acquisition (JPMorgan paid $1.7 billion) left of their own accord to join smaller firms with less capital. Masters said these were "very interesting career decisions."

The defections were all the more interesting, because Masters began her career as a JPMorgan commodities trader. RBS Sempra's oil traders gave Masters a vote of no confidence. Their flight was a loss of "key people," whom she said she needs to replace.

Masters is poised for more debacles, proclaiming:

> *All it's going to take is a little pop to the upside. We could be producing a 30 to 35 percent ROE and looking like gods.*

Good luck with that. Masters also noted that this potential windfall might come at the expense of others:

> *We've got too many banks chasing too little volume and margins have compressed.*

The United States is trying to pull out of the greatest financial tailspin in its history. Dice-rolling braggadocio by a key officer at one of the nation's largest banks is exactly the kind of thing Congress, taxpayers, and voters should find scary.

Ramp up Risk and Cross Your Fingers

Big unanticipated market moves always result in big winners and big losers among big gamblers. After the fact, most winners claim they were smart—not just lucky.

When bank managers take a big gamble and lose hundreds of millions of dollars, they don't call it reckless; they spin it as an error of "judgment." The directive is to "put on risk" and "generate results." This may be why Masters cautioned employees:

> *I don't want us talking to the outside world, neither about successes nor about failures.*

JPMorgan is making big bets and crossing its fingers in a dangerous and volatile market.

Masters takes "pleasure" in the "ballsiest" business, and she wants her traders to get lucky. Moreover, she's engaged in internal spin control and plans a "deep dive" with the Board and the CFO. This may reduce her chances of walking Wall Street.

No one should be concerned for the job security of managers like Masters at JPMorgan, and that is precisely the problem. Delusional risk-taking and lack of transparency at Too-Big-To-Fail banks—especially in the areas most vulnerable to rampant speculation—were ignored by so-called financial reform.

Jamie Dimon and Robert Rubin: Evasive on "Fraud as a Business Model"

November 12, 2010

Foreclosure fraud isn't about losing paperwork or having incorrect paperwork. It is about committing fraud and trying to manipulate the U.S. legal system. No one—not even a bank—can show up in court with phony evidence.

State Attorneys General decry foreclosure fraud, because among other things, people signed affidavits making representations that were untrue. This is fraud on the court. All of these foreclosures may be vacated.

Corrupt people in Congress and corrupt regulators cannot intervene for the banks this time. Banks have to face state courts, and many Attorneys General are happy to take them on.

Banks that committed fraud on the court do not get a do-over. Even if they can show up later with correct documents, it does not erase the original crime of fraud on the court. Anyone who presented phony documents as evidence in court broke the law.

Former Ohio Attorney General Richard Cordray advised banks that engaged in fraud on the courts (by submitting falsified affidavits) to negotiate meaningful loan modifications.

Jamie Dimon's Evasion

Jamie Dimon, CEO of JPMorgan Chase, said that JPMorgan did not foreclose on people who didn't deserve it. Dimon was dismissive saying JPMorgan might have to pay some penalties, but it should just carry on with foreclosures. Financial reporter Annie Lowrey noted that JPMorgan's third quarter 2010 report contradicts its CEO:

> But the financial statement itself proved the lie. The bank said it was carefully checking 115,000 mortgage affidavits. It set aside a whopping $1.3 billion for legal costs. And it put an extra $1 billion into a now $3 billion fund for buying back bunk mortgages and mortgage products. [73]

JPMorgan's role in alleged foreclosure fraud had already been made public when Dimon made these ill-considered statements.

In a CNBC interview, Former Ohio Attorney General Richard Cordray refuted baseless claims made by Ally Bank, formerly known as GMAC Bank, which was bailed out by TARP. Ally said that it didn't know of instances of improper foreclosures. Cordray shot back that every foreclosure done with falsified affidavits was improper. It's fraud on the courts. He stated that as yet, no one knows the scope, but it could be tens of thousands or hundreds of thousands of instances of fraud on the court.

The fact that this happened repeatedly doesn't make it more excusable, it makes it worse. Ally Bank, Bank of America, and JPMorgan have admitted to this practice. Apparently they had "fraud as a business model."[74]

The good news for banks is that Richard Cordray was not reelected to the post of Ohio's Attorney General. The bad news for banks—and the good news for Ohio—is that Cordray may become an Ohio Supreme Court Justice.

Robert Rubin Dodges Responsibility

The Economist's Buttonwood Gathering in New York on October 25 featured Robert Rubin, former senior advisor of Citigroup (also former Treasury Secretary under President Bill Clinton, and former Co-Chair of Goldman Sachs) as head of the first panel. He led a role-play about what might happen if one of the United States defaulted on its debt in the year 2013.

States cannot declare bankruptcy, but neither Rubin nor any other panel member mentioned it. Instead of putting states on notice now that they have to get their budgets in order—even if it means cutting back on promises—the panel suggested that the Federal Government should bail out the states.

When it came time for Q&A, I asked the first question and framed it by pointing out the irony of this panel discussing a potential state default and systemic risk. While many states have been fiscally irresponsible, their distress is now acute due to fraudulent lending further damaging the economy leading to reduced tax revenues.

Moreover, weak states also have higher borrowing costs, since municipal bond insurers' credit ratings imploded after they sold credit default swap (CDS) protection on value destroying securitizations (CDOs).

Rubin's Citigroup bought credit default swap protection from Ambac, one of the two largest municipal bond insurers, on Citi's value destroying mortgage backed securitizations.

During Rubin's watch as Citigroup's "risk wizard," Ambac sold protection on Citi's toxic CDOs including Diversey Harbor ($1.875 billion), Ridgeway Court Funding I ($1.57 billion), Ridgeway Court Funding II ($1.95 billion), Adams Square II ($510 million), 888 Funding ($500 million), Class V Funding III ($500 million). Citi settled many of these contracts with Ambac for deep discounts. (The Fed did not have taxpayers' interests in mind when it settled AIG's transactions with Goldman Sachs and others for 100 cents on the dollar.)

Ambac filed for Chapter 11 bankruptcy on November 8, 2010, two weeks after Rubin's shameful performance on this panel.

Robert Rubin didn't express an ounce of regret (or context) for his role in the crisis. On the contrary, he was insufferably smug. In his opening remarks, Rubin self-servingly asserted that no one could foresee the crisis in 2007, despite ample public evidence to the contrary. Citigroup and Ambac never came up.

The Biggest Headache for Investors in Groupon and Facebook

March 3, 2011

Groupon makes its money by selling coupons for goods and services. It partners with local merchants. When you buy a coupon for a merchant's discount on Groupon, it reportedly takes a 50% cut in the U.S.

Groupon has had a few embarrassments. On Valentine's Day, FTD's flowers were priced lower than Groupon's "deals" and the online discounter had to apologize to customers. Moreover, merchants often put conditions and restrictions on Groupon discounts that dilute the value of the deal, similar to restrictions on redeeming air miles. Even so Groupon's valuations have ranged from $1.2 billion to $6 billion to $15 billion all in the space of a year. What's it really worth? More on that later.

Facebook is free and "always will be." It makes its money from ads and revenues from games (if users don't block them), albeit phone apps so far do not display ads. Michael Arrington at *Techcrunch* reported that Facebook is secretly building its own phone to control its own operating system.[75] He noted that Li Ka-Shing is a Facebook investor, and he is an investor in the rumored INQ and Spotify phone project. While Facebook may remain free, it would have to figure out a way to get users to pay their phone bills.

Facebook has tremendous potential to exploit its 500 million users. In fact, one of Facebook's fundraisers is a genius at exploitation. Goldman Sachs, the Great and Powerful Oz of Finance (just don't look behind the curtain), has already opined on Facebook's value. In January 2011, it valued Facebook at $50 billion when it sought to raise $1.5 billion in Facebook financing.

Rich Teitelbaum of *Bloomberg News* reminded the financial world that Goldman Sachs Asset Management's anemic track record suggests that Goldman may not be the best go-to source for putting a value on an asset. Despite Goldman's public relations hype that it employs the "best and brightest," it trailed the average return of its peer group in every category. Goldman has an incentive to dangle a high valuation on Facebook in front of clients:

> Jim Clark of Netscape and Silicon Graphics fame was irritated that Goldman wanted to fee stuff its Facebook offering with a 4 percent placement fee, a half percent expense fee, and a snatch-back of 5 percent of investors' potential profits.
>
> A few months earlier, Clark had invested in Facebook through another financial firm at a lower price, and the other firm wouldn't potentially gouge him with Goldman's 5 percent pleasure-of-your-company tax. "I don't think it's reasonable," Clark told Bloomberg. "It's just another way for [Goldman] to make money from their clients." The question remains whether Clark bought his stake at a reasonable price.[76]

In January 2011, SharesPost Inc. valued Facebook at $82.9 billion on the secondary exchange. Whatever price the market will pay today, one has to be concerned about what it will pay tomorrow. Even if the future value of Facebook is say, $4 billion, Goldman will rake in fees.

Impermanent Value

Both Facebook and Groupon became successes because they are web based networks that required few management skills, minimum capital to start, and there were no barriers to entry. That is also their biggest problem. The ugly truth is that no one can tell you what they are worth as businesses.

Groupon's successful-so-far revenue model is its curse. It's both trying to hold its position in "established" markets, and it's trying to expand. The problem is that web users in other countries have noticed Groupon's success and the fact that Groupon has been paying high premiums for local established discounting web sites just to get at the client distribution lists.

Groupon's competitors are both buying sites for the same reason as Groupon, and local entrepreneurs can easily copy Groupon's business model. It seems all it takes is a good web developer, a two-page merchant agreement, and an accounting firm that can handle the taxes as a site expands internationally. Groupon may have a head start, but it has no long-term competitive advantage. That puts its margins, its market share, and its ability to expand and hold its position in new markets at risk.[77]

Smart investors look for highly skilled managers in industries with a long-term competitive advantage in a stable industry run by decision makers with a "here-today, here-forever" mentality. Between Groupon and Facebook, it seems Facebook has the better chance of making a case, but it hasn't made one so far.

Facebook seems to be thinking of ways to create a loyal user base by penetrating deep within its user base. It certainly has a shot, but it is unclear whether it can maintain a competitive advantage.

Users are fickle, and young users will gravitate to the next exciting new thing. The rapid success of Catherine Cook's myyearbook.com has to give investors pause. She started the site 6 years ago as a 16-year-old high school student with a $250,000 investment from her brother, and the site is valued at $20 million. While it's no threat to Facebook, it has a fresh look, is responsive to users, and offers new spins such as allowing users to buy each other gifts and "lunch money."[78][79]

Investors may wonder when the next bright young kid will eat Facebook's lunch and make it look like a site for old fogies. Facebook may adapt, but it would do itself favors by disclosing its revenues, and how it plans to face up to potential competitors.

Mark Zuckerberg's Value Problem: "My" Facebook Profile Was a Fraud, So Was "Warren Buffett's"

July 14, 2011

I don't use Facebook. Neither does Warren Buffett, but phonies have used his name on Facebook. Earlier this month, an imposter created "my" profile on Facebook. In order to get the fake removed, Facebook required an uploaded scan of a government issued I.D. that shows a photo and birth date (for example, a driver's license or passport). Facebook suggests one black out the most sensitive information and claims it will delete this scanned information from its servers once identity has been verified.

In other words, after an impostor faked my identity, I was the one who had to put myself further at risk by providing a verifiable scanned government I.D. to prove I had the right to complain about the fraud enabled by Facebook.

The Antisocial Network

There was no mechanism to email a human, who could have easily verified my identity without the need for me to upload a scan of a government issued I.D. (after blacking out the document number). There was also no way to even submit the report using the "Reports" link without the upload.

Christopher Soghoian, a privacy advocate at the Center for Applied Cybersecurity Research at Indiana University told the *Wall Street Journal*: "People do not like Facebook. They do not trust Facebook. Facebook gets people to give up information under the claim that it's private and then it's made public. And your only option is to shut down your account."[80]

I now completely agree with Mr. Soghoian. I don't like Facebook, and I don't trust Facebook. You don't even need an account to be punked by Facebook. When you've been impersonated, Facebook asks for private information and claims it will delete it from its servers, but given that it has failed to protect private information in the past, why should anyone trust this claim? Yet I had no choice but to supply the information in order to get cooperation from Facebook to take down the fraudulent profile.

The Facebook Team responded three days later reporting it had removed the profile. If you expect niceties such as "sorry for the inconvenience," forget it. That might be fine if you are imposing on Facebook, but when Facebook's protocol has imposed on you, something more is required, if Facebook ever wants to be taken seriously as a valuable business.

Investors Should Take Note of Phony "Users"

Mark Zuckerberg said that Facebook is "free" and always will be. But it isn't true for all of its users. Facebook claims "750 million active users," and some, the "whales," must eventually provide profitable business.

Facebook requires revenues, and it requires an eventual demonstration of ongoing profits to keep investors happy. That means it needs users to buy goods and services so that Facebook gets a cut of the action. It's an indirect cost imposed on the Facebook users that support the network. If Facebook loses those willing buyers, it loses the whole ballgame.

Eventually investors will want to know the number of profiles of people in the demographic sectors that are most likely to buy goods and services. If one had a mind for mischief, then one could mislead investors by, intentionally or otherwise, allowing phony profiles of whales. In my case, Facebook did just that. Investors should ask if this is a habit.

Reasonable Questions

What is Facebook's strategy? Where is its audited balance sheet? Which users provide the most revenue? Of target demographic profiles, how many are fakes? How many authentic users does Facebook actually have? Does Facebook know how many user profiles are genuine, and if so, how does it know?

Based on my experience, Facebook doesn't know who is real and who isn't real. Many people may not even be aware there is an impostor profile of them on Facebook, and if they are aware, they may resent the hoops they have to jump through to get it removed. I know I was tempted to shrug and let it go, but I didn't.

Investors should take that into account when evaluating Facebook's "users" and the potential for revenues they represent.

The "Social Network" Broke the Social Contract

If you eat in a cafeteria that asks you to dispose of your trash and put away your tray after you eat, you cooperate, because you are holding up your end of the social contract. You clean up for the next person, whom you've never met. You trust that others understand and honor this social contract, too. You trust that someone who has never met you will have the courtesy to clean the table before you arrive for your next meal. It doesn't make you superior. It just means you understand the utility of honoring the social contract. On your next visit, you won't have to carry your tray to a table covered with trash. But if others break this social contract, you'll find another place to eat where the people are smart enough to cooperate with the social contract, because it is a nicer place to hang out.

Facebook may think it's too cool to honor the web's social contract. It may believe its image says "we are the Borg," but to me it says "we are the slobs," and we're not interested in running a business. Facebook's attitude is futile, and I won't be assimilated.

Users who believe they're getting something free may tolerate it, but people who spend money, actual customers, will find a better place to hang out as soon as an alternative becomes available. As I mentioned in an earlier commentary, "The Biggest Headache for Investors in Groupon and Facebook," bright young people are doing interesting things on the web that may one day challenge Facebook on features alone. If newcomers are trustworthy and courteous, Facebook will lose its revenue generators.

Facebook will have a hard time keeping its inflated stock market valuation—currently roughly $84 billion for its privately traded shares—once investors face up to its flawed business model. For my part, I can say that if you ever see a profile of "me" on Facebook, it will be another impostor.

CHAPTER 4 Gold and Silver

Washington Must Ban U.S. Credit Derivatives as Traders Demand Gold

March 8, 2010

Congress should act immediately to abolish credit default swaps on the United States, because these derivatives will foment distortions in global currencies and gold. Failure to act now will only mean the U.S. will be forced to act after these "financial weapons of mass destruction" levy heavy casualties. These obligations now settle in euros, but the end game is to settle them in gold. This is so ripe for speculative manipulation that you might as well cover the U.S. map with a bull's-eye.

Credit default swaps are not insurance. If you buy fire insurance on your home, you must own the house. If you buy credit protection on the United States, however, you do not need to own U.S. Treasury bonds. If your protection gains value after you buy it—not because the U.S. defaults, but because of market mood changes—you can resell that protection and make a profit.

Lower credit risk means a lower price for protection. Zero implies zero risk. The higher the basis points, the higher the implied risk. When U.S. credit default swaps were first introduced, the price of protection was around two basis points. According to *Bloomberg*, the price for five-year protection was around 38 basis points (per annum) on Friday. But the price in the over-the-counter market—where this stuff actually trades—was almost double or around 75 basis points.

Since most traders in U.S. credit default swaps don't think the U.S. will default any time soon, why are they trading U.S. credit default swaps? They are speculating on price movements the way a day trader buys and sells stocks to speculate on stock price movements.

Volume in U.S. credit default swaps is relatively small, but it can explode rapidly, just as volume expanded rapidly for credit default swaps on mortgage debt in 2006 and 2007.

Speculators Want U.S. CDS Payoffs in Gold

Remember AIG? When prices moved against AIG on its credit default swap contracts, AIG owed cash (collateral) to its trading partners. AIG paid billions of dollars and owed billions more when U.S. taxpayers bailed it out in September 2008.

U.S. credit default swaps currently trade in euros. After all, if the U.S. defaults, who will want payment in devalued U.S. dollars? The euro recently weakened relative to the dollar, and market participants are calling for contracts that require payment in gold. If they get their way, speculators on the winning side of a price move will demand collateral paid in gold.

The market can create an unlimited number of these contracts very rapidly. The U.S. wouldn't have to ever default to trigger a major disruption in the gold market. Spreads (or prices) on the credit default swaps could simply move based on "news," and demand for gold would soar.

If this speculation drives up the price of gold, and the available gold supply becomes limited, are you willing to post your children as collateral? I am pushing the point so that we put a stop to this before it is too late.

Global Disaster in the Making

More than a year has passed since former Treasury Secretary Henry Paulson went to Congress in September 2008 to plead for special powers and TARP money to bail out U.S. financial institutions. Yet there has been no meaningful financial reform.

The European Union has its own challenges. German Chancellor Angela Merkel recently called for limits on credit derivatives on Greece, since the European Union is concerned about misuse of credit derivatives for speculation. Chancellor Merkel did not go far enough.

World leaders shouldn't merely ask for limits on sovereign credit derivatives. They should demand a ban on all sovereign credit default swaps.

Washington Must Ban U.S. Credit Derivatives: Games and Gold (Part 2)

March 12, 2010

In an earlier post, I wrote that Congress should act immediately to abolish credit default swaps on the United States, because these derivatives will foment distortions in global currencies and gold. Credit default swaps on the United States currently settle in euros, but there is talk of creating new contracts calling for settlement in gold. This is just a trial balloon discussion at the moment, but it is one that Congress should immediately deflate along with all credit derivatives on the United States.

Most traders in U.S. credit default swaps don't think the U.S. will default as long as we have money printing presses, so they are speculating on price movements. If speculators manage to get contracts to settle in gold, speculators on the winning side of a price move will demand collateral paid in gold.

Gold is Collateral on the London CME

Presenting gold to satisfy demands for Performance Bond Collateral has been allowed on the London CME in a limited way since October 2009.[81]

> CME Clearing is introducing an enhancement to the existing Performance Bond Collateral schedule. Effective October 19, 2009, firms will be able to post physical gold to CME Clearing to cover non-segregated (NSEG) Performance Bond requirements. Initially, gold will be able to be posted to JPMorgan Chase Bank in London, England. In the near future, we hope to add additional depositories.

There will be a firm asset limit of $200 million. These guidelines are subject to change and will be evaluated on a regular basis.

Sovereign Credit Default Swap Contracts: Tower of Babble

The credit default swap market has a history of conflicts, and the worst of them occur when it is time to settle up. For example, hedge funds Eternity Global Master Fund Ltd. and HBK Master Fund LP thought they purchased protection against an Argentina default and sued when J.P. Morgan refused to pay off on Argentina credit protection contracts Eternity had purchased.

J.P. Morgan's posture was different when it wanted to collect on the protection it bought from Daehon, a South Korean Bank. J.P. Morgan claimed the slightly different contract language met the definition of restructuring under the credit default protection contract it had with the South Korean Bank.

Regulators "Can't Find" Evidence of Market Manipulation

European regulators said they saw no evidence of manipulation in the Greek credit default swap market, because they examined DTCC data. DTCC doesn't capture all trades. Regulators wouldn't have found evidence of the rampant manipulation in the U.S. mortgage backed securities market, either, since those trades were not captured on any clearing exchange. Moreover, already flawed "ISDA standard" documentation does not have to be used for opaque credit derivatives, including those that may reference sovereign debt. Allan Sloan at the *Washington Post* asked the right questions:[82]

How much of this stuff do the Street people own? Where is it? What kind of securities has it been pushed into? No one knows. The one thing you can bet on, though, is that unraveling it all is going to be horribly complicated. Why? Because for Wall Street, complexity equals profitability.

I am not against covered short selling or puts, and some short sellers have done better work than main stream media in uncovering accounting manipulation and over-borrowing. But the credit default swap market has a history of manipulation, and we are in the middle of a global financial crisis. Speculators can potentially destabilize a country or a company that's already in trouble.

Time for Reform is Overdue

More than a year has passed since former Treasury Secretary Henry Paulson went to Congress in September 2008 to plead for special powers and TARP money to bail out U.S. financial institutions. Yet there has been no meaningful financial reform.

Lehman was not alone in fudging its accounting and over-borrowing. All of our legacy investment banks: Lehman Brothers, Goldman Sachs, Morgan Stanley, Bear Stearns, and Merrill Lynch had borrowed too much money, all of them used gimmicks to disguise debt, and all of them—including Goldman Sachs—would have gone under in 2008 without the bailouts.

World leaders should not be surprised that many countries also disguise debt and fudge their accounting. A good first step to reform of the financial system is to take away financial instruments that are ripe for abuse, starting with a ban on all sovereign credit default swaps.

How to Corner the Gold Market

March 30, 2010

First, let your greed overcome all regard for the stability of the global market, and overcome your aversion to illegal activities. Stay away from people like me, and fly under the radar, because I'd like to see you thrown in jail. Most Washington officials, regulators, and Wall Street managers are probably safe to hang around, especially if you cut them in for a piece of the action or give them vague promises of a future lucrative job.

Next, cultivate relationships—or plant someone—on as many of the gold exchanges as possible in London, New York, Chicago, Hong Kong, Sydney, and Dubai. Get to know key people at one or more of the bullion banks: JPMorgan Chase, UBS AG, ScotiaMocatta, Barclays Bank, and Deutsche Bank AG. Get to know as many mine producers as possible (China has been buying gold mines), and watch the sales of mines, particularly to China. Get to know all of the refiners.

Set up some new offshore corporations, subsidiaries of existing corporations, and a hedge fund or two of your own to engage in some gold trading.

Get to know as many hedge fund buyers as possible, and encourage everyone to buy physical gold. Remove the gold from custodian banks, and stash it in a vault solely under the control of the hedge fund. Use your network of people with net worth of $1 billion or more to get them to buy gold, too. Then work on the "small" investors with only $100 million or more net worth. Keep the key decision making group as small as possible to make it harder for anyone in your group to try to back out.

Pump up the gold story. Get your friends to tell retail investors to buy some gold every month. Get your buddies in the financial business to offer exchange traded gold funds (ETFs) that claim to buy physical gold. This will sound safe to retail investors, but in fact, the ETFs are very risky. This will serve your purpose when you are ready to start a panic. These particular ETFs will allow the "gold" to be commingled with the custodian's gold, and the custodian can lease out the gold. Moreover, the "gold" custodian can give it to a sub custodian that the manager doesn't know. The sub custodian can give it to yet another sub custodian unknown to the original custodian.

The manager will never audit the gold, and the gold is not "allocated" to a particular investor. Since this is an "exchange traded" gold fund, investors will probably assume the gold is regulated by the Commodity Futures Trading Commission (CFTC), but it isn't. By the time investors wake up to the probability that there is very little actual gold backing their investment, your plan will be ready to execute.

Locate the naked shorts, the bullion dealers whose short positions are greater than their long positions. After you complete your plan, the naked shorts will have to pay whatever you can squeeze out of them to cover the contracts they have with you.

Now you are ready to execute your plan.[83]

Step 1: Let everyone in the futures markets know you are buying gold, speculating in gold, and want to take physical delivery. It helps that China openly announced it wants to increase its gold reserves; the market isn't looking too hard at you. At first, act like you're naïve. Buy on margin and pyramid up by reinvesting your profits when you have them. This part is legal, but you don't want to draw too much attention to yourself. Your buddies in the market will distract attention from you by buying gold and putting on straddles (selling the near months and buying in future months). No one will suspect collusion.

Step 2: Get the banks to let you finance your gold. They will lend you most of the value of your gold, especially if you do not argue about the interest rates they charge. Since they are borrowing from the Fed or another Central Bank at nearly zero, they consider the difference they get from you (backed by your gold) as gravy. As the price of gold rises, they will lend you more, and you can add to your gold position.

Be careful with the loans, though. In March, 1980, Paul Volcker was Chairman of the Federal Reserve. As the Hunts tried to corner the silver market, Volcker inadvertently ruined their plans. Volcker raised interest rates to fight inflation and issued a special credit restraint to banks admonishing banks not to provide financing for speculators in gold and silver. Borrowing costs rose, while silver prices dropped. The former billionaires were bankrupted by Volcker's prudence. Fraud is not for sissies. But don't worry too much. No one in Washington is really listening to Paul Volcker today. They just trot him out for a photo-op, and then dilute any "rules" he suggests to render them totally ineffective.

Step 3: Book up all of the space at gold refiners, so that no one else can do it. Buy as many gold mines as possible, and do not hedge (sell gold forward). Since the price of gold is going up, persuade other mines to keep as much of new production as possible off the market, while you execute your plan to push up prices. Keep the part about your attempt to manipulate gold prices a secret. You won't be 100% successful with all the mines, but you don't have to be, and every bit helps. Besides, if these other mines insist on hedging (by selling gold forward), your plan may drive them into bankruptcy, and then you can buy them cheap.

Step 4: Create credit derivatives contracts that give you the option to ask for your pay-off in gold. Make the reference credit the United States or the United Kingdom and create extra triggers like credit downgrades or other events that make it easier for you to demand payment in gold. The steps you use here to manipulate the gold market can be adapted to the credit derivatives market, so even if you can't trigger the event, you can make the spreads move in your favor and demand collateral in gold. Hide the credit default swap contract from the eyes of the clearing exchanges by embedding them in a securitization, a credit-linked note, or a sovereign fund product. The investors that invest in these products never read the documentation, so when you trigger the event, they won't realize they are caught in a short squeeze—scrambling for your gold at the high prices you set—until it is too late.

Step 5: Pick the future month to make your big move. You will go long gold futures and demand physical delivery. Your buddies will all go long, too. Mix it up a little by buying some straddles to make it appear you are just a regular speculator, and throw everyone off the scent. Balance your straddle so it is relatively neutral, and the initial long position continues to apply pressure. When the long side of your straddle becomes due, demand physical delivery (this will be before your other long position) to keep up the pressure.

Step 6: Secretly and habitually start making some large early purchases in non-U.S. markets. That way, when the U.S. markets open, gold should follow the upward trend. Create chaos by doing as many of the following as possible in the shortest time possible. Move any remaining gold you have in trading depositories to private storage. Get some banks to issue research reports on how the bullion banks don't have enough gold to cover their massive short positions, and talk about the tight gold supplies. Trigger some of those credit default swaps. Inform the investors in non-allocated "paper" gold ETF's just how stupid it is to give their money to a "manager" that doesn't audit the gold, insure the gold, prevent leasing of the gold, allocate the gold, or otherwise prove the gold is backing the fund.

Step 7: The bullion banks and dealers that have over-hedged their physical gold with short positions will now be squeezed and have to meet margin calls. You and all of your speculator friends will look bad, so now is the time to use a ruse. Offer to cancel some of your forward contracts in exchange for early delivery of gold. This will temporarily relieve the bullion dealers' pain on their short positions, and give you control over even more of the gold supply.

Step 8: You and your friends have pinched off the gold supply and control most of the free gold supply having locked it up in your own vaults and warehouses. You are all long a lot of futures contracts, and you will all demand physical delivery. You now have the naked shorts exactly where you want them.

Step 9: Rely on bankruptcy and bailouts to get what you want. Normally, you would be afraid that you would never get paid, because your demands would bankrupt the naked shorts. But the naked shorts are likely to be unwary hedge funds or other sophisticated investors, and no one cares if you bankrupt them. Other naked shorts are likely to be the bullion banks, and they are all being bailed out by the Central Banks who will lend them what little gold they have left and then beg the IMF for whatever they have. In lieu of that, you can set a very high cash price and take cash. In the gold feeding frenzy you have created, you can gradually unload some of your physical gold. If you managed to bankrupt any gold mines, circle back and see if you can scoop them up for a song.

China is a wild card. If it is not part of your scheme and decides to lend its gold, it could dampen your profits or even upset your short squeeze. But China may not want to help out your victims. Why should they? If China buys enough gold mines and increases its reserves enough, it may be in its interest to befriend you. Your combined ownership will have made the futures markets irrelevant. Together you will not only have cornered the gold market, *you will have cornered gold.*

Gold Game Changer: J.P. Morgan Accepts Bullion as Money

February 7, 2011

J.P. Morgan Chase & Co. announced on February 7, 2011 that it will accept physical gold as collateral for investors that want to make short-term borrowings of cash or securities.[84]

Presenting gold to satisfy demands for performance bond collateral has been allowed on the London CME in a limited way since October 2009. As of November 22, 2010, the Intercontinental Exchange Inc. (ICE) has accepted gold bullion as collateral on all credit default swaps and energy transactions.

I don't recall the G-20 declaring gold a new currency. Yet JPMorgan Chase and a couple of financial market exchanges have effectively declared that gold is an alternative currency.

In other words, gold is money.

Abolish Credit Default Swaps on Sovereign Debt

In an earlier post, I wrote that Congress should act immediately to abolish credit default swaps on the United States, because these derivatives will foment distortions in global currencies and gold. Credit default swaps on the United States currently settle in euros, but there is talk of creating new contracts calling for settlement in gold. Congress should immediately ban all credit derivatives on the United States, since the opportunities for mischief making outweigh the hedging value.

Most traders in U.S. credit default swaps don't think the U.S. will default as long as we have money printing presses, so they are speculating on price movements in U.S. Treasury bonds due to potential increases in interest rates. If speculators manage to get contracts to settle in gold, speculators on the winning side of a price move will demand collateral paid in gold.

Destruction of the Volcker Bubble Deflator

In 1979/1980 the Hunt brothers tried to corner the silver market. In March 1980, Paul Volcker (who was then Chairman of the Federal Reserve) went to DEFCON 1 and directed banks to cut off funding to precious metals speculators. That directive included billionaires like the Hunt brothers. The Hunts couldn't borrow money against their long silver positions to meet their margin calls. Volcker popped the silver bubble and the Hunt brothers were bankrupted.

Since gold is now accepted collateral, there will always be a way to borrow against one's gold position, so speculators that create leveraged long gold positions can always find a way to fund margin calls. The Volcker bubble deflator is no longer relevant.

Trifecta of Absent Financial Regulation: CDS, Currencies, Commodities

How much mayhem could "creative" minds generate in the credit default swap markets, the currency markets, and the gold market? Quite a bit, since customized credit default swaps can be embedded in all manner of financial investments, and they can be written to offload unexpected risks on naïve investors.

The Dodd-Frank "financial reform" bill doesn't address customized over-the-counter credit default swaps, and the bill doesn't do anything at all to rein in speculation in the currency markets or the commodities markets.

Disclosure: I currently own some long positions in precious metals including gold. This is not an offer or solicitation for purchase or sale of any security and is not an investment recommendation of any kind and should not be construed as such. These comments reflect my views as of February 7, 2011, and are subject to change at any time based on market and other conditions.

Today's Silver Scandal

May 5, 2011

Under-30 silver traders weren't alive to see the billionaire Hunt brothers bankrupted by silver trades, and those under-45 years old probably never read about it. The Hunts' silver debacle occurred after the "soybean caper," but before the CFTC fined them $500,000 in a July 1981 out of court settlement for blatant violation of commodities laws in their attempt to corner beans. The Hunts had borrowed money to buy silver and leveraged themselves in silver futures in an attempt to corner the market.

On March 14, 1980, the CFTC staff reported to their commissioners that the Hunt brothers could handle their short-term losses as silver prices fell, because "they bought at low prices." The CFTC was right about the low purchase prices (around

$15 on average), but it was wrong when it thought the Hunt brothers could handle the losses.

Simultaneously, then Fed Chairman Paul Volcker instituted a new directive to U.S. banks as part of his anti-inflation policy. It was a "special restraint" on lending to speculators with holdings in commodities or precious metals. The banks knew better than to mess with Volcker, and they immediately closed the lending spigot to speculators in gold and silver.

Within three days, the Hunt brothers' cash had nearly run out, and they couldn't meet a margin call. Two days later, they had to deliver silver instead of cash in order to meet the margin call. Other speculators were having trouble raising cash against their silver, and prices dropped like a stone.

Back to the Future

Some believe the recent general commodities pullback was triggered by the series of CME margin hikes on silver within the past week, after the recent exponential run-up in silver prices. Whether or not that is true, holders of leveraged long commodities positions should have warily watched the action in the silver market. Some silver speculators may not have seen the margin hike as a constraint on lending, but it should have been a red flag for any speculator with a leveraged long position. Moreover, after silver markets closed, silver prices were getting "banged" lower in what looked like suspicious market manipulation.

Speculators rushed in as prices recently soared and rumors swirled that there will be a delivery default at the CME including one of the TBTF banks with a huge short position that it cannot cover. Are the rumors true? I don't know since those in charge of investigating these matters haven't put evidence in the public domain, even after a senior member of the CFTC claimed there was blatant silver manipulation.

The fastest way to collapse a recent run up in prices is to choke off the ability of those with leveraged long paper positions to raise cash. Another way is to rapidly hike margins; those with insufficient ready cash will be forced to liquidate. As they liquidate to meet margin calls, prices fall, and it creates a cycle which feeds on itself. I have no explanation for the recent ramp up in silver prices any more than I have an idea of where spot silver prices eventually hit bottom.

This isn't the first time there has been extreme price action and volatility in the silver futures markets, and it will not be the last. If anyone thinks that the Commodity Futures Trading Commission (CFTC) has the right stuff to regulate the commodities markets, look no further than its failure to check manipulation in the silver market.

The CFTC has the mandate to "regulate" tens of trillions of dollars in credit derivatives, but it is actually in the business of anti-regulation.

Price Manipulation: Look for Motive

January 19, 2012

Regulators haven't been able to keep up with price manipulation in the commodities markets or any other market. Why do games persist? The short answer is because they can, and because they can be very profitable in the short run.

If you've Googled gold or silver, you've probably come across sites that are breathless about the possibility of manipulation of metals prices. The problem with the Internet is that it's new, too new to capture the rich history of the financial markets. Manipulation of metals prices—and the prices of many other commodities—is an old tradition. Here's one example adapted from *An Alchemist's Road: My transition from medicine to business,* by Dr. Henry Jarecki (Dr. Jarecki is currently Chairman of Gresham Investment Management LLC.), October, 1989. This publication is not available on the Internet.

The Silver Arbitrageurs

In the 1960s Alan Rosenberg, a coin dealer, sold dollar bills that were silver certificates to a firm called Metals Quality. At the time, the Federal Reserve converted dollar silver certificates to a set amount of silver. Before the Fed finally discontinued the conversion, the converted silver was worth more than a dollar. The difference became great enough that it paid to buy up the certificates for slightly more than a dollar, convert the certificates to silver, and sell the silver for a profit. This is one of the rare instances of a true arbitrage.

Not everyone wanted to go through the trouble of handling the conversion, so people like Rosenberg collected certificates and sold them for more than one dollar each, but for less than the price of the silver represented by the certificate. It was worth it to Rosenberg to have someone else do the work of squeezing out the last bit of value.

That's where Metals Quality came in. It bought certificates from coin dealers and currency exchanges and handled the conversion to silver and sold the silver for a profit. Metals Quality paid Rosenberg for his silver certificates based on the first Comex price of silver for the day (less something for the trouble of the conversion and some profit). It made no difference whether the first price of the day was based on one contract or 100 contracts. Each contract represents 10,000 ounces of silver.

The Silver Foxes

Rosenberg figured out a way to make some extra money when he sold his certificates. He instructed his broker to go into the commodities trading pit first thing in the morning and bid up the price of the first silver contract each day.

Rosenberg overpaid and lost money on the contract's 10,000 ounces when he sold the contract later in the day. By then, the price fell back to the actual market manipulation-free price. But as a result of his price manipulation, Rosenberg sold say 100,000 ounces to Metals Quality for an extra 3 or 4 cents per ounce. His profits from the price manipulation on 100,000 far exceeded the loss and trouble on the 10,000 ounces for which he artificially overpaid.

Eager to make an even bigger profit margin, Rosenberg called Henry Jarecki, then owner of Federal Coin & Currency. Like Rosenberg, Jarecki collected bulk quantities of silver certificates for sale to Metals Quality. Rosenberg hoped that Jarecki would help him manipulate the first Comex price, the first silver trade on Comex in the spot month. Rosenberg figured Jarecki would help him pump up the price that Metals Quality would pay, and they could split the loss on the 10,000 ounces that had to be sold later at a lower price. Of course, that loss would be absorbed by the profits they made by getting Metals Quality to pay an above market price, and Rosenberg's loss would be only half his previous loss. His net profit would increase by the amount he reduced his initial loss.

The only flaw in Rosenberg's loss-sharing idea is that he didn't know that when he spoke to Henry Jarecki, he was speaking both to Federal Coin & Currency and to Metals Quality.

Silver Price War

Rosenberg was costing Jarecki money, because Jarecki sold his silver on the usually lower London fixing price the previous night and was buying the certificates from coin dealers like Rosenberg at the higher manipulated first Comex price.

Without explaining anything to Rosenberg, Jarecki sent a broker into the trading pits to do the opposite of Rosenberg's broker. Jarecki's broker sold the first contract very low, so he bought coin dealers' silver certificates cheaper than where he had sold silver on the London fixing price the night before.

After waging this price war for a while, the two brokers struck a bargain. On one day Rosenberg's broker would buy the silver high, and the next day Jarecki's broker would sell silver very low. After a week or so, they decided it was counterproductive and they gave it up.

Jarecki was lucky, because the costly silver price manipulation came to his attention through a serendipitous tip-off from the manipulator. When people slugged it out in the commodities pits, they often made their own justice. By the time regulators caught up with a price manipulator (if ever), it was too late to protect an aggrieved party.

Moreover, it isn't easy to prove someone is manipulating prices by taking a small loss for a potentially much bigger gain. Many feel this is just being sharp.

Absent Regulation

Anomalous price moves are a red flag, and it seems regulators aren't even looking at them. If regulators ever did decide to launch a genuine investigation, the place to start is with those who gained the most in the short run—or those who avoided the most short run loss—from the price moves.

The idea that the Commodity Futures Trading Commission (CFTC) can regulate credit derivatives when they aren't up to the task of regulating commodities is among the more ludicrous results of our financial crisis "regulation." The MF Global debacle and the price action in precious metals—especially around options expiration dates—show how lost our regulators are and how mistaken their overseers in Washington remain.

CHAPTER 5 Criminal Behavior

Madoff Deserves Lots of Company

December 13, 2008

If justice is to be served, Madoff deserves many things, including many new acquaintances.

A Giant Ponzi Scheme

Bernard Madoff confessed—not the securitization "professionals" who work or worked for famous investment banks, certain CDO managers and certain hedge funds. On the plus side, U.S. taxpayers are not bailing out Madoff. News reports indicate he doesn't owe a certain famous large investment bank any money.

The *Wall Street Journal* missed a golden opportunity. It wrote that if Madoff's alleged losses exceeded $50 billion, it would "dwarf past Ponzi schemes."[85] Yet, Madoff is a piker.

The largest Ponzi scheme in the history of the capital markets is the relationship between failed mortgage lenders and investment banks that securitized the risky overpriced loans and sold these packages to other investors—a Ponzi scheme by every definition applied to Madoff. These and other related deeds led to the largest global credit meltdown in the history of the world.

Investment banks raised money from new investors to pay back old investors (mortgage lenders' dividends to shareholders and creditors of mortgage lenders which often included themselves).

When mortgage lenders imploded, investment banks sped up opaque securitizations to offload worthless tranches of CDOs mixed in with others to careless so-called sophisticated investors along with naive investors. Raising money from new investors to pay back old investors, even if you are the old investor covering up losses is a Ponzi scheme. [Added May 8, 2009.]

SEC Strategy

The SEC's enforcement strategy seems to be 1) ignore the charity of strangers such as Harry Markopolos: "Madoff Securities is the world's largest Ponzi Scheme."[86] 2) "investigate" and drop the matter, and then 3) wait for the Perp to crack under the strain of being ignored and confess.

The SEC employed a similar strategy with respect to the investment banking securitization activities it "regulated" over the past several years. Congress and others agree, claiming there will be time to find out who is responsible later. *Bail now, scapegoat later.*

Complicated and Cryptic

Madoff claimed his business was too complicated for outsiders to understand. He was "cryptic" about the firm's business. He ran a secretive business, and kept his financial statements under lock and key. Just who does Madoff think he is—the Treasury Secretary or the Chairman of the Federal Reserve?[87]

Investment banks and other "bailees" have hundreds of billions of dollars' worth of assets in opaque accounting buckets known as Level 2 and Level 3. Good luck trying to find details.

Bonuses

Madoff wanted to pay his employees bonuses, earlier than usual, right after owning up to his problems.

Troubled investment banks that engaged in troubling activity want to pay employees bonuses, too. They have owned up to nothing, and it looks as if they will get away with it.

Premise of *Fortune* Cover Story is Incorrect

January 11, 2009

The premise of this week's *Fortune* cover story, "Sending Wall Street to Jail," (January 19, 2009) is not only incorrect, it lacks *Common Sense*.[88] The article seems unable to muster outrage. In the words of Thomas Paine: "a long habit of not thinking a thing wrong, gives it a superficial appearance of being right."

Fortune talks about the difficulty of proving criminal intent when the SEC, Fed chairman and others thought (or more to the point, studiously avoided rational thought) things had gotten as bad as they could get. Since when are the popular delusions of those outside one's firm a defense for willfully failing to mark your positions to market and material accounting weaknesses, if not misstatements?

The magazine gives the benefit of the doubt to senior managers who were way off the mark in their earnings releases and says "we're not talking here about ...Ponzi schemes." In a few cases, the latter is actually true, but in others, we should be talking about Ponzi schemes and asking why the SEC did not shut down the securitization groups at some of the major investment banks doing business in the United States.

Investment Fund Managers: Nine Warning Signs

February 9, 2009

Lately, we've heard a lot about hedge funds and other types of investment funds that have been both unlucky and dishonest. The overwhelming majority of these managers are men, because the world of finance is dominated by men. A woman can feel at a disadvantage, but when dealing with the wrong crowd, even savvy male money managers sometimes feel at a disadvantage. How can you tell if you should be worried?

These nine warning signs alarm the savviest money managers in the world:

- **A cult figure.** If the manager is a cult figure and has no independent third party that verifies his returns, you are probably already in trouble. Do-it-yourself reporting doesn't cut it when it comes to your money.
- **The fund has a "gate,"** meaning it can hang onto your money. The fund manager may have a period of time where he can prevent you from withdrawing your money, or can impose a penalty for early withdrawal. Sometimes the fund manager can change the rules later to prevent you from withdrawing your money. Sometimes there is a legitimate

reason for this, such as in a real estate partnership, but hedge funds that invest chiefly in stocks shouldn't tie up your money.

- **Small-time banks and accountants**. Investment funds should be separate from a fund manager's other accounts and placed in a custodial account with a well-known bank. The fund manager should also have a credible auditor.
- **Poor transparency.** You can't get documents that tell you what the investment manager is investing in and the manager can change his strategy at will. Even a current list of investments won't tell you what the manager is doing ten minutes from now.
- **The manager has absolute power** over his investments and his staff, so there are effectively no risk controls beyond the manager's whims. Your manager should be able to explain in simple terms how risk is controlled.
- **Lots of leverage.** If you bought an uninsured car and put 20% down, you wouldn't drag race on New Year's Eve.
- **A single strategy**. If one strategy dominates the fund performance, it's a red flag. One investment strategy does not fit all markets.
- **Unlimited expenses**. Most funds have a cap on expenses plus management performance fees. Ask your manager where you can find the fees in the documents, and ask for a thorough explanation. Then ask someone else and try to match the responses.
- **Deflects questions.** Any question is a reasonable question when you are giving your money to someone else to manage. If your manager seems condescending or answers your questions with jargon, you are being mistreated. It's a red flag if your manager shows irritation, impatience, or refuses to give reasonable clarification when asked. But beware of the charming manager who only seems to answer your questions, but whose answers and explanations are not satisfactory. Con artists are always pleasant while you're being hustled.

Wall Street's Fraud and Solutions for Systemic Peril

September 29, 2009

Last week I gave a presentation to members of the International Monetary Fund (IMF) explaining the corrosive atmosphere that allowed the largest Ponzi scheme in the history of the capital markets to flourish. The following is a brief summary.

Wall Street gave mortgage lenders large credit lines (similar to credit card debt) and packaged the loans into private-label residential mortgage backed securities (RMBS). Most of the RMBS was rated "AAA," since subordinated investors absorbed the risk of a pre-agreed amount of loan losses. But many RMBSs were backed by portfolios comprising risky fraud-riddled loans.

Most of the "AAA" investment was imperiled, and subordinated "investment grade" components were worthless. Wall Street disguised these toxic "investments" with new value-destroying securitizations and derivatives: Collateralized Debt Obligations (CDOs and CDO-squared), Structured Investment Vehicles (SIVs), Real Estate Mortgage Investment Conduits (REMICs and Re-REMICs), Asset Backed Commercial Paper (ABCP), and related credit derivatives.

Meanwhile, collapsing mortgage lenders paid high dividends to shareholders (old investors) and interest on credit lines to Wall Street (old investors) with money raised from new investors in doomed securities. New money allowed Wall Street to temporarily hide losses and pay enormous bonuses. This is a classic Ponzi scheme.

Securities laws chiefly apply to financiers (the underwriters and traders) that create, sell, and trade securities. Underwriters are responsible for appropriate due diligence, an investigation into the risks. Rating agencies do not buy and sell securities, but they should have their special NRSRO designations immediately revoked as a start. One former rating agency official even suggests liquidation.

If you know or should know that investments are overrated and overpriced when they are sold, those facts must be specifically disclosed. If you fail to disclose material information, expect to be investigated for fraud. If you have a mortgage subsidiary, expect it to be investigated, too.

Wall Street protests that it sold toxic assets to sophisticated investors obliged to perform independent due diligence, so those investors may have trouble claiming damages. But the ballgame has changed. Massive fraud damaged the U.S. economy. (Housing prices didn't just fall; they plummeted as the fraud unraveled.) U.S. taxpayers became unwilling unsophisticated investors funding Wall Street's bailout.

The Fed uses tax dollars to keep some of our largest banks—weakened by reverse-Glass-Steagall mergers with troubled entities—from collapsing under heavy loan losses.

Wall Street's huge bonus payments were based on suspect accounting. Failure should not result in fortune. Yet, Wall Street once again proposes to pay out exorbitant bonuses.

Many banks' current illusion of profitability is only made possible by taxpayers' enormous subsidies including low cost borrowing, higher interest payments on bank capital deposits, a credit line for the FDIC (to be repaid with banks' subsidized profits), and continued government debt guarantees on bank debt. A large share of certain banks' subsidized profits is due as reparation to unsophisticated investors, the U.S. taxpayers.

Delusional Complacency

When you leverage fraud riddled fixed income securities, there is nowhere to go but down in a hurry. Confusion after the fraud falls apart leads to a vicious cycle of selling, as investors and lenders shun both good and bad assets. The deflating debt bubble is followed by a classic liquidity crunch.

By the end of 2006, public reports of implosions of large mortgage lenders eliminated CEOs' plausible deniability. By January 2007, many (including me) publicly challenged the failure to account for losses. Instead, toxic securitization *accelerated* in the first half of 2007—classic malfeasance as a Ponzi scheme collapses.

In August 2007, I projected hundreds of billions in principal losses for mortgage loans alone—not counting other troubled asset classes, derivative duplication, and leverage. Fed Chairman Ben Bernanke contemporaneously said mortgage loan losses would be $50-100 billion.

At a lunch following my presentation, a senior officer claimed the IMF had estimated global losses of $1 trillion in its April 2007 Global Financial Stability Report.[89] I averred the IMF's Report followed a growing wave of billions in write-downs; by then *Bloomberg News* had reported potential global losses in the high hundreds of billions of dollars (Feb 2008). (Everyone's estimates were too low.) Not so, other senior IMF officers said; they were "early" and had great political "courage." But their heads were up their own hindsight bias. The IMF's estimate was in the April 2008 Report, after Bear Stearns' March 2008 implosion. I later sent the IMF official a link to the April 2007 Report, and he admitted he misspoke. Blind to fraud, the IMF had missed the message.[90]

The IMF is not a financial regulator. Actual regulators did worse. The SEC dropped seminal investigations and failed to investigate ongoing securities fraud. In the spring of 2007, the Fed and the U.K.'s FSA reported that the degree of leverage in the global financial system was less than at the time of Long Term Capital Management, but in reality it was much greater.[91] They are now repeating their mistakes. Winston Churchill said we must alert somnolent authority to novel dangers; but our regulators are complacent, and the dangers are not novel.

Existing Solutions to Halt Growing Systemic Risk

An IMF official asserted: "You can't prove fraud" and insisted it was in the interest of risk managers not to let their institutions collapse. This IMF officer isn't just soft on crime; he's in denial. Failure to recognize fraud led to statements like the one that opened Chapter 2 of the IMF's April 2006 Global Financial Stability Report:

> There is growing recognition that the dispersion of credit risk by banks to a broader and more diverse group of investors, rather than warehousing such risk on their balance sheets, has helped to make the banking and overall financial system more resilient.

The IMF's source was a 2006 speech made by Treasury Secretary Timothy Geithner, then president and CEO of the New York Fed.[92] The IMF gets the lion's share of its funding from the

United States and the United Kingdom, its stakeholders. Geithner's views have more influence than those of former Fed Chairman Paul Volcker, who calls for a return of Glass-Steagall, a separation of traditional commercial banking from high-risk activities.

Wall Street supplies a swinging door of jobs for its financial regulators, and—in the case of many members of Congress and our Presidents—campaign contributions. This dependence is known as "capture," and the result is that instead of reining in Wall Street, dependent thinking enables mayhem.

In the recent Ponzi scheme only the agents—mortgage lenders, rating agencies, fund managers, securitization professionals, CFOs, CEOs, and other fee or bonus beneficiaries—prospered. Controls and risk management were undermined. The financial institutions and their shareholders, for which these agents are failed stewards, collapsed. Investors in toxic securitizations lost money. Had regulators done their jobs, they would have shut down Wall Street's financial meth labs, and the Ponzi scheme would have quickly choked to death from lack of monetary oxygen.

After the Savings and Loan crisis of the late 1980s, there were more than 1,000 felony indictments of senior officers. Recent fraud is much more widespread and costly. The consequences are much greater. Congress needs to fund investigations. Regulators need to get tough on crime.

Troubled financial entities should be put into receivership and restructured. Old shareholders will be wiped out. Debt-holders will take a haircut (discount) along with a debt for new equity swap to recapitalize the entity. But the job won't be complete until we separate high risk activities from traditional banking in a return to a Glass-Steagall like structure with regulators that indict fraudsters, snuff out systemic fraud, and allow honest bankers to prosper.

The fact that many U.S. banks stuck to traditional banking and protected shareholders during this crisis is under-publicized, but their prudence worked.

We have the solutions. We need the will to implement them.

Endnote: In April 2005, I gave a presentation to the IMF including a discussion of flawed ratings of "super-senior" and "AAA-rated" structured products. Thereafter, loan fraud accelerated and securitization standards deteriorated, yet the IMF's April 2006 report stated: "As a practical matter, the investors who may be least likely to appreciate such nuances (e.g., smaller regional banks and retail investors) typically only purchase the most senior (least risky) credit products." In reality, many "super-senior" tranches and the "AAA" tranches subordinate to them had substantial principal risk.

Banging the U.S. Stock Market

May 10, 2010

Chicago residents grew up to the sound of local early morning radio rundowns of pork belly futures and other exchange traded commodities. Every trick in the book from manipulation of soybeans to silver has played out in Chicago's trading pits. Every market professional I've talked to in Chicago since Thursday is of the same opinion. It makes no difference whether human beings or computers are front running and manipulating trades. The gyrations in the market last week have the look and feel of classic market manipulation.

If you want to manipulate a market, deregulate it as much as possible. Then make it as "dark," and fast as possible. Make it hard for outsiders to view your trades as they get done, and make it even harder for anyone to figure out why you are trading. Get as much monopoly power as possible over the market. Get funding at the cheapest possible rate. The best possible rate is the near zero cost funding available from the Federal Reserve.

Next, get your "men" stationed in the most influential positions at the exchanges. Make sure your cronies have shock and awe market dominance through, say, High Frequency Trading algorithms that now make up the majority of stock trades.

Then, make sure you have advance information of major market-moving events. A bailout announcement by the European Union would do nicely. A few days before the announcement, "bang" the market. Pound down the value so you can monetize put options and other bearish instruments. Trigger customers' stop-loss orders, and pick up bargains at their expense. Then cash-in again when the market pops up on bailout news.

To paraphrase Paul Erdman's 1975 tongue-in-cheek observation: "The lack of discretion in financial and political circles these days is appalling."

Meanwhile, take the heat off of yourself by leaking "fat finger" rumors to CNBC, since they can be relied upon to repeat as gospel any self-serving news you throw at them. *Did someone type billions? It should have been millions.* If we want to rescue the market from the *Jaws* of future disasters, we have to recognize that "this was no boating (or typing) accident." The system itself is flawed.

The NYSE was supposed to provide market liquidity. Trading safeguards are no good unless they are system-wide. The current and former heads of the NYSE, billed as the "best and the brightest," i.e., the most connected, should be asked a few questions about High Frequency Trading and "liquidity" providers. Our mega-bank trading desks that control most of the volume on the exchanges should be called in for an accounting and justification of their trading activities. Trading patterns during last week's debacle and over the last year should be examined.

Unfortunately, as others have observed before, the SEC is both largely incompetent and captured. They are learning to crawl in the space age. Moreover, the next stop for SEC officials seems to always be a highly paid influential job at a law firm, fund, or other entity that heavily relies on Wall Street for revenues. Financial reform requires radical overhaul of our "regulators."

As for Wall Street mega-bank reform, Congress seems disinclined to break up our Too-Big-To-Fail banks, define proprietary trading, or sever Goldman Sachs, Morgan Stanley, and proprietary trading at large banks from the Federal Reserve's, i.e., taxpayers' heavy subsidies.

If everyone wants to stick to the story of "woe is us, we had no idea things could go this wrong," then fine. No one is in control; no one is in charge; and no one can competently regulate our current system. This is a compelling argument for immediate radical financial reform.

Update May 11, 2010: The *Wall Street Journal* published an article suggesting that a trade by Universa crashed the market. Nassim Taleb, author of *The Black Swan*, with a second edition just coming out today, advises the hedge fund.[93]

The *WSJ* article misleads the public about an important event. This trade did not crash the market. The other side of Universa's trade would have been "delta hedged," meaning the futures contracts required to hedge the trade would have been meaningless to the market, or one could have bought offsetting puts or an options spread trade to hedge. This trade was immaterial to the events on Thursday. The transaction is immaterial and was not responsible for the market move.

The put options would expire worthless if the S&P were just above the strike in June. According to the WSJ article, the strike appears to be 800, but the article is a bit vague. Assuming the strike is 800, the contracts would only make some money at expiration if the S&P were below that, and the contracts would only make $4 billion if the S&P went to zero. Even on a high volatility day like last Thursday, Universa could have made money on the price of the put options, but even if it cashed out at the top of the market, it would only have made around $25 million after investing $7.5 million, and again, that is if Universa were lucky enough to sell at the highest level for the options for the day.

IKB's CEO Found Guilty of Market Manipulation—Some U.S. Bank CEOs Should Also Face Charges

July 16, 2010

Financial news media is abuzz with analyses of Goldman Sachs's settlement with the SEC for $550 million in a case of alleged fraud regarding the packaging and selling of a CDO called Abacus. Goldman Sachs admitted to no wrongdoing. The settlement is less than Tiger Woods's potential $700 million divorce settlement—and Tiger didn't help bring the economy to its knees (he also publicly admitted his transgressions and expressed regret)—but it's a start.

The SEC might want to look into the deals that Goldman Sachs underwrote on which other banks bought protection from AIG as well as the deals upon which Goldman Sachs itself bought protection from AIG. If all of these banks buy the securities back at the original price of par (100 cents on the dollar less interim principal payments), the tens of billions of dollars of proceeds can be used to pay back AIG's public debt. Instead, taxpayers heavily subsidize Goldman Sachs.

IKB received $150 million of the SEC's settlement with Goldman, recovering all of the money it lost on its investment in the investigated Abacus CDO. The bigger story is that the former CEO of IKB, Stefan Ortseifen, was found guilty of market manipulation by a German court. Yesterday, the *Wall Street Journal* reported the story on the second page of its markets section (C section), and it deserved more prominent coverage:[94]

At the heart of the case was a press release that IKB issued on July 20, 2007, as credit markets worsened, assuring investors that its exposure to the subprime fallout was limited and that it remained on track to meet its profit outlook.

Ortseifen was fined €100,000 (around $127,000) and given a 10-month suspended sentence. That strikes me as a pretty light sentence for fluffing the truth about the fact that at the time, IKB was actually being crushed by its losses. IKB eventually needed a bailout of more than €10 billion (around $12.7 billion) in government-backed loans. The court's fine probably didn't even make a dent in Mr. Ortseifen's wallet, but it's a start.

In this post-Sarbanes-Oxley world, U.S. CEOs and CFOs should also be held accountable for their rosy statements during this period, along with their SEC filings.

While the Goldman Sachs settlement is a victory of sorts for the SEC, it shouldn't distract us from the larger issues. Massive widespread malfeasance helped bring the global economy to its knees.

CHAPTER 6 Pundits and Junk Science

Reporting v. PR: Meredith Whitney and AIG

March 23, 2009

Much of the financial media blows in the wind of PR machines. AIG, Washington, Congress, various former investment banks, banks and others worked overtime to spin financial information over the past several years forcing competent reporters to engage in time intensive research on complex financial products. Other times, the press simply misinterprets the facts.

Last week, Charlie Rose billed Meredith Whitney on his show as the woman who gave early warning about AIG. I found that surprising given that as far as I know, she did not. The *L.A. Times'* review of *House of Cards*, a book about Bear Stearns, says author William Cohen gave Whitney credit for warning for some years that trading in credit derivatives and mortgage backed securities set us up for a credit implosion. This is not her expertise, but it is mine, and to the best of my knowledge she did not. Ironically, Whitney rated Bear Stearns *perform* and only downgraded it to *underperform* on March 14, 2008 as it tumbled 53% in one day. Whitney rated Lehman *outperform* in March 2008, while beleaguered Bear Stearns merged with JPMorgan Chase. She downgraded Lehman to *perform* towards the end of March 2008, and Lehman went under the following September.[95]

Few specifically and publicly warned of the global financial meltdown in advance—when something could have been done about it—as far as I know, Whitney was not in that number. Warren Buffett, Jeremy Grantham, Jim Rogers, and I (among others) were. My early warnings of credit derivatives, structured products, and structured vehicles are well documented in articles and books over many years (see Endnotes. In August 2007, I spoke up about AIG to Warren Buffett, Jamie Dimon, and the *Wall Street Journal*.

Meredith Whitney seems best known for her analysis of Citigroup at the end of October 2007. Jim Rogers appeared with

Whitney earlier in the year on *Cavuto on Business* and stated he was *short* Citigroup (he shorted C in late 2006/early 2007), and he said Citigroup was going to $5. Whitney rated Citi *sector perform* from October 3, 2005 until October 31, 2007.[96] The stock lost 7.9% versus a 7.5% gain for the Philadelphia Stock Exchange/KBW Bank Index during this period. The following summarized the timeline to the best of my knowledge:

January 3, 2007 – October 31, 2007: Citigroup stock is $55.66 on January 3, 2007. It steadily drops to $42.25 by October 31, 2007. Legendary investor Jim Rogers is *short*, says Citi will fall to $5 when he appears on *Cavuto on Business* with Meredith Whitney. She rates Citigroup sector and refutes Jim Rogers.

October 31, 2007: Jim Rogers is still *short*. By now prominent analysts including Richard Bove, Charles Peabody and Michael Mayo have already told clients to *sell*. Whitney rates Citigroup sector underperform, but says it could trade in the low 30's. She states Citi must cut its dividend. But it's much too late to issue a warning about structured products, since problems were by now well-known and activity had already ground to a halt. Citigroup is $42.45 on October 31, 2007 and is below $30 by December 27, 2007 and still falling.

October 31, 2007 – March 19, 2009: Citi drops steadily. It hits $5 in January 2009, and it dips to $3.61 on March 19, 2009. Whitney became more negative. Jim Rogers took his profit.

At the end of October 2007, Whitney said Citigroup needed to cut its dividend. It was a refreshing contrast to some of her competitors. She rated the dropping stock *sector underperform*, but said it "could trade in the low $30s."[97] To my mind, Whitney's was not an early call; the stock had been dropping steadily throughout the year. Jim Rogers had been *short* the stock for almost a year. Citigroup had already reported a $6.5 billion write-down for the third quarter of 2007. Whitney was ahead of many analysts who missed Citigroup's problems, but at least three prominent competing analysts had previously told their investors to *sell*.

When it comes to press coverage of our major financial institutions, the stakes are higher and the issues are not innocuous.

When I challenged AIG's second quarter 2007 financial reporting, it was based on my analysis of a $19.2 billion super senior credit default swap position.[98] With respect to potential principal loss or a mark-to-market loss, AIG had problems (even if AIG positioned some of its other contracts as "insurance" it still had to post collateral).

This was after the implosion of Bear Stearns Asset Management's two doomed hedge funds brought about by investment banks challenging the pricing of their "highly rated" assets and making collateral calls. [I publicly opposed Bear Stearns Asset Management's proposed Everquest IPO and cited a dodgy Citigroup CDO therein, among other issues, in May 2007. This was one of the triggers of the price inquiries.]

Yet AIG's PR spin was so effective, that the financial press backed off for the time being. AIG spins its PR like a top. It realizes what an effective strategy this is in deflecting financial reporters from the truth.

AIG asserted that it could not imagine any scenario under which its positions would have losses. Despite evidence to the contrary, AIG claims the unimaginative employees in its AIG Financial Products unit are the "best and brightest." In early 2008 it entered into retention bonus contracts for these employees, yet there were many structured products professionals in New York looking for work.

How the employees of AIG Financial Products came to be so exalted above other finance professionals, and distinguished like some new species, is worth inquiring into.

Looking back on true early warnings and how they were dismissed and discredited helps us understand the issues now threatening the global economy and the failings in our system. It is important to identify who provided thoughtful analysis when it mattered most, because that can be helpful as we work on solutions.

*****

Taleb Kills $20 Billion Mythical Swan

June 1, 2009

A recent *GQ* article quoted Nassim Nicholas Taleb as saying that in the falling market he "made $20 billion for our clients, half a billion for the Black Swan fund."

> I went for the jugular—we went for the max. I was interested in screwing these people—I'm not interested in money, but I wanted to teach them a lesson, and the only way you can do it is by trying to take it away from them. We didn't short the banks—there's not much to be gained there, these were all these complex instruments, options and so forth. We'd been building our positions for a while...when they went to the wall we made $20 bln for our clients, half a billion for the Black Swan fund.[99]

I checked with Nassim Taleb regarding the $20 billion in gains and asked if he were misquoted. He responded via email: "The quote is inaccurate. THe [sic] 20 billion might correspond to the face value of positions." This response is both vague and different in character from the mythical $20 billion in gains inaccurately quoted in *GQ*'s article. The total gains could be a tiny fraction of what Taleb loosely describes as "face value."

Why is *GQ's* mistake important? In my opinion, public claims of enormous private hedge fund gains require credible back up, and one would think that *GQ* would have known that before it inaccurately quoted Taleb as having made a bell ringing gain of $20 billion for clients. Presumably, the error referred to outside clients, not the black swan fund itself, but it could have the side effect of attracting investors to the black swan fund, similar to advertising or salesmanship.

The black swan fund's strategy is purportedly to buy out-of-the-money put options on stocks and broad market indices and hedge tail risk for clients. The strategy may produce long periods of mediocre—or even negative—returns followed by a large gain and vice versa. No one can tell you for certain exactly when (or for how long) large gains are possible. Initial success in a newly created fund may not be replicated in the future, and there is always the problem of scaling. Scaling refers to the fact that an individual fund may make a high return on an initial investment, say 100% on $100 million, but lose 10% on $1 billion.

The Market Can Stay Irrational Longer Than You Can Stay Solvent (or Patient)

We know that big unanticipated market moves always result in big winners and big losers. After the fact, many winners claim they were smart—not just lucky.

In my opinion, any claim of enormous gains for any strategy—including a black swan fund—should be explained and balanced with caveats. The siren song of enormous gains is always enticing, but the actual swan song may be off key.

A black swan fund strategy may produce future huge gains, but it may also produce mediocre returns (or even slowly burn cash for long periods) before producing another huge gain. The waiting period for the next big payday could be brief, or it could be longer than your investment horizon.[100]

Endnote: The GQ article had been posted on Taleb's web site sans notes or corrections and flagged as one of two articles being "most representative overall profiles." Other media referred to the *GQ* article and incorrectly attributed $20 billion in gains to Taleb ["Nassim Taleb is the Lebanon-born derivatives trader known for...having made clients of his Black Swan fund $20 billion from shorting the markets last autumn." under "Tinkerman," *The Times*, April 7, 2009. *The Times* referred to the correction on July 3, 2009 after other media outlets noted my commentaries and reported the error.]. It was brought to my attention in May, and I contacted Taleb about GQ's reportage of the $20 billion gain on May 19.

After my initial inquiry, Taleb added "(with typo on the 'billions')" to his web site's link to the article, but he added no further clarification of the numbers at that time.

Almost one month after several web-based media outlets questioned *GQ*'s reportage, Taleb provided more information. At the end of June 2009, Taleb added a correction note to the article he originally posted as "most representative" with no clarification. Instead of making "$20 billion for our clients, half a billion" for the

Black Swan funds [per the original article and Taleb's uncorrected original web site posting], and instead of making "**almost** [emphasis in original] half a billion for the black swan funds," [per a December 2008 email to Will Self that Taleb later put in the public domain on June 30, 2009], Taleb's late June 2009 correction now says the $20 billion was notional exposure in future value of options, and the funds made between "a quarter and a half a billion."

Hat tip to alert readers and Chicago's option market makers. Thanks also to Nassim Taleb for confirming the inaccuracy of the quote. Will Self, the author of the GQ *article, did not respond to an email sent to his agency.*

Taleb's Stranded Swan?

June 3, 2009

Before penning my previous commentary, I contacted Nassim Nicholas Taleb to check whether there were any inaccuracies in a *Wall Street Journal* article about the performance of his previous black swan fund, Empirica Kurtosis Ltd. The article said the fund had a 60% return in 2000 followed by "losses in 2001 and in 2002." In 2003 and 2004 it had low single-digit gains, a period when hedge funds posted average returns of 20% and 9% respectively. The fund's size was around $375 million when most of the assets were returned to investors.

In my query to Taleb, I also asked for confirmation that the fund experienced a voluntary wind-up...more on that later.

Taleb did not respond. Considered with his previous coy reply regarding *GQ*'s mythical $20 billion, I gave up hope of clarification. I enjoy debating philosophy, but debate is no substitute for size of actual gains.[101]

I was particularly interested in Empirica Kurtosis's reported anemic performance in 2001, because according to Taleb, the 9/11 terrorist attacks of 2001 were a "black swan" event.

How can a black swan fund do so poorly when the black swan finally appears?

Imagine a scenario: When the black swan appears, investors panic. The fund manager wants to cash in gains when volatility soars. Nervous investors want the manager to buy more "insurance," when it is expensive and ill-considered. But investors should not be blamed for a black swan fund's anemic performance any more than a pilot would blame nervous passengers for a bumpy plane ride. Management takes credit (and juicy fees) for the gains, so it should take responsibility for overall performance. This scenario may not be relevant for Empirica Kurtosis, but then, what is the explanation?

What about the voluntary wind-up I mentioned earlier?

Taleb's web site stated EMPIRICA WAS NEVER CLOSED [emphasis in original].[102] That may be true if one is only referring to Empirica LLC, a risk management operation. But in my opinion, it is incomplete to assert this without mentioning the voluntary wind-up of Empirica Kurtosis Limited.

Taleb never responded to my query about the wind-up. The Bermuda-based trustee was more helpful and confirmed that Empirica Kurtosis Limited was indeed wound up in 2004/2005.

Winners' Swan Dive

Big wins and big losses always occur after any market move. Winners are eager to claim they were smart—not lucky.

The big picture should be big enough to provide perspective. A black swan fund may have a good year followed by losses and mediocre returns. Empirica Kurtosis Limited may have become an example of a black swan fund with clipped wings.

Excerpted Transcript May 8, 2007—*The Colbert Report* (Stephen Colbert interviews Taleb):

> **Taleb:** Take Google, September 9/11, the rise of the internet, Harry Potter...They were unexpected and no one saw them coming, and after they happened, oh yah, it was so explainable by historians, scholars and academics, but before they happened, they were so unexpected.
>
> [Later]
>
> **Colbert:** So you say...9/11 could not be predicted.
>
> **Taleb:** It is very very hard to predict these events.

[Apparently Taleb never heard of the August 2001 presidential briefing: "Bin Laden Determined To Strike in U.S." based on a July 2001 intelligence report.][103]

Colbert: ...I'm glad to hear that, because that means the 9/11 Commission was a waste of time. Because we shouldn't have investigated why it happened, right?

Taleb: You need you need [sic] to investigate to see if it is predictable or not...

Colbert: But why? Why investigate something that can't be predicted, because there is nothing to learn from it.

Taleb: No, after the fact, Okay, you have to look at...uh...first of all you can learn something from the event, it's not like you can't learn at all.

Colbert: Okay

Taleb: But 9/11, 9/11, what I'm saying is that it's there is so many events like 9/11 that could have taken place, you see, so, it's just to see if there's responsibility, is there any vigilance or no vigilance. This is why we investigated 9/11.

Colbert: Is Iraq a Black Swan? We couldn't have ever foreseen it would go poorly, we would never have known that was not going to go well...

Taleb: No, wars, wars, yah, listen, wars since Napoleon...we learned that wars...wars are more and more unpredictable, more and more complex, the link between action and consequence becoming fuzzier, and I think that the war in Iraq was a mistake...we should have seen that it could have led to these dire consequences. [Only since Napoleon?]

Colbert: We should have but we didn't, therefore we couldn't.

[Later]

Colbert: It seems like you're essentially saying the future is unpredictable.

Taleb: No, I'm saying, yes, my idea in the book is to show two things: number one that the future is rather unpredictable, it is dominated by Black Swans and these black swans are not predictable, and the second point that is quite central, is that we humans...all right?...try to concoct stories to convince ourselves that the future is more predictable than it actually is...[Like Taleb's Napoleon story?]

Colbert: The future is essentially not predictable.

Taleb: Yes, it's not.

Colbert: By that logic, doesn't it mean that in the future you will be able to predict things, because you are predicting that you cannot predict things?

Gasparino's Glass Jaw Was CNBC's Draw

July 22, 2009

Why didn't CNBC give early warning of Wall Street's implosion? Perhaps because CNBC's on air reporting usually isn't hard hitting, despite what media articles may say. It's a good thing former pugilist, Charlie Gasparino, didn't try for the Golden Gloves.[104]

Gasparino's July 14, 2009 rant about Goldman Sachs was very late to the party.[105] On the topic of Wall Street, the only "f-bomb" Gasparino failed to drop is the fraud pulled off by Wall Street firms when they failed to properly mark their books and fueled massive problems for the American economy.[106] On July 20, Gasparino was easily fooled by Goldman's assertion it is responsible for a public service (liquidity and a backstop) and failed to analyze the key legitimate issues that need to be addressed by reformers: Goldman's (and Wall Street's) undue influence over Treasury and Fed officials and Wall Street's need to make reparations to the U.S. Treasury.[107][108]

Goldman runs a hedge fund. This observation isn't new, and Goldman is not alone among our large banks in running invisible hedge funds. Many others raised substantive issues about Goldman and Wall Street long before Gasparino, and they haven't caved.

There are many good reporters who actually read documents, analyze them, and know how to sift good information from bad, but Gasparino isn't one of them these days. Here's a tiny Bear Stearns sample:

"Jimmy Cayne built Bear Stearns from the ground up with one key ingredient: guts. We induct a Wall Street icon" by Charles Gasparino *Trader Monthly* Jun-Jul 2007 [*Trader Monthly* ended operations February 2009]. At the beginning of August 2007, Gasparino's mantra was: "When I had dinner with Jimmy Cayne on Sunday night."

Footwork Needs Work

After-the-fact reporting is not the same as being "ahead" of everyone else. Here's Charlie in Oct 2007 discussing Merrill with me.[109] Not only was CNBC very late to the party regarding the meltdown, Gasparino makes a typical assertion: "When we reported [Merrill's write-downs] here three weeks ago…ahead of anyone else…" right after I point out I wrote an article about Merrill's short-able positions, "The Predators' Fall," ten months earlier (and gave warnings about Wall Street's phony products, overrated products, and excessive leverage much earlier than that).

Gasparino Can't Take a Punch

As for Gasparino's on air etiquette, *Squawk Box's* Joe Kernen has the right attitude. In this January 2008 clip, around 3:44 minutes in, Charlie protests to me: "Would you just let me finish, would you just let me finish! You sound like me, now…let me finish."

Joe Kernen laughs: "So you know you do it, I didn't know you knew you did it, Charlie!"[110]

Disclosure: Near the end of 2007, a producer for CNBC's *Squawk Box* asked me if I wanted to go on regularly with Charlie, because I took him in stride. I declined.

*****

Where Were Drama Pundits When It Mattered?

July 29, 2009

Hundreds of people from clergymen to lawyers have claimed decorations for bravery that they never earned.[111] Why should finance be any different?

Meredith Whitney's Unreported Death Threats (See also: "Reporting v. PR")

In the early part of 2007, Meredith Whitney appeared on *Cavuto on Business* with Jim Rogers and opposed his viewpoint. She rated Citigroup "sector perform." Rogers was *short*. By the end of October 2007, three other prominent analysts already had a sell on Citi; Whitney followed by rating it sector underperform and said Citigroup could trade in the low $30s and would have to cut its dividend. The dividend cut was a good call. Rogers made it months earlier when he shorted the stock. It was too late to give an early warning about Citigroup's toxic assets. Securitization had already ground to a halt, and everyone was taking losses. Citi hit $5 in January 2009, just as Rogers said it would.

According to *Reuters*, Whitney said she got "several death threats" as a result of her Citi call.[112] The rumored death threats were widely reported. But who told the press about death threats? Security consultants advise the target of death threats not to discuss it, particularly not with the press. The threats were downgraded faster than Whitney downgraded Citigroup—a *Fortune* interview said she received "one death threat." Whitney rated Bear Stearns *perform* and downgraded it to *underperform* on March 14, 2008 as it tumbled 53% in one day.[113] Clues to Bear Stearns' problems were publicly reported in May 2007 when the Everquest IPO became news, and CDOs from BSAM's hedge funds landed on Bear Stearns's balance sheet.[114] Reportedly, Whitney hesitated Bear's fateful week of March 2008 due to her perceived pressure over her Citi dividend call, but pressure or not, she was already too late.

Jim Rogers also warned about Lehman when Bear Stearns imploded in mid-March 2008, but Whitney continued to rate Lehman outperform. Whitney downgraded Lehman to "perform" at the end of March 2008—so much for taking a hint or issuing an early warning. Lehman went under September 2008.

I first took an interest when Whitney was billed as the woman who gave early warning about AIG, because she did not as far as I know. In August 2007, I challenged AIG's earnings—specifically its failure to take losses on credit derivatives protecting "super senior" structures, the type of products on which we eventually paid out TARP money.

When asked by an economist to comment on my analysis of her calls that did not attract alleged death threats, Whitney retorted: "She is just jealous."[115] Not true. My feeling is akin to that which I have for Rosie Ruiz, who appeared to run a marathon in record time, but had merely jumped in at the end of the race—it's a different feeling entirely.

Nassim Nicholas Taleb's Backfiring Blunderbuss (See "Taleb Kills $20 Billion Mythical Swan" and "Taleb's Stranded Swan?")

According to *The Guardian*: "to establish his credentials as the sage of our current predicament, Taleb frequently refers to an August 2003 article in *The New York Times* in which he correctly predicted [Fannie Mae] had underestimated the risk of [a big move] in interest rates that would destroy the value of their portfolio."[116] [117] By the time Taleb spoke up in August of 2003, many others had already raised issues not only about the models, but also about the GSEs' massive exposure to a handful of counterparties, a risk Taleb missed. The *New York Times* article also asserted that Fannie Mae's business plan seemed safe, "since people typically do not default on their mortgages," so it would not establish *anyone*'s credentials as the sage of our current predicament.

Malfeasance, not models, disrupted the global economy, and Taleb still gets that part wrong. Black Barts imitating the gentleman highway robber—not black swans—caused most of the damage.

Taleb's Empirica Kurtosis "black swan" fund had negative returns in 2001, the year of the 9/11 black swan event. Taleb later claimed he only called it a hedge fund "in May-Oct 2001." Perhaps he meant something else, because Empirica Kurtosis wound up at the beginning of 2005 with lackluster returns, and performance specifics are not public, but it may have been a stranded swan.

In the spring of 2009, Taleb prominently posted a *GQ* article on his web site that (inaccurately) attributed $20 billion in gains to a strategy employed by a new fund that Taleb advises. I had contacted Taleb about the obvious (to me) error and written that the mistake was not Taleb's. But silence may be interpreted as endorsement whatever the source of the original error. The error suggested his strategy had proven to be scalable (would apply to large investments), while the fund was attracting new investors. But there is actually no empirical evidence.

Taleb asserted the article was about philosophy, and one should ignore the numbers. *The Times* (among others) didn't seem to see it that way. *The Times's* original reference to *GQ's* article focused on the erroneous $20 billion in trading gains *months* before Taleb made his correction in the face of media pressure.[118] As for Taleb's eventual explanation that the "$20 billion" referred to a "notional" amount of derivatives that produced between $250 to $500 million in gains, it raises further strategy questions.

Taleb has appeared in public with Arianna Huffington who has credited him with courage, yet he plays the victim and resorts to unwarranted name calling when asked legitimate questions.[119] He has said Myron Scholes belongs in a retirement home and called Nobel Prize winners charlatans. Viciousness isn't the same as courage. It takes courage to be transparent not just when results look fabulous (temporarily or otherwise), but when they don't make you look as favorable.[120]

Gasparino's Shadow Boxing (See also: Gasparino's Glass Jaw Was CNBC's Draw)

I did not give enough credit to some of CNBC's on air reporters when I wrote it should be viewed solely for entertainment. CNBC's Diana Olick did brilliant (and early) reporting during the onset of the housing crisis—the best on any news channel at the time. CNBC's David Faber provided context to the global financial meltdown and our nagging debt hangover. They aren't alone in good reporting at CNBC.

But Charlie Gasparino's reportage was more entertainment than substance in my opinion. I'm told Gasparino said he normally doesn't respond to "people who do not matter on Wall Street" (people like me who have appeared with him on CNBC) and called me a "publicity hound." He said it to *Dealbreaker*, a Wall Street Tabloid, because it was looking for something to publicize.

Gasparino also bashed bloggers, including *Crossing Wall Street's* Eddy Elfenbein (his real name) and Tyler Durden at *ZeroHedge*. (I would explain the pseudonym "Tyler Durden," but 1st Rule: You do not talk about [IT], and 2nd Rule: You DO NOT talk about [IT].) Why should anyone take his posturing seriously? Gasparino's blogger bashing got further publicity, but not for opinions that matter.[121]

Serious Issues For Serious People

This roundup is the last of my commentaries on pundits who may—inadvertently or otherwise—be associated with claims that their opinions carry more weight than others. All opinions, no matter what the source, should be backed up with facts. That goes double for hype. Legitimate questions deserve answers. Backlash unaccompanied by a fact-based argument is pointless. Many people are deterred from raising legitimate issues, because those who want "the worship of jackals by jackasses," as H.L. Mencken put it, tend to lash out. That isn't the only reason people lash out, of course. Some people simply have very thin skins. If so, perhaps they shouldn't make provocative public comments.

We have tough issues to confront, and all of us should be prepared to deal with tough questions and have their representations, conceptions, misconceptions, and theories scrutinized. No pain, no gain. In my experience, people with the most substance are also the most pleasant when asked questions that most people find awkward. They realize that raising issues is often awkward for both the questioner and the person responding. Serious people are prepared to engage in serious discourse.

Looking back on true early warnings and how they were dismissed and discredited helps us understand the issues now threatening the global economy and the failings in our system. It is important to identify who provided thoughtful analysis when it mattered most, instead of those that simply said they did.

Michael Lewis: Junior Salesgirlieman

March 15, 2010

I was in the Salomon Brothers' 1985 training class that Michael Lewis lampooned in his amusing book, Liar's Poker. Imagine my surprise to see him billed as a trader on 60 Minutes, since he was actually a junior salesman. Well-heeled male peacocks strutted the trading floor, and junior salesmen were girlie-men, mere eunuchs serving their pashas.

Michael hit the roof when I ribbed him about the mischaracterization. (We are not colleagues but have exchanged the occasional email.) Yet, in January 2007 he didn't spare the "wimps, ninnies, and pointless skeptics" at Davos. I wasn't at Davos (Michael wasn't either), but he derided people who staked their reputations—as I staked mine—on the fact that the financial system was in peril. One might think he'd have a thicker skin, when turnabout was fair play and truth was his casualty.

Michael had asserted "Davos Man...will brood about virtually anything, no matter how little he knows about it." He ridiculed their concern of a pending crisis due to the surge in derivatives demand and called it "this year's case in point." Then Michael showed how dangerous it is to be a brilliant writer with a poor command of facts and their true meaning:

> None of them seemed to understand that when you create a derivative you don't add to the sum of total risk in the financial world; you merely create a means for redistributing that risk. They have no evidence that financial risk is being redistributed in ways we should all worry about.[122]

Actually, there was a lot of evidence that risk was being "redistributed" in ways we should all worry about. Predatory lending was a national scandal. I was well-published on phony securitizations, phony AAA ratings, phony accounting—and the mother of all risk—excessive leverage on securities that could only plummet in value.[123]

Other serious people also spoke and wrote eloquently and accurately about the risks. They were often ridiculed by mainstream media girlie-men and intimidated by their bosses. Some—like my friend, Arturo Cifuentes—stood their ground and were maliciously fired for it.[124] Meanwhile, Michael was still cheerleading Wall Street:

> But the most striking thing about the growing derivatives markets is the stability that has come with them.

Derivatives had destabilized the global financial system, albeit Michael was clueless. Leverage was much more dangerous than at the time of Long Term Capital Management's implosion. Then Michael gave us the payoff:

> If they really believe the markets mispriced risk...they must also believe they could make vast sums of money if they quit their day jobs and opened a hedge fund to take the other side of stupid trades.

Exactly. That is what I wrote to risk managers at the same time Michael was penning his screed. I told them to get out of investment banks and short those trades, since bank managers had their boots on the necks of risk managers, as regulators and the media licked the managers' boots.[125]

Michael had it wrong in more than one profound way. The markets weren't just "mispricing risk," those in-the-know were manipulating prices—covering up malfeasance and losses. Meanwhile, some members of the fourth estate used their pernicious pens as pawns in the cover-up.

All of the legacy investment banks enabled predatory lending, yet they now perpetrate what Elizabeth Warren calls the "myth of the immoral debtor." Wall Street banks were the key architects of the financial meltdown. The Fed provided cheap money, but irresponsible financiers exploited it. Banks massively over-borrowed, their agents extracted billions in bonuses, and now they blame hard-working taxpayers. These predators call this "God's work," while most of the media covers-up for them.

Michael Lewis is Wrong Again: It was Fraud

Michael wrote me that he read my book on structured finance while he was working on his book, because "it inspired one of the main characters" of *The Big Short*. Yet, he mangled the facts in his eagerness to create a story, since it is again fashionable—and profitable—for Michael to bash Wall Street.

Michael told *60 Minutes* (March 14) the financial crisis is a story of mass delusion, but he's only deluding himself.[126] It takes courage to tell the real story. This is actually a story of Wall Street's massive, wide-spread, multi-year fraud, including accounting fraud.[127]

I appeared on *60 Minutes* (February 14) and said Wall Street's dealings with mortgage lenders, securitizations, derivatives, and investors were a massive Ponzi scheme, the biggest crime ever against the American economy.[128] Wall Street and Washington hope you are gullible enough to believe otherwise.

The *Washington Post* says his book reads like the "same smart-alecky Michael Lewis," a biased account of industry players "whom he holds up to ridicule for their arrogance." I'm sure I'll enjoy it for the irony.

Wealthy Patriots Wage Class War

December 12, 2011

A strange thing happened in Chicago on Thursday, December 8. An audience of well-heeled professionals, a mixture of Democrats and Republicans, packed a room at the Drake Hotel to hear Robert Shiller, a Yale professor, give a presentation on the housing market. A few members of the audience were in the top 1%, and the balance of the audience was probably in the top 2%-5%. At the end of the presentation, there was a bi-partisan revolt.

The Chicago Mercantile Exchange (CME) and the Chicago Council on Global Affairs (CCGA) jointly sponsored the presentation. I'm a donor to CCGA's president's circle. Professor Shiller, deemed one of the country's foremost housing authorities, proposed a futures index for hedging and a new type of mortgage loan product along with some historical filler. In the context of our recent housing debacle, he never once uttered the word "fraud."

Fraud "Blind Spot"

Shiller's speech was 2 ½ years after I appeared on C-Span talking about the many aspects of widespread interconnected mortgage fraud that damaged the global financial markets. I summarized fraud's significant role in the 2008 financial crisis in a book called *Dear Mr. Buffett.*[129]

Shiller's speech was months after Congressional investigations showed how Wall Street firms provided financing for fraudulent loan activity of a number of different loan originators by creating fraudulent securitizations.

His speech was also months after widespread reports of robo-signing of affidavits and other types of foreclosure fraud. Banks showed up in court with fraudulent documents, which is fraud on the courts.

The Yale professor's speech was just four days after *60 Minutes* blew open widespread loan origination fraud at Countrywide. The firm created fraudulent documents. Separately it was reported that in Countrywide's Chicago office, 90% of loan applications were altered and income was sometimes inflated by Countrywide employees, not by borrowers.

Countrywide settled a well-publicized fraud lawsuit for $8.68 billion with several states including Illinois.

Shiller's talk was the day after former Illinois Governor Rod Blagojevich was sentenced to 14 years in prison after his corruption conviction.

Shiller spoke on the same day that Jon Corzine, former CEO of bankrupt firm MF Global (former Democratic Governor of New Jersey, former Democratic Senator from New Jersey and former CEO of Goldman Sachs), testified before Congress that he had no intention to break the rules but he just doesn't know what happened to an estimated $600 million to $1.2 billion of customers' assets. MF Global was among other things a Futures Commission Merchant (FCM) and Shiller was proposing a futures index. Customers' money disappeared from segregated accounts that should have been intact but were not.

*****

Audience Calls for Integrity

Michael Moskow, current vice-chairman and senior fellow on the global economy at CCGA and former head of the Chicago Federal Reserve, stood at the podium as Robert Shiller took questions from an upset audience. One attendee noted in an email to me that questioners were professionals, "not the Occupy Wall Street crowd who were accused of inciting 'class warfare' at the podium."

During the brief Q&A two men, one a former long-term Wall Street professional, asked questions about how we move forward when there is so little confidence. They cited the lack of integrity in the global financial markets.

After that, I asked how one creates a futures index (as Shiller proposed) in which one can have confidence without acknowledging the existence of fraud and vigorously prosecuting fraud. There was fraud by loan originators, fraudulent securitizations, and even fraud in the residential mortgage backed securities (RMBS) that backed a different hedging instrument, the ABX index.

The first time the word "fraud" was uttered that evening was when I posed my question.

Shiller himself never used "fraud." The most he would say in his so-called response was "some people aren't very nice." Really? It sounded rehearsed, and it struck most people in the audience as a shameful cop-out. If this is what economists are teaching students at universities, students should demand a refund of their tuition. Kindergarten children are given better warnings about strangers with candy.

"Countrywide Broke the Law. Homeowners Did Not."

Even worse Shiller, intentionally or otherwise, distorted my meaning. He claimed borrowers inflated income, without citing a source. Some of that occurred, but that wasn't what I referred to in my question. I corrected Shiller. I had clearly referred to instances where Countrywide altered documents and put in higher income amounts so that the mortgage loans would be approved for people that could not afford them. [Illinois Attorney General Lisa Madigan stated: "Countrywide broke the law. Homeowners did not."] Moreover, Shiller completely dodged the issue of fraudulent securitizations and foreclosure fraud.

CCGA and Academia Need to Get Their Crimes Straight

As if in a continuation of his answer to my question, Shiller mentioned he had spoken with a cab driver (apparently the source of all man-on-the-street information for academics) and the cab driver had no savings, only debt. Robert Shiller and Michael Moskow, the retired head of the Chicago Fed, appeared smug to me about this anonymous struggling working man's plight.

They seemed to be promulgating what Elizabeth Warren calls the "myth of the immoral debtor." Yet being in debt or even going bankrupt is not a crime in the United States. Loan originators' submission of fraudulent documents is a crime. Securities fraud is a crime. Foreclosure fraud is a crime.

Afterwards, several people came to me and to the other questioners. Much of the audience complained to CCGA's conference organizers. All were disappointed in Professor Shiller. A male CPA in the audience later contacted me via my website and wrote that he was glad I had put the question to Shiller: "though I have a great deal of respect for him, I was disappointed in his 'response' (if you could call it that)."

One woman who earned a Ph.D. in history found Shiller's response to me "incoherent:"

> I was with my husband, brother, and his wife. I chatted with the stranger next to me and at least two people escaping at the same time [leaving after the speech]. No one could believe what a huge "fail" the evening had been...the failure of our political and expert classes to address the core issues...have alienated even those working in the financial industry—right up into the rung below the top of the

food chain...this feels like the Ancien Régime's last days.

Class Warfare

Alumni of the Federal Reserve, corrupt politicians, and willfully blind academics would be correct to say that evening was a case of "class warfare." Well-heeled U.S. patriots declared war on the lack of class demonstrated by their financial peers.

“Allow me to issue and control a nation’s money, and I care not who makes the laws.”

—Mayer Amschel Rothschild

CHAPTER 7 Politicians' Inaction

President Obama's Right to Free Speech

May 10, 2009

President Obama enjoys the same rights as the average citizen, even when he engages in political grandstanding and advocates substantively bad economic policies.

Clifford Asness, Principal of AQR Capital Management, seems to disagree. He calls the president's recent remarks about hedge funds "libelous," but he may have meant to write slanderous.[130]

President Obama called hedge fund managers "speculators" who were "refusing to sacrifice like everyone else" and who wanted "to hold out for the prospect of an unjustified taxpayer-funded bailout" of Chrysler.

Hedge fund managers are outraged, and Asness calls himself "unafraid" and paints himself a hero for speaking out against a popular President. He thinks hedge fund managers are caving out of fear.

I agree with Mr. Asness that neither the United Auto Workers nor its pension fund should receive special treatment. Hedge fund managers are obliged not to "sacrifice" their clients' money or agree to payouts that would have been out of order under bankruptcy.

In Mr. Asness's parlance it is "stealing" to "sacrifice" clients' money. Mr. Asness says it is the job of hedge fund managers to maximize the outcome for their investors, but in this unregulated industry, many high profile hedge fund managers helped themselves to investors' funds or made material misrepresentations to investors.

I don't recall Mr. Asness's letter expressing outrage about outright theft by hedge fund managers. Then there is the more benign but galling hubris of "quant funds" that touted how their models enabled them to outperform the market—until they wildly underperformed the market during the current debacle. It probably felt like a "sacrifice" to their investors. Mr. Asness is not defending Eagle Scouts, albeit there are many hedge fund managers of high integrity, even when their returns are not high.

Mr. Asness writes that "the President screaming that the hedge funds are looking for an unjustified taxpayer-funded bailout is the big lie writ large." He adds it is "because hedge funds have not taken government funds that they could stand up to this bullying." Yet indirectly at least, some hedge funds have been beneficiaries of the taxpayer funded bailout, and some were direct contributors to the need for bailouts. Hedge funds may not have had a starring role in the financial meltdown, but they were supporting actors.

Where was Mr. Asness's outrage about the role of certain hedge funds in value destroying securitizations that fueled the financial meltdown? In my opinion, several hedge funds deserve scrutiny by the Department of Justice for their role in disastrous CDOs. If the worst hedge funds get is a misdirected scolding, then some of them are getting off too lightly.

Taxpayers are on the hook both directly and indirectly. When the creditors of Bear Stearns Asset Management's (BSAM) hedge funds demanded that Bear Stearns step in, it did. BSAM's other hedge funds may have had their credit lines yanked if Bear Stearns had not bailed out the creditors of two of its problem funds. Those money-losing hedge fund assets ended up on the balance sheet of Bear Stearns. Now JPMorgan Chase is holding the bag. I'll bet some of those assets or like-kind assets ended up in the $30 billion Maiden Lane vehicle that has already been written down by $4.4 billion.

Citigroup took $9 billion of assets on balance sheet from Old Lane Partners, the hedge fund Vikram Pandit ran before he became CEO of Citigroup. Merrill Lynch, prior to its merger with Bank of America, supplied hedge funds with non-recourse financing, and those financed assets may boomerang back on its balance sheet. The U.S. taxpayer bailed out AIG's credit default swap counterparty/creditors that included some hedge funds. Taxpayers handed over TARP money partly to fund these debacles. Many prime brokers are able to continue funding hedge funds only because the government (the taxpayer) is providing them with unprecedented funding. Saying that hedge funds have been truly off balance sheet is—to use Asness's words—"the big lie writ large."

Mr. Asness ends with this taunt: "I am ready for my 'personalized' tax rate now." *Would that be the 'personalized' tax rate currently paid by most of his fellow citizens on their income?* Mr. Asness should not be suggesting that other citizens—even when that citizen is the President—should have fewer citizenship rights than he, especially since he (along with other hedge fund managers) enjoys tax breaks on his hedge fund management fees unavailable to the average wage earner. Perhaps Mr. Asness is afraid hedge fund managers are caving from fear that their privileged tax breaks will be revoked.

President Obama's apparent financial naiveté—or perhaps a willingness to destroy capitalism by changing the rules—is indeed annoying. It is especially annoying to me if it was partly inspired by the actions of some hedge funds. But Mr. Asness is correct when he says: "I'm entitled to my voice and to speak it loudly...in this great country." That is why I take issue when Mr. Asness seems to characterize a public Presidential scolding as illegal.

In this great country, POTUS is equally free to vent his frustration as Mr. Asness. Nothing about President Obama's remarks seemed slanderous; it is called free speech. POTUS has a right to spout bad financial policies in public. I disagree with POTUS that bond investors should take a back seat to union interests. But I also disagree that hedge fund managers should have the same easy access to leverage and tax breaks that they enjoyed in the past, since both investors and taxpayers have ultimately paid for the mistakes of hedge fund managers.

Washington's Bipartisan Betrayal: The 2015 Global Financial Crisis

December 31, 2009

The time has come for new year's resolutions. The House passed the Wall Street Reform and Consumer Protection Act of 2009 (H.R. 4173) on December 11, 2009. It gives $4 trillion in "emergency funding" to our largest banks during the next financial crisis. Instead of reform, Congress offers even bigger bailouts. Unless we change direction, we will have another crisis by 2015. Congress has made all the wrong moves to guarantee it.

The economy did not just have a heart attack; we are suffering from financial appendicitis. Instead of doing the necessary surgery, Congress is prescribing potent addictive painkillers.

How did we get here? Housing is the largest component of our economy. Cheap money from the Federal Reserve, crippling of states' rights to rein in mortgage lenders, and failure to enforce securities laws allowed the largest Ponzi scheme in the history of the capital markets to flourish.

Wall Street's shadow banking system gave mortgage lenders large credit lines (similar to credit card debt) and packaged the loans into private-label residential mortgage backed securitizations. Most of each deal was rated "AAA," since subordinated investors absorbed the risk of a pre-agreed amount of loan losses. But hundreds of billions of dollars in private-label deals were backed by portfolios comprising risky fraud-riddled loans. Most of the "AAA" investment was imperiled, and subordinated "investment grade" components were worthless. Wall Street disguised these toxic "investments" with new value-destroying securitizations and related credit derivatives: Collateralized Debt Obligations (CDOs and CDO-squared), Structured Investment Vehicles (SIVs), Real Estate Mortgage Investment Conduits (REMICs and Re-REMICs), Asset Backed Commercial Paper (ABCP), and related credit derivatives. Wall Street also engaged in suspect securitizations of some credit card receivables, auto loans, bank trust preferred securities, commercial real estate loans, and a variety of corporate loans.

Meanwhile, collapsing mortgage lenders paid high dividends to shareholders (old investors) and interest on credit lines to Wall Street (old investors) with money raised from new investors (perhaps your pension fund) in doomed securities. New money allowed Wall Street to temporarily hide losses and pay enormous bonuses. This is a classic Ponzi scheme.

When you leverage fraud riddled fixed income securities priced at 100 cents on the dollar, there is nowhere to go but down in a hurry. Confusion after the fraud fell apart led to a vicious cycle of selling as investors and lenders shunned both good and bad assets. The deflating debt bubble was followed by a classic liquidity crunch resulting in a global crisis.[131]

Wall Street protests that it sold toxic assets to sophisticated investors obliged to perform independent investigations of the risk. That argument no longer applies. U.S. taxpayers became unwilling unsophisticated investors funding Wall Street's bailout.

Other parties—mortgage bankers, credit rating agencies, hedge funds, credit rating agency, insurers, mortgage brokers, regulators, Congress, and the Federal Reserve Bank—were supporting actors. If Wall Street's financial meth labs had been shut down earlier, the money machine would have stopped running.

Recent arguments blame Fannie Mae and Freddie Mac, the indirect mortgage lending giants. This is misguided. The largest slug of new risky products and bad loans were created to fuel Wall Street's private-label securitizations. Fannie and Freddie were more at the effect than the cause (not blameless, but not the largest cause of the housing bubble). Now that shadow banking is dead, they are being stuffed with even more bad product to pick up the slack.

Fannie Mae and Freddie Mac are the new motor for no-money-down mortgage loans and a host of new problems. The fraudsters involved with our last crisis went unpunished, and they will help create our next crisis. This brewing fraud fest will result in greater misery and systemic risk. Instead of reform, Congress responded on Christmas Eve by agreeing to cover unlimited loan losses.[132]

Bank depositors' money is guaranteed, if deposits are below the current FDIC deposit insurance limits. Banks did not need to be bailed out to protect depositors. We bailed out banks' other creditors with public money. We are printing so much money that now depositors should worry about inflation.

Inflation is the great destroyer. Inflation will wipe out investment gains (and more) much more quickly than taxes. If you earn, say, 5% on your deposits, 5% inflation will wipe out your gains, (and you aren't earning 5% on your deposits or treasury notes in the first place). That is worse than any current or proposed tax rate, since that would translate to a 100% tax rate.

Wall Street, Fannie Mae, and Freddie Mac supply a swinging door of jobs and paid projects for its financial regulators,

Congressmen, appointed administration officials, and investigation committee staffers. Many members of Congress and our Presidents have received massive campaign contributions funded by Wall Street. This dependence is known as "capture," and the result is that instead of reining in Wall Street, dependent thinking enables mayhem.[133]

We have an alternative to bailouts, one that does not violate the spirit of democracy. Troubled financial entities should be put into receivership and restructured. Old shareholders will be wiped out. Debt-holders will take a haircut (discount) along with a debt for new equity swap to recapitalize the entity. But the job won't be complete until we separate high risk activities from traditional banking in a return to Glass-Steagall, indict fraudsters, snuff out systemic fraud, and allow honest bankers to prosper.

After the Savings and Loan crisis of the late 1980s, there were more than 1,000 felony indictments of senior officers. Recent fraud is much more widespread and costly. The consequences are much greater. Congress needs to fund investigations. Regulators need to get tough on crime.

The fact that many U.S. banks stuck to traditional banking and protected shareholders during this crisis is under-publicized, but their prudence worked.

We have the solutions. We need the political will to implement them.

CHAPTER 8 Rating Agencies

Revoke Rating Agencies' NRSRO Designation for Structured Products

September 17, 2009

The IMF invited me to present my views on the global financial crisis as detailed in my book, *Dear Mr. Buffett: What an Investor Learns 1,269 Miles from Wall Street* on Monday, September 21. Among other recommendations, I will suggest Congress approve more funding for investigations that should lead to felony indictments of financial professionals involved in the largest Ponzi scheme in the history of the capital markets. Predatory securitizations of fraudulent loans, the credit derivatives that referenced them, and fraudulent accounting enabled former investment banks and some legacy banks to raise money from new investors to pay back old investors (themselves and mortgage lenders) in what was known to be an unsustainable and fraud riddled business model.

The rating agencies have been in the news as they fend off lawsuits for their ratings of ABS CDOs (collateralized debt obligations backed by asset backed securities). The rating agencies claim their ratings are protected by free speech, and they may or may not be successful in defending themselves in court. In my book, *Structured Finance*, I explain the rating agencies' history of failure (in my opinion) to competently rate hundreds of billions of dollars' worth of these and other structured products. The relevant rating agencies involved in these ratings are the top three: Moody's Corporation; Standard & Poor's (S&P), part of McGraw-Hill Cos., Inc.; and Fitch, owned by France-based Fimalac SA.

The rating agencies are quick to point out that they do not perform due diligence on the data they use and take no responsibility for unearthing fraud; they merely issue "opinions." But rating agencies can demand to see evidence of appropriate due diligence from the underwriters, who are obliged to perform it.

Instead, rating agencies failed to adhere to basic statistical principles.

Meanwhile, the SEC seeks comments about the steps it should take to regulate the rating agencies. In my letter to the SEC dated February 13, 2007, I called for the SEC to revoke the rating agencies' registration as Nationally Recognized Statistical Rating Organizations (NRSRO) for structured products. The SEC failed to act in 2007, but it can correct that error and do it now.

In addition to criticizing rating agencies for their ratings of CDOs, I mentioned another class of structured products, CPDOs that were rated "AAA" at the time I wrote the letter. I asserted CPDOs had substantial principal risk. That meant these "AAA" rated products deserved a junk rating. By January 2008, within a year of my warning, Moody's noted that two of the originally AAA-rated CPDOs would unwind causing substantial principal loss to investors. In fact Moody's, the rating agency that bases its "AAA" rating on expected loss, belatedly projected investors would have a *90 percent loss.* Although I had flagged the looming danger to investors' principal, the SEC did nothing.

Ackman Versus Wall Street's Ponzi Scheme

May 4, 2010

When nobody seems to be losing money, nobody cares. If a corrupt scheme is "making money," everyone involved—from the culprits to the dupes—viciously attacks anyone who tries to expose it. Bill Ackman, manager of hedge fund Pershing Square Capital Management, L.P., learned this lesson the hard way.

"Friends in High Places"

In 2002, Ackman used credit derivatives (and shorted stock) to place a "short" bet against MBIA, the largest of the municipal bond insurers. (Ackman later bet against other bond insurers.) Joseph "Jay" Brown, then MBIA's Chairman and CEO, met with Ackman in 2002 about a negative report Ackman was about to release. In Christine Richard's new book, *Confidence Game,* Ackman recalls this power-play:

> You're a young guy, early in your career. You should think long and hard before issuing the report. We are the largest guarantor of New York state and New York City bonds. In fact, we're the largest guarantor of municipal debt in the country. Let's put it this way: We have friends in high places.[134]

Ackman published the report on his fund's web site: "Is MBIA Triple-A?" Among other issues, Ackman questioned MBIA's foray into credit derivatives and synthetic CDOs.

Here's some ironic background you won't find in *Confidence Game*. In 2003, Jack Caouette, then Vice Chairman of MBIA, wrote a blurb for my book on the dangers posed by credit derivatives and synthetic CDOs, *Collateralized Debt Obligations & Structured Finance*:

> Caveat Emptor! Never in the history of finance has this warning been more appropriate. With the development of esoteric structured finance techniques, the savvy as well as the novice are exposed to a bewildering array. An outstanding mixture of exposition, mathematics and skepticism.

Ackman's concern was reasonable. Structured finance is easily gamed, and fraud was common.

Ackman's early bet didn't pay-off, and he was not just ignored, the financial media raked him over the coals. Moreover, Ackman was correct about several other accounting issues unrelated to synthetic CDOs.

Ackman persisted, MBIA protested, and in early 2003, the SEC and New York Attorney General's office investigated him. The NY AG's office, then headed by Eliot Spitzer, grilled Ackman for six days. Ackman's activism eventually led to a two-year investigation of MBIA resulting in its restating seven years of earnings and a $75 million fine.

Ackman didn't stop. He hired a top forensic accounting expert and several times brought evidence of fraudulent accounting to Moody's, the leading credit rating agency. Meanwhile, MBIA restated its numbers twice. At the end of 2005, Ackman wrote Moody's board of directors:

> Moody's Aaa rating is so powerful and credible that investors don't do any due diligence on the underlying credit. Every day that Moody's incorrectly maintains an Aaa rating on MBIA, these extremely risk-averse investors unwittingly buy bonds that are not deserving of Moody's Aaa rating.[135]

MBIA escalated its risk. MBIA wrote credit derivatives on new "Triple-A" risk backed by malignant mortgage loans, including built-to-fail mezzanine CDOs. It didn't matter how much "confidence" Wall Street, rating agencies, bond insurers, and regulators had in maintaining a collective financial lie, MBIA was unstable.

In February 2008, MBIA cut its dividend and suspended structured finance activities. Jay Brown wrote MBIA's investors that Ackman's "campaign" was an attempt to destroy his business. Ackman's shorts weren't the problem. MBIA could have used some shorts of its own, since it was long with too little coverage. MBIA had insured rotting mortgage risk with too little capital to maintain even an investment grade rating.

By June 2008, MBIA and Ambac, the largest municipal bond insurers, lost their "AAA" ratings and slid fast from there. At the end of 2008, Ackman took $1.1 billion in gains for Pershing Square, enough to offset losses in other investments, some of which subsequently rebounded.

Bankers Get Bonuses, USA Gets the Great Recession

Wall Street banks with financial ties to mortgage lenders fueled bad—and often fraudulent—mortgage lending, created phony mislabeled securities, and off-loaded the temporarily disguised risk on bond insurers (MBIA, Ambac, AIG, FGIC, and more) and naïve investors to keep the Ponzi scheme going. A housing bubble fueled by corrupt finance damaged the U.S. economy, and taxpayers bailed out the chief culprits.

Those with "friends in high places" did the most damage to the nation's economy and personally profited the most. It's also noteworthy that Ackman's outrage was not directed at investment banks with whom he traded and that underwrote fraudulent value-destroying CDOs, fed him internal CDO data, internal CDO models, and information on MBIA's and Ambac's positions, all of which bolstered his confidence to continue with his short positions. The high pay of Wall Street and its cronies doesn't reflect efficient markets or individual brilliance; it's a market failure.

The Great Bailout protected debt holders and some shareholders in corrupt financial institutions. Culprits involved in phony securitizations that damaged the economy have windfall gains and are now heavily subsidized with taxpayer dollars. Bill Ackman's ordeal shows us how much endurance will be required to reverse these mistakes and reform the financial system.

In the interest of full disclosure, I attended Bill Ackman's book launch party and am quoted in the book.

Tavakoli Structured Finance Revokes Credit Rating Agencies' NRSRO Designation: Issues and Solutions for Restoring Credibility to the Credit Rating Agencies and Rehabilitating the Alternative Banking System

July 26, 2011

I. REVOCATION OF THE NRSRO DESIGNATION[136]

Ten rating organizations are designated Nationally Recognized Statistical Rating Organizations: Moody's Corporation; Standard & Poor's Ratings Services (S&P, part of McGraw-Hill Cos., Inc.), Fitch, Inc., Best Company, Inc., DBRS Ltd., Egan-Jones Rating Company, Japan Credit Rating Agency, Ltd., Kroll Bond Rating Agency, Inc. (f/k/a LACE Financial Corp.), Rating and Investment Information, and Realpoint LLC. Moody's and S&P are the most influential and have the most market share. Ratings, particularly those of Moody's and S&P, are built into the global regulatory and market framework.

Ostensibly the U.S. Securities and Exchange Commission (SEC) qualifies the NRSRO designation. The SEC's series of failures to check the creation and sale of hundreds of billions of dollars of blatantly misrated securitizations leading up to the financial crisis are beyond the scope of this report. It's worth noting, however, that if the Food and Drug Administration failed to check the sale of tainted meat that repeatedly sickened a large segment of the population, we would demand a top to bottom overhaul of the organization and its methods.

In February 2007, the SEC sought comments about the steps it should take to regulate the rating agencies. In my letter to the SEC dated February 13, 2007, I called for the SEC to revoke the rating agencies' designation as Nationally Recognized Statistical Rating Organizations (NRSRO). Ratings for structured products were based on smoke and mirrors.

In upholding the NRSRO designation the SEC and Congress are as irrelevant to the truth as Galileo's inquisitors when they forced him to recant his upholding of Copernicus' idea that the earth moves around the sun. Fundamental truths are not changed by arbitrary legislation like Congress's Credit Agency Reform Act of 2006, meant to improve ratings quality, or by the SEC's regulation. Since the SEC failed to act, I now revoke the NRSRO designation for all credit rating agencies for every class of credit rating with the exception of corporations not engaged in structured finance in a meaningful way. Specifically, this revocation is for the following rating classes: structured financial products including, but not limited to, structured credit products, asset backed securities, and synthetic securitizations; financial institutions (including brokers or dealers and hedge funds), insurance companies, and sovereigns that have bailed out their banking systems and continue to fund them.

This report provides further background on this action focusing on the top two rating agencies, Moody's and S&P, and suggests a multi- year process required to restore a credible NRSRO designation for the rating agencies.

*****

A. Rating Agencies' Role in the Financial Collapse: The Sovereign Effect

The U.S. and European economies are experiencing credit turmoil that is a side effect of the collapse of the alternative banking system, sometimes referred to as the "shadow" banking system. This is the financial system created using a combination of structured finance techniques employed over more than twenty years including special purpose vehicles, securitization, interest rate derivatives, commodity derivatives, currency derivatives, and credit derivatives.

At its best, the alternative banking system was a financial growth engine that provided a mechanism for efficient financing and risk distribution for borrowers that otherwise found it difficult to access traditional bank financing. The downfall of this system was due to a series of failures, chiefly the role of the largest banks that underwrote phony securitizations and failed to follow established laws governing the underwriting of the securities they sold. This was abetted by failures at the rating agencies, regulators, monoline insurers, and ancillary finance partners of investment banks: mortgage lenders, mortgage servicers, legal advisors, accountants, student loan providers, auto loan providers, credit card issuers, and academic consultants.

Most of the market for ratings is dominated by Moody's and Standard & Poor's, especially the U.S. market, where these two U.S.-based rating agencies have been entrenched and have most of the historical data. Fitch has played a more minor but significant role as both a primary and swing provider in the rating of structured financial products.

In the run up to the current crisis, the rating agencies misrated mortgage securitizations called Residential Mortgage-Backed Securities (RMBS) that included loans with poor underwriting standards and fraudulent loans; this risk wasn't captured in the ratings. (APPENDIX II.) As mortgage lenders failed, new investors had to be found to pay off old investors i.e., mortgage lenders and the banks that funded them. When the business model became unsustainable, it devolved into a Ponzi scheme. (APPENDIX III.) The errors compounded with misrated Collateralized Debt Obligations (CDOs) and CDO-squared products that were securitizations of misrated tranches. (APPENDICES IV. and V.) Credit derivatives technology added hidden risks and amplified problems. From the start "AAA"-rated tranches of these deals showed the high probability of significant principal loss. (See Section VI. for a more detailed discussion.) These were just a few of the rating agencies' egregious debacles. This report will discuss a few more, but it is still a partial list.

In a July 2011 report, The Joint Forum at The Bank for International Settlements' (BIS) Committee on Banking Supervision issued a report titled: "Report on Asset Securitisation Incentives." Characteristic of most central banks and regulators in the global financial system, it did not identify the key rating agency issues and when it comes to other aspects of securitization, the word "fraud" is not mentioned anywhere in the report. This sort of denial enables repeat offenders.

This is ironic, because BIS enabled "super senior" tranches, supposedly the top-most "AAA" tranches of CDOs that used credit derivatives technology, since it awarded lower regulatory capital requirements for these tranches. The "super senior" tranches of synthetic CDOs, securitizations that use credit derivatives technology, made up most of each deal. This will be discussed in more detail later in this report.

The BIS report noted that from 1990 to 2006, the peak year for ABS issuance, "AAA" rated assets ballooned from 20 percent of rated fixed-income issuance to almost 55 percent. Many of these came at the tail end of this period when the "AAA" ratings were unwarranted, in fact many warranted a junk rating at the outset, but BIS didn't mention that part. It also left out that in the first half of 2007, virtually every "AAA" of ABS CDOs warranted junk ratings.

Prior to the effective halt of private label securitizations in the latter part of 2007, the alternative banking system provided an outlet for more than 70% of bank loans. By June, 2008, just three months before the September 2008 financial meltdown, CDOs in default already exceeded $200 billion. More troubles were subsequently exposed in CDOs and a variety of other products. Investors included insurance companies, bank investment portfolios, mutual funds, pension funds, hedge funds, and other money managers. Every sector of society was affected as misrated products caused actual principal losses combined with loss in value due to declining market prices and illiquidity.

The perceived ability to remove ever increasing risk from the balance sheets of the largest banks through misrated securities backfired as risk boomeranged back onto the balance sheets of underwriters. Liquidity—coming up with needed cash—is now a global problem, since investors are wary of lending money (by investing) against potentially misrated assets.

Advance hedging and raising capital requirements would only have helped mitigate some of the failures of risk transference: failure of credit default swap counterparties, consolidation of assets of flawed-at-creation special purpose vehicles, and consolidation of failed "independent hedge fund" assets.

The general financial meltdown experienced in September 2008 was accompanied by the suppression of facts and self-serving misinformation by many of the key players. Capital buffers and hedges were insufficient, and the controversial choice was made to recapitalize the banks without inquiry into the causes and culprits. Unfortunately, the bailout was also done without conditions and no meaningful steps have been taken that will prevent a similar global financial catastrophe.

As of 2009, "AAA" issuance from Sovereigns that still have that rating ballooned to outstrip the "AAA" ABS issuance of 2006. This is no surprise. Government bailouts to recapitalize the banks meant that new sovereign debt had to be issued. Capital spending, the biggest driver of economic growth was starved of funds.

As a result of the enormous bailouts, sovereign debt ballooned imperiling the "AAA" ratings of many sovereign entities while debt issuance continued to expand. "AAA" asset issuance stood at around $5 trillion in 2006, and in 2009 it was around $6 trillion. A significant chunk had shifted from imploded ABS CDOs to "AAA" sovereign debt. (APPENDIX VI.) Sovereign ratings are lagging indicators of risk and are readjusted by the rating agencies only after the damage is already blindingly obvious and well-reported by other more reliable sources.

Dodd-Frank will not avert a future crisis any more than Sarbanes-Oxley was effective in averting the last crisis. Banks can appear to take mortgage loan risk on balance sheet, but can lay it off through derivatives or through structural games. The provisions in Dodd-Frank are easily thwarted through opaque structured finance. Another problem is that risks have ramped up in other opaque areas: currency derivatives, credit derivatives, interest and market-linked derivatives, and commodities derivatives and speculation. This report, however, will continue to focus on the rating agencies.

This report deals with only one critical aspect of what it will take to rehabilitate the alternative banking system. It is a necessary—but not sufficient condition—to address the various issues that have contributed to the credit rating agencies' history of failure.

B. Rating Agencies' Current Practice Is Junk Science

One cannot understand the strengths and weaknesses of any model unless one understands the risk characteristics of the target portfolios' assets. This is accomplished by examining the underwriters' due diligence, and demanding even more thorough due diligence from the underwriter, if it is warranted. Since this granular work wasn't properly done by any reasonable professional standard, the rating agencies computer models employed inputs that were simply guesses (or worse, deliberate masks of the risk) instead of a rational assessment of value.

Rating agencies correctly point out that deal sponsors and investment bank underwriters are responsible for due diligence on the underlying collateral. Although the rating agencies do not perform due diligence for investors, they can demand evidence that proper due diligence has been performed before attempting to apply their respective ratings methodologies. In fact, it is not possible to perform a sound statistical analysis without it.

Statistics is the mathematical study of the probability and likelihood of events. Known information can be taken into account, and likelihoods and probabilities are inferred by taking a statistical sampling. The rating agencies have not lived up to the NRSRO designation by any reasonable professional standard.

For example, in the mortgage loan securitization market, a statistical sampling of the underlying mortgage loans should verify the integrity of the documentation, the identity of the borrower, the appraisal of the property, the borrower's ability to repay the loan, and so on. Rating agencies should take reasonable steps to understand the character of the risk they are modeling. Yet, they seemingly rated risky deals without demanding evidence of thorough due diligence, or if they did, they ignored or didn't understand the implications.

It seems the rating agencies either did not refuse to "rate" securitizations that lacked this evidence, or they ignored reports that revealed fatal asset flaws for many structured finance transactions. In more colloquial language, the rating agencies just made stuff up.

When rating agencies use old data for obviously new risks, it's financial astrology. When rating agencies guess at "AAA" ratings (without the data to back it up), it's financial alchemy. When rating agencies evaluate no-name CDO managers without asking for thorough background checks, it's financial phrenology. In other words, the rating agencies practice junk science. The result is that junk, i.e., non -investment grade tranches of securitized assets routinely got "AAA" ratings prior to the meltdown of 2008. So-called super-safe "super seniors" were junk.

The rating agencies' have turned their names to mud, and Congress and the SEC do not seem to have the expertise to even correctly identify the issues. When they adopted arbitrary rating labels as benchmarks, the BIS, Fed and SEC enabled junk science. Investors do not have an alternative to this flawed system other than to do their own fundamental credit analysis.

II. NOT MERE OPINIONS: PART OF REGULATORY AND MARKET FRAMEWORK

The rating agencies assert that they issue mere opinions, but the NRSRO designation gives ratings the appearance of being issued from a position of authority. Regulators and investors rely on this pseudo-authority. When named as defendants in legal disputes, rating agencies hid behind the shield of journalist-like privilege keeping notes confidential. Rating agencies claimed they only issue opinions, however negligent they were in adhering to any reasonable professional standard when formulating those opinions. Dodd-Frank takes steps to increase transparency, but 1) it hasn't yet been implemented, 2) the approaches to several key identified problems have yet to be defined, and 3) the Act altogether missed some of the key issues. This will be addressed in more detail in Section VIII.

Bank regulators and insurance regulators have enacted capital rules for banks based on ratings. Many investment funds and investors have charters requiring them to only buy products that have been rated by one or more of the top three rating agencies. Since there is no independent standard to define the meaning of a rating, the rating agencies have unintentionally been given the power to change regulatory requirements. This is an extraordinary result given that the rating agencies are private companies.

Although they shouldn't, many investors rely on the rating and the coupon when buying structured financial products. For many investors a high coupon did not indicate high risk. Some naïve and misguided investors viewed the extra compensation as the privilege of those fortunate enough to have enough high net worth to be offered complex products. These investors did not think they were taking on extraordinary credit risk and extraordinary "financial engineering" when they bought products with the "AAA" rating. They thought they were buying sound, albeit less liquid products, and the extra coupon was viewed as compensation for less transparency and less liquidity.

Money market funds and pension funds rely on ratings. Pension funds are required to buy investment grade rated investments. The SEC is proposing that mutual funds should not rely on ratings, but the SEC is missing a piece. The SEC should not allow an investment below a previously required rating. For example, if an investor relied on an "AAA" rating before and it did not work out, that should not mean the investor should ignore the requirement and invest in something with a lower rating, either. Rather, the investor should still be required to have an "AAA" rating and should be required to determine that the value of the investment lives up to the rating.

Ratings are relied upon as if they are based on reliable and reproducible methods, but they are not, especially when it comes to structured products.

A. Ratings Cartel: Moody's, S&P, and Fitch

In 2003, I formally explained flaws with rated structured products in a book, *Collateralized Debt Obligations & Structured Finance*. I discussed these issues with the rating agencies and in various forums. There were already serious problems with inflated "AAA" ratings in securitizations that had inherent structural flaws, problems with supposedly investment grade rated collateral, and conflicts of interest that held investors' capital hostage to the self-interest of "managers" and investment banks. Those conflicts of interest often resulted in substantial principal losses to investors, and the risk was not captured in the ratings. The fact that all three top rating agencies (the only raters relevant to the issue) failed seemed more than a coincidence.

Instead of taking measures to address these flaws, the rating agencies ramped up their flawed structured products ratings business.

This tactic was temporarily successful because the top rating agencies act as a quasi-cartel, and their fees magically converged. They have each participated in overrating "AAA" structured products backed by dodgy loans that took substantial principal losses. As I will explain later, by the end of 2006 it was clear that it wasn't merely a question of misguided technique, the rating agencies' integrity was questionable, and "AAA" ratings were meaningless.

Moody's and S&P (Fitch was the exception) presented a fairly united front in defending their methods up to the September 2008 financial meltdown. Fitch, which also participated in overrating CDOs, seemed more responsive in downgrading structured products, but none of the three has meaningfully addressed the serious problems I discuss next.

III. RATING AGENCIES LACK REASONABLE STANDARDS: DODD-FRANK'S MISSES

The Dodd-Frank Act has not yet been implemented. Even when implemented, it will miss problems it should have addressed. This portion of the report addresses what can go wrong and all that has already gone wrong with the rating agencies. Dodd-Frank identified some, but not all of these problems. Subsequent sections illustrate these problems and the consequences they caused and will cause again. Section VIII. explains what Dodd-Frank got partially correct and what needs to be corrected to plug the gaping holes in the legislation and restore credibility to the rating agencies and the alternative banking system.

A. Rating Scales Are Self-Defined: Benchmarks and Methodologies Change Arbitrarily

Rating agencies define their own risk scales. (APPENDIX VII.) In other words, there is no independent, authoritative, or consistent definition of ratings benchmarks. Methodologies and models change at will. Global banking regulators and insurance company regulators have defined regulations and capital requirements that refer to these insubstantial ratings. An unintended consequence of the changeable ratings is rating agencies that were not elected and are not part of government have the ability to legislate by changing the meaning of their ratings.

Moody's awards a rating based on its estimate of expected loss, a single piece of information, and assigns a rating based on the safest (least expected loss) to the riskiest (highest expected loss): Aaa, Aa1, Aa2, Aa3, A1, A2, A3, Baa1, Baa2, Baa3, Ba1, Ba2, Ba3, B1, B2, B3, Caa1, Caa2, Caa3, Ca, C. Anything above Baa3 is considered investment grade, and anything below that is considered speculative grade. Standard & Poor's awards ratings based on default probabilities and labels products AAA, AA+, AA, AA–, and so on. Fitch uses the same labels as S&P. As with Moody's, anything above BBB– is considered investment grade and anything below is considered speculative grade. I'll use "AAA" to denote the highest rating, but will specifically name Moody's, which uses the "Aaa" notation, when I am making a point specific to Moody's.

"Super Senior" tranches are what I called "the greatest triumph of illusion in twentieth century finance," in my 2003 book on CDOs. I asked where the regulators were, since this fantasy would lead to bitter disillusionment for investors. Supposedly, former "AAAs" were subordinated to this tranche. In other words, the "AAA" tranche became the "first loss" tranche for the so-called super senior. There was no standard definition for this tranche, and when I specifically asked Moody's for the definition in 2002, it abdicated responsibility for coming up with one. I pointed out the former "AAA" was not the same as the new "AAA" that had become the "first loss" for the "super senior." Yet the label was identical. One market definition for "super senior" was that the probability of loss was 10^{-6}, meaning there was a one in a million chance of the investor taking the loss. Nothing could have been further from the truth. Some investors in late vintage "super senior" CDOs (2006-2007) lost all but a small single digit percentage of their initial investment. (APPENDIX VIII.)

Even the BIS bought into the "super senior" nonsense and awarded lower regulatory capital requirements for it. In 2002, I spoke to the head of market risk at the Chicago Fed about the problem and he dismissed it saying efficient markets meant the problem would be resolved in 18 months. How did that work out? In 2003, I wrote Jaime Caruana, then head of the BIS, but received no response.

At the beginning of 2005 I wrote an article for *Risk Professional* rating the rating agencies. Moody's claims its ratings reflect expected loss, a mathematical concept based on the probability of default and loss severity. Moody's occasionally changes the expected loss that corresponds to a given rating. S&P emphasizes probability of default, and occasionally changes the probability of default level that corresponds to its ratings. Fitch's model produced unreliable results, since Fitch kept changing its correlation matrix. Structurers using Fitch's model dubbed it the "Fitch Random Ratings Model."

There is tremendous moral hazard built into this system. The rating agencies enjoy extraordinary power. There is enormous incentive to fudge over serious mistakes. If an investment grade rated securitized asset shows increasing default rates in the asset portfolio, a rating agency might be tempted to change the definition of a rating rather than confront the inaccuracy of the rating, given that regulators and markets make decisions that are ratings-driven. Moreover, in order to gain market share, rating agencies may change their definitions and methodologies to win business from banks.

Since many money managers cannot buy bonds that are not rated investment grade, and since some are required to sell bonds that fall below investment grade, ratings have a huge impact. This is why when Moody's admitted that impairment rates show no difference in performance between CDO tranches with a junk rating of BB– and an investment grade rating of BBB, it should have been headline financial news in mainstream financial newspapers, but it wasn't. That problem was later swamped by misrated "AAA" structured products that were in reality non-investment grade junk.

It would seem logical that rating agencies' ratings could be mapped onto each other, but they cannot. One would think that rating agencies would at least be internally consistent, but that isn't necessarily so, especially when it comes to securitizations.

B. Rating Agencies' Excuses for Heterogeneous, Multi-year Failures

The rating agencies' problems run deep. In late 2003, the *Financial Times* took rating agencies to task for misrating debt issued by scandal-ridden Parmalat, Enron and WorldCom. Fitch protested that "credit ratings bring greater transparency." Standard & Poor's retorted that "rating agencies are not auditors or investigators and are not empowered or able to unearth fraud."

I responded to rating agencies' protests. There was ample evidence that investors were misled if they believed rating agencies provided greater transparency for structured financial products. Investors relying on ratings to indicate structured products' performance were consistently disappointed in a variety of securitizations. S&P provided a timely example after it downgraded Hollywood Funding's deals backed by movie receipts from "AAA" (the highest credit rating possible meant to be safe from loss of principal) to BB (a noninvestment grade, i.e., junk rating, meaning principal is at risk and the investment is not suitable for investors expecting reasonable safety).

Bond insurers raised fraud as a defense against payment, and S&P had thought payment was unconditional. In other words, S&P had a fundamental misunderstanding about the primary character of the risk. If S&P read the documents at all, then it lacked the competence and expertise to understand the meaning of the documents.

By this time, the rating agencies had morphed into a cartel of sorts. They competed for market share and raced each other's "standards" to the bottom. This wasn't merely a failure of the rating agencies, however, it was a clear failure of regulators, since a loud alarm was already blaring from a series of similar rating "mishaps." Rating agency failures were manifest in the rating of securitizations of manufactured housing loans, metals receivables, furniture receivables, subprime mortgage loans, and more.

When rating agencies make mistakes in securitizations backed by debt, the losses tend to be permanent and unfixable. The sole source of income is the portfolio of assets. When they repeatedly fail to understand the risk of the underlying assets—as they have done over several years for a variety of securitizations—they blow the entire job.

IV. MISRATING COMMERCIAL FINANCIAL SERVICES' SECURITIZATIONS 1995-1998

The Commercial Financial Services' (CFS) debacle provides a stunning early example of the rating agencies' incompetence. Rating agencies downgraded around $2 billion in securitizations backed by charged-off credit card receivables managed by Commercial Financial Services from investment grade to junk overnight.

Court cases involving alleged fraud at Commercial Financial Services were litigated for years in the U.S. courts. Facts were reported in the mainstream financial press and became public knowledge, yet regulators took no steps to correct problems with the rating agencies.

The proceedings of the public criminal trial of CFS's former head, Bill Bartmann (*United States of America v. William R. Bartmann*), after which he was acquitted, gives insight into the flawed processes of the rating agencies, their cozy relationships with securitization professionals, and the failure of their regulators. Yet all involved were free to make the same mistakes in future asset-backed securitizations, particularly in the subprime mortgage market.

All of the top three rating agencies, Moody's, Standard & Poor's, and Fitch overrated CFS's asset backed securitizations. (Duff & Phelps Credit Rating Co. rated CFS's transactions and is now a part of Fitch. Fitch IBCA also rated CFS's securitizations.) Only Moody's declined to rate CFS's later transactions, but it did not withdraw ratings on deals it had already rated. All three rating agencies gave investment grade ratings to securitizations that merited a junk rating.

A. Underwriter Hired Analysts Who Rated the Deals

Underwriters hire employees of the rating agencies, and this can be a conflict of interest for rating agency employees. In this example, I focus on S&P. Chase Securities, lead underwriter for CFS, hired analysts from Standard & Poor's familiar with its methodology to work on CFS's securitizations. In fact, they were hired for their "expertise." An analyst later testified that he did not use his statistics training in his work. Another analyst had special knowledge of S&P's approach to evaluating CFS's securitizations. He testified that he either authored the S&P credit memo or had close involvement with S&P's credit memo that was passed on to Chase Securities.

The collateral for the securitizations, charged-off credit card receivables, were illiquid assets, and there were no publicly available prices. The only transactions were private and involved CFS and a handful of other participants. The ultimate value of the assets was projected based on an untested model and CFS's representations of their ability to collect cash flows in the form of lump sum settlements or payments on "performing" loans in static pools of loans.

B. Rating Agencies Relied on Biased Proxy Data and Ignored Statistical Principles

S&P relied on data supplied by CFS, even though CFS had little experience with charged-off credit card receivables and claimed to have developed a proprietary model that was untested over time. Since a long period of historical data on charged-off credit card receivables was not available, CFS used data on unsecured consumer loans on which it had collected. Testimony by the Chase employee that formerly worked at S&P and testimony by an S&P employee revealed that CFS's data did not include loans on which CFS was unsuccessful in achieving collections.

Among the weaknesses of this analysis were two key problems with the data:

1. Unsecured consumer loans were only a proxy for credit card receivables. The loan types had similarities, but also had important differences. The correlation between the payoff behaviors was unknown, and

2. S&P did not verify how the loans were chosen as data. They did not verify whether the loans had been chosen randomly. This wasn't a representative sample of what might happen with charged-off credit card receivables, since it was reasonable to expect that CFS would not be able to collect on some of those loans. By including only loans on which collections occurred, the data was biased.

C. Rating Agencies Ignored Statistical Principles and Red Flags for Three Years

In his testimony, the former S&P employee said that he did not use his statistics training in his work regarding CFS, even when hired in Chase Securities' research area with a dotted line reporting relationship to the Managing Director and Group Head of Asset Backed Origination and asked to draft a memo on this topic to his new boss.

S&P and Chase Securities became comfortable with CFS's model, not because it was accurate, not because the results correlated with actual charged-off credit card collection data, not because it correlated with even the unsecured consumer loan data provided by CFS, but because it consistently produced results that made the loans used as collateral in the securities appear much better than CFS's biased collection data provided on unsecured consumer loans.

D. Rating Agencies Ignored an Audit and "A Classic Situation for Fraud"

Yet there was nothing that verified the accuracy of the model's results. S&P and Chase Securities did not verify the utility of the data provided by CFS and did not make sure the data was unbiased. A later audit report of the collectability of the loans revealed that CFS's representations of the collectability of the loans were grossly inaccurate, yet this report was ignored.

The model results were arbitrary. As part of its ongoing due diligence failure, Chase Securities failed to validate the model at the outset or at any other time in its relationship with CFS, and S&P failed to ask for any validation. This was particularly odd due to a senior Chase credit officer's concerns that CFS presented "a classic situation for fraud."

These problems occurred throughout a three year period, yet Chase Securities and the rating agencies did not uncover problems or publicly reveal red flags, of which there were many. Only Moody's withdrew from rating further securities after CFS evolved to a new structure, but Moody's did not downgrade securities it had already rated. Instead, issues became public due to the charity of a stranger. In the early fall of 1998, the rating agencies received an anonymous letter concerning the cash flows of the securitizations issued by CFS. The letter alleged that about 20 percent of cash collections on assets for the securitizations came from asset sales, even though the securitizations were supposed to be static pools from which only assets on which collections were zero or not cost effective could be sold. Furthermore, the sales were made to a newly incorporated company and the officers of the company were unknown.

On October 21, 1998, Duff & Phelps Credit Rating Co. (DCR) downgraded CFS's securitizations six notches from single A to BB—from solidly investment grade to well below investment grade. DCR cited CFS's reliance on sales of the securitizations' assets to make payments due to investors. A couple of days later, Fitch IBCA lowered the rating of CFS's securitized transactions to CC, 10 notches below investment grade. It claimed it relied on CFS's representations that assets sales did not represent a significant amount of monthly collections, yet Fitch IBCA had apparently done no independent investigation of sales of which it was already aware. Moody's and S&P also downgraded the transactions below investment grade. Shortly thereafter, all of the rating agencies stopped rating CFS's securitizations.

On December 11, 1998, CFS filed for bankruptcy protection in the U.S. Bankruptcy Court for the Northern District of Oklahoma after its unsecured creditors threatened to file an involuntary bankruptcy petition. Jay L. Jones, then an executive officer of CFS and owner of the mysterious company that bought loans at inflated prices from CFS, pleaded guilty to a single count of conspiracy as part of a plea agreement in exchange for testimony against Bartmann, who was later acquitted. Jones was eventually convicted, sentenced to five years in prison for his role, and was released in January 2007. In a separate lawsuit, Chase Securities settled out of court for an undisclosed amount.

While rating agencies may not be responsible for performing due diligence, they need to see evidence of appropriate due diligence in order to rely on data used to perform a fundamental statistical analysis. As circumstances change and a growing stream of red flags are revealed, due diligence standards become more stringent. The fundamental bases for value in CDOs are the value of the underlying assets and the cash flow. The timing, frequency, magnitude, and probability of receipt of the cash flows are affected by a variety of factors. Just as in any financial transaction, common sense, checks on the character of securitization managers, and one's ability to grasp the fundamentals of what is happening with the cash flows are key. Yet, time and again, rating agencies fail to follow fundamental principles of statistical analysis and make the same mistakes.

V. CONSTANT PROPORTION DEBT OBLIGATION SCANDAL 2006-2008: LEVERAGED CREDIT BETS

Securitizations are not the only area where rating agencies doled out phony "AAA" ratings. Ratings on leveraged synthetic credit products are often misleading. A recent example is the "AAA" rating achieved by products like the constant proportion debt obligation (CPDO), which is largely a leveraged bet on the credit quality and market spreads of indexes based on U.S. and European investment-grade companies. Besides credit risk, there is a substantial amount of financial engineering risk. Potential losses are due to defaults or market value changes (when spreads widen). The high leverage puts investors' principal at risk, since it acts as first-loss protection on the leveraged exposure to the indexes.

A. CPDOs: Phony "AAA" Ratings for New Structured Credit Products

Constant Proportion Debt Obligations appeared on the market in 2006. I immediately flagged CPDOs as deserving a non-investment grade, i.e., junk rating. Yet, Moody's and S&P awarded CPDOs "AAA" ratings. These leveraged bets on the credit quality and market spreads of indexes based on U.S. and European investment-grade companies put investors' principal at significant risk.

Investors essentially took the risk of the first losses on leveraged exposure to the indexes, and there was no margin of safety. Scenario analysis revealed the flaws. I told the *Financial Times* in November 2006, "rating agencies have proved that when it comes to some structured credit products, a rating is meaningless. All AAAs are not created equal, and this is a prime example."

The rating agencies' careless enabling of this product through phony "AAA" ratings had an important side effect. U.S. pension funds found that the distortions in the market created by CPDOs caused them to lose money on both their investments and their hedges.

After rating an early CPDO transaction "Aaa," Moody's was criticized by industry professionals, including me. Moody's then changed its rating methodology applying a different standard for subsequent transactions. Investors were attracted by the "Aaa" rating and the high coupons. The investment banks selling them were attracted to upfront fees of 1 percent plus annual servicing fees of up to 0.1 percent.

In May 2007, the *Financial Times* reported that Moody's original "Aaa" ratings for CPDO were the result of a computer "bug," and the ratings should have been (according to Moody's) four notches lower.

It is difficult to tell whether Moody's was taking half-measures to try to cover for its previously indefensible position, or whether it is really that flat out incompetent. In any case, four notches was inadequate, since that still left CPDOs with an investment grade rating. In February 2007, I had already written the SEC (and copied officers of all three rating agencies) that CPDOs had substantial principal risk, i.e., CPDOs merited junk ratings, and this was soon proved correct.

B. Moody's Is Exposed Having Changed CPDO Rating Methodology

Moody's documents showed that after it corrected the "bug," it changed its methodology resulting in the ratings staying "Aaa" until January 2008, when credit spreads moved and proved the original ratings were ludicrous. The CPDOs were then downgraded several notches. As previously noted, even this was inadequate. Moody's seemed to be floundering.

The part about Moody's changing its methodology was not news to me. I had included that information in the letter to the SEC on proposed regulations in February 2007. I do not recall who told me about the change. If it was a secret, it was an open secret. All three rating agencies' models have more patches than Microsoft software.

C. Moody's: Both Methodology and Integrity Were Questionable

Moody's "Aaa" rating seemed to be due to something more than a serious disagreement with my opinion. Moody's internal memo said that the bug's impact had been reduced after "improvements in the model." This suggests that there may be a cause and effect. The initial reality of inconvenient lower ratings may have been covered up by the methodology change.

D. CPDO Investors Lost Most of Their Principal on New "Aaa" Rated Products

By January 2008, just under a year after my written comments to the SEC, Moody's analysts wrote that two of the originally "Aaa" rated CPDOs would unwind and investors would lose approximately 90 percent of their principal. The irony is that Moody's is the rating agency that claims its "Aaa" rating is based on expected loss.

E. Standard & Poor's Also Claimed a Model Error and Defended Its Unsound Methodology

Standard & Poor's had also rated CPDOs "AAA." In fact, it was the first to do so, and Moody's later followed suit. S&P vigorously defended its ratings methodology, even after it downgraded CPDOs. S&P later disclosed that it too found an error in its computer models, but said: "This error did not result in a ratings change."

S&P claimed its error was caught and remedied by its ratings process. Yet S&P's ratings process didn't catch the fact that the "AAA" products were incompetently rated at the outset when in fact the products deserved a junk rating.

In other words, S&P admitted to a model error while defending an unsound methodology. Its methods were in fact so unsound it initially awarded the "AAA" rating (as did Moody's, so one should again question the "independence" of the rating agencies), admitted to a model error while temporarily defending an indefensible rating, and within a few months experienced the public humiliation of high principal losses on what was now obviously a product that merited a junk rating from the beginning.

VI. RATING AGENCIES' ROLE IN THE FINANCIAL MELTDOWN

In a repeat of the failings of previous debacles such as the previously noted CFS scandal, and despite examples of fraud and misconduct in mortgage loan origination revealed in the FAMCO and Ameriquest scandals, the rating agencies once again failed to live up to a reasonable professional standard in rating hundreds of billions of dollars of securities backed by mortgages, all of the products derived from them, all of the entities that issued them, and the entities that invested in them.

Although the subprime crisis has been a euphemism for the financial meltdown, various other financial products were overrated. Banks that created them and held them in inventory were also overrated. Banks that engaged in leveraged structured credit transactions and credit derivatives—all the major banks—were overrated. Sovereigns that these banks called home were also overrated.

The following examples focus on the problems of misrated mortgage backed securities or multi-sector CDOs that included mortgage-backed securities, since the housing market is such a large part of the U.S. economy and the implosion of these products affected banks, monoline insurers, insurance companies, pension funds, individual retirement accounts, mutual funds, and foreign investors.

The financial implosion of 2008 was not a "black swan" event or an unforeseeable problem. The following examples are not meant to be comprehensive or cover every institution in every category. Rather, I offer examples that typify preventable events and the ongoing failure of regulators to rein in the instigators of the collapse. The banks that ran the alternative banking system played a starring role while the rating agencies played a key supporting role.

A. Misrated From the Start: RMBSs, CDOs, CDO-Squared

Banks gave corrupt mortgage lenders with unsustainable business models large credit lines (similar to credit card debt) and packaged the loans into overrated private-label Residential Mortgage Backed Securities (RMBS). (APPENDIX II.) Most of the RMBS was rated "AAA," since subordinated investors absorbed the risk of a pre-agreed amount of loan losses. But many RMBSs were backed by portfolios comprising risky fraud-riddled loans. Moreover, portfolios of mortgage loans often included loans for which the representations and warranties were breached. Most of the "AAA" investment was imperiled, and subordinated (lower rated) "investment grade" components were worthless. As mortgage lenders failed, new investors had to be found to pay off old investors i.e., mortgage lenders and the banks that funded them. When the business model became unsustainable, it devolved into a Ponzi scheme. (See APPENDIX III.)

The worst of the subprime loans were among the cohort originated from the end of 2004 through 2007, and these entities were primarily funded through credit lines and private label securitizations engineered by Wall Street banks including JPMorgan Chase, Citigroup, Bank of America, Merrill Lynch (now part of Bank of America), Lehman Brothers (now bankrupt), Morgan Stanley (now a bank that can borrow from the Fed), Goldman Sachs (now a bank that can borrow from the Fed), Bear Stearns (now a part of JPMorgan Chase), and others.

The rating agencies misrated Collateralized Debt Obligations (CDOs) that were re-securitizations of tranches of RMBSs. (APPENDICES IV. and V.) These so-called CDOs of Asset Backed Securities (CDOs of ABS), often used credit derivatives technology to transfer risk in a way that amplified risk to investors. These CDOs of ABS were often "multi-sector" deals and assets included not only misrated tranches of RMBSs but misrated tranches of other asset backed securities including student loans, auto loans, credit card receivables, consumer loans, and other tranches of misrated CDOs (which had other misrated CDO tranches in their asset portfolios). (APPENDIX IX.)

These errors compound when tranches of securitizations with flawed ratings are used as collateral in other CDOs. From the start "AAA"-rated tranches of these deals showed a high probability of significant principal loss. A product called CDO-squared included the mezzanine (middle-risk but still investment grade) tranches of misrated CDOs (which had other misrated CDO tranches in their asset portfolios) that were virtually worthless. The result was that "AAA" tranches of CDOs had enormous risk of principal loss at creation and merited non-investment grade, i.e., junk ratings.

The problem was magnified further when hedge funds applied leverage to these products, virtually guaranteeing eventual disaster. Flawed products purchased at par with the use of leverage are on a one-way trip down net asset value's slippery slope. Yet rating agencies handed out "AAA" ratings on vehicles like structured investment vehicle "lites," also known as SIV-lites. These vehicles employed short-term financing on long-dated assets that had flawed ratings. Structured Investment Vehicles (SIVs) and Asset Backed Commercial Paper Conduits (ABCP) were created to further temporarily offload "highly rated" tranches of CDOs. Real Estate Mortgage Investment Conduits (REMICs and Re-REMICs) were plagued with similar problematic ratings as RMBS and CDO products.

B. Credit Derivatives: Documentation Risk Not Captured By Ratings

Credit derivatives allowed the multiplication of risk. A fraud-riddled loan could be used over-and-over again in deal-after-deal, since the physical asset did not need to be part of the portfolio. The same was true of tranches of securitizations backed by fraud riddled loans. Instead, it was referenced as a "notional" asset. The notional risk could be transferred more than once. This seemed to happen only with the worst loans and worst tranches. Some RMBSs and CDOs were built to fail. This was very convenient for short sellers.

Credit derivatives and total return swaps added "financial engineering" risk to securitizations, and this risk was not captured by the ratings. These over-the-counter products at times included "documentation risk" detrimental to the investor.

C. 2006 Onward: Tail End of a Ponzi Scheme

HSBC took a $6 billion subprime write-off for the fourth quarter of 2006. None of the U.S. banks followed suit, although they should have. Many (including me) publicly challenged the failure to account for losses. By 2007, there was no excuse for the rating agencies, the SEC, and the banks that brought corrupt deals to market.

Instead, toxic securitization accelerated in the first half of 2007—classic malfeasance as a Ponzi scheme collapses. I projected hundreds of billions in principal losses for mortgage loans alone—not counting other troubled asset classes, derivative duplication, and leverage.

By 2006, to keep what had now devolved into a Ponzi scheme going, more loans and securitizations were required. This is the classic end play of a Ponzi scheme. (APPENDIX III.) Lending standards plummeted and fraud by mortgage lenders accelerated to attract more borrowers. Collapsing mortgage lenders paid high dividends to shareholders (old investors) and interest on credit lines to Wall Street (old investors) with money raised from new investors in built-to-fail CDOs. New money allowed Wall Street to temporarily hide losses and pay enormous bonuses.

While this business at first may not have appeared to be Ponzi scheme, it crossed the breakeven point and the cover-ups began prior to 2007. By the end of 2006, public reports of implosions of large mortgage lenders eliminated CEOs' and rating agencies' plausible deniability, albeit problems were manifest well before then.

In August 2007, I explained to the *Wall Street Journal,* which reported the matter, that AIG had materially mismarked a more than $19 billion "super senior" credit default swap position that it was required to mark-to-market (market prices determine value). AIG said it would never experience a loss and took no accounting loss whatsoever. AIG's market price loss was already material, and the underlying CDOs would soon have substantial principal loss (leading to losses for AIG) on just this one position alone. It also had other problematic positions on its balance sheet. A few months later auditors said AIG showed material weakness in its accounting. By September 2008, AIG was bailed out unjustly enriching its credit default swap and securities lending counterparties, including Goldman Sachs. Henry Paulson was CEO of Goldman at the time the problematic trades were put on, and he was Treasury Secretary with influence over the AIG bailout that enriched Goldman Sachs without conducting an investigation.

This is particularly poignant, because under Hank Paulson's leadership, Goldman Sachs Alternative Mortgage Products, or GSAMP, was alleged to have created Garbage Sold At Mythical Prices. A complaint of alleged fraud on the part of Goldman Sachs detailed its close relationships with troubled mortgage lenders, Countrywide, New Century, and Fremont. A complaint showed Goldman knew of "an accelerating meltdown for subprime lenders such as New Century and Fremont." Despite known serious loan problems, Goldman continued to securitize the loans and sell them in packages of residential mortgage backed securities.

An RMBS known as GSAMP-2006 S3 was among $494 million of securities bought by institutional investors in April 2006 and was created and distributed by Goldman Sachs Alternative Mortgage Products (GSAMP). *Fortune's* Allan Sloan and Doris Burke followed the deal as its value slid ever downward as well as the fudgy way the deal's deteriorating value seemed to be overstated by the trustee's report. "Defaults and rating downgrades began almost immediately. In July 2008, the last piece of the issue originally rated below AAA defaulted—it stopped making interest payments. Now every month's report by the issue's trustee, Deutsche Bank, shows that the old AAAs—now rated D by S&P and Ca by Moody's [junk ratings]—continue to rot out...[by the end of October] only $79.6 million of mortgages were left, supporting $159.9 million of bonds...But even worse, those mortgages aren't worth anything like their $79.6 million of face value... the remaining bonds are worth maybe 10% of face value."

D. Raters' Role in Violation of Securities Laws: "Investment Grade Rated" Was Junk

Note that if you take a mezzanine (investment grade but lower rated than "AAA") tranche of GSAMP's previously mentioned RMBS, at the outset it has little value. In other words, "assets" such as these with "solid investment grade ratings" are nearly worthless junk. Yet mezzanine tranches such as these were routinely securitized into CDOs without disclosure that the rating labels were at the outset materially misleading.

The Congressional subprime probe revealed that due diligence reports such as those provided by Clayton Holdings Inc. showed grave problems with the original loans, yet these reports were either ignored or suppressed and this material information was not disclosed in deal documents when securities were sold.

Securities laws chiefly apply to financiers (the underwriters and traders) that create, sell, and trade securities. Underwriters are responsible for appropriate due diligence, an investigation into the risks. If you know or should know that investments are overrated and overpriced when they are sold, those facts must be specifically disclosed. Even sophisticated investors can be victims of fraud if they performed adequate due diligence and difficult-to-uncover material facts were withheld.

Rating agencies cannot competently rate securities without someone performing due diligence on the underlying collateral, and raters have to thoroughly examine it. Multi-year problems in the mortgage loan market combined with risky new products and lower underwriting standards were waving red flags. Although the rating agencies are not responsible for performing due diligence, under any professional standard they are required to review evidence of appropriate due diligence, and the bar for the definition of "appropriate" becomes higher in the face of more red flags.

In other words, it appears the rating agencies enabled the sale of mislabeled securities either through willful negligence or technical incompetence. Either way, the rating agencies do not merit the NRSRO designation.

E. Merrill Lynch's Example of Ponzi Finance

Merrill Lynch was a part owner of California-based Ownit Mortgage Solutions. Ownit made second-lien mortgages, issued 45-year ARMs, and originated no-income-verification loans. In the words of William D. Dallas, its founder and CEO: "The market is paying me to do a no-income-verification loan more than it is paying me to do the full documentation loans."

Michael Blum, Merrill Lynch's head of global asset-backed finance sat on Ownit's board. Neither Ownit nor Merrill can claim the relationship was arm's length. Revenue was up around 33% in the first three quarters of 2006, but Ownit was losing money. In November of 2006, JPMorgan Chase told Ownit that its $500 million credit line would disappear on December 13. Ownit went bankrupt at the end of December 2006.

When Ownit imploded, Blum faxed in his resignation to Ownit's Board of Directors. In this post Sarbanes-Oxley world, one might have expected Blum to insist on a thorough audit of Ownit instead of faxing in his resignation, particularly since Merrill didn't stop securitizing Ownit's loans. For example, Merrill brought an RMBS to market in early 2007 that included Ownit's piggyback loans (second liens). Around 70 percent of the borrowers had not provided full documentation of either their income or assets, and most borrowers had a 100% loan to value ratio, meaning the mortgage balance was at least as great as the value of the property being mortgaged. At the time, home prices were weak and falling.

The deal's documents omitted the fact that Merrill was Ownit's largest creditor. In early 2008, the "AAA" tranche was downgraded to junk. Moody's forecast that the original portfolio could lose around 60 percent of its value. In other words, the permanent value destruction of principal would be around 60 percent. Bond Fund of America was among the burned investors.

Instead of halting securitization activity to review loans, Merrill accelerated CDO activity in the first half of 2007. That was just a few months before private label mortgage securitization ground to a halt in the U.S. JPMorgan, Ownit's credit line provider, was no better, even if its CDO volume was lower than many other banks. For example, it is being sued for a deal called "Squared" brought to market in May 2007.

CDOs were often offloaded on naïve investors. Funds in Europe and the United States—including local government run funds—often find they did not understand the risks of complex structured financial products they own, because they relied on the "AAA" ratings for guidance. These Main Street government investors have no choice but to cut costs, aggressively go after back taxes, and—if the problem is bad enough—raise taxes. Main Street's list of investors that feel burned is long and growing.

For example, the Springfield (Massachusetts) Finance Control Board alleged that Merrill Lynch & Co. sold it "AAA" rated CDO products backed by subprime debt without fully disclosing the risk. State law limits Springfield's investments to government securities and short-term liquid investments. Regarding Springfield, I told the *Wall Street Journal:* "Merrill has to know its customers and sell them what's suitable and appropriate. These CDOs are not."

There is often a difference between an investor with a lot of money to manage and a sophisticated investor. That is why many compliance departments at investment banks ask that brokers and institutional salespeople to "know your customer." Investments must be "suitable and appropriate" for investors. The idea is to sell complex products to investors that have the ability to understand and analyze the risk.

Springfield Finance Control Board was fortunate that its troubles received publicity. The "AAA" rated tranches were overrated and at the outset merited a "junk" rating. The three CDOs that Springfield originally purchased for $13.9 million in the summer of 2007 were valued by Merrill at around $1.2 million by January 2008. In the wake of negative publicity, Merrill repurchased the CDOs for the full amount of $13.9 million.

F. Merrill Lynch: Signs of A Classic Control Fraud

Through a variety of tricks and gimmicks, Merrill tried to hide risk that couldn't be offloaded on unwary investors in a desperate game to avoid taking substantial accounting write downs in the first half of 2007. This presents all the earmarks of a classic control fraud. I reviewed all 30 of Merrill's ABS CDOs brought to market in 2007 representing a notional amount of $32 billion. Without exception, all of them presented a classic situation for fraud. By June 10, 2008, all 30 had one or more "AAA" tranches downgraded to junk by one or more rating agencies. (APPENDIX X.)

Among the CDOs were multi-sector CDOs with a lot of mezzanine CDOs from other failing deals. When Merrill couldn't find investors, it stuffed junk into new CDOs to hide losses by creating an artificial "bid" and covering the problematic tranches with phony investment grade ratings on new tranches. Merrill also issued CDO-squared products. One example is a CDO-squared called Durant issued in June 2007. Its portfolio consisted almost entirely of credit default swaps referencing mezzanine tranches of other very problematic CDOs with a couple of mezzanine CLO tranches and subprime home equity loan tranches thrown in. This entire CDO was a piece of junk right from the start. I am not just making these comments today, I made them publicly and ongoing before these phony deals came to market.

Six months later, in January 2008, Durant was in liquidation. (APPENDICES X. and XI.)

Rating agencies and the SEC had no excuse for allowing deals like this to come to market (or appear to come to market, since Merrill also retained a lot of cynically repackaged and misrated risk, another characteristic of control fraud), particularly in 2007 when it was obvious mortgage lenders were imploding. In an article for *Risk Professional* (then called *GARP Risk Review*) at the beginning of 2007, I specifically mentioned Merrill's securitization activity and that risk managers should get out before they become scapegoats. These problems were known, but by allowing securitization activity like this to continue, the rating agencies and the SEC enabled a cover-up of accounting losses through the issuance of phony securitizations.

G. Monoline Insurers

Throughout 2006-2008, the situation of the financial guarantors was much more desperate than the ratings reflected. The largest U.S. municipal bond insurers (called monolines even though they dabbled in other areas), Ambac and MBIA were still rated "AAA" in January 2008. The rating agencies expressed concern, but they performed ludicrous stress tests using insufficient default scenarios and recovery values that were much too high. I released a rebuttal. On the basis of projected loan losses alone, monolines were undercapitalized and did not merit an "AAA" rating. Although the insurance companies and the rating agencies denied it at the time, it was clear they would experience significant principal losses.

Once again, I was at odds with the slow response time and artificially high ratings of the rating agencies. As I noted in my report at the time, the situation was much worse than losses due to the fraud riddled loans. The CDOs also had stunning financial engineering risk. The monolines had insured CDOs and some late vintage multi-sector CDOs that were particularly ugly. MBIA had insured some of Merrill's 2007 CDOs. The deals had enormous "cliff" risk from near worthless collateral used in the original portfolios. The rating agencies seemed to ignore this or perhaps they didn't understand it.

APPENDIX XII shows problematic CDOs insured by Ambac and MBIA, the largest bond insurers—but not the only bond insurers to implode after being misrated—and lists the underwriters and so-called managers of those deals. The deals are shown to be contemporaneous with my challenge of the rating agencies' analysis. Based on their public statements, the rating agencies seemed incompetent. There is a possibility that they understood the problem and lied to prevent a public panic, but if so, they were very good at covering up any hidden expertise. Ambac and MBIA subsequently imploded. Ambac and MBIA later negotiated discounted settlements for many of these CDOs and some of the deals are in the midst of legal disputes.

H. Rating Agencies' Misrepresentations Throughout 2007 and Beyond

In the face of trenchant criticism, the rating agencies continued to make excuses for their poor performance, saying the overwhelming majority of ratings actions (downgrades and declarations of events of default) had been directed at the weakest-quality subprime securities. They pointed out that few "AAA" tranches had been downgraded (by them).

The rating agencies claimed that "AAA" tranches were unlikely to experience a loss. This was laughable misdirection by the rating agencies. SIV-lite debt (SIV-lites invested in "AAA" CDOs) was subsequently downgraded to CCC from "AAA" almost overnight. "AAA"s from CPDOs, ABCP, CDOs, and CDO-Squareds, were downgraded to junk.

The rating agencies' assertion at the time that it doesn't matter much if only BBB-rated and lower tranches are downgraded was also misdirection. In the past, when BBB and below tranches were downgraded, "AAA" tranches were not downgraded because the deals were usually older deals and the higher-rated tranches were largely amortized with only a small principal balance remaining. There was very little risk to the higher-rated tranches. But many of the subprime-backed deals that had been downgraded were recent 2006–2007 vintages. More than 300 tranches of these new securitizations were placed on downgrade or negative watch by the rating agencies. No reasonable financial professional accepted that the "AAA" tranches of such deals were as creditworthy as the previous "AAA" tranches of non-mortgage and non-leveraged loan deals in which the lower tranches had not been downgraded.

If this were not bad enough, liquidity dried up due to oversupply of misrated product and too little demand for hard-to-value securities. The market not only penalized CDOs with wider credit spreads to account for the greater credit risk, but also penalized these tranches for their opacity. Prices decoupled from fundamental value causing even further price drops. The rating agencies assert that the entire price drop was due to lack of demand and illiquidity, but the cause of the lack of demand was the fact that many structured products were incorrectly rated at creation.

In other words, either through intention or incompetence the rating agencies lied in the sense that they made false statements that had grave consequences for investors and the global financial markets.

VII. SOVEREIGN RATINGS

Sovereigns that bailed out banks are saddled with much greater government debt than before the crisis. In the spring of 2007, the Fed and the U.K.'s FSA reported that the degree of leverage in the global financial system was less than at the time of Long Term Capital Management, but in reality it was much greater. Global regulators are now repeating their mistakes. The risks in the interconnected global banking system have moved to currency trading and currency derivatives (remember the contribution of knock-in options to the 1995 currency crisis), leveraged loans, credit derivatives, market-linked derivatives, speculation in commodities, and both foreign and domestic government debt. Winston Churchill said we must alert somnolent authority to novel dangers; but our regulators are complacent, and the dangers are not novel.

With respect to the recent crisis, highly leveraged fixed income assets posed perils to the global banking system. When excessive leverage is combined with fixed income assets acquired at par, there is extreme risk. If the assets decline in value and liquidity becomes tight, it can cause a vicious cycle of selling that feeds on itself. If one combines that with foreign currency risk, one adds to the potential pain. If that is further accompanied by a price reduction that is due to a permanent or at least sustained price decline in underlying assets, it is virtually impossible for an undercapitalized overleveraged entity to recover from even a temporary liquidity shock. If a country cannot quickly refinance (roll financing), the collapse is quick and brutal. This isn't a new discovery, this is simply a fact.

The structured component of international finance is so influential that the failure of the rating agencies to competently rate structured financial products—and their overall incompetence with derivatives—means that their sovereign ratings are largely meaningless. The various issues with Portugal, Ireland, Italy, Greece and Spain (the PIIGS) are beyond the scope of this report, but the rating agencies, already at sea, seem to be somewhat influenced by politics as downgrades lagged and in some cases continue to lag reality. The result is that ratings adjustments come long after the need for a downgrade is obvious. To be clear, this has nothing to do with the theory of efficient markets. The rating agencies seem to flounder and arrive late to the party.

Banks that engaged in leveraged borrowing and that trade derivatives including currency derivatives, credit derivatives, commodity derivatives, and interest rate derivatives are not within the ability of the rating agencies to competently rate. Since Governments' and Central Banks' finances are intimately tied with the global banking system, the rating agencies do not competently rate sovereign debt.

A. Sovereign Rating Example: Iceland's "Aaa"

Moody's misguided "Aaa" ratings were not limited to securitizations. In 2007, financial professionals derided Iceland's inflated "Aaa" rating due to the risk posed by excessive leverage and excessive borrowing in foreign currencies. A cult YouTube video, apparently out of Bombay, India in 2007 mocked Moody's and its "Aaa" Iceland rating. It was widely circulated among financial professionals.

Moody's tried to temper its decision in a January 2008 report: "Iceland's Aaa Ratings at a Crossroads." It wrote: "Iceland enjoys high per capita incomes, well-developed political, economic and social institutions, favorable demographics and a fully-funded public pension system...Its government debt ratio is less than half the average of the Eurozone member countries." Moody's did all it could to rationalize its decision to maintain the "Aaa" rating.

As was true of many of Moody's "Aaa" ratings, it was forced to give up the game. In October 2008, Iceland temporarily suspended stock trading and seized Kaupthing, the country's largest bank, as its banking system collapsed and plunged the country into bankruptcy. Iceland's external debt was around $70 billion at current exchange rates (then €50 billion) or around $218,000 for each of its 320,000 citizens.

B. United States: "AAA" in Label Only

The financial debacle was enabled by a classic control fraud within our largest banks. Wall Street's huge bonus payments were based on suspect accounting, and bankers continue to seek those rewards by ramping up risk within the banks. Many banks' current illusion of profitability is currently only made possible by taxpayers' enormous subsidies including low cost borrowing, higher interest payments on bank capital deposits, a credit line for the FDIC (to be repaid with banks' subsidized profits), and continued government debt guarantees on bank debt. A large share of certain banks' tax-subsidized profits is due as reparation to unsophisticated investors, the U.S. taxpayers. While the Fed prints money, it seeks to keep short-term interest rates artificially low, essentially robbing investors who earn such low interest rates on "safe" investments, that after inflation, they are earning negative real returns.

The Fed uses tax dollars to keep some of our largest banks—weakened by reverse-Glass-Steagall mergers with troubled entities—from collapsing under heavy loan losses. U.S. taxpayers became unwilling unsophisticated investors funding Wall Street's bailout.

In the wake of the global financial crisis, *Bloomberg* estimated that by March 21, 2009, pledges by the Federal Reserve, Treasury Department, Federal Deposit Insurance Corporation topped $12.8 trillion. The U.S. GDP was $14.2 trillion. At the time the pledges represented more than $42,000 for every man, woman and child in the U.S.

Massive hiding-in-plain-sight fraud damaged the U.S. economy. Housing prices didn't just fall; they plummeted as the fraud unraveled. By the end of 2010, four million home loans were more than 50% underwater with an average of $107,000 negative equity; this alone is around $428 billion in negative equity. 7.8 million loans were 25% or more underwater. Most of these damaged borrowers were paying higher interest rates than the national average, couldn't refinance, and were ineligible for HAMP, a government initiated refinancing program.

Securitized assets were dumped on the balance sheets of the Fed (and the Fed supplied near zero cost funding to plug holes in bank balance sheets and special government guarantees on bank debt), special purpose entities set up by the Fed, Fannie Mae, Freddie Mac, and the FHA (through government guarantees). Government guarantees allowed for new issuance of securitized mortgage loans that otherwise would have no buyers, since the rating agencies are widely mistrusted.

The effect of existing government entitlements and obligations combined with expanding bank debt, flawed loans, flawed securitizations, and leverage significantly weakened the U.S. economy stunting growth as money was diverted to the banks and away from capital spending, the biggest driver of any economy.

The damage of financial malfeasance was so extensive and the protocol of the bailout so profligate that the "AAA" rating of the United States has been rendered an incorrect but politically expedient label. The U.S. issues its debt in dollars, and if necessary can engage in a silent default by devaluing the U.S. dollar. To some extent, that has already happened.

The U.S. dollar is still the world's reserve currency. It is also an "intervention" currency, and an "invoice" currency for much international trade. Central banks hold dollars as a reserve, and private agents hold dollar denominated investments. So far, the U.S. has the most well developed short-term financial markets, so when there is a "flight to quality," which these days means the lesser of other evils, foreigners rush to liquid financial instruments like T-Bills.

Unlike the Yuan, the U.S. dollar is freely exchangeable in most of the world. The U.S. buys its major imports such as oil in dollars. But change is already in process. Iran has said it will accept Yuan for oil. There is talk of oil prices being expressed in a basket of currencies that will include gold. Gold is already being accepted as collateral on derivatives exchanges, and in this sense, gold is now recognized again as money for trading purposes.

The problem for the U.S. is that despite the temporary advantages, the world is diversifying into other currencies, including gold. The Yen and Deutsche Mark (before the Euro) were the former candidates for diversification. Future candidates may be the Yuan and perhaps a new Euro (if Germany prevails in getting its way). That will push up the value of those currencies and push down the value of the dollar.

Even if this doesn't happen right away, the U.S. is in a weakened state and it is not immune to shocks. Recall the 1973 oil embargo, for example. Oil prices quadrupled overnight and the dollar fell from 350 yen to 250 and from 3.25 Swiss francs to 1.80. Two hour moves eclipsed the previous two decades. Then there was the 1995 U.S. dollar crisis brought about by the "tequila effect" when one of our debtors, Mexico, neared default and had to be bailed out.

When foreigners lose confidence in the United States, they don't suddenly sell all of their assets or pull out all of their money (although some of that does happen), the immediate effect is a fast fall in the dollar. The Fed has compensated for the explosion in new debt by purchasing government bonds, but this strategy may not be sustainable, and if not, there may be a swift rise in interest rates.

The current "AAA" rating of the United States is not on merit, but it is a convenient fiction for the global financial markets, because no one yet has an alternative. It would be more accurate to say that the United States remains investment grade, because of our current role in the infrastructure of the global economy. Whether or not the rating agencies put an explicit downgrade on the United States is largely irrelevant. The United States has seen huge U.S. dollar fluctuations and higher interest rates in the past, and on its current course will see them again. The fundamentals of the U.S.'s increasing debt load, massive future entitlements, high unemployment rate, and weak economy with no meaningful growth plan speak for themselves.

VIII. RESTORING CREDIBILITY: WHAT REGULATORS MISSED AND WHAT THEY GOT RIGHT

The U.S. based rating agencies, Moody's and S&P are subject to Congressional legislation and ostensibly regulated by the SEC. The Dodd-Frank Act attempted to address issues with the rating agencies, and it made several good suggestions, but missed key problems. Japan has a set of rules for the rating agencies, and Europe is developing a separate set of rules. Ratings are used globally, and it seems rating companies should be regulated by an international body.

A. Create Objective Benchmarks and Rating Scale: Revoke the Raters' Ability to Legislate

Neither U.S. nor European regulators address the problem of rating agencies' ability to make up their benchmarks and rating scales and change them at will. The discussion below has been further developed from the work of Dr. Arturo Cifuentes, a former Moody's rating methodology developer, and Jose Miguel Cruz in their "White Paper on Rating Agency Reform," issued from the department of industrial engineering at the University of Chile in May, 2010.

Moody's and S&P each have a nine category scale with 21 notches. (See III. A. And APPENDIX VII. Note that "D" is not counted in the nine category scale, since it denotes default.) There is no reason to consider the ratings as having equivalent meanings. Moody's and S&P base their scales on different concepts, expected loss and probability of default, respectively. The rating agencies employ different computational methods and different models. They each use their own data sets.

It is more than a little interesting to note, that the ratings are often similar, even when they are egregiously wrong, and even though they supposedly employ different theoretical frameworks.

For example, both Moody's and S&P awarded "AAA" ratings to CPDOs, a product developed in late 2006 that merited a non-investment grade rating, i.e., a junk rating and quickly fell apart. (See Section V.) It begs the question of whether the rating agencies are actually independent or whether they are being consistent with each other to maximize revenues.

Solution: A third party (the SEC, for example, unless it is replaced as the regulator, and it should be) should define the benchmarks and the rating scale. The rating agencies would no longer be free to choose benchmarks and effectively redefine the meaning of ratings. Rating agencies would only be entitled to issue ratings, i.e., determine where the creditworthiness fits in relative to the pre-defined benchmarks that correspond to the rating scale.

If a combination of levels of probability of default and loss given default (from which recovery value is determined) is used to create a rating scale—an appealing prospect—then two supplementary rating scales are in order. One scale would reflect the probability of default and one scale would show the loss given default.

Said another way, the ratings scale and the cutoffs would be objective and the same cutoffs and scales would be used by all rating agencies. The rating agencies would have no ability to change the cut-off values.

Implementation would require some global buy-in, and a comment period of say, three months, from stakeholders. Legacy ratings would be mapped to the new scale with the proviso that the mapping might be flawed due both to the flaws inherent in the original ratings process, and the fact that the theoretical approaches were originally different.

B. Solution: Eliminate "Mezzanine AAA" Tranches and "Super Senior" Tranches

Neither U.S. nor European regulators address the problem of "first loss AAA" tranches and "super senior" tranches. Many "AAA" tranches had insufficient subordination to ever merit that rating based on the quality of the assets in reference portfolios. But even solving the problem of quality of assets in the portfolio does not solve the conceptual problem of "super seniors" being somehow superior to what was formerly a genuine "AAA." The definition of "super senior" and the benchmark requirements to merit the designation were left undefined by the entire industry.

Super seniors were meant to be super safe, and even BIS enabled them by awarding favorable regulatory capital treatment to them to accommodate banks. In fact, "super seniors" are a gimmick created to achieve favorable regulatory capital treatment.

Not only did "super seniors" make a mockery of the "AAA" label, they did not live up to their name. Many investors in "super seniors" lost almost all of their initial investment when they invested in late vintage CDOs. Investment banks and banks that retained "super seniors" on their balance sheets and "insured" them to try to obtain income via a flawed regulatory capital and economic "arbitrage" ended up with heavy losses. (See also Section III. A. and APPENDIX VIII.)

C. Focus Is On Wrong Metrics with Uninformed Guesses as Model Inputs

Neither U.S. nor European regulators address the rating agencies' apparent incompetence. For example, the heavy reliance on correlation models is the wrong way to go about determining whether any benchmark meets the requirement of a rating when the most important metrics are probability of default and loss given default (or said another way, recovery value in the event of default). It would have been more productive to spend all of the time and effort determining probability of default and recovery value and none of it on correlation.

In fact, the exercise of understanding the granular risk well enough to determine probability of default and recovery value gives one a much better understanding of correlation and how correlation among assets changes and converges under different scenarios. Once one understands that, one is keen to abandon the unstable correlation metric in favor of the granular approach. This may be part of the reason my analyses prove superior to the rating agencies time and again. Another reason may be conflicts of interest within the rating agencies themselves. Revenues were more important than ratings accuracy. (See Section VIII. E.)

Rating agencies adapted the Gaussian Copula model and black box correlation models for structured financial products. Correlation models try to determine if a portfolio's assets will behave similarly when a reference asset strengthens or weakens. The models are highly unstable. They are like a chair that collapses beneath you as soon as you sit on it. Small changes to model inputs result in huge changes to the results. (See article following the letter in Appendix I.)

If you play with coins or dice, you know exactly what your inputs are and you can model all potential outcomes. You can examine the coins (heads or tails per coin), and you can model all of the possible outcomes. You can examine dice (one to six dots on each face of each cube), and again, a mathematical model can describe all potential outcomes. We may use a Monte Carlo model (or other model) to randomize the inputs (the flips and tosses), but we do not have to guess at the inputs for dice and cards; they are known in advance and the relationship between the inputs does not change.

Unlike cards and dice, the inputs to credit models are not exact representations of reality, they are estimates of variables. The inputs to credit models are a guess, but they should be educated guesses—not the complete stabs in the dark used by the rating agencies.

We rely on data approximations to come up with the inputs in the first place, and the relationships between the inputs can change. For example, most of the data describing how one corporation behaves in relationship to another is based on market prices such as stock prices or the prices of credit default swaps based on corporate debt. Moreover, there is very little of this already suspect data to work with. The results are guesses about relative price or yield spread movements, which result in a guess about the correlations. When a credit upset occurs in a financial sector, correlations that were previously fractional numbers tend to converge to one. Everything seems to fall apart at once. A model will calculate the wrong answer to nine decimal places, but it cannot tell you it is the wrong answer.

The biggest problem with correlation models is that even if they temporarily get the correct answer, they do not tell you what you need to know. The models estimate asset correlations instead of the necessary default correlations. Furthermore, the overwhelming flaw in the methodology is that if you want to make up a default correlation between two companies, you must make the false assumption that default probability does not vary, but of course it does.

Even if the models measured the default probability of individual companies—and they do not—if a company defaults, you still have to guess the recovery rate, the amount left over, if any, after all obligations are paid.

You cannot solve for two independent items of information from a single piece of information such as a letter grade or a price. You cannot get both the probability that a company will default and the amount of money you will have left if it does default.

Solution: Modelers must understand the granular credit risks in a portfolio. There is nothing wrong with employing a shortcut like a correlation model (even though there are better techniques), but a correlation model is not a substitute for examining due diligence to understand the character of the granular risk in a portfolio. For example, new risky mortgage loan products with corrupt underwriting standards failed in the same way no matter where they were located, and recovery values were much lower than the assumptions used by the rating agencies. This was knowable in advance. Mortgage loan originators had a known history of fraud. (Examples include FAMCO, Ameriquest, manufactured housing loan originators.) Yet in the recent debacle, rating agencies' correlation assumptions were grossly incorrect at the outset.

D. Rating Agencies Must Review Evidence of Underwriters' Due Diligence

Both the Dodd-Frank Act and proposals by European regulators call for more transparency about underlying collateral, but don't hold rating agencies explicitly accountable for demanding thorough due diligence from underwriters, especially in the face of red flags that suggest third party fraud audits may be in order. A fraud audit doesn't mean anyone is being accused of fraud, only that the audit will be thorough enough to uncover it if it exists. In the case of mortgage lenders and the underwriters themselves, one would have found the reports of Clayton Holdings that suggested that the securitizations created by underwriters were invalid as many loans' representations and warranties had been breached, and the documentation of loan transfers seemed missing. Beyond that, the credit quality of the loans was so poor that the ratings were invalid.

The rating agencies are swift to point out that they do not perform due diligence on the data they use and take no responsibility for unearthing fraud; they merely provide an opinion. In past legal battles, rating agencies successfully claimed journalist-like privileges, refused to turn over notes of their analyses, and continued to issue opinions. Independent organizations exist, however, that perform rigorous due diligence for a fee. Underwriters can hire them, and rating agencies can demand to see the results. These reports include loan reviews, and audits ranging in thoroughness from a cursory review to a fraud audit depending on the circumstances.

The consequences of the unwholesome mix of lax underwriting standards and new risky loan products combined with varying degrees of overreaching, predatory lending, real estate speculation and outright fraud, were discoverable with reasonable due diligence. The egregious overrating of securitized products was completely preventable in the course of competent analysis.

The rating agencies could have—and should have—asked issuers and investment bank underwriters to demonstrate that they had performed a statistical sampling and verification of underlying loans in the proposed portfolios. This includes independent checks of appraisals, checks that mortgages have not been mis-sold, background checks of mortgage brokers, background checks on mortgage lenders, background checks of CDO managers, verification that the homeowner can cope with the reset when a "teaser" period comes to an end, and income verification on "stated" income loans.

The rating agencies underestimated default probabilities, underestimated loss given default, and overly relied on historical data when assigning ratings. In a repeat of past mistakes, the basis of the analysis was flawed, and the amount of protection required to award the various ratings was insufficient at the outset.

Solution: This requires a multi-part solution. Rating agencies may need an upgrade in the caliber of the people they hire, particularly since they've gotten probability of default and loss given default incorrect even on a granular basis (Enron and other granular risks). The Dodd-Frank Act calls for more transparency of the data and the criteria used by the rating agencies. That is a good idea, but as stated before, there should be third-party criteria for the benchmarks (the cutoffs) and the rating scale that corresponds to those benchmarks. A further step is to redirect the focus of the rating agencies from correlation to probability of default and loss given default.

E. Rating Accuracy Should Be the Only Measurement of Success

Neither the Dodd-Frank Act nor the European regulators clearly address the problem of conflicts of interest within the rating agencies. Dodd-Frank asks for two independent members in the administrative and supervisory board whose compensation isn't linked to rating agencies' results, presumably revenue targets. Agencies should focus on ratings issuance and not simultaneously provide advisory or consultancy services. The rules nebulously call for employees with knowledge and experience. The rules also call for staff turnover to avoid employees getting too close to entities they rate.

The problem with this approach is the rating agencies will claim they already do all of the above. They will insist their people have the correct knowledge and experience. The key problem, however, is that business managers with revenue and market share targets sacrificed ratings accuracy. There were no consequences for this behavior. The rating "agencies" are companies, and shareholders like to see revenue growth.

The awarding of so much power to the rating agencies created a welfare state of ongoing fees. Even today, there is rating shopping for products like Re-REMICs. This indicates how ineffective the regulators have been and how ineffective the proposed rules will be in future.

It's time to make the goal and the measurement clear. The rating agencies are private companies owned by shareholders and management will therefore always push for ways to increase revenue in order to get higher compensation. Regulators can counter this by insisting on only one measurement of success. Rating accuracy can be the only measurement of success.

Using rating accuracy as a measurement of success, Moody's, S&P, and Fitch, the top three rating agencies, have all been failures. The NRSRO designation is completely unwarranted, and this is why I've revoked it. Beyond that, regulators should consider disqualifying rating companies from issuing any ratings whatsoever if there is a repeat of past "mistakes."

Solution: The consequence of making rating accuracy the only metric of success is that rating agencies/companies will have an incentive to purge management and withhold bonus compensation from managers that are not capable of producing accurate ratings for fear of losing the right to issue any ratings at all.

Regulators can rate the rating agencies on the basis of accuracy and put companies on probation, meaning the companies can lose the right to issue any ratings. Whether or not regulators choose to take this step, the NRSRO doesn't apply to any of the existing rating agencies, and in order to win that designation—which is above and beyond the previously mentioned ability to issue ratings—the rating agencies must demonstrate that they have completely overhauled methods and can produce accurate ratings.

F. Conflicts of Interest: Chinese Wall Is Needed

Within the rating agencies, analysts often report to business managers interested in building market share and revenues whether or not it comes at the expense of ratings accuracy. There is no "Chinese Wall" to protect ratings analysts from business managers whose bonuses depend on increasing revenues and market share.

Solution: Since the rating agencies are private companies, they can choose their own system of compensation. Maximizing revenues at the expense of rating accuracy is contrary to public interest. Raters should be shielded from marketing managers and corporate management, and their compensation should be based solely on rating accuracy. See also the solution for Section E.

G. Conflicts of Interest: Joint Ventures

Rating agencies market risk consulting and models to banks and investors. At times, rating agencies have engaged in joint ventures with banks. For example, S&P entered into a joint venture with Bank of America Securities in the spring of 2003 to market Bank of America's Lighthouse model. Bank of America Securities and S&P used the model to determine credit option adjusted spreads (OAS) and ratings analysis for credit portfolios. BAS's senior manager wrote an email to his staff lauding the benefits of the joint venture with S&P: "This could be a significant development for us and give us entre into a lot of accounts in both Europe and US that we might not have by coordinating with S&P... If we handle this the right way, it could be a powerful tool, especially to clients below our radar screen or outside our reach internationally that S&P might have influence over." BAS described a very cozy—and potentially very lucrative—relationship.

Solution: The Dodd-Frank Act and the European regulators recognize this as a problem and recommend this type of consulting should not be simultaneous with ratings issuance, but they don't go far enough. This sort of consulting business should be spun off. The stakes are so high for the rating "agencies" that if rating companies want to participate as raters in the global financial markets, they should have a single focus.

H. Conflicts of Interest: Banks and Rated Entities Hiring Raters' Employees

Banks often hire rating agency analysts for their connections and influence within the agencies. There have been cases in which analysts hopeful of employment at a bank rated that bank's securitizations created and sold for a given issuer/sponsor and later worked on securitizations of the same issuer/sponsor once employed by the bank. This poses another type of conflict of interest for the rating agencies. Analysts are tempted to be accommodating. (See Section IV. for the Commercial Financial Services's example.)

Solution: The Dodd-Frank Act asks for not-yet-created rules to adopt an employee look-back so that rating agencies can review ratings when an employee seeks or obtains employment with an entity that is subject to a credit rating. This is a good idea. A better idea is to ask if the incentives within the rating agencies and the lure of potentially lucrative jobs outside rating agencies resulted in collusion between rating agencies and banks to egregiously misrate securities at the outset, since that was the ratings result. The tough question was avoided in favor of a not-yet-defined rule. Another part of this solution should be to prohibit employees from accepting such employment for a period of two years, especially since remaining rating agency employees that engage in the look-back review are still subject to the same conflicts of interest that inspired the look-back review.

I. Mistaken Idea: Rating Agencies Design Securities

For all of their mistakes, the rating agencies have been unfairly characterized as having been the architect or co-architect of asset backed securitizations. While it is true that rating agencies were often over-accommodating to underwriters, they don't design transactions by giving excessive guidance to bankers. Any project that requires approvals will have give-and-take in order to see the task to completion. The contribution of the dialogue between rating agencies and bankers to our current crisis has been blown out of proportion. That may serve the interests of banks that want to deflect attention from their failures in their duties as underwriters—not to mention their failure to comply with securities laws—but it does not help to define or solve the real problems.

Solution: See Section E.

J. A Mistaken Idea On Fees, and the Real Fee Issue

Bankers raise capital by selling the bonds and equity investments that result from a securitization of assets. A small portion of the capital is earmarked to pay the law firms, rating agencies, accountants, administrators, trustees, banks' structured finance professionals, banks' salespeople and traders, and so on. The idea that bankers pay rating agencies a rating fee thus creating a conflict of interest is a mistaken area of focus. In fact, proceeds from the investors from whom the capital is raised are paying the rating agencies' fees. If investors in a deal agree they want an unrated deal, they can forego the rating altogether, albeit that is not practical for institutional investors whose charters or regulators require rated products. If one wants to use the argument that receiving pay from proceeds creates a conflict of interest, then one must apply it to the lawyers, accountants and any other professional not directly employed by the underwriter.

While it is a concern, this issue has been blown way out of proportion. It would be more accurate to say that in the pressure to gain market share and increase revenues, rating agencies deliberately lowered standards to win business any way they could. This would likely have been a problem even if investors paid them directly.

Solution: Both the Dodd-Frank Act and the European Regulators got the solution even when they didn't correctly define the problem. Most of the rating agencies' fees from a securitization are paid as a large upfront fee with a small ongoing maintenance fee until the securitization either unwinds or matures. If rating agencies' fees are paid over time, their interests would be better aligned with investors.

The rules should go a step further. It would also be a pious idea to make fees contingent upon the accuracy of the ratings for investment grade rated notes. One could achieve this by subordinating rating agencies' realigned ongoing fee payments to the payments to the investment grade rated note investors.

The further issue is the compensation of the management of the rating agencies. Again, making ratings accuracy the only measurement of success (from a regulatory point of view) and ranking and disqualifying rating agencies from being eligible to issue ratings whatsoever would be an effective incentive to realign priorities within the rating agencies. Irrespective of the previous comments, I revoke the NRSRO designation—which is separate from the ability to issue ratings—of all the rating agencies.

K. Ban Credit Derivatives and Total Return Swaps in Rated Structured Financial Products

Neither the Dodd-Frank Act nor European regulators tackle this issue head on. Credit derivatives technology was used to reference the worst credits more than once in more than one securitization. Total return swaps were also employed in some CDOs. All of these transactions are over-the-counter (OTC) meaning these derivatives are not transparent and do not trade on exchanges. Buried within the documentation are numerous ways to stuff hidden risks into the portfolio. This discussion is beyond the scope of this report, but rating agencies have proved themselves inadequate to the task of unpacking these risks and putting a sensible rating on securitizations that include these risks.

In fact, many "experts" in credit derivatives have been caught off guard by hidden risks. There have been many private disputes about the meaning of the language in over-the-counter documentation. Making the documents public on a web site may provide more disclosure, but that isn't the same thing as transparency.

Solution: Ban the use of credit derivatives and total return swaps in rated structured finance transactions.

L. Other Derivatives in Rated Structured Financial Products

Neither the Dodd-Frank Act nor European regulators deal with raters' ability to cope with derivatives. Based on my past interaction with the rating agencies, they do not have sufficient competence in foreign exchange derivatives (and quantoed deals), commodity derivatives, or interest rate derivatives to award credit ratings to deals that include the risk presented by the derivatives, even when the derivatives are labeled as "hedges."

Solution: See Section E.

M. "Managed" Deals

Neither the Dodd-Frank Act nor European regulators address this. In the CDO debacle, most of the deals were "managed." There is evidence that deal managers had a variety of unacceptable issues including but not limited to 1) shady backgrounds that were discoverable in the course of normal due diligence, 2) close ties with banks that underwrote deals and a dependence on those banks for fee revenue, 3) conflicts of interest with CDO investors and other funds managed by the "manager." Some of these managers were fly-by-night operations that went bankrupt or are now effectively without any business.

Partial Solution: Background checks are a partial solution, but the reality is that when a manager has a conflict of interest with the CDO investor, it has never turned out well for investors, and ratings have proved meaningless. There are ways of putting "handcuffs" on managers by writing trading rules into the documents, yet even these rules can be thwarted.

N. An Observation: "Agencies" are Companies; Shareholders Cannot Govern Rating Agencies

Neither the Dodd-Frank Act nor European regulators address this. The rating agencies are shareholder owned entities and are in the unusual position of having enormous power, which they've perverted and abused. They can at will change the definition and methodology for their ratings and thus the capital reserved by several financial entities. By getting the ratings so risibly wrong on investment grade products, they've enabled a global financial meltdown.

Warren Buffett, CEO of Berkshire Hathaway, has sometimes said that shareholders must demand changes to limit compensation and excesses of company officers, but he himself did no such thing when it came to Berkshire Hathaway's investment in Moody's, at least while it raked in fees from rating structured products. At the end of 2007, after the issuance of misrated private label securitization had ground to a halt, Berkshire Hathaway still owned 48 million shares of Moody's Corporation, the same number of shares Berkshire Hathaway owned in 2005. The shares represented just over 19 percent of Moody's capital stock. To the best of my knowledge, at no time did Buffett interfere or attempt to positively influence the behavior of the rating agencies when it came to the misrated financial products that damaged the financial system. Yet at the time, Buffett was not completely unaware of the problem.

It's ironic that Buffett makes no secret of the fact that he himself disregards ratings when making investment decisions. He is concerned with the ratings of Berkshire Hathaway only to the extent that other investors rely on them. Ratings affect Berkshire Hathaway's cost of borrowing and its ability to attract insurance premiums. Buffett has recently been selling off blocks of his shares of Moody's.

The role of the rating agencies has been so pervasive and influential that it cannot be left up to "efficient market" forces—proven to be inefficient and distorted through crony capitalism—or to shareholders to correct problems.

Solution: Regulators cannot make shareholders do anything, but they can change the incentives. (See Section E.)

O. Thwarting Dodd-Frank: Risk Retention and "Conflict of Interest" Transactions

The Dodd-Frank Act provided a reason for me to laugh out loud at a couple of sections. First, it is useful to point out that had existing securities laws been enforced, the "added" prohibitions in the Dodd-Frank Act wouldn't be necessary. Yet regulators and Congress abdicated. The clock on the Statute of Limitations is running out for enforcement (five years for securities fraud). Denial of widespread malfeasance and fraud leads to the type of ineffective legislation evident in the Dodd-Frank Act.

In an attempt to say "We Fixed It!" the Act proposes stern sounding prohibitions that any competent structured finance professional can thwart. The first is the idea of risk retention. Congress may recall Goldman's CEO, Lloyd Blankfein, claiming that Goldman retained the "first loss" risk of CDOs. I can think of several ways in which Blankfein can make that statement with a straight face, while Goldman may have had virtually no risk whatsoever.

Dodd-Frank asks for at least 5% risk retention and the position must be unhedged. In addition, the waterfall of the cash flows must be made available. I can think of several ways to thwart this rule's intention. Here's just one way that doesn't even involve derivatives. As I explained in my 2003 book, one can create a CDO in which the "first loss" risk is actually safer than the "AAA" tranche of the CDO since cash flows are diverted to the "first loss" risk holder in a hidden way. I defy regulators to read the deal documentation and figure it out. So much for Dodd-Frank's "risk retention."

Moreover, it pays to state the blindingly obvious. The Act is relying on clever people who thwarted existing disclosure requirements, and who remain unpunished, to now follow the disclosure requirements of the Act. Good luck with that.

Solution: The goal is to prevent corrupt underwriters from selling junk as "investment grade," and from selling junk as "AAA." The global financial community has chosen to hide under their desks rather than confront this issue. Given this reality, it may be more effective to insist that "AAA" meets third-party global benchmarks and has a global meaning. If rating agencies cannot produce ratings that live up to that meaning, they should no longer be allowed to issue ratings.

IX. CONCLUSION

The global market and regulatory framework has been built around credit ratings, even though savvy market professionals know better than to rely on them. Banks, hedge funds, insurance companies, pension funds, and corporations are all affected by ratings. Even the over-the-counter trading market is affected by ratings. Collateral requirements for swap counterparties are just one example of a ratings driven requirement. Banks have different capital reserve requirements depending on the ratings of assets. Insurance companies, pension funds, and mutual funds all have ratings requirements in their regulations or charters. Ratings driven regulations have been adopted globally, albeit regulations vary by venue.

Yet there is global distrust of the rating agencies. Congress and the SEC have not faced up to the key problems. The Dodd-Frank legislation in the United States illustrates Congress's poor grasp of many of the issues and its inability—or unwillingness—to address them. Rating agencies have not been held accountable for past poor performance. The possibility of malfeasance or collusion with fraud has been skirted rather than addressed.

The Dodd-Frank Act proposes that financial regulations eliminate references to credit ratings for stock brokerages and money funds, but this has not yet been implemented. Likewise, banking regulators are pushing back on Dodd-Frank and asking for rewrites; in other words, they are stalling. The mistake in the Dodd-Frank Act is that there is no reliable globally recognized system with which to replace ratings as an indication of credit risk. Banks, insurance companies, pension funds, mutual funds, and other investors should do their own credit assessments, but the reality is they relied on rating agencies, and they continue to look to them for guidance.

Until there is an objective reproducible and reliable method of providing credit ratings to securitizations, it will be impossible to rehabilitate the alternative banking system. If one is to wean the global financial system off of government guaranteed debt, there has to be a viable means of agreeing on creditworthiness.

The top rating agencies, Moody's and S&P, have a multi-year history of failure in rating some granular corporate credit risks and have a spectacular history of failure in rating heterogeneous structured credit products and securitizations. In particular, in rating securitizations, they have not followed statistical principles by any reasonable professional standard. None of the other rating agencies show evidence of filling this role, and would have to qualify in order to credibly rate these products. For this reason, I've revoked the Nationally Recognized Statistical Rating Organization (NRSRO) designation for all of the rating agencies for all but corporations that do not engage in a major way in structured financial products.

Just because the problem of creating a viable global credit rating system is difficult doesn't mean it shouldn't be done. In fact, it is precisely because it is difficult that there is a great need to thoroughly address the issue. The rating "agencies" are actually corporations, and they are domiciled in different countries. Nonetheless, an international regulator can determine which of these corporations will eventually earn the NRSRO designation. Meanwhile, it can determine which rating agencies will be allowed to continue to issue ratings, albeit without the NRSRO designation.

In revoking the NRSRO designation, I'm making the statement that I'm better qualified to opine on this than Congress or the SEC, since this is a matter of reasonable professional standards in following statistical principles. The top rating agencies, the ones most relevant to the global financial community, do not meet the standard. The "Nationally Recognized Statistical Rating Organization" label cannot be legislated or awarded by regulators when it is demonstrably false any more than they can enact legislation to make the sun move around the earth.

The solution is to raise one or more rating agencies up to standard to merit the NRSRO label. Meanwhile, rating agencies can continue to issue ratings but must commit to coming up to standard. Those that cannot should have the privilege of issuing ratings completely revoked. The second part of the solution is to develop global third party benchmarks and global third party rating scales and make accurate ratings the only measurement of success.[137]

"Why has government been instituted at all? Because the passions of men will not conform to the dictates of reason and justice, without constraint."

—Alexander Hamilton 1757-1804

CHAPTER 9 Fannie Mae and Freddie Mac

"Fraud As a Business Model"

September 6, 2011

There were many factors that contributed to our recent financial bubble: deregulation, cheap money from the Fed, failure to enforce remaining regulations, crony capitalism, hubris, speculation, leverage, and fraud among other problems. While fraud wasn't the only issue, it was and is a significant contributor to the credit bubble. Restraining fraud is a necessary but not sufficient condition for a sound financial system. Congressional investigations in recent years have put ample evidence of fraud in the public domain.

To illustrate just one type of malicious mischief, Senator Carl Levin (D. Mich.), Chairman of a senate investigative panel, issued a memo stating that Goldman "magnified the impact of toxic mortgages." *The Wall Street Journal* reviewed data showing that a $38 million subprime-mortgage bond created in June 2006 was referenced in more than 30 debt pools causing around $280 million in losses to investors by 2008. In other words, Goldman kept repackaging, reselling or protecting (buying credit default protection on) losers. It took the wrong kind of nerve for Goldman's CEO to say he was doing "God's work."

Arianna Huffington pointed out that the financial system is rigged and that offenders get off lightly:

> Until the Securities and Exchange Commission sued Goldman Sachs for fraud in April of 2010, it was easy to forget that we have a regulatory agency designed to protect the public from the pillaging of corporate America. Six months earlier, the SEC has arranged a settlement with JPMorgan that showed how rigged the system is. The banking giant agreed to pay a $25 million penalty and cancel $647 million in fees owed by Alabama's Jefferson County as the result of a

> complicated derivatives deal that blew up in the county's face. As part of the settlement, JPMorgan neither admitted nor denied wrongdoing—despite overwhelming evidence that it had engaged in plenty of wrongdoing.[138]

On Friday, September 2, 2011, The U.S. Federal Housing Finance Agency (FHFA), the regulator for taxpayer-subsidized mortgage lending guarantors Fannie Mae and Freddie Mac, filed lawsuits against 17 of the world's largest banks over suspect mortgage loans which helped exacerbate the U.S. housing crisis. Both Fannie Mae and Freddie Mac were placed in conservatorship in September 2008 after they nearly collapsed. The FHFA claims banks misrepresented the value of the mortgage loans and mortgage securities they underwrote, arranged, and sold.

So far the banks being sued include Bank of America Corp along with its Countrywide Financial Corporation and Merrill Lynch & Company divisions, Goldman Sachs Group Inc., JPMorgan Chase & Co., Citigroup Inc., Deutsche Bank AG, Barclays PLC, Nomura Holdings Inc., Morgan Stanley, Ally Financial Inc., Credit Suisse Group Inc., First Horizon National Corp, General Electric Co, the HSBC North America Holdings unit of HSBC Holdings, The Royal Bank of Scotland Group PLC and Société Générale SA. The FHFA is just getting started.

Critics of Fannie Mae, Freddie Mac, and their previous regulator, OFHEO, say that they were sophisticated investors, and they should have known better. William K. Black is a former bank regulator who played a role in hundreds of successful prosecutions after the Savings and Loan Crisis. He told the *Wall Street Journal*: "It's a great myth that you can't defraud sophisticated financial parties."[139] Particularly when loans are fraudulent and material information was not disclosed.

The Financial Crisis Inquiry Commission published evidence from the testimony of officials of Clayton Holdings (among others), a due diligence firm, that underwriters and rating agencies ignored evidence of suspect loans and did not disclose this information to investors.[140]

The FHFA's complaint involves tens of billions of dollars in potential recoveries that will benefit taxpayers. Yet, as Arianna

Huffington points out, banks continue to find ways to get Americans to subsidize problems that the banks themselves were chiefly responsible for creating. Consumers struggle to keep up with payments as the unemployment rate rises along with prices for food, energy and healthcare. Meanwhile, job creation hovers near zero.

When consumers fail to keep up, banks, trying to offset losses in other areas, turn around, hike interest rates, and impose all manner of fees and penalties—all of which makes it less likely consumers will be able to pay off mounting debts.[141]

Money is being put in taxpayers' pockets in the form of "recoveries" while being extracted again in the form of subsidies and cheap funding to shaky banks that continue to award record pay and record bonuses as they gouge consumers. We can expect more of the same if we continue to let banks off with a slap on the wrist for malfeasance—along with a taxpayer subsidized fine—while banks neither admit nor deny wrongdoing.

Banks won't change until we follow the law and take "prompt corrective action." Banks that committed widespread fraud should be placed in receivership. Bank of America was cited by William K. Black and L. Randall Wray in their October 2010 post as the place to start, and I agree.[142]

On December 8, 2010, I presented an analysis to the Federal Housing Finance Agency (FHFA) in Washington D.C. of key causes of our current financial crisis: "Repairing the Damage of "Fraud as a Business Model."[143] The phrase "fraud as a business model" comes from a comment referenced in the presentation made by Richard Cordray, then the Attorney General of Ohio and the current Director of the Consumer Financial Protection Bureau, when he discussed foreclosure fraud.

*****

"If the American people ever allow private banks to control the issue of their currency, first by inflation, then by deflation, the banks and corporations that will grow up around them will deprive the people of all property until their children wake up homeless on the continent their Fathers conquered."

—Thomas Jefferson 1743-1826

CHAPTER 10 Warren Buffett's Twist: "Please, sir, I want some more."

Warren Buffett's Wall Street War

October 20, 2009

In a January 2009 interview with NBC's Tom Brokaw, Warren Buffett criticized leveraging "to the sky," and creating "phony instruments [RMBSs, CDOs, et al.] that fool other people so you stick money in your pocket." In 2002, he claimed over-the-counter derivatives are "financial weapons of mass destruction" and participants who account for them have "enormous incentives to cheat."

Warren Buffett, the blogosphere's "Oracle of Omaha," often chastises the financial community. If you cost him money, he's liable to write an expose. He posts annual shareholder letters on a low-tech website and seems to labor under the assumption that rational people eagerly read his blog. Congress and regulators are dismissive of Buffett's hyperbolic rhetoric; it is fit only for a banana republic.

In 2003, Buffett wrote of the manufactured housing industry's "business model centered on the ability...to unload terrible loans on naïve lenders...The consequence has been huge numbers of repossessions and pitifully low recoverie[s]." Buffett alleged that the manufactured housing industry's consumer financing practices were "atrocious," and securitizations provided the money to fuel the financing.

Berkshire Hathaway's investment in the distressed junk debt of Oakwood Homes lost money after the designer and manufacturer of modular homes went bankrupt in 2002. Buffett claimed "Oakwood participated fully in the insanity."

Warren Buffett's diatribe suggested that most of the manufactured housing industry was involved along with several Wall Street firms that underwrote the securitizations. Using money from new investors to pay returns to old investors in unsupportable investments is called a Ponzi scheme.

Oakwood's loans to purchasers of manufactured homes were made possible by a line of credit from Credit Suisse First Boston (Credit Suisse). The credit line was similar to a credit card except that Oakwood had to put up the home loans as collateral. Credit Suisse earned fees for the loans and further fees when it packaged (securitized) Oakwood's loans. Credit Suisse (the old investor) bought the securitized loans and then sold them to new so-called sophisticated investors.

Sales of manufactured homes declined. Loan delinquencies (late payments) and repossessions rose. Oakwood Homes had crushing debt and falling income for at least three years before it filed for bankruptcy in November 2002. But securitizations had temporarily inflated the bubble for the collapsing enterprise. A June 2008 court opinion said Oakwood's aggressive lending practices led to the high number of repossessions and a debt load that Oakwood could not support. Oakwood's liquidator said the transactions it did with Credit Suisse were "value destroying."

Someone should have muzzled Warren Buffett back in 2003. The Slumbering Esquires' Club might have believed Buffett's preposterous theory that after private securitizations became popular, the "industry's conduct went from bad to worse." Buffett's wacky warnings could have jeopardized Wall Street's subsequent mortgage lending securitization Ponzi scheme.

The SEC might have investigated Lehman Brothers' questionable shenanigans, especially after it was held liable in 2003 by a California jury for allegedly helping FAMCO cheat borrowers. The SEC might have looked into the unsavory practices at Goldman Sachs Alternative Mortgage Products, Bear Stearns, Merrill Lynch or the entire private securitization industry, and their mortgage lending subsidiaries.

While the SEC slept inside a collapsing debt bubble, the Omaha conspiracy theorist spooked Goldman Sachs into believing it needed his money. In the fall of 2008, Buffett closed a deal for $5 billion in Goldman Sachs's preferred stock paying a 10% annual dividend. Goldman even gave Buffett warrants to buy $5 billion in common stock at a price of $115 any time before October 1, 2013. [The Fed let Goldman buy back its warrants for chump change.] Buffett's warrants are now about $3 billion in-the-money and worth much more—a sweetener for his crispy calamari.

Hank Paulson, Ben Bernanke, and Tim Geithner ignored the historic ravings of the most successful living investor, and fueled some of the bombers piloted by Wall Street before finance's Pearl Harbor. After they used taxpayer money to save the system and enriched the culpable with no strings attached, Buffett said "it could have turned out a lot differently," and called each of them a four-letter word. The label was undeserved.

Four-letter words aside, Warren Buffett raised a good point. It could have—and should have—turned out a lot differently. But it's not too late. Buffett called the crisis an economic Pearl Harbor and said that "Wall Street owes the American people one at this point." During World War II, we imposed an excess profits tax. We should impose a 95% excess profits tax—or windfall profits tax—on certain financial institutions (including Goldman Sachs) enriching themselves with ongoing low-cost Fed funding and debt guarantees.

Warren Buffett did not call for a windfall profits tax, but we should consider it with a host of other reforms.

Adapted from Dear Mr. Buffett. What an Investor Learns 1,269 Miles from Wall Street.

Warren Buffett, Stop Using My Credit Card!

November 23, 2009

I like Warren Buffett. I even wrote a book about the financial crisis contrasting his principles of prudent finance with recent excessive leverage, bad lending, and malfeasance. Buffett is not a regulator, an altruist, a consumer advocate, or an elected official. As CEO and largest shareholder of Berkshire Hathaway, his goal is to maximize shareholder value.

U.S. capitalism has morphed into a financial oligarchy. If Buffett's choice is between getting along in the financial community or the public interest, public interest loses. But he didn't cause our financial crisis, and he spoke out in advance about excessive leverage and bad lending. The financial markets are now wildly distorted. Others have funding advantages Buffett can only dream about, so he exploits an advantage when it becomes available.

I have been a trenchant critic of rampant financial malfeasance, and Buffett has only wished me well and told me to "keep writing." For my part, I try to keep in mind that we view the world through different lenses.

On October 25, 2009, when *BBC's* Evan Davis interviewed him, Buffett surprised me. It started out so well, but after six minutes the interview went sideways.[144] [Not shown in this clip Buffett said his $5 billion investment in Goldman Sachs' preferred stock (plus free warrants) last year was, in part, a bet on a US government bailout.[145] He thought the U.S. taxpayer got a good deal, but we got a worse deal than Buffett negotiated.][146]

At 3:14 min: Buffett explains that if there were only 50 people on a fertile island, we wouldn't take the five smartest people out of the 50 and give them the most money and tax breaks for trading rice futures and speculating: "*Hell no*! We'd get everybody producing rice. The idea that people that move money around are some favored class—and they are in this country, even in terms of taxes—strikes me as getting pretty far away from where we should be."

At 6:00 minutes: Buffett claims shareholder losses obviated moral hazard. *Not true*. In control frauds (first identified by William K. Black), financial institutions are destroyed, and shareholders lose. Only the *agents*: CEOs, CFOs, and highly paid employees are enriched.[147] Unlike Buffett, these agents are "stewards," not major owners. Moral hazard remains an intractable problem.

At 6:25 minutes: Buffett claims taxpayers have not bailed out anybody, because tax rates have not gone up (yet), and "tax receipts are way down this year." Chinese and Japanese buying U.S. government bonds have bailed out financial institutions. *Not true unless we default or destructively print inflationary dollars.* Tax receipts are down because of *unemployment*. U.S. taxpayer credit bailed out financial institutions, and we will have to pay back our debts.

Imagine this scenario: Warren grabs my credit card and charges twelve suits. When I object that I don't want to bail out his wardrobe, he chuckles and says, *don't worry, you haven't paid anything yet. The bank that issued the credit card bailed out my wardrobe, and it hasn't even had time to charge you interest on my purchase.*

When I protest that I'll have to eventually pay off both the balance and accrued interest, he tries flattery. *You are so productive that by the time you have to pay this off, you'll have so much more wealth that you won't even notice these charges. You've always been good for it before, and you'll figure out how to pay!*

Don't fall for it.

Government debt, like your credit card, is a type of money. It must be paid off with our future taxes generated from our production (unless you wish to destroy the economy by printing excess money). The fruits of your labors should be used in the way you see fit.

We must stop subsidizing speculators with cheap funding and tax breaks. We have to hold people accountable for malfeasance, break up large financial institutions, and allow them to fail instead of bailing them out. As for high pay and tax breaks for speculators, even Warren Buffett says: "*Hell no!*" But he won't help us make changes. U.S. taxpayers will have to figure it out, or we will pay.

Disclosure: At the time of this writing, Tavakoli is a Berkshire Hathaway shareholder.

Recapped in *BBC*'s mp3 podcast of Oct 26, 2009:[148]

Evan Davis: When you invested in Goldman Sachs (GS), what gave you the confidence to do that?

Warren Buffett: It was a very scary time.... I did not feel that we would be dumb enough really in a really basically prosperous country to let the misfunction (sic) of the financial engine bring down the country. But there was a time there where you wondered about that.

Evan Davis: I want to be clear here. When you made that investment, was it essentially a bet on GS performance or the performance of the authorities?

Warren Buffett: Both. Both. I mean you had to count...on Washington in effect not becoming so dysfunctional or blind to the problem or whatever it might be that it would let the whole country topple. But you also had to count on the fact that GS itself was basically a sound institution.

Clarification: Contrary to Buffett's assertion, Goldman Sachs wasn't sound. It was saved thanks to government bailouts, cheap public funding, debt guarantees, and a new bank holding company status conferred by the government on August 14, 2009. Goldman became a protected financial holding company ensuring there wouldn't be a future run on Goldman Sachs.

Warren Buffett and Charlie Munger: Winning the Class War

September 21, 2010

Fed Economists Gara Afonso and Anna Kovner with MIT finance professor Antoinette Schoar offer new evidence suggesting that although credit terms were tougher for large underperforming banks in the two days after Lehman's bankruptcy, the much-hyped market "freeze" was a myth.[149]

Thomas Paine, one of the Founding Fathers of the United States, urged Colonists not to trust the words of "interested men" tied by money and status to the British government and British royalty: "It is the good fortune of many to live distant from the scene of sorrow; the evil is not sufficiently brought to *their* doors to make *them* feel the precariousness with which all American property is possessed."

Warren Buffett Jumped the Squid

Today's interested men defend the bailouts and subsequent absence of felony indictments. They include Warren Buffett, Chairman and CEO of Berkshire Hathaway, and Berkshire's Vice-Chairman, Charlie Munger. I wrote a book, *Dear Mr. Buffett: What an Investor Learns 1,269 Miles from Wall Street*, about the financial crisis contrasting their formerly avowed principles of prudent finance with Wall Street's malfeasance. But they are not regulators, altruists, or elected officials. As officers and major stakeholders of Berkshire Hathaway, their goal is to maximize shareholder value. If the choice is between Berkshire's gain and public interest, public interest loses.

Buffett heaped praise on Berkshire's investments in Goldman Sachs and Wells Fargo (among others), while overlooking problematic activities within these bailed-out financial empires.

Warren deserves great credit for donating most of his wealth to charity, but one must deduct serious points because some of "his" wealth was appropriated from unwilling fellow citizens.

Charlie Munger's War

Andrew Frye of Bloomberg News reported Charlie Munger's recent remarks to law students at the University of Michigan. Munger suggests we shouldn't be "bitching about a little bailout;" we should have wondered why the bailout wasn't even bigger. (Click here for video.)

Taxpayers have already been saddled with crushing debt that transferred benefits to those most connected with Washington. *Bloomberg News* estimates the financial rescue already approaches $12.8 trillion in combined lending, spending, guarantees, and commitments. Taxpayer-subsidized banks that played a key role in getting us into this mess continue to pay their officers handsomely for failure. There were alternatives to Washington's largesse: controlled bankruptcy, conservatorship, and restructuring.

Washington's overheated money printing to support the bailouts has the nation in the grips of stranguflation. Lost jobs and reduced salaries combined with rising food and energy prices feel like hyperinflation to those most in need. Meanwhile, deflation has hit middle class investments and pension funds, and uncertainty about the future leaves them vulnerable. *Third World America* reveals that some former middle class Americans are using credit cards charging high interest rates to buy essential items including food.

Munger conjured the specter of Germany's Weimar Republic in an attempt to justify the bailouts: "We ended up with Adolf Hitler." *ZeroHedge*, home to finance's mainly masked throw downs, spoke for many (including me), when it retorted that Germany's hyperinflation was born from "wanton money printing" and set the stage for Hitler.

When it comes to bailouts that will hit middle class taxpayers most, Munger has a double standard:

> The 86 year-old told the 25 million of Americans who comprise the 16.7% of the underemployed population in the country, to "suck it in and cope."

> Not only that, but apparently, all those who have been without a job for 99 weeks and more and no longer have recourse to insurance benefits, should "thank God for bank bailouts." Why of course he would say that: after all $26 billion worth of direct BRK investments were the recipient of over $95 billion in bailouts.[150]

We bailed out banks that were the key architects of much of our national misery and currency destruction. Those living in poverty will have a much more difficult time bettering themselves, as much of the middle class sinks.

Updated Disclosure on September 21, 2010: I currently have no position (long or short) in Berkshire Hathaway.

Buffettgate: An Unenforced Policy Isn't a Policy

April 6, 2011

Several years ago I had dinner with one of my former managers. His firm had just settled a discrimination lawsuit for $1 million due to the actions of one of his salesmen. Top management blamed my colleague, because he had lost control of the situation.

I remembered the salesman, a loud bully. A group of us would arrive early and read the paper. My first morning, he snatched the *Wall Street Journal* from my hands and swaggered to his desk. I walked over and pointedly recovered it. This continued until the third morning, when I took back my paper and accidentally spilled his coffee. I apologized. I can be a little clumsy when retrieving my property, and I was likely to become even more unpredictable. He stopped grabbing my paper after that.

The salesman had tormented a new sales assistant, and this time he went beyond childishness. His least offensive remark to the young man was to regularly call him "Jew boy." The assistant lawyered up, and the result was the lawsuit against the firm.

My colleague felt he was being unjustly blamed. "We have a policy against discrimination," he protested. Yet he had heard the slurs, witnessed the salesman berating the assistant, and had done nothing.

"So you say," I responded. "A piece of paper with words on it doesn't constitute a policy. A policy that isn't enforced isn't a policy; it's a cover story." The sales assistant's lawyers successfully made the same argument.

Berkshire Hathaway's Cover Story

Today's *Wall Street Journal* noted that Warren Buffett, the CEO of Berkshire Hathaway, had a policy against insider-trading that restricted officers, including David Sokol, from investing in "securities of other public companies in which Berkshire has invested or may in the future invest."[151] The reporters thought the memo might give comfort to those concerned about potential ethical breaches by Berkshire Hathaway's autonomous management.

David Sokol bought shares in Lubrizol the day after meeting with Citigroup bankers to discuss potential acquisition candidates for Berkshire Hathaway. At least that was what the Citi bankers understood to be the purpose of the meeting. Sokol's actions were inappropriate. Front-running is an offense for which a banker or investment banker would be fired. Citi's bankers were shocked when they learned of Sokol's purchases. Moreover, it appears his actions were "expressly prohibited" by Berkshire Hathaway's "policy."[152]

Yet, Buffett seems to support and excuse Sokol's actions:

> "Neither Dave nor I feel his Lubrizol purchases were in any way unlawful. He has told me that they were not a factor in his decision to resign."[153]

Why didn't Buffett make it a factor and ask Sokol to resign?

During an initial meeting with Sokol about Lubrizol, Sokol told Buffett he owned shares in the company, but Buffett didn't ask him for further information including details of the timing, price, and number of shares. Warren Buffett devotes 12 hours a week to playing bridge. After the cards are dealt, players engage in an auction in an attempt to determine the value and number of the cards in each suit held by their partners. Yet Buffett states he did not inquire further about a senior Berkshire Hathaway officer's investment in an acquisition candidate.

Charlie Munger, a member of Berkshire Hathaway's board of directors, called Sokol's purchases "a glitch."[154] Sokol tried to excuse his own actions by telling CNBC that Munger had bought a 3% stake in Chinese electric car and battery maker BYD, prior to Berkshire's acquiring a large stake in that company. The facts of Munger's purchases (through a fund) were different, and Munger hedged: "I don't want to criticize his comparisons." Perhaps because doing so would highlight that Sokol's behavior was unethical.

Warren Buffett may be more diligent when he plays cards than in enforcing the policies he wrote for Berkshire Hathaway. Principles only matter when they are inconvenient. A policy that isn't enforced isn't a policy. Neither Warren Buffett nor Charlie Munger will publicly consider that there is anything even potentially immoral or unethical about Sokol's behavior. The SEC may find it goes even beyond that, when it completes its inquiry.

Warren Buffett and the Boys of Wall Street

May 9, 2011

One of my long-time New York friends said: "If you have three people working in a McDonald's there will be politics and grandstanding. Wall Street isn't much different." There's more fame, and the fortune is much greater, but he's on to something.

One of the reasons Warren Buffett has cultivated an image of trustworthiness is because his public persona seemed to be above it. Some contrast from my personal experiences may illustrate the point.

A Question of Character

A top hedge fund manager's emails were made public as the result of discovery in a lawsuit. He derided the CEO of an insurance company using profane imagery and referred to the Canadian CEO, who was born in India, as a "schwarze," a pejorative term for people of African heritage. In a *Reuters* article, I was quoted as saying the language speaks to character.[155] The hedge fund manager emailed me to insult mine for speaking up (not to express regret for his choice of words revealed by *Reuters*). Perhaps he feels the best defense is a lame offense.

When performing due diligence, investors consider capacity, capital, and character. The hedge fund manager may underestimate how offensive his language appears to many people, including me. He may also disregard the multi-national and multi-racial make-up of the families of investors and colleagues.

People are sometimes unfairly judged by their age, race, birthplace, gender, height, deformities, or handicaps. Those are factors that are completely beyond their control. Yet, I got the impression the hedge fund manager felt it was unfair for anyone to judge him for words that were completely within his control.

"What Motivates You?"

Late last year, another "top" hedge fund manager (with a mixed track record), I'll call him the Yeti, said he'd like to talk to me about an idea he had that I should start a fund of funds. I found this a bit odd. I'd explained to him that I've publicly stated for years that I believe fund of funds managers add zero or negative value. Those that invested clients' funds with Madoff are a recent example. If I were going that route, I'd start a fund. Nonetheless, he thought it worth discussing, so I met with him in his New York offices.

I was feeling particularly good that morning, and it showed. My mood seemed to annoy him. He asked a smarmy and chilling question: "What motivates you, Janet, is it *sex*?" I should add that he's married and cultivates a press image as a family man. He's also more than ten years my junior. He explained that I could hire only female employees, and then he'd introduce me to some people; I'd make a large fortune. He continued with his supposed motivation: "money makes sex a lot easier to get."

"It's dangerous to use one to try to get the other," I responded. (Depending on the circumstances, it can also be illegal.)

What was the purpose of that meeting? Apparently, the Yeti was hoping to be educated as to why money cannot buy a better personality.

Not long after that, I publicly and separately disagreed with the Yeti on a business issue. He complained via email that our relationship was over. But there was no "relationship," and nothing wholesome would develop from his "ideas." Meanwhile the financial press profiles the Yeti as a role model, which is an abominable snow job.

Buffett's Gentle Treatment by the Financial Press

It's easy to like Warren Buffett; he's a relief in comparison. No financier has as long a track record or has garnered so much good press for so long as Warren Buffett, the CEO and largest shareholder of Berkshire Hathaway. His language and business demeanor has been exemplary, and his public statements against malfeasance and hubris have been a welcome oasis in a business riddled with multi-decade frauds and scandals. He's been the rock star of the financial world.

It's as if there was a pact among the financial press to overlook foibles as long as no scandal could be directly tied to Warren Buffett's actions. Suddenly that's changed.

Bloomberg's Jonathan Weil reminded the financial community that the press has given Warren Buffett very gentle treatment in past scandals. Buffett stayed mum during the financial crisis as Moody's (Berkshire owned around 19% of the stock at the end of 2007) handed out "AAA" ratings on junk bonds. He headed Coca-Cola's audit committee, and the SEC issued a cease and desist order against the company for misleading earnings statements in the 1990's. Warren Buffett knew about contracts between Berkshire's GenRe unit and American International Group Inc. for which GenRe paid a $92 million fine and four executives were sentenced to prison.[156] The SEC claimed Berkshire and its audit firm, Deloitte, violated the SEC's auditor independence rules when one of Deloitte's advising partners traded in and out of Berkshire's stock; Berkshire concluded Deloitte was independent anyway, and the SEC didn't object.[157]

It's noteworthy that none of the financial journalists with the most access to Buffett raised the issue that Buffett himself appears to have violated Berkshire's disclosure policies as stated in a recent Berkshire Hathaway audit report on David Sokol's violation of Berkshire's insider trading policies. The "duty of candor" the non-independent audit committee applied to Sokol, a former executive, should also apply to Warren Buffett.[158]

If It Isn't "Unlawful," Why Did Buffett Give the SEC "Very Damning Evidence?"

In a March 30 press release, Buffett announced David Sokol's resignation and praised his track record. At Berkshire Hathaway's April 29 annual meeting, he told of how Sokol turned down $12.5 million in incentive pay several years ago. Buffett didn't mention that Sokol was Chairman of MidAmerican when plaintiffs in a lawsuit questioned Sokol's calculations. A judge ruled there was a "breach of obligation" and awarded $32 million plus stock in a project company in damages.[159]

In his March 30 release, Buffett wrote that Sokol's purchases of shares of Lubrizol, a company targeted as a Berkshire Hathaway acquisition candidate, were not a factor in his decision to resign. Jonathan Weil retorted that the line "wasn't remotely credible." Buffett himself admitted at his annual meeting the trades were a firing offense.

Buffett tried to dodge the key issues at the annual meeting by saying that people were bothered by his March 30 release because they missed "some big sense of outrage." Actually, the public has had enough phony outrage. Missing were candor and material facts.

The most important fact was that while Buffett wrote on March 30 that neither he nor Sokol felt the trades were "in any way unlawful," after a month of press uproar, Buffett admitted at his annual meeting that on the day he wrote his release he turned over evidence to the SEC's enforcement division that was "some very damning evidence, in my view."

Now the rating agencies are reviewing weak corporate governance at Berkshire Hathaway and may downgrade the company's credit rating. That would lead to relatively higher funding costs which would create a drag on returns.

Buffett didn't think this incident would damage his reputation, but perhaps as Jonathan Weil points out, it's because the press has gone easy on him in the past. Buffett isn't being judged on appearances. He's being judged by words and actions completely under his control.

The bank hath benefit of interest on all moneys which it creates out of nothing.

—Theodore Roosevelt 1858-1919

CHAPTER 11 The "Regulators"

Inside the Wall Street Journal's Future of Finance Initiative

December 14, 2009

Last week I was a participant in the *Wall Street Journal*'s Future of Finance Initiative in England. *WSJ* has written a summary of the conference highlights, and missed some key points. Allow me to fill in the blanks.[160][161]

Paul Volcker, former Fed Chairman and current Chair of the President's Economic Advisory Board, made the most worthwhile comments.[162] Moral hazard was not discussed in the open forums, so Volcker reminded the assembly. Yet even Volcker did not broach the topic of fraud.

Alistair Darling, Chancellor of the Exchequer, spoke on the opening evening. I asked him why massive financial fraud remained unaddressed.[163] Darling appeared momentarily confused and seemed to suggest this was exclusively a U.S. problem to be handled by the courts. I pushed back on this notion. By the time one needs a lawyer, it is too late. I noted that we, the middle aged financiers in the room, are responsible for taking action. If we don't face this issue head on, we will never restore trust in the financial system.

Ana Botin, Banesto's Executive Chairman, suggested that the risk manager should report to the board. Then she blew it with the assertion—made several times—that the CEO can also be Chairman. (Ken Lewis defended his dual role as CEO and Chairman of Bank of America at a Fed conference in 2003. How did that work out?)

I didn't challenge Botin's assertion, because I used my two minutes (literally) during the "Too Big to Fail" breakout session to (unsuccessfully) try to carry the point that when banks fail, we should allow shareholders to be wiped out, and debt holders should take losses. (Under that scenario, most of the current managers would be booted out.) Instead, the group posted the need for a "living will" to be designed by the managers that made life support during our recent crisis a debatable necessity.

Elizabeth Corley, CEO of Allianz Global Investors in Europe, presented conclusions from her panel's discussion of the "Regulatory Frontier."[164] The panel's idea of upgrading regulatory resources was to deploy senior financial institution officers to regulators for two or three years and vice versa. Meanwhile, the financial institutions should chip in to maintain the regulators' former high pay. Howard Davies of the London School of Economics saved me from having to explain the concept of regulatory capture. After he spoke, I was the only one to clap. Apparently everyone else thought the panel was titled the "Predatory Frontier."

Robert Diamond, president of Barclays PLC, sounded like a financial holocaust denier.[165] He seemed to think that the idea of breaking up banks has only to do with the threat to the financial system, if they fail. The point is that some of these institutions threatened the financial system—and continue to threaten the financial system—because they are too big to manage.

Diamond seemed to dislike the term "socially useless" to describe recent financial innovation and defended Barclays' proprietary trading. Since Barclays has dropped its suit involving its total return swap with Bear Stearns' imploded hedge funds, Diamond may have already forgotten this relevant example of financial innovation gone wrong. Hedge fund investors were wiped out, the hedge funds' dodgy assets landed on Bear Stearns's balance sheet, and later on JPMorgan Chase's balance sheet, after it acquired Bear Stearns. Our past crisis taught us that hedge funds are not independent of the banking system. This transaction wasn't merely socially useless, it had negative social utility.

Mario Draghi, Bank of Italy's Governor and Chairman of the Financial Stability Board, seemed to think that hedge funds are independent. This is simply incorrect. If the example above didn't persuade him, he might consider the assets that came back onto bank balance sheets and contributed to market instability. For example, in March of 2008 as Bear Stearns bit the dust, the Carlyle Group's CCC fund assets and the assets of Peloton's funds boomeranged back on bank balance sheets at the most inopportune time.

Bob Diamond defended structured credit products saying there is a real purpose for structuring credit for pension funds. He was probably unaware that state pension funds in the United States were damaged by the unintended consequences of a "AAA" rated structured credit product. The pension funds were wise enough to avoid investing in the product, yet as I explained in my February 2007 letter to the Securities and Exchange Commission, large fixed income pension funds were unintentionally harmed by the market distortions caused by this financial innovation.

My letter to the SEC cited this financial innovation as an example of why the special NRSRO designation of the rating agencies should be revoked. The product did not deserve its "AAA" rating. It had substantial principal risk and deserved a non-investment grade, or junk rating. Within a year all of these new "AAA" innovations blew up. Moody's estimated that investors in one of them would get back only around ten cents on the dollar.

Not all financial innovation is harmful, but it is undeniable that in recent years it was a runaway train that nearly derailed the global financial system. You wouldn't have realized that, if you listened to most of the participants. They chiefly represented the interests of large financial institutions, and the financial system is still attached to the privileged placenta of central banks doling out taxpayer subsidies. Most of the conference reflected the insulated thinking of this protective womb.

Treasury Cover-Up of Goldman's Role in AIG Crisis

December 22, 2009

In November 2009, I wrote in the Huffington Post that Goldman Sachs Group nearly bankrupted AIG. In December, the *Wall Street Journal* explained to the general public that Goldman fueled AIG's gambling and played a much bigger role in the mortgage bets that nearly felled American International Group (AIG) than the Treasury, the Fed, or Goldman itself publicly disclosed.

The November 17, 2009 SIGTARP report missed the most damaging facts. Intentionally or otherwise, it was evasive action or just plain whitewash. The report failed to clarify Goldman's role in AIG's near collapse, and that of all the settlement deals, the U.S. taxpayers' was by far the worst.

Goldman originated or bought protection from AIG on about $33 billion of the problematic $80 billion of U.S. mortgage assets that AIG "insured" with credit derivatives, about twice as much as the next two largest banks involved.

Goldman acted as middle-man on $14 billion of that amount, after it took the risk of mortgage assets originated by other banks and insured all of it with AIG. Goldman may wish to claim it "was only following orders," but since Goldman also originated many of the mortgage assets ultimately protected by AIG, it should have been well aware of the risk posed to itself and to AIG. The risk was then Goldman's. If AIG failed, Goldman Sachs would have had to make good on those trades. Goldman stuffed so much risk into A.I.G. that Goldman nearly killed its own "hedge."

In November 2008, the New York Fed paid 100 cents on the dollar for the $14 billion of mortgage assets related to Goldman's trades. Goldman estimated the assets had lost $9.6 billion, or around two-thirds of their market value. Overall, the government's bailout of AIG allowed Goldman to avoid losses on its trades covering $22 billion in assets.

The U.S. taxpayer deserved a much better deal. In late July 2008, SCA, another bond insurer, settled similar contracts for only around thirteen cents on the dollar. In August 2008, Calyon, a French bank also involved in AIG's transactions, settled disputed financial guarantees with FGIC, a bond insurer facing bankruptcy, for only ten cents on the dollar. Ambac, another bond insurer in need of capital, recently canceled similar trades for ten cents on the dollar.[166]

Defenders argue that circumstances surrounding AIG were different from the other bond insurers. They are correct; *the circumstances were worse.* The Fed should have made sure any payments that originated from AIG, before or after the bailout, were only temporary loans to be repaid as soon as possible.

This link[167] provides a snapshot from January 2008 of two of Goldman's value-destroying securitizations that were protected by AIG. (You will have to enlarge the image after clicking, and the document is a bit awkward.) The first is Abacus 2005-2; Goldman originated and bought protection on these mortgage assets. The second is Davis Square Funding IV. Goldman originated this deal, and French bank Societe Generale bought protection from AIG against it.

Inside Goldman's mortgage assets were value-destroying assets created by other Wall Street firms. Everyone bought each other's junk so prices stayed artificially high, and the risk could be dumped on someone else. Of course, this doomed strategy eventually fell apart. At the time of the AIG bailout, losses were quickly eating away at the insides of these products cooked up in Wall Street's financial meth labs.

Among the many shards of glass masquerading as gems, you will find Tourmaline CDO 2005-1. It was managed by Blackrock, the manager of the AIG assets that the Fed purchased with public money. Perhaps the Fed's theory in handing out no bid contracts to Blackrock has something to do with the diligence displayed by a fox watching a hen house.

The Fed gave the U.S. taxpayer a raw deal. At the time Goldman got its give-away, Henry Paulson was treasury secretary—he was also Goldman's CEO when it put on its trades with AIG—and former Goldman chairman Stephen Friedman was then chairman of the New York Federal Reserve Bank. Goldman CEO Lloyd Blankfein was the only Wall Street executive at one of Paulson's bailout meetings. Goldman was inside the tent advising on the most self-serving way to save itself and gain unfettered access to public funds.

In the fall of 2008, Goldman Sachs became a bank holding company before switching to a less regulated financial holding company in August 2009. This prevented a run on Goldman Sachs and gave it permanent access to Fed funds, taxpayer money. Goldman pays rates near zero for short-term borrowing while it earns profits on the higher rates paid on the capital it is required to deposit with the Fed. Goldman also issued nearly $21 billion in debt guaranteed by the FDIC. Most valuable of all, however, is the perception that Goldman is so well-connected, that the government will never let it fail.

Goldman paid mega bonuses in past years subsidized by selling hot air. Now it proposes to again pay billions in bonuses based on earnings made possible by taxpayer dollars.

Now that the crisis is over, we should ask Goldman Sachs—and all of AIG's other trading partners involved in these trades—to buy back these mortgage assets at full price. Alternatively, we can impose a special tax. Instead of calling it a windfall profits tax, we might label it a "hot air" profits tax.

A Goldman spokesman denies it could have known these mortgage assets were a problem, but Goldman also acknowledged I had warned about them—and the grave risks they posed—at the time they were created. It said my opinion was in the "minority." As it happens, Goldman's opinion was proved tragically wrong, and mine was proved correct. It is not in the public interest to rely on Goldman's opinion about the greater risk it now poses to the global markets, and the Treasury should exact a much greater financial cushion.

The global financial crisis and the special circumstances surrounding AIG's bailout were extraordinary. It is unconscionable to reward value destroying activity that damaged not only AIG, but enabled massive damage to the U.S. economy. It is in the public interest to claw back public money. Goldman should buy back these mortgage assets at full price, or we should impose a reparations tax. Furthermore, Goldman should pay off its FDIC guaranteed debt, and once again become an investment bank with no access to Fed borrowing, *before* it pays taxpayer-subsidized bonuses to its employees.

Timothy Geithner, I Call Your Bluff

January 7, 2010

The Treasury responded to reports that the New York Fed asked AIG to suppress and delay facts about the bailout. Meg Reilly, a Treasury spokesperson claimed: "In the transaction at the heart of this dispute...the FRBNY [Federal Reserve Bank of New York] made a loan of $25 billion which is on track to be paid back in full with interest." She claims the loan is currently "above water."

In the first place, that loan is not the heart of the dispute. Nonetheless, the FRBNY should immediately release the details of all of the Maiden Lane III assets backing that loan and show the current prices BlackRock has placed on them. Based on the current market, it is extremely likely that the loan is *underwater.*

The assets backing the loan are so-called super senior and AAA rated collateralized debt obligations (CDOs). Similar CDOs trade for under ten cents on the dollar, not close to the average price of 35 cents for the loan's assets shown in a recent Fed report. The Fed claims prices climbed 4.5%. Yet in the secondary market, prices have dropped.

The Fed awarded no-bid contracts to BlackRock to manage and price these assets (among other things). Given BlackRock's track record as a CDO manager, I have no reason to believe its prices are reliable.[168]

BlackRock managed Pacific Pinnacle CDO ($1 billion; closed 1/1/07; event of default 2/4/08); Pinnacle Point Funding ($2B closed 6/7/07; acceleration 12/13/07); Tenorite CDO I ($1 B closed 5/11/07; liquidation 2/7/08); and Tourmaline CDO III ($1.5 billion closed 4/5/07; event of default 3/31/08). (Earlier I wrote a commentary that included a 2005 CDO called Tourmaline, managed by BlackRock. It ended up being part of a CDO bailed out by the Fed.) I highlight BlackRock's 2007 CDOs similar to those it now manages for the Fed, because in 2007 mainstream media was already reporting on the potential for CDOs of this type to blow up. I wrote an article for the precursor to *Risk Professional* in early 2007 warning about the type of value-destroying CDOs that AIG insured. I had also issued earlier warnings on other types of value-destroying CDOs.

If the Treasury wants to publicly claim the loan is not underwater, now is the time to prove it, even though this particular loan is not the key issue.

As Representative Darrell Issa explained in his letter to the Fed, at the heart of this dispute is my assertion that Treasury Secretary Timothy Geithner, in his former role as President of the FRBNY, paid 100 cents on the dollar to settle AIG's credit default swap contracts, and he wildly overpaid. Other bond insurers including Ambac, MBIA, and FGIC have settled similar contracts for as little as ten cents on the dollar.[169]

The general public was kept unaware of several politically explosive facts. Risky subprime loans partly backed CDOs that AIG insured. Goldman Sachs played a key role in AIG's distress with both credit default swap transactions and CDOs that Goldman underwrote. The identities of the banks—including some foreign banks—that received payments were not revealed until five months after the bailout. The November 2009 TARP Inspector

General's report failed to mention that Goldman originated or bought protection from AIG on about $33 billion of the problematic $80 billion of U.S. mortgage assets that AIG "insured" with credit derivatives, about twice as much as the next two largest banks involved.

The TARP report also failed to highlight the character of the synthetic CDOs underwritten by Goldman Sachs that remain on AIG's books. There is nothing wrong with hedging or taking the opposite view to one's customers. There is nothing wrong with using credit derivatives to accomplish this goal. But there are serious questions about whether residential mortgage backed securities and downstream CDOs were value-destroying and misrated.

Wall Street was chiefly responsible for the "financial innovation" that did massive damage to the U.S. economy. I assert there should be fraud audits of Wall Street's securitization activities.

Given the extraordinary circumstances surrounding AIG's trades, the global financial crisis, and the AIG bailout, it is time to reopen this issue. AIG's counterparties can repurchase the approximately $62 billion of CDOs from Maiden Lane III at full price. The price can be adjusted for interim principal and interest payments, as applicable.

If the Fed really believes they are worth 35 cents on the dollar, then these counterparties will be getting a windfall versus ten cents on the dollar. As for Goldman Sachs's approximately $8.2 billion in CDOs (including synthetic CDOs) that are still on AIG's books, they can be settled at ten cents on the dollar, and excess collateral currently held by Goldman can be returned. This is the value at which other bond insurers have settled similar deals. The return of payments to AIG can be used to pay down its public debt, *before* banks pay tax-payer subsidized bonuses to their employees.

Show Bernanke and Geithner the Door

January 22, 2010

Both the United States and the United Kingdom have had a coordinated non-response to financial reform. If a drunk driver killed your neighbors and crashed the car into your house, you wouldn't expect a police officer to hand the offender a bottle of whiskey and the keys to a bigger, faster, and more powerful car. You would be outraged if the officer said he would only impose a fine, and then made you lend the drunk the money to pay the fine. Yet this is the modus operandi of our financial system, and now financial drunk drivers refuse blood tests and huff that their seat belts were fastened.

Both Federal Reserve Chairman Ben Bernanke and Treasury Secretary Timothy Geithner missed the critical warning signs of our recent financial crisis. In April of 2009, Steve Forbes called Geithner "the most formidable impediment to an economic recovery." Ben Bernanke repeats past mistakes and hands out cheap money with insufficient conditions or regulation. Both economists have been economical with the truth. There were alternatives to their actions during the crisis that are based on sound financial principles and do not violate the spirit of democracy.

President Obama has proposed a baby step towards financial reform. He proposes to limit ill-defined proprietary trading, limit banks' borrowings, and prevent banks from investing in hedge funds and private equity funds. Banks' lobbyists and PR spin-doctors are already working overtime to thwart him.

Mainstream financial media got it badly wrong when it said that the proposal was based on populist anger. It may have motivated President Obama to (only partly take) Paul Volcker's advice, but sound financial principles back that advice.[170]

Some bank stocks fell in price after the President's remarks yesterday. That was because savvy investors knew that speculators might no longer be able to report high risk-based earnings subsidized with taxpayer dollars. In this case, a fall in stock prices for banks driving down Wall Street should be viewed as a healthy sign. A few bank stocks rose, because they rely on traditional banking backed by sound financial principles.

Goldman Sachs's stock went down a few percentage points. It became a newly created "bank," to get on the taxpayer give-away gravy train. JPMorgan Chase claims only 1% of its revenue comes from proprietary trading, yet even before its merger with Bear Stearns, JPMorgan's market share of credit derivatives was greater than 50% for U.S. banks. That meant you could combine the credit derivatives of all other domestic banks, and JPMorgan's positions were greater. Those are just two examples. Banks' "non-proprietary" trading desks are often invisible hedge funds.

Taxpayers currently subsidize banks with cheap money supplied by the Federal Reserve. Even banks that nearly crashed our economy borrow at nearly zero interest rates, while some consumers pay nearly 30% on credit card debt.

Banks enjoy a Term Asset-Backed Securities Loan Facility (TALF) that allows them to borrow against problem assets. New banks have each issued tens of billions in FDIC guaranteed debt through the Temporary Liquidity Guarantee Program (TLGP). Banks get interest payments on the excess reserves they keep with the Fed. Accounting rules were changed in April 2009, so banks make up their own prices for assets and more easily hide losses. These are only a few of many newly-created hidden subsidies.

Taxpayers are paid only peanuts in fees for these massive subsidies while being squeezed with high interest rates and mortgage foreclosures—after our economy was devastated chiefly by several banks' malicious mischief.

What has the financial crisis taught us? Among other things, we should show Bernanke and Geithner, enablers from the previous administration, the door. Paul Volcker is right to ask for a return to Glass-Steagall. It worked until it was eroded over several decades by bank lobbying. Banking and speculative trading activities—even when done for "customers"—don't mix.

"Financial innovation" must be limited, since much of it in recent years was the financial equivalent of card cheating. Banks should not be allowed to sponsor hedge funds and private equity funds, and furthermore, they should not be allowed to lend to them through prime brokerage units or other means. Financial institutions must be allowed to fail. Hedge funds require regulation. Malfeasance should be investigated and prosecuted. Credit derivatives should be traded and cleared through exchanges and made transparent. Compensation and financial incentives at banks must change. Bank employees cannot continue to reap huge rewards at no personal risk while shoving risk into the global financial system.

President Obama promised us change, and he should seize this opportunity to demand sweeping financial reform.

Congress Exposes Profiteering in AIG's Deals: Delay Enabled Cover-Up

January 28, 2010

Yesterday the House released some missing details of the AIG bailout.[171] The public knew that the Fed paid 100 cents on the dollar to AIG's trading counterparties to resolve its credit default swaps, but the details of the assets behind the trades were kept secret.

Plenty of Time to Renegotiate AIG's Contracts

The first bailout of AIG occurred in September 2008 when the FRBNY extended an $85 billion credit line to AIG. By the September 2008 initial bailout, Goldman Sachs had extracted $7.5 billion in collateral from AIG, and other banks that bought Goldman's CDOs also extracted billions from AIG.

Goldman CEO Lloyd Blankfein claims he had no idea AIG had trouble producing collateral. I knew AIG was headed for grave trouble more than a year before the September 2008 bailout and raised the issue with both Warren Buffett and JPMorgan Chase CEO Jamie Dimon. Goldman Sachs claims to be a superior risk manager, yet asks the public to believe that it was clueless about AIG's distress, even though Goldman itself was a key contributor to it.

Then Treasury Secretary Henry Paulson was CEO of Goldman Sachs at the time it put on these trades with AIG. Lloyd Blankfein was (and remains) CEO of Goldman and was the only Wall Street CEO at one of Paulson's bailout discussions. Stephen Friedman, then Chairman of the NY Fed, also served on Goldman's board.

Details That Could Anger the Public

An analysis of the previously secret details shows that at the time of the November 2008 buyout, some CDOs had implied prices of around 60 cents on the dollar. Others had implied prices of around 20 cents on the dollar.

Not revealed by the new report is that many of the assets backing some of the CDOs have a high risk of severe or total principal loss (many have actual losses). These CDOs have "cliff risk," as in falling off of one. (There is currently no reliable secondary market, and similar CDOs have traded as low as one penny.) One such CDO is Davis Square IV, a CDO on which French bank Societe Generale bought protection from AIG. The CDO is a poster child for Wall Street's key contribution to a financial crisis that devastated the U.S. economy.

Goldman Sachs created and closed Davis Square IV in April of 2005. The CDO was managed by Trust Company of the West (TCW). The original portfolio included mortgage-backed securities from Goldman Sachs Alternative Mortgage Products, Merrill, and problem mortgage lenders Countrywide, New Century, Novastar, First Franklin, and Fremont (among others). Assets include home equity loans, midprime loans, subprime loans, and adjustable rate mortgages. The CDO also includes other CDOs.

AIG's Joe Cassano said AIG was basically out of the business of guaranteeing mortgage product at the end of 2005, yet the report shows around 14% of the CDOs on which AIG sold protection appear to be from 2006, 2007, or 2008 representing around 30% or $19 billion of the $62.13 billion notional amount purchased by the Fed. Furthermore, CDOs from 2006 and 2007 are buried within the portfolios backing the original CDOs. For example, TCW traded mortgages from 2006 and 2007 vintages into the portfolio backing Davis Square IV. These "assets" are among the worst of the lot.[172]

CDO managers may disclose conflicts of interest, but a conflict of interest shouldn't mean that new assets "managed" into your portfolio are highly likely to do you harm. TCW and Goldman Sachs had a relationship that benefited TCW, which earned fees from deals like Davis Square IV. Davis Square IV included several tranches of Goldman's Abacus deals, including $53.5 million from 2006. By September 2008, Goldman's CDO, Abacus 2006-12, was already downgraded from AA2 to Ca, a junk rating—it means you are likely to lose your shirt. Another part of this CDO in Davis Square IV's portfolio was downgraded from A3 to Ca. Three of Goldman's slices of Abacus 2006-15 also made their way into Davis Square IV, and they were also all downgraded to Ca, a junk rating, by September 2008.

Among other eyebrow raising assets in Davis Square IV, one finds a CDO called Pinnacle Point Funding 2007-a. This CDO was managed by Blackrock. It closed June 7, 2007, and went into acceleration (not a good sign) on December 13, 2007. Davis Square IV's "investment" was originally rated triple-A. By the time of AIG's September 2008 bailout, it was already downgraded to C, a junk rating, by Moody's. Yet the Fed awarded no-bid contracts to Blackrock to manage the assets it bought from AIG.

Profiteering and Track-Covering: Possible Reasons for Redaction

The financial windfall conferred by AIG's bailout, the self-serving claim that the crisis prevented negotiation, and the subsequent cover-up of details were very much to the benefit of Goldman Sachs and its current and former officers involved in the bailout discussions.

In the example above, I show the Davis Square IV portfolio as of January 2008. One would need similar snapshots of all the CDOs to figure out who did what to whom. The fact that the Fed and SEC suppressed potentially explosive facts is bad enough, but the delay in making the information public has given interested parties a window of opportunity to cover their tracks by dumping the worst of the assets, thus hiding them forever from public view.

Suppressing the details of AIG's trades made it easier for AIG's counterparties to cover-up profiteering and then exploit public funds. If details of these trades had been made public in September 2008, a reasonable negotiator would have demanded that the billions of dollars that had been extracted from AIG (including the $7.5 billion Goldman extracted by then) should be recharacterized as a loan.

Instead, the Fed gifted tens of billions of dollars to banks that supplied the financing for bad loans that damaged the U.S. economy. More than that, these banks engaged in suspect deals that covered up losses and allowed them to continue to report apparent "profits" and pay inflated bonuses. Meanwhile, their securitization activities continued to harm the economy during a period when the United States was at war.

Goldman is not solely responsible, but it had a large role in AIG's crisis and a unique position of conflicted interest and influence over the terms of the bailout. Now that the crisis is over, this issue should be reopened, and billions in collateral should be clawed back to pay down public debt, before Goldman Sachs pays more than $16 billion in taxpayer subsidized bonuses to its employees.

Congress's FCIC Nearly Nailed Former Citigroup Executives to the Wall—Then Blew It

April 8, 2010

Phil Angelides, Chairman of the Financial Crisis Inquiry Commission, had Robert Rubin, former senior advisor Citigroup (also former Treasury Secretary under President Bill Clinton, and former Co-Chair of Goldman Sachs), and Chuck Prince, former CEO of Citigroup, in the palm of his hand today. He asked them why they weren't alarmed for Citigroup in May of 2007, when the Bear Stearns hedge funds ran into trouble. He recalled they imploded in June 2007 and joked that it happened around the time of his birthday. Rubin and Prince shrugged it off, and Rubin said that he didn't know about Citigroup's CDO troubles until the fall of 2007.

Separately, Tom Maheras, then a top fixed income executive at Citigroup, said in the fall of 2007 that Citigroup's "super senior" CDOs were worth 100 cents on the dollar.

Angelides may not have realized it, but there were facts in the public domain that tie Citigroup very closely to the fate of Bear Stearns's hedge funds. Either these top people from Citigroup didn't ask their subordinates about their exposure—and the nature of their exposure to the Bear Stearns hedge funds—or the controls in Citigroup broke down. Rubin testified today: "I don't think Citi is too big to manage." Yet, these events suggest something is seriously amiss.

In my book on the financial meltdown, *Dear Mr. Buffett,* I explain how I knew Citigroup was in trouble and its involvement in value-destroying CDOs purchased by Bear Stearns Asset Management's imploding hedge funds. At the time, I spoke to investigative reporters Matthew Goldstein ("Bear Stearns's Subprime IPO," *BusinessWeek,* May 11, 2007.) and Jody Shenn ("Bear Stearns Funds to Transfer Subprime-Mortgage Risk with IPO," *Bloomberg News,* May 11, 2007) about Bear Stearns and the disturbing assets, including some created by Citigroup, revealed by an SEC filing it made in May 2007 for a proposed initial public offering (IPO):

> I went to the SEC's web site, and as I scanned the document I thought to myself: Has Bear Stearns Asset Management completely lost its mind? There is a difference between being clever and being intelligent. I was surprised to read that funds managed by BSAM invested in the unrated first loss risk (equity) of CDOs. In my view, the underlying assets were neither suitable nor appropriate investments for the retail market.
>
> I did not have time for a thorough review, so I picked a CDO investment underwritten by Citigroup in March of 2007 bearing in mind that if the Everquest IPO came to market, some of the proceeds would pay down Citigroup's $200 million credit line.[173] [Emphasis added] Everquest held the "first loss" risk, usually the riskiest of all of the CDO tranches, and it was obvious to me that even the investors in the supposedly safe "triple-A" tranches were in trouble. Time proved my concerns warranted, since the CDO triggered an event of default in February 2008, at which time Standard & Poor's downgraded even the original safest "triple-A" tranche to junk.

All the banks that lent to Bear Stearns Asset Management's (BSAM) two problematic hedge funds pressured the managers to mark down the prices of their assets by late May and early June 2007—even the prices of "AA" and "AAA" rated assets. Before the hedge funds went under, BSAM circulated bid lists for the assets, and the prices were atrocious.

How is it that given Citigroup's huge loan and creation of CDOs that these two funds bought didn't draw the attention of Citigroup's senior management? Citigroup was deeply involved, and there was obvious danger to its own balance sheet.

Chairman Angelides was apparently unaware that Citigroup had reason to be deeply alarmed by the events that caused the

Bear Stearns hedge funds to implode. He missed a golden opportunity to ask Citigroup's former executives about their seeming obliviousness to this enormous risk.

More to the point, Angelides might ask these executives why Citigroup's officers made rosy public statements and why Citigroup's financial filings with the SEC did not show huge accounting losses for the second quarter of 2007 (and earlier).

After the negative publicity, the Everquest IPO did not come to market.

President Obama: Bring Back William Black

April 25, 2010

William K. Black, a regulator during the dark days of the Savings & Loan Crisis, gave the most sensible testimony about the financial crisis heard in Washington so far.[174] Fraud thrives and spreads in a regulatory free, highly paid, criminogenic environment. Cheaters prosper driving honesty out of the market.

> Firms such as Citigroup and Merrill Lynch [and others] were able to create complex securities backed by recklessly underwritten [often fraudulent] mortgages, knowing that they could pass the risk along to someone else who had less information about the underlying loans. [The] $62 trillion credit derivatives market allowed Wall Street to lend without having confidence in the men and women it lent to. Wall Street hedged away the risk of lending and in the process undermined the entire system.[175]

It's time to bring back Black and resolute regulators like him. Our proposed "financial reform" bill is a sham, and the health of our society and our economy is at stake.[176]

Failed Regulators Are Still in Charge

Our financial "investigations" aim to miss. First, the media writes breathless articles portraying Washington's financial "investigators" as "tough." Each new commission is billed as our

"Pecora" moment. The "investigators" hire teams of staffers who badger people like me for charity with insightful questions like: "What's a CDO?" Treasury, Federal Reserve, and Wall Street notables loudly complain about "unfair" and "harsh" investigators. Then everyone marches to the Hill where the committee pelts Wall Street executives with verbal marshmallows. Here are just four examples:

The FCIC: Phil Angelides, Chairman of the Financial Crisis Inquiry Commission, had Robert Rubin, Citigroup's former senior advisor (also former Treasury Secretary under President Bill Clinton, and former Co-Chair of Goldman Sachs), and Chuck Prince, former CEO of Citigroup, in the palm of his hand. He failed to question them about Citigroup's sales of complex CDOs and a $200 million loan to the failed Bear Stearns hedge funds, even though it was public information and a classic situation for securities fraud.

The SEC: The SEC filed a recent complaint of alleged fraud in a civil lawsuit against Goldman Sachs. The complaint did not mention that Goldman may have used the subprime mortgage-linked security at issue to unload other complex bonds it created. The complaint strikes me as an SEC publicity stunt. Wall Street banks had deep ties (and often ownership) with corrupt mortgage lenders and created phony securities that funded loan fraud. Corrupt finance—enabled by the SEC's multi-year failures—amplified the problem. The SEC (rating agencies, and more) behaved as collaborators, and now they seem to want credit for bringing one seemingly incomplete complaint against a sapling, while the forest fire rages on.[177]

Senate's Permanent Subcommittee on Investigations - "Trial by Email": The leak of Goldman's emails suggests that shorting as a hedge is the same thing as betting against clients. ("Blankfein E-Mail Shows Firm Profited Betting Against Mortgages," Christine Harper, *Bloomberg*, April 24, 2010.) It's not necessarily so.[178] Even if facts show it is true, there is a much bigger issue. Wall Street banks bet against our entire society when they created and sold phony securities that fueled fraudulent mortgage lending. That activity was profitable for some firms

(Goldman) and unprofitable for others (Lehman, Citigroup, Merrill Lynch, and more). Yet in every case, it was control fraud. CEOs and bankers grew rich while the financial institutions that employed them often imploded. The agents of the fraud prospered while American society and the American economy were massively damaged. ("Wall Street's Fraud and Solutions for Systemic Peril, " Tavakoli, *TSF*, September 29, 2009)

TARP "Investigations": Unintentionally or otherwise, the TARP Inspector General's November 17 "SIGTARP" Report appeared to be evasive action or just plain whitewash. A week before that particular SIGTARP report was released I disclosed key information that the SIGTARP report didn't even mention. With better access, a budget, a mandate, greater staff, and more time, the "investigator" did a poor job, yet is lauded in much of the media and in Washington as "tough." After damaging facts become public, SIGTARP "catches up." It's an embarrassment. ("Goldman's Undisclosed Role in AIG's Distress," Tavakoli, *TSF*, November 10, 2009.)

I urge the President to play the race card—the human race card. The Founding Fathers sought to protect the Republic from this tyranny of private interests. This was meant to be a place where all members of the human race have a fair opportunity to thrive.

These show trials and faux "investigations" distract us from the real job of reform and protect Wall Street's interests. It's time to bring back Black—or regulators like him—and truly give us our "Pecora" moment.

CHAPTER 12 Media Circus

ProPublica's (and *NY Times'*) "Untold" Magnetar Story Creates Excuses for Wall Street and Washington

April 19, 2010

ProPublica, Planet Money, and radio show *This American Life* recently carried stories about Magnetar, a hedge fund that profited from the housing crisis. Unfortunately, many thought it was a fresh revelation. Magnetar wasn't a previously unknown hedge fund. Magnetar did not create the synthetic CDO structure, and the magnitude of Magnetar's role in the subprime crisis has been overblown.[179]

The *New York Times* recently wrote that the synthetic CDO story has only begun to emerge in recent months, and referenced the *ProPublica* story. I was mentioned as an early critic of synthetic CDOs.[180]

Yet, more than two years ago the *Wall Street Journal* featured Merrill Lynch, Magnetar, N.I.R. and others involved in a failed synthetic CDO called Norma in a PAGE ONE investigative report on December 27, 2007, and followed up with another article on Magnetar's strategy. Even earlier, on December 17, 2007, *WSJ* had a front page article in its markets section reporting a potential legal battle involving MBIA, Wachovia, Deutsche and UBS for the cash of Sagittarius, a synthetic CDO (in which Magnetar had also invested) that had declared an event of default. The *Wall Street Journal* had done many investigative articles on value-destroying CDOs, some even earlier.[181]

The *Wall Street Journal* did some brilliant investigative reporting in the fall of 2007, and Washington did nothing. The reports were early enough to plan for the worst, take corrective action, and minimize damage. The news appeared before Bear Stearns imploded in March 2008, and the financial crisis came to a head in September 2008.

[I was quoted in all the *WSJ* articles referenced in this commentary, which is why the links were handy. *WSJ* also published many other synthetic CDO exposes as did other financial media. See also my endnote on Magnetar.]

Classic and Massive Ponzi Scheme

My book on the financial crisis, *Dear Mr. Buffett* (Wiley 2009), explains how Wall Street banks were the key architects of the largest Ponzi scheme in the history of the capital markets. Phony debt packages (RMBS, CDOs) supplied the money for unwise—often predatory and fraudulent—mortgage lending. Banks had close business relationships with (and often direct investments in) mortgage lenders and mortgage loan servicers.

Wall Street banks stuffed bad loans and bad loan packages into even more complex packages—including synthetic CDOs—to disguise problems and continue to earn bonuses. As everything started to fall apart, banks accelerated the scheme. They produced the most complex value-destroying deals in the shortest period of time. These are the classic characteristics of a Ponzi scheme, which is illegal.

Washington Ignored Pre-Crisis Media Reports

Synthetic CDOs made the financial crisis worse. Many types of financial entities were involved, and the following media warnings are only two examples that should have spurred Washington and regulators to act.

In May 2007, ten months before Bear Stearns imploded, *Business Week's* cover story exposed value-destroying synthetic CDOs in Bear Stearns Asset Management's hedge funds. (*Bloomberg News* also covered the story). The hedge funds imploded in June 2007, and Bear Stearns absorbed the hedge funds' "assets." In March 2008, JPMorgan Chase bought Bear Stearns to save it from collapse. Citigroup created synthetic CDOs with the failed Bear Stearns hedge funds. Citigroup also gave the hedge funds a $200 million loan, so it's remarkable none of this came up in last week's FCIC hearings.

In a *Wall Street Journal* article in August 2007, I asserted AIG failed to write down losses for its credit derivatives linked to synthetic CDOs. In early October 2007, the *Wall Street Journal* wrote about a value-destroying synthetic CDO involving nowdebased bond insurer MBIA. In the *WSJ's* January 14, 2008 article on Magnetar's strategy, Calyon was identified as the underwriter of a synthetic CDO called Cetus. Calyon was one of AIG's trading partners involved with other CDOs (unrelated to Magnetar)—including some done jointly with Goldman Sachs—that were purchased in the AIG bailout. AIG should never have been bailed out without pre-conditions.

Officials did nothing while the banks damaged the economy, but they acted very quickly when they needed to save the banks. In the months preceding the crisis, officials said the problem could be contained, but main stream media articles already showed they needed to perform investigations and institute financial reform.

End Note: Synthetic CDOs were well-known to professionals years before Magnetar got involved. Synthetic collateralized debt obligations, which use credit derivatives technology, made the mortgage crisis worse by enabling the cover-up of losses. In 2003, I wrote a book on the dangers of synthetic CDOs, called "*Collateralized Debt Obligations & Structured Finance.*" It includes the structure used by Magnetar and other hedge funds in the recent mortgage debacle, but the example used corporate credit risk (Wiley, 2003, Chapter Pp. 181, 194-196 in particular, combined with short mezz Pp. 261-265). I don't know the first person to use that structure, but it wasn't new. The second edition released in 2008 explains the role of structured finance in the subprime crisis in more detail. Synthetic CDOs and many other new structures were used. [I sent gratis copies of each edition to the head of every branch of the Federal Reserve system when they were first published. I also sent a copy to the Chairman (Greenspan and later Bernanke) and received an acknowledgement.]

The first edition (2003) was written before subprime lending exploded. In subsequent years, I warned about new growing problems with subprime (ABS CDOs and synthetic CDOs) at CFA conferences, professional conferences, in numerous articles, in main stream media, and at the International Monetary Fund (April 2005). The 2008 edition consolidates some of those warnings and explains the deterioration in the financial markets due to many types of corrupt structured financial products.

One of the key people at **Magnetar,** David Snyderman, was in the structured products group at Citadel in August 2004 (and joined Magnetar in mid-2005). At that time, the group he headed asked me to meet with them after reading my CDO book. They said my book gave them the idea to apply the structure to the other loan markets, but banks had already approached many hedge funds with this trade to get around post-Enron accounting issues (among other reasons). The documentation for mortgage loans had already been developed, albeit ISDA didn't issue a template until June 2005; as usual it was behind market practitioners. As I recall, Snyderman did not attend his group's meeting on that day. I declined to get involved, since my book was written as a warning, not a manual for mischief. To the best of my knowledge, the entire group left Citadel shortly thereafter and scattered to various shops.

In 1998, I wrote the first public book that explains problems with credit derivatives, *Credit Derivatives* (Wiley, 1998), before Long Term Capital Management blew up. Banks had a lot of risk to hedge funds using certain types of credit derivatives (total return swaps and esoteric credit derivatives), and I wrote that banks' exposure was too great, because hedge funds were overleveraged and could easily blow up. At the time, I sent gratis copies to the heads of several Federal Reserve Banks.

Tavakoli's Top Ten Business Books (satire)

December 13, 2010

1. *New Century: Fooling Me All of the Time or Why Improper Practices Only Matter When I'm Short and Not Earning Double-Digit Dividends,* by David Einhorn, author of *Fooling Some of the People All of the Time.*
2. *The Race to Stop the Collapse of Goldman Sachs and Exploit the Crisis,* by Henry M. Paulson, author of *On the Brink: Inside the Race to Stop the Collapse of the Global Financial System.*
3. *The End of Wall Street and the Global Takeover by Financial Oligarchs,* by Roger Lowenstein, author of *The End of Wall Street.*

4. *If Everyone is a Devil, Then No One is Responsible, Particularly not any Wall Street Bank that Your Husband May End Up Getting Paid Big Bucks to Defend*, by Bethany McLean and Joe Nocera, authors of *All the Devils Are Here.*
5. *Blame the Meltdown on Outliers Instead of Outright Liars*, by Scott Patterson, author of *The Quants: How a New Breed of Math Whizzes Conquered Wall Street and Nearly Destroyed It.*
6. *Crybaby Game: I'm Taller than You Are, and My Banking Friends Didn't Instigate Securities Fraud, Those Damn Bond Insurers are to Blame*, by Christine Richard, author of *Confidence Game: How Hedge Fund Manager Bill Ackman Called Wall Street's Bluff.*
7. *Trust Bernanke To Fund*, by Andrew Sorkin, author of *Too Big to Fail.*
8. *The Big Shortcut: Skip Hard-Hitting Facts and Excuse Fraud as Delusion*, by Michael Lewis, author of *The Big Short.*
9. *The Greatest Trade Ever: It Beats Investigative Journalism*, by Gregory Zuckerman.
10. *Buffett Dearest: If You Had a Hot Line to the Treasury, You'd Sell Your Principles Too*, by Janet Tavakoli, author of *Dear Mr. Buffett.*

Best All-Time Business Book: *The Best Way to Rob a Bank (Again and Again) Is to Own One: How Banking Executives and Politicians Looted the Global Financial System*, by William K. Black. Kindle Price: $12 Trillion (bail-out costs including government guarantees and back-stops).

2011: The Year *60 Minutes* Misled Americans About Municipal Bonds

December 20, 2011

In previous posts, I've mentioned serious fiscal problems that need to be addressed at state and local levels. This varies by region and some issues are potentially solvable.

I live in Illinois, which is ground zero for fraud, corruption, underfunded pension funds and general fiscal mismanagement. It's an example of one of the worst fiscal messes in the United

States. This year Illinois hiked personal income taxes from 3% to 5%, and increased corporate taxes. We'll be slammed with hidden tax increases in utilities, purchases, and more. When now Mayor Rahm Emanuel left his post as White House Chief of Staff to run his election, the Chicago mayoral race centered partly around steps, including budget cuts, needed to solve Chicago's serious fiscal issues.

On December 19, 2010, I was (at first) happy to see *60 Minutes* highlight fiscal problems of states and municipalities. It explained how Illinois was late on payments to service suppliers, and it's a huge problem for people doing business with the state. The state's pension fund is underfunded and although *60 Minutes* didn't mention it, state pension funds are the prey of Wall Street cronies that stuff them with losses and then propose fee-loaded leveraged financial products that are bets to make up the shortfall. Then *60 Minutes* went completely off the rails by suggesting that these problems would lead to widespread defaults on municipal bonds in 2011.[182]

A "Performance"

Instead of focusing on the implication of these problems to public services including police protection, fire departments, city maintenance, and city jobs (among other things), *60 Minutes* let a pundit claim these problems translate into near-term massive municipal bond defaults. Meredith Whitney, the pundit, had written a report, "Tragedy of the Commons," which supposedly backed her claims.

Contrary to *60 Minutes*' assertion, Meredith Whitney, a banking analyst, did not have a great track record. Gullible reporters had given her great PR for an October 31, 2007, call on Citigroup that had been correctly made many months earlier in her presence by my friend Jim Rogers, a legendary investor. They appeared on television together, and at the time she refuted Rogers. I was later bemused to see that either she or her PR flacks apparently took credit for my early warnings about serious problems at AIG.

Whitney told *60 Minutes*: "You could see 50 sizable defaults. Fifty to 100 sizeable defaults. More. This will amount to hundreds of billions of dollars' worth of defaults....It'll be something to worry about within the next 12 months."

A Wild Guess

Subsequently, Whitney wouldn't justify her analysis saying "Quantifying is a guesstimate at this point."[183] *60 Minutes* admitted it had never reviewed her much-touted report. The report never mentioned sizable defaults, only that there "invariably" would be defaults. *Bloomberg* also reported that *60 Minutes* was wrong about her "untarnished' track record. Since she started her company in 2009, about two-thirds of her stock picks underperformed market indexes. A 2008 *Fortune* cover story ranked Whitney 1,205th out of 1,919 equity analysts the previous year, based on stock picks.

Whitney told Bloomberg's reporters: "A lot of this is, you know it, but can you prove it? There are fifth-derivative dimensions that I don't think I need to spell out to my clients." As a derivatives expert I can attest that this is gibberish. But I want to hear her explanation of "fifth-derivative dimensions," because I adore a good belly laugh.

Genuine Research via Bloomberg

Bloomberg is also the financial news service that has done great early work on fraud and related municipal bond defaults, because that's a worthy story. Municipal credit issues are granular and the severity of the problem—or non-problem—depends on the specific situation.

In September 2005, *Bloomberg* broke a story about Jefferson County's hair raising problems, "The Banks that Fleeced Alabama," by Martin Z. Braun, Darrell Preston and Liz Willen. According to the article, "taxpayers blame the $160 million in fees JPMorgan Chase and other banks have charged to arrange the county's financing—in deals that were never put out to bid." This year, Jefferson County filed for bankruptcy.

As the year wore on, Meredith Whitney waffled and by May she told a *Bloomberg* radio host: "In the cycle of this municipal downturn, I stand by it. But we never had a specific estimate for that." Fortunately, Joe Mysak, a *Bloomberg* print reporter, exposed that for the nonsense it was. Whitney had indeed given a one-year time frame on *60 Minutes* and had called for hundreds of billions of dollars in defaults with 50 to 100 or more sizable defaults.[184]

A Stellar Performance

Whitney's prediction of "hundreds of billions" of defaults was way off the mark. Even with Jefferson County's $943 million filing, defaults for 2011 were down from 2010. Bonds that dipped into reserves to make payments totaled only $24.6 billion according to Richard Lehmann, publisher of the Distressed Debt Securities Newsletter. Defaults defined as bonds that missed payments are down to only $2.1 billion from $2.8 billion in 2010. In 2011, municipal bonds had stellar performance as an asset class returning more than 10% of potentially tax exempt returns. They beat the S&P, treasuries, corporate bonds and most commodities.[185]

CNBC Schools 60 Minutes

As for the actual analysis in Meredith Whitney's "Tragedy of the Commons" report, it seems that it had serious flaws, at least when it came to Nevada.

Nevada State Treasurer Kate Marshall appeared on CNBC to debunk Whitney's claim that Nevada's municipal bonds were troubled. Marshall challenged Whitney's analytics saying (among other things) that Whitney apparently misinterpreted a PEW report on pension plan liabilities. Nevada only represented 1/16th of the plan, and state employees pick up half the tab. Marshall then explained why Nevada's municipal bond claims paying ability is much better than it would appear to the casual observer. The economy was still tough, but Nevada managed in anticipation of the ongoing crunch. Property tax revenues dropped, but sales tax revenues were up, gambling revenue was up, and business modified tax revenues were up. Her cash position in June 2011 was much better than 2010.

CHAPTER 13 The Eurozone

Wall Street's Advice to the IMF: Control Your Alleged Rapists! (satire)

May 22, 2011

We are outraged by your lack of empathy for your victims! We're not talking about the targets of your sexual advances, of course. We mean us.

You're supposed to be bailing out trading partners, bankers in weak foreign countries bankrupted by bailouts. Remember, you pigs are supposed to be financially raping the citizens of the PIIGS (Portugal, Italy, Ireland, Greece and Spain). We'll get back to that shortly, but first we have to address some housekeeping.

Jeopardizing Our Health

Condoms aren't foolproof, and HIV doesn't care how much you paid for a hooker in Thailand. It has come to our attention that you have allegedly been customers of our New York based suppliers of prostitutes, and we're furious.

We need you to stick to the job. Moreover, if you had just listened to our advice to Joran van der Sloot, you wouldn't be caught allegedly doing anything in the wrong place at the wrong time.

Targets Can Shoot Back

As for the handling of your internal matters, it was a nice touch to call newly resigned IMF head and alleged sex offender Dominique Strauss-Kahn's 2008 affair with a subordinate a "serious breach of judgment" and impose no real consequences. It was a great move to reportedly decline investigations and consequences for other managers involved in suspect activities. It's well known that a permissive atmosphere enables harassment (and more) and dismays the targets who perceive they will get no support. This is exactly the kind of thing we do all the time, but you have to save all this good stuff for your next high profile job in finance or politics.[186]

Until now, your internal targets felt so intimidated you were able to sweep all this under the rug. You can't count on that anymore with all the new publicity you've brought on yourselves.

Targets have caught on that they have nothing to lose and at least can gain back the self-esteem you've tried to destroy. Targets' careers are already embattled, so it is in their interest to take action, and they're not going to apologize for standing up for themselves.

Moreover, it's a snap to see through the flaws in the IMF's new "policy." You say that when it comes to intimate relationships, you will investigate if there is evidence of harassment. Obviously, the complainer will have to produce the evidence. But how has letting you handle things worked out so far for targets?

Targets will never buy that nonsense now. They'll tell you to stuff it and act independently. Targets have a right to treat this as a matter of personal safety. When it comes to the topic of their personal safety, you have nothing to add.

The IMF Can't Even Negotiate "Consensual Sex"

Even when sexual relations between your bosses and subordinates apparently begin as consensual, the IMF inspires targets to rebel. According to the *New York Times*: "One woman is said to have slept with her supervisor, who then gave her poor performance reviews to pressure her into continuing with the relationship."[187]

We must point out that if you want someone to continue a sexual relationship, tell them their performance was great. In the battle of the sexes, he declared thermonuclear warfare!

Remember Whom You're Supposed to Be Screwing

This may sound as if we've developed a conscience, but don't worry, we haven't. The truth is that we need you to do as we say and not as we do for a change.

We need you to keep bailing out weak countries like Ireland. Many of Ireland's bankers fled the country, and the people of Ireland are drowning in their debt.

We love the way the IMF forced a loan on the Irish to pay off the government debt that was forced on them to pay off the bankers' debts. To get the bailout loan, the Irish government had to slash spending, lay off tens of thousands of public workers, lower wages, increase taxes, and cut health care budgets. The bankers got away with financial murder, and the citizens are paying for it, just the way we like it.

Instead of letting banks fail or restructuring banks, we need you to do the same thing to Greece and possibly other countries, too. The Greeks are already protesting: "We're not Ireland!" Your recent scandals may encourage them to get even more insistent and come up with an alternative of their own.

We do lots of business with these foreign banks and governments. So stop spending so much energy trying to screw each other and spend it screwing the citizens of countries with governments that need bailouts because they bailed out bankers.

Clean up your act, so that we don't have to clean up ours!

Euro Endgame

June 1, 2011

The European Central Bank (ECB) is facing a dilemma similar to that faced by major U.S. banks in the 1980s with defaulted loans to Latin America. The PIIGS (Portugal, Ireland, Italy, Greece and Spain) collectively require debt write-downs that exceed banks' capital and reserves, and the tantrums of Jean-Claude Trichet, President of the ECB, won't change that fact.

The crazy but true strategy so far has been "Don't call bad debt, bad debt"—at least not openly. The continued attempt to "convert" bad loans to good loans by lending bad debtors more money so they can pay interest on bad loans, makes it temporarily unnecessary for Eurozone Banks and other debt holders to take write-downs.

Greece provides one example. The current last-ditch attempt by the IMF and Eurozone Banks is to impose on Greece exogenous wage deflation under the guise of "internal devaluation," higher retirement age and pension reforms, reduced spending protocols, and "privatization" of Greek assets by foreigners. Greece is coming under pressure to sell crown jewels like Thessaloniki Water and

Sewage and Piraeus Port Authority. Greek citizens may view that as robbery, since it will only provide enough to make interest payments on debt for a short period to help the ECB cover up its problems. This benefits the Eurozone banks that are in denial, but it doesn't help Greece.

The most egregious mistake is the attempt to impose exogenous reform of Greece's inefficient and often ineffective tax collection system. Similar to Iceland, Greek citizens may object to outside interference, demand a vote, and repudiate Greek debt, especially since there is a widespread perception that crony capitalism enriched irresponsible bankers and connected government officials while saddling disenfranchised Greek citizens with a multi-generation bill. Greeks invented democracy and they may be inspired by a slogan of the American Revolution: "No Taxation without Representation!"

Greece will have to impose fiscal restraint. The austerity measures forced on Greece from the Eurozone will be more onerous than those Greece will have to impose on itself, if it takes back control of its own currency and devalues it.

Euro: Super Deutsche Mark with a French Accent

The immediate crisis is in Greece, but it is not alone. It is futile to blame the citizens of deadbeat borrower countries, and given the flaws in the European Union, it isn't entirely their fault. The Euro is a super Deutsche Mark with a French accent. There was no Renaissance of manufacturing and productive jobs in the outer reaches of the Eurozone.

When you're overleveraged, your entire future depends on cash flow, and the cash flow isn't there for countries like Greece. The ECB is threatening to cut Greece off from bank liquidity—triggering Greek bank failures—if there is any restructuring of Greek debt. But the cash flow isn't there to service and repay existing debt, and even selling off assets won't change the long-term situation for Greece.

The ECB alone bought €75 billion in government bonds, and €45 billion or around 60% of them are Greek debt. Despite JPMorgan's estimate of around €81 billion in capital and reserves for other European banks to sustain a 50% haircut in various government bonds, it likely isn't enough given that government bonds aren't the only challenges the banks face.

The ECB's problem and the problem for many Eurozone banks is that they do not want to mark their bonds to market. They don't want to know what the debt is really worth, and it's not worth anything near what they're telling themselves it is worth. Threatening Greece so that they can cover up the problem is only a temporary fix, and it isn't fooling anyone.

Deep Discounts: If PIIGS Owe You Money, You're in Trouble

Given that no one wants to face the magnitude of the problem, it is difficult to say how bad this can get, but history gives us an example of what needs to be done. In the late 1980s if U.S. banks had marked-to-market their Latin American debt, the losses would have wiped out the capital of Bank of America and Manufacturers Hanover (now part of JPMorgan Chase). Citibank was close to being wiped out. Other banks were also on the ropes: Irving Trust (now part of Bank of New York Mellon), First Chicago (now part of JPMorgan Chase), and Continental (later seized by the FDIC due to other bad loans).

By the end of 1987, Latin American debt ranged from around 15 cents on the dollar for Bolivian debt to around 35 cents on the dollar for Argentine debt. Market value estimates at the time recognized a valid appraisal method based on the fact that the U.S. had forgiven a large chunk of Mexico's debt and restructured it.

After Latin American countries defaulted on debts, the subsequent granular restructuring negotiations resulted in various dollar-denominated Brady Bonds, named for then U.S. Treasury Secretary Nicholas Brady. Each country negotiated its own terms. In the earlier Mexican debt restructuring for example, half of the $20 billion debt was forgiven, and the principal of the other half of the debt was secured with a zero coupon UST bond then trading at around $2 billion of the $10 billion face value (the other half of the original debt). Mexico then had to meet the interest payments to service the $10 billion bond.

Greece is a sovereign country. The ECB is acting as if it can dictate terms to Greece, but as U.S. banks found out, when someone owes you a lot of money and they cannot pay it back, you are in as much trouble—and sometimes in more trouble—as they are.

Endgame for the Euro

The crisis the Eurozone now faces is that citizens of countries with the most fiscally irresponsible governments and banks may be of a mind to vote out their current governments and repudiate their debt. If the ECB keeps storming out of meetings and isn't willing to engage in meaningful negotiations, then it will be in Greece's best interest to exit the Euro. The ECB can threaten all it likes, but it is dealing with sovereign states.

Greece can exit the Euro, implement its own austerity programs, force a renegotiation of its debt, and devalue its own currency. If politicians dig in their heels at the expense of Greek citizens, the Euro will likely end not with a whimper, but with a bang, and other distressed debtor countries may follow suit.

"Standard" Credit Default Swaps on Greece Are a Sham and It's Not a Surprise

October 27, 2011

At least it's not a surprise to any financial professional that has paid attention to the false reassurances that the International Swaps and Derivatives Association, Inc. (ISDA) has given over the years to naïve participants in the credit derivatives market.

"Customers" that accepted ISDA documentation when buying credit default protection on Greece are now discovering that ISDA defends the position that a 50% discount on Greek debt is "voluntary" and therefore not a credit event for credit default swap payment purposes according to its documents.[188] This makes the ISDA "standard" credit default swap (CDS) ineffective as a hedge for the widened spreads (reduced price) of Greek debt, and it makes it ineffective as a protection against default using reasonable standards of impairment to define default. ISDA can defend ambiguous definitions so that payment on the credit default swap is virtually impossible.

First Step in a CDS: Protect Yourself from the ISDA Cartel

As previous sovereign problems have illustrated, the only way to buy protection is to rewrite the flawed ISDA "standard" document and agree to new more sensible terms, before concluding the initial trade. One has to first protect oneself from the ISDA cartel "standard" documentation before one can buy sovereign default protection, or any other protection for that matter.

I explained the need to rewrite ISDA documentation in some detail to the IMF in April 2005. In the intervening years ISDA documentation changed, but the need to rewrite it remained the same. I cannot stress enough that the International Swaps and Derivatives Association, Inc. (ISDA) "standard" documentation touted by that organization does a grave disservice to unwary credit default protection buyers. The first thing a credit derivatives trader needs to do when presented with such a document is to rewrite it and agree upon new terms before the trade. There is no such thing as "standard" documentation in the credit derivatives market, particularly the sovereign credit derivatives market.

Credit default swap documentation has a long history of problems. This isn't the first time investors have been burned in the sovereign credit default swap market. Hedge funds Eternity Global Master Fund Ltd. and HBK Master Fund LP thought they purchased protection against an Argentina default and sued when J.P. Morgan refused to pay off on Argentina credit protection contracts they had purchased.

At issue was the definition of restructuring. Did Argentina's "voluntary debt exchange" in November of 2001 meet the definition of a restructuring? The Republic of Argentina gave bondholders the option to turn in their bonds in exchange for secured loans backed by certain Argentine federal tax revenues. J.P. Morgan claimed this didn't meet the definition of restructuring, at least for the protection it sold to Eternity.

J.P. Morgan's story was different when it wanted to collect on the protection it bought from Daehon, a South Korean Bank. J.P. Morgan claimed its slightly different contract language met the definition of restructuring under the credit default protection contract it had with the South Korean Bank.

In other words, J.P. Morgan made sure its contract language would allow it to get paid when it bought protection and would make it harder for its counterparty to get paid when it sold protection.

Language Arbitrage: You're Not a Sucker, You're a Customer

Banks that play this game call it "language arbitrage." Anyone that bought sovereign credit protection on Greece after accepting ISDA "standard" documentation without modifying the language now finds that they are on the wrong side of an "arbitrage." An arbitrage is a riskless money pump. In this case, it means that money has been pumped out of credit default protection buyers with no risk to their counterparties, the financial institutions that ostensibly sold them credit default protection on Greece.

CHAPTER 14 MF Global Implodes

Credit Derivatives and Leverage Sank MF Global

November 4, 2011

MF Global imploded this week due to proprietary "repo-to-maturity" transactions that are in substance total return swaps, a type of credit derivative. MF Global failed to meet margin calls on credit derivatives linked to risky fixed income debt. Regulators haven't learned much from American International Group's (AIG) and Long Term Capital Management's (LTCM) debacles. Like the "repo-to-maturity" transaction, a total return swap is an off balance sheet transaction treated as a sale, but the total return receiver, MF Global, is long both the price and credit default risk of the reference assets. The total return payer, not MF Global, is technically the legal owner of the reference assets. The attraction of this arrangement is financing and leverage. Naturally, ratings downgrades will trigger increased margin calls. This is all business as (un)usual.

MF Global Admitted "Diverting" Money from Segregated Accounts

What isn't usual is diverting money from segregated customer accounts. It's too late to blame "sloppiness, bookkeeping, or accounting." MF Global admitted it "diverted" money from customers' segregated accounts.

The fact that MF Global was exposed to default risk and liquidity risk because of its "repo-to-maturity" transactions and that the risk was linked to European sovereign debt was disclosed in MF Global's 10K for the year ending March 31, 2011, a required financial statement filed with the SEC.[189] The CFTC and other regulators had the information right under their noses, but it appears they didn't understand that they were looking at a leveraged credit derivative transaction that could lead to margin calls that MF Global would be unable to meet.

Even if all the money can eventually be recovered, it doesn't change the fact the MF Global took impermissible steps.

Liar's Poker

Here's a crazy but true side note. Michael Stockman, the chief risk officer of MF Global (as of January 2011), was in our Liar's Poker training class lampooned by another classmate, Michael Lewis.

More Liar's Poker

Last week when customers asked for excess cash from their accounts, MF Global stalled. According to a commodity fund manager I spoke with, MF Global's first stall tactic was to claim it lost wire transfer instructions. Then instead of sending an overnight check, it sent the money snail mail, including checks for hundreds of thousands of dollars. The checks bounced. After the checks bounced, the amounts were still debited from customer accounts and no one at MF Global could or would reverse the check entries. The manager has had to intervene to get MF Global to correct this.

Rogue Trader and Questionable Risk Management

Gary Gensler, Jon Corzine's former Goldman Sachs colleague and current head of the Commodity Futures Trading Commission (CFTC), had reason to be concerned about MF Global's risk management. In early 2008, a rogue trader racked up $141.5 million in losses in unauthorized trades that exceeded his trading limits.[190] It seems he accomplished this in under seven hours. In August of this year, MF Global and the underwriters of its 2007 initial public stock offering (IPO) paid around $90 million to settle claims by investors that they were misled about MF Global's risk management prior to the rogue trader's actions. Since 2008, MF Global's financial condition has been nothing to brag about.[191]

CFTC's Unprecedented Failure to Move Customers' Assets Before FCM's Bankruptcy

The exchange-traded futures markets have been shaken to the core. The Bankruptcy Code apparently conflicts with the

Commodity Exchange Act, so customers of MF Global have less protection than they otherwise might have had. In the past, the exchanges and CFTC "always" moved customer positions before a Futures Commission Merchant (FCM) declared bankruptcy. The CFTC had ample reason to have contingency plans for MF Global based on publicly available information. Yet the Gensler-led CFTC hasn't followed this historical precedent when an FCM led by his former Goldman colleague teetered on the edge of bankruptcy.

Endnote: The "repo-to-maturity" transaction which was treated as a sale is indeed in substance a total return swap, contrary to what damage control spin-doctors may say. The "repo-to-maturity" label is simply a wolf in sheep's clothing. Total return swaps (and the transactions labeled "repo-to-maturity") are also a credit derivative. MF Global itself disclosed the fact it sought sale treatment for this "repo" transaction while retaining the price and default risk. Regulators seemed at a loss as to how to interpret the substance versus the form. For more on credit derivatives and total return swaps, see also either the first or second editions of my book (Wiley 1998, 2001): Credit Derivatives & Synthetic Structures: A Guide to Instruments and Applications.

*****

MF Global Revelations Keep Getting Worse

November 21, 2011

- Shortfall estimated at $1.2 billion or more (up from $600 million)
- "Repo-to-Maturity" is a "Total Return Swap-to-Maturity," a Type of Credit Derivative
- Probable Shortfalls Throughout 2011
- Regulators Waive Required Tests for Jon Corzine
- Questions About How MF Global Became a Primary Dealer
- MF Global Wrote Rubber Checks for some Electronic Checks for Others
- Tip-Offs for Some Customers?
- CFTC's Gary Gensler Didn't Act
- MF Global Debacle Damages a Key Global Market

When MF Global collapsed on October 31, it was the biggest financial firm to collapse since Lehman in September 2008. Then Chairman and CEO Jon Corzine is connected to the head of one of his key regulators, the Commodity Futures Trading Commission (CFTC), through his former protégé at Goldman Sachs, Gary Gensler. Prior to becoming the CEO of MF Global, Jon Corzine was the 54th Governor of New Jersey, a U.S. Senator from New Jersey, and the CEO of Goldman Sachs.

Corzine also knows the Fed's William Dudley, a key member of the Fed's Open Market Committee, from their days at Goldman Sachs. The Fed approved MF Global's status as a primary dealer, a participant in the Fed's Open Market Operations, less than one year after Jon Corzine took its helm and beached it on a reef called leveraged credit risk.

MF Global's officers admitted to federal regulators that before the collapse, the firm diverted cash from customers' accounts that were supposed to be segregated:[192]

> MF Global Holdings LTD. "violated requirements that it keep clients' collateral separate from its own accounts...Craig Donohue, CME Group's chief executive officer, said on a conference call with analysts today that MF Global isn't in compliance with the rules of the exchange and the Commodity Futures Trading Commission."[193]

Cash in customers' accounts may be invested in allowable transactions, and MF was allowed to make extra revenue from the income. But what isn't allowed, and what MF Global apparently admitted to doing, is to commingle customers' money with its own and take money from customers' accounts to meet margin calls on MF Global's own allowable transactions. Even if all of the money is eventually clawed back and recovered, this remains an impermissible act. Moreover, full recovery—even if it is possible—is not the same as restitution. People have been denied access to their money, and businesses and reputations have been tarnished.

In layman's terms, you may buy a Rolls Royce with customers' excess cash, sell it at a profit, and pocket part of the profits. You may buy a Rolls Royce and try to resell it at a profit with your firm's cash. But you aren't allowed to take customers' money to make the car payments on your firm's Rolls Royce. If one engages in this impermissible activity, it becomes almost impossible to cover up if you have an accident driving your Rolls Royce.

Implausible Denial and an Ugly Surprise

On November 1, Kenneth Ziman, a lawyer for MF Global, relayed information from MF Global to U.S. Bankruptcy judge Martin Glenn in Manhattan: "To the best knowledge of management, there is no shortfall." If that sounded like a cover-up, it was, unless of course you prefer to believe that the "best knowledge" of management is actually no knowledge at all.

How long does it take to find more than $600 million to $1.2 billion of customers' money? MF Global's books seem so messed up that one person couldn't have created this chaos alone. A lot of people had to agree to throw away controls, standards, and procedures. I doubt this happened just in the final week or two before MF Global blew itself up.

> According to a U.S. official, MF Global admitted to federal regulators early Monday [October 31, 2011] that money was missing from customer accounts. MF Global acknowledged a shortfall in a phone call amid mounting questions from regulators as they went through the firm's books.[194]

The initial bankruptcy estimate was a shortfall of around $600 million. As of Monday November 21, MF Global's liquidating trustee believes the shortfall may be as much as $1.2 billion and possibly even more. (The final figure was $1.6 billion.)[195]

"Repo-to-Maturity" is a "Total Return Swap-to-Maturity," A Type of Credit Derivative

If you call a total return swap-to-maturity a "repo-to-maturity," you are much less likely to freak out regulators. Many regulators still remember that Long Term Capital Management (LTCM) used total return swaps (among other things). Jon Corzine should remember, too, since he was closely involved with LTCM when he headed Goldman Sachs. In September of 2011, FINRA seemed to catch on that MF Global's transactions were riskier than it previously thought and asked for more capital against these trades.

Part of AIG's acute distress in 2008 was due to credit default swaps, another type of credit derivative, linked to the risk of shady overrated collateralized debt obligations. The basic problem was risk on fixed income assets that could only go down in value combined with lots of leverage.

I'd like to interject a side note. I understand that some pundits tried to say that the *New York Times's* Gretchen Morgenson was incorrect when she wrote MF Global was felled by derivative bets.[196] She is correct. The pundits leaped to the conclusion that when she referred to credit derivatives and "swaps" that she meant credit default swaps, but she was referring to total return swaps, a type of credit derivative. (Later in the article she discussed a different topic, lack of transparency in credit default swaps, another type of credit derivative.)

MF Global's problematic trades were different from AIG's, but they were also derivatives, in fact, they were a form of credit derivative. The "repo-to-maturity" transaction was just a form over substance gimmick to disguise this fact. Specifically the transactions are total return swaps, a type of credit derivative, and the chief purpose of these transactions is leverage.

A total return swap-to-maturity includes a type of credit derivative. It allows you to sell a bond you own and get off-balance sheet financing in the form of a total return swap. Alternatively, you can get off-balance sheet financing on a bond with risk you want (but do not currently own so there is no need to sell anything) and take the risk of the default and price risk. (Price risk can be due both to credit risk and/or interest rate risk.) This is an off-balance sheet transaction in which the total return receiver (MF Global) has both the price risk and the default risk of the reference bonds. In this case, MF Global had the price risk and the default risk of $6.3 billion of the sovereign debt of Belgium, Italy, Spain, Portugal, and Ireland. As it happened, the price fluctuations of this debt in 2011 weren't due to a general rise in interest rates, they were due to a general increase in the perceived credit risk of this debt.

Repo transactions are on balance sheet transactions, but they don't draw as much scrutiny from regulators. There was just one little problem. MF Global wanted the off-balance sheet treatment of a derivative, a total return swap, but it didn't want to call it a total return swap, so it used smoke and mirrors. Even if MF Global engaged in a wash trade at the end (if there is no default in the meantime) to buy back the bonds, MF Global would receive par on the bonds from the maturing bonds. The repurchase trade at maturity is a formality with no real (or material) economic consequence.

In other words, the "repo-to-maturity" exploits a form-over-substance trick to avoid calling this transaction a total return swap. Accountants paid by the form-over-substance seekers and asleep-at-the-switch regulators will sometimes, at least temporarily, go along with this sort of relabeling.

The fact that MF Global was exposed in a leveraged way to default risk and liquidity risk because of these transactions and that the risk was linked to European sovereign debt was disclosed in MF Global's 10K for the year ending March 31, 2011, a required financial statement filed with the SEC. The CFTC and other regulators had the information right under their noses, but it appears they didn't understand that they were looking at a leveraged credit derivative transaction that could lead to margin calls that MF Global would be unable to meet.

The result is that yet another large financial institution has been felled when it couldn't meet margin calls due to the credit risk of fixed income assets combined with high leverage in an off-balance sheet transaction. The ugliest part of this story, however, isn't that MF Global got in over its head, it's that the bankruptcy trustee estimates customers' money to the tune of $1.2 billion or more is still missing.

Probable Shortfalls Throughout 2011

MF Global reportedly employed 35:1 leverage—some reports are 40:1—against a portfolio comprised around 20% of European Sovereign risks including Belgium, Italy, Spain, Portugal, and Ireland. MF Global would have had several trading days in 2011 with moves of 5% to 10% on this sovereign risk. MF Global was so thinly capitalized that this trade alone could eat up half of its capital. Any of MF Global's other asset positions moving the same way in 2011's highly correlated markets would have put MF Global in a position of negative equity. From a risk management point of view, examiners have to consider the very strong possibility that MF Global had several negative equity days throughout 2011.

How did MF Global meet margin calls throughout 2011? It seems an investigation into money flows throughout 2011 is in order.

By the end of October, the combination of a $90 million August legal settlement against MF Global coming due, increased capital calls by FINRA, and margin hikes from counterparties worried about MF Global's credit made it impossible for MF Global to cover up its shortfall.

Regulators Waive Required Tests for Jon Corzine

Jon Corzine resigned as Chairman and CEO of MF Global on November 4, 2011, just days after the October 31 bankruptcy announcement.[197] As a matter of corporate governance, holding the position of Chairman and CEO meant that Corzine had a lot of concentrated power with little oversight. Many question the wisdom of a corporate structure that allows officers to hold this dual position. (Ken Lewis, the former Chairman and CEO that merged Bank of America into the poorhouse held this dual role, too. Lewis defended this practice at the Federal Reserve Bank of Chicago's Bank Structure Conference in 2003.) Corzine was the former governor of New Jersey and had been out of the active markets for twelve years. Prior to that, until 1999 he had been the CEO of Goldman Sachs.

The Financial Industry Regulatory Authority Inc. (FINRA) gave Jon Corzine a waiver from his Series 7 and Series 24 exams when he took the helm of MF Global in March 2010. The former is required for anyone involved in the investment banking or securities business including supervision, solicitation, or training of persons associated with MF Global, and that included Corzine. As an officer of MF Global the latter was required for Corzine, since he had been out of the business for around 12 years or more than six times the 2 year expiration date for reactivating these qualifications.[198]

Jon Corzine to Credit Derivatives Head: Next Time "Double Up" (See note below)

The test waiver by regulators seems to be blatant cronyism, because Corzine not only hadn't been involved in the day-to-day markets for more than a decade, his responsibilities at MF Global included active decision making. The waiver wasn't justified. Corzine reportedly authored the strategy for the MF Global killing trades, and he also had authority on the trading floor.

Jon Corzine pushed traders to increase their risk. According to an MF Global employee, Corzine knelt down beside Jim Parascandola, head of credit derivatives trading, and told him that next time he should "double up" on his winning protection bets on brokerages. Traders loved Corzine, because he pushed them to increase risk. Now the traders aren't lifting offers, they're pounding the pavement. ***Update*:** Subsequent to this report Jim Parascandola told me that he was never told to increase the size of any position, albeit his trades were profitable.

MF Global Becomes a Primary Dealer Unregulated by the Fed: How Did That Happen?

MF Global's financials were shaky ever since Man Group spun it off in 2005 and saddled it with a lot of debt. Yet MF Global was added to the Fed's list of 22 primary dealers in February 2011, less than one year after former Goldman CEO Jon Corzine officially came on board. Primary dealers buy and sell U.S. treasuries at auction and are a counterparty to the Fed's Open Market operations.[199]

William C. Dudley is the president and chief executive officer of the FRBNY. He is also vice chairman of the Federal Open Market Committee (FOMC) and VP of the Markets Group, which oversees open market and foreign exchange trading operations and provisions of account services to foreign central banks and manages the System Open Market Account. Dudley is a former partner at Goldman Sachs (1986-2007), and he was Goldman's chief economist.

David Kotok of Cumberland Advisors has raised important questions about the fact that the Fed has dropped its role of surveillance of primary dealers. Besides trading treasuries, the big benefit to primary dealers is the perception that the Fed will provide funding to primary dealers during a systemic liquidity crunch. Just before Bear Stearns imploded, the Fed changed the rules so that non-U.S. banks, along with brokers that were primary dealers (as MF Global later became), were allowed to borrow through a program called a Term Securities Lending Facility (TSLF) to finance mortgage backed securities, asset backed securities, and more. TSLF's start date was too late to help Bear Stearns, and the program has now been discontinued, but the perception of a Fed safety net has precedence.

Why did the Fed award prestigious primary dealer status to a shaky operation like MF Global, an entity it does not regulate?

MF Global Stalled and Wrote Rubber Checks

The week before the bankruptcy, when customers asked for excess cash from their accounts, MF Global stalled. According to a commodity fund manager I spoke with, MF Global's first stall tactic was to claim it lost wire transfer instructions. Instead of issuing an electronic check or sending an overnight check, MF Global sent paper checks via snail mail, including checks for hundreds of thousands of dollars. The checks bounced. After the checks bounced, the amounts were still debited from customer accounts, and no one at MF Global could or would reverse the check entries. The manager has had to intervene to get MF Global to correct this, and still hasn't gotten the entries corrected.[200]

Tip-Offs for Some Customers?

In August, customers started pulling billions of dollars out of their segregated accounts with MF Global. It was the biggest outflow of funds since January 2009. The bankruptcy trustee may claw back transfers of funds from MF Global as it was teetering, because it is likely that employees within MF Global were well aware of the problems and tipped off key customers.[201]

Yet Gary Gensler, head of the CFTC, did not investigate or begin transferring accounts out of MF Global before the bankruptcy, and that is unprecedented for the CFTC. Given that Gary Gensler was a protégé of Jon Corzine at Goldman Sachs, one should question why Gary Gensler didn't act and why he should be allowed to remain head of the CFTC.

CFTC's Gary Gensler Didn't Act

Gary Gensler, Jon Corzine's former Goldman Sachs colleague and current head of the Commodity Futures Trading Commission (CFTC), had reason to be concerned about MF Global's risk management. In early 2008, a rogue trader racked up $141.5 million in losses in unauthorized trades that exceeded his trading limits. It seems he accomplished this in under seven hours. In August of this year, MF Global and the underwriters of its 2007 initial public stock offering (IPO) agreed to pay around $90 million to settle claims by investors that they were misled about MF Global's risk management prior to the rogue trader's actions. Since 2008, MF Global's financial condition has been nothing to brag about. Now the settlement is in jeopardy due to the bankruptcy. [Michael Stockman, the chief risk officer of MF Global as of January 2011 (after the previous mentioned incident) was in my Liar's Poker training class lampooned by another classmate, Michael Lewis.]

In the past, the exchanges and CFTC "always" moved customer positions before a Futures Commission Merchant (FCM) declared bankruptcy. The CFTC had ample reason to have contingency plans for MF Global based on publicly available information. Yet the Gensler-led CFTC hasn't followed this historical precedent when an FCM led by his former Goldman colleague teetered on the edge of bankruptcy. Gensler has recused himself from the CFTC's probe of MF Global.[202]

The exchange-traded futures markets have been shaken to the core. The Bankruptcy Code apparently conflicts with the Commodity Exchange Act, so customers of MF Global have less protection than one might expect. The Securities Investor Protection Corporation (SIPC) is not the FDIC. Account holders have no idea how long it will take to get back all of their money, if it is there to be recovered, and right now, it appears a lot of it cannot be found. This is why many traders sweep all of the excess cash out of their accounts each day, and only put in cash when required.

MF Global Debacle Damages a Key Global Market

The "risk wizards" of Goldman Sachs once again look like market wrecking balls. The futures market is a globally connected market and it is a key mechanism for farmers, metals miners, and metals fabricators (among others) to hedge their risk. Confidence in the futures market has been shaken. No one knows if their money is safe, but what is more disturbing is the appearance of crony capitalism once again giving favored treatment, lax regulation, and absent oversight to a crony capitalist that abused all of these perks to blow up a large financial firm and damage a key global market.

Is Crony Capitalism Wrong?

December 3, 2011

On Nov. 29, 2011, *Bloomberg* magazine's Richard Teitelbaum published an article revealing a secret meeting on July 21, 2008, with then secretary of the treasury and former Goldman Sachs CEO Hank Paulson, and around a dozen hedge-fund managers and Wall Street executives.

Five of the hedge fund managers were former Goldman Sachs employees. The meeting was held at the offices of the founder of hedge fund Eton Park Capital Management, Eric Mindich, a former 15-year employee of Goldman Sachs who rose to be the senior strategy officer of Goldman's executive office. He is also current chair of the asset managers' committee of the President's Working Group on Capital Markets.

Then Secretary Paulson asked the hedge fund managers what the market might think if he placed mortgage giants Fannie Mae and Freddie Mac into conservatorship, a move that would have wiped out value for the shareholders and possibly wiped out value for subordinated debt holders.

According to the article, one hedge fund manager had a short position in these stocks when he walked into the meeting. He was shocked that Secretary Paulson blabbed specifics, and the hedge fund managers therefore believed the Treasury Department would implement the plan. Seven weeks later, it did.

The hedge fund manager called his lawyer at a break in the meeting, and his lawyer told him Paulson had divulged non-public material information. His lawyer advised him to stop trading in the shares of these companies immediately. Ironically, that meant the hedge fund manager could not cover his short positions, so he profited by riding the value of the shares all the way down to the bottom. If he hadn't been at the meeting, and if he had any doubts, he might have covered his short position earlier and made less money. One will never know, because Secretary Paulson tied the hedge fund manager's hands.

But the more interesting implication is for the other managers in attendance. If they didn't already have a short position in Fannie Mae and Freddie Mac, they now had non-public material information that would allow them to almost certainly profit mightily by initiating such a trade. They could even be more confident in shorting other financial institutions that would likely take a shellacking.

Richard Teitelbaum quoted me: "What is this but crony capitalism? Most people have had their fill of it."

Meanwhile, then Secretary Paulson told the public a different story than he told the meeting attendees. According to *Bloomberg's* research, earlier that day, Paulson told the *New York Times* that the

Federal Reserve and the Office of the Comptroller of the Currency were inspecting Fannie and Freddie's books and he expected the result of this would inspire confidence. The *New York Times's* article appeared the following day. Any investor in the shares of Fannie and Freddie would be less likely to sell their shares in the face of this reassuring message.[203]

There is no way of knowing [without an investigation into non-public trading records] whether the hedge fund managers initiated new trades as a result of this meeting, but the key issue is that then Secretary of the Treasury Paulson communicated non-public material information that could financially benefit the recipients at the public's expense.

Apparent Damage Control: That's How They Roll

On Wednesday, Nov. 30, 2011, I got a call from a staffer for Congressman Michael Quigley (D., IL.). Congressman Quigley represents Illinois's 5th district. He replaced Rahm Emanuel, the current mayor of Chicago, in a special election after Rahm resigned to become White House Chief of Staff. (Note added 12/4: Rahm Emanuel was on Freddie Mac's Board in 2000 and 2001, a period during which its regulator said the board "failed in its duty to follow up on matters brought to its attention.") Rod Blagojevich preceded Rahm Emanuel. Blagojevich was elected governor in 2002 and was subsequently impeached for corruption and misconduct and convicted of one count of lying to the FBI. He awaits sentencing.

Congressman Quigley's staffer called because he saw my quote in the *Bloomberg* article. He claimed he was looking for clarification of my position, and I stated the article accurately reflected my viewpoint. But the staffer seemed to me to defend the meeting.

The staffer said this kind of meeting "happens all the time." I retorted, "Really? What's the excuse?"

He then claimed he was just trying to play "devil's advocate." But don't we have a surplus of those?

The staffer claimed that people want to discuss regulations with people who might be affected. I responded that this excuse is ludicrous. Then Secretary of the Treasury Paulson discussed material non-public information about the restructuring of Fannie

Mae and Freddie Mac with people who were in a position to profit at the expense of the public. I cut the phone call short at that point.

I would like to give my local politician the benefit of the doubt that a staffer wasn't acting as an errand boy trying to send a message, but that phone call didn't give me much to work with. It seems that whether it is Henry Paulson working for a Republican administration or a Democratic errand boy doing apparent damage control, it looks as if we're steeped in bi-partisan sleaze. If the staffer was merely playing the fool, then U.S. citizens needn't suffer them gladly. [Note added December 6, 2011. Please see clarification below. Mr. Quigley clarified that we share mutual position.[204]]

Breach of Then Treasury Secretary Paulson's Duty as a Public Steward

This is from the Department of Treasury's website:

> Treasury's mission highlights its role as the steward of U.S. economic and financial systems, and as an influential participant in the world economy.[205]

It seems to me that the secretary of the treasury is a civil servant and a public steward. When then Secretary Paulson offered material non-public information to hedge fund managers that could profit by trading shares (initiating new shorts) of Fannie Mae and Freddie Mac while telling the public a different story, he breached those duties.

Public service is just a social contract, and as one fund manager observed, "So are the Ten Commandments."

What do we, as Americans, stand for and how much of this can we stand? What are we willing to tolerate or not tolerate from our public servants? Where did we go so wrong that congressional staffers—most probably errand boys—imply that crony capitalism is business as usual?

In case our politicians or their staffers may have any remaining questions, let me be clear.

The above meeting is an example of crony capitalism, and it is wrong.

Note added December 6, 2011. The following is an excerpt from Mr. Quigley's (U.S. Representative for Illinois' 5th District) post, "Paulson's Actions Raise Serious Ethical Questions"

> I share the outrage of concerned citizens like Richard Teitelbaum, Janet Tavakoli, and Professor William Black of the University of Missouri - Kansas City. During a time of budget-busting bailouts and skyrocketing debt, it is wholly inappropriate and wrong that an elite group of insiders would be able to profit by their personal connections to Washington policymakers. Last week, my staff spoke to Ms. Tavakoli and others to ascertain the scope of Secretary Paulson's potential wrongdoing, and subsequently sent a letter requesting an oversight hearing on this matter to Chairman Patrick McHenry of the Subcommittee on TARP, Financial Services and Bailouts of Public and Private Programs, of which I am the ranking member. Unfortunately, I believe Ms. Tavakoli misunderstood the reason for our call and hope that this post clarifies our mutual position.

Corzine Dodges the Fraud Question

December 9, 2011

It's as if Jon Corzine's PR machine is in top spin mode. You'll recall Jon Corzine is the former head of Goldman Sachs and former CEO of MF Global that appeared in front of Congress yesterday to answer questions about an estimated $600 million to $1.2 billion in missing money from the segregated accounts of customers of MF Global. Prior to becoming the CEO of MF Global, Jon Corzine was the 54th Governor of New Jersey, a U.S. Senator from New Jersey, and the CEO of Goldman Sachs.

Yesterday and today, I heard confusion about whether or not MF Global's diverting customer funds was allowable and the possibility that customers will eventually get the money back.

Let me be clear. The diverting of customer funds from segregated accounts is not legal or allowable, and even if the money is later "found" it is fraud.

Jon Corzine was a bond trader in his past life and he says he doesn't know where the money is and that he didn't understand the details of the operations of MF Global, which appear to be a mess due to negligence or intent.

Corzine Knew or Should Have Known About an Alleged Federal Crime

Corzine may truthfully say he doesn't know exactly where the money is at the moment, but as head of MF Global and as the proponent of risky leveraged sovereign bond trades, he knew or should have known that MF Global didn't have enough cash (or collateral) to support those trades.

Instead of unwinding the trades, it appears that MF Global illegally wired money from customer accounts to satisfy margin calls on MF Global's trades. If that illegal activity happened, Corzine as a bond trader aware of risk and as the head of MF Global, knew it or should have known it. This should be the focus of Congress' investigation. Wire fraud is a federal crime.

"Finding" Money Doesn't Excuse Fraud

Let me address the implication of the potential to "find" the money. The money may indeed be "found." If the bonds mature and pay off one hundred cents on the dollar, it may be possible to claw back money from MF Global's trading partners without much of a fight. Otherwise there may be a legal battle for money that as creditors of MF Global, they were never entitled to in the first place.

The rights of MF Global's customers are superior to the claims of these creditors. But eventually replacing the filched funds is not the same as restitution, since reputations and businesses have already been ruined. Damage has also been done to the trust in the global futures market and Futures Commission Merchants (FCMS).

Never Allowable to Filch Customers' Funds

The key issue is that it is never allowable to divert money from customers' segregated accounts. CFTC Commissioner Jill E. Sommers did a good job of stating that in her testimony yesterday.[206] Moreover, if any trades mimicking Corzine's were done on behalf of the tiny minority of customer accounts that could engage in this trade, the trades would have to be segregated and credits or losses would show up in the relevant customers' accounts.

That still doesn't explain the missing funds in most customer accounts. Most customer accounts would not even be eligible for the "Corzine sovereign bond trade." Why is that? Here's an excerpt from Sommers' testimony:

> Under Section 4d of the CEA, customer segregated funds may be invested in: general obligations of a sovereign nation (to the extent the FCM holds customer funds denominated in that sovereign nation's currency).

Most MF Global customers now missing money did not hold foreign currency accounts.

Pushing the idea that this trade was "allowable" for some customer is a distraction trick to avoid the question of whether MF Global impermissibly wired money from customers' accounts to satisfy margin calls for its own trades. Wire fraud is a federal crime.

At Issue is Massive Fraud

The issue under investigation is what appears to be a bold and massive fraud, and Jon Corzine offered no alternative explanation, in fact it seems he cannot explain anything about the firm he ran to anyone's satisfaction.

Jon Corzine may not know where the money is right now, but as head of MF Global, he knew or should have known his trades needed collateral and that customers' money went missing to satisfy part of that need. If it is proved that fraud occurred—and money missing this long is a very suspicious sign—it's not plausible to me that Jon Corzine was unaware it was happening at MF Global.

It seems Jon Corzine would have Congress believe he's hopelessly incompetent, because it is better to have them believe that than the business for which he was responsible was breathtakingly wrong.

Rehypothecation Is An Old Story: MF Global's Story Is a Different Story of Filched Funds

December 16, 2011

Yesterday Congress held another hearing on MF Global. One representative seemed to suggest that MF Global's movement of money to the UK may have somehow been allowable under Rule 1.25. It was as if a Member of Congress had become Corzine's PR flack, an apologist for Corzine, and was trying to create a false excuse for Corzine. Jon Corzine has been a big Congressional fundraiser and bundler, and it is interesting to see how cheaply some Members of Congress can be bought.

Rule 1.25 wouldn't allow investment in foreign sovereign debt for U.S. dollar accounts, and even if it did, the accounts' assets must be segregated. Rule 1.25 does not allow anyone to filch funds from customers' accounts.

Accounts at MF Global are missing money and have no corresponding asset entries. There is a shortfall of an estimated $600 million to $1.2 billion.

Congress keeps asking how we can prevent this in the future, and I have an answer for them. Run firms with honest people that can reasonably explain the workings of their business to other honest and reasonable men. Reasonable explanations took a holiday from the Congressional hearings.

CFTC Commissioner Jill Sommers did a good job of explaining MF Global's problem in earlier testimony. The cases in which investment in foreign sovereign debt for customers' own accounts are limited to the extent of their foreign exchange deposits (so a small minority of accounts), and it is never allowable to transfer money out of the customer accounts to commingle with MF's investments.

Lies, Cover-ups, and Rubber Checks While Corzine Headed MF Global

The behavior of some Members of Congress is disgraceful because so many honest people were cheated. Here's just one example. While Jon Corzine still headed MF Global, customers requested wire transfers of their money, but MF Global stalled, rubber checks were written and sent to customers, and the checks bounced.

Yet on November 1 while Corzine still headed the firm, Kenneth Ziman, a lawyer for MF Global, relayed information from MF Global to U.S. Bankruptcy judge Martin Glenn in Manhattan: "To the best knowledge of management, there is no shortfall." That wasn't the truth.

> According to a U.S. official, MF Global admitted to federal regulators early Monday [October 31, 2011] that money was missing from customer accounts. MF Global acknowledged a shortfall in a phone call amid mounting questions from regulators as they went through the firm's books.[207]

We bailed out large failed financial institutions with invisible support amounting to trillions of taxpayer dollars and visible support amounting to billions of taxpayer dollars. Hardworking farmers and others that had accounts with MF Global have been left to twist in the wind. Innocent reputations and businesses have been damaged due to MF Global's shortfall.

Filched Funds

We already know for a fact that many US dollar accounts were not intact. Money was missing and there were no asset entries as was required. There's not enough perfume to make this pig smell good. At issue is MF Global's use of segregated customer funds and commingling of segregated customer assets to cover its own shortfall.

Another Potential Crime: Did MF Global Misrepresent Source of Funds to the Fed?

Why did the Fed award prestigious primary dealer status to shaky MF Global, an entity it doesn't regulate and for which it doesn't provide surveillance? Did MF Global subsequently make misrepresentations to the Fed?

MF Global's financials and risk management procedures were shaky ever since Man Group spun it off in 2005 and saddled it with a lot of debt. In fact, in August of 2011, MF Global settled a lawsuit for misrepresentation of the quality of its risk management procedures. Yet MF Global was added to the Fed's list of 22 primary dealers in February 2011, less than one year after former Goldman CEO Jon Corzine came on board. Primary dealers buy and sell U.S. treasuries at auction and are a counterparty to the Fed's Open Market operations.

William C. Dudley is the president and chief executive officer of the FRBNY. He is also vice chairman of the Federal Open Market Committee (FOMC) and VP of the Markets Group, which oversees open market and foreign exchange trading operations and provisions of account services to foreign central banks and manages the System Open Market Account. Dudley is a former partner at Goldman Sachs (1986-2007), and he was Goldman's chief economist.

The biggest benefit to primary dealers is the perception that they are protected by a Fed safety net. This belief is based on precedence, since the Fed has already provided funding to primary dealers during a systemic liquidity crunch. Just before Bear Stearns imploded, the Fed changed the rules so that non-U.S. banks, along with brokers that were primary dealers (as MF Global was), were allowed to borrow through a program called a Term Securities Lending Facility (TSLF) to finance mortgage backed securities, asset backed securities, and more. TSLF's start date was too late to help Bear Stearns, and the program has now been discontinued, but the precedence has been set.

As MF Global's financial condition deteriorated in September and October, MF Global was required to increase its reserves to cover potential Fed losses if MF Global went under, as it eventually did. In Congressional testimony yesterday, New York Fed General counsel Thomas Baxter testified that MF Global said that money posted to the Fed did not come from customers' accounts, and MF Global gave those representations to the Fed in writing. Baxter testified: "If that representation turns out to be false, a federal criminal offense has been committed."

This will be up to investigators to determine, however, since there is no public evidence. Nonetheless, it raises disturbing questions as to why the Fed awarded primary dealer status to an operation like MF Global in the first place.

CME Head Terry Duffy: Under Corzine, Inaccurate Report Kept Regulators in the Dark

Throughout the Congressional hearings, Jon Corzine kept testifying as to how he had no explanation or even expert opinions on what happened at MF Global. He often referred to the fact that he's no longer with MF Global or that events happened after he left. Terry Duffy testified to events that happened under Jon Corzine's leadership:

> CFTC and CME staff and auditors returned to the firm on Sunday, Oct. 30, and were informed by this discrepancy was caused by "an accounting error." Our auditors, working with the CFTC, devoted the rest of the day and night, to find the so-called "accounting error." No such error was found.
>
> Instead, at about 2 a.m. Monday morning, Oct. 31, MF Global informed both the CFTC and CME that the shortfall was real and that customer segregated funds had been transferred out of segregation to the firm's broker dealer accounts.
>
> After receiving this information, CME remained at MF Global while (the firm) attempted to identify funds that could be transferred into segregation to reduce or eliminate the discrepancy.
>
> A CME auditor also participated in a phone call with senior MF Global employees, wherein one employee

> indicated that Mr. Corzine knew about the loans made from the segregated accounts."
>
> [On Monday, October 31] MF Global revised its segregation report for Thursday, Oct. 27, indicating that the alleged $200 million in excess segregated funds should have been reported as a deficiency of $200 million. This shortfall on segregation on Thursday, Oct. 27, was hidden by the inaccurate report, a telling sign to keep regulators in the dark.
>
> It remains to be seen whether this failure to disclose permitted additional segregated funds to be improperly transferred.
>
> Throughout this time, the firm and its employees were under the direction and control of MF Global management. Transfers of customer funds effectuated by MF Global for the benefit (of the firm) constitute very serious violations of our rules and of CFTC regulations.

A very good summary of Terry Duffy's testimony and its implications can be found at *National Hog Farmer*.[208] It provided the best early financial coverage on this topic.

Allowable Rehypothecation: Problematic, But A Different Problem Than MF Global's

There has been a lot of misinformation about rehypothecation, an old term that seems to have been newly rediscovered by bloggers. To be clear, allowable rehypothecation is not the dark question that has been raised about MF Global. Filching funds as I described above is illegal. Writing rubber checks is illegal.

My favorite rehypothecation story involves Henry Jarecki, then head of Mocatta Metals and current head of Gresham Partners LLC. I'm sure he'll tell the story better and give you more details than I. But here is the basic story, and it is a parable of this problematic but legal practice.

Around 1979, Mocatta Metals owned 30 million ounces of silver that Jarecki leased to industrial users. He was long silver outside the exchanges, and he hedged by being short silver on the exchanges using futures contracts. But all the price action was on the exchanges where prices were soaring. Jarecki used cash to meet margin calls. People started getting nervous and rumors circulated, because most people were unaware he owned a huge silver position.

Meanwhile, the Hunts had borrowed $50 million from Mocatta to buy more silver and had deposited 10.7 million ounces with Mocatta as collateral for the loan. Jarecki rehypothecated the Hunts' silver, meaning he used it as collateral for his own borrowing. This wasn't prudent, but it was definitely legal. After the Hunts posted the silver as collateral with Mocatta, the price of silver tripled. The Hunts were nervous after hearing the rumors about the cash margin calls for Mocatta's futures hedges, and they showed up in Henry Jarecki's office in a very bad mood.

The Hunts knew the value of their collateral at then market prices far exceeded the cash value of their loan, and they wanted the loan size increased so they could buy more silver. Jarecki agreed to a bigger loan, but the increase wasn't big enough to satisfy the Hunts, who became suspicious that Jarecki was in financial trouble. The Hunts then said they wanted to prepay the loan and take back their silver. Jarecki responded that the loan terms didn't allow for early repayment. Now the Hunts were afraid and angry.

If Jarecki had to buy the Hunts' silver in the open market or if he had to cancel his futures trades with no offset to meet the Hunts' demands, it would have created a liquidity crisis for Mocatta. Instead, Jarecki solved everyone's problems. He arranged an exchange of futures for physicals (an EFP to cancel out his and the Hunts' futures positions in exchange for a special agreement on the silver) and sold the Hunts 23 million ounces of silver for cash at what was then the top of the silver market.

Honest People Don't Look for Malicious Loopholes

At all times the Hunts had cash in exchange for their assets, there was a full accounting, and Mocatta Metals was good for its obligations. In fact, Mocatta Metals immediately satisfied the

Hunts' demands. Even better, it sold the Hunts more silver, which the Hunts wanted. Honest people don't exploit customers by citing malicious loopholes, they come up with creative solutions to more than satisfy customers.

Mocatta used creativity to prevent a liquidity crunch. Even in its best form, rehypothecation can create a liquidity crisis and panic due to the basis risk. Mocatta averted that and everyone was satisfied. It's poetic justice that Mocatta was also lucky in its timing in the silver market.

But as I said at the outset, allowable rehypothecation is not what has everyone up in arms about the missing money at MF Global.

Congresswoman Marcy Kaptur Confronts MF Global and Wall Street

December 26, 2011

On October 31, MF Global went bankrupt under circumstances that suggest a classic situation for fraud. MF Global's Chairman of the Board and CEO was Jon Corzine, former Goldman Sachs CEO, former U.S. senator (D., New Jersey), and former governor of New Jersey. On November 4, 2011, Corzine resigned as head of MF Global. Customer money to the tune of $600 million to $1.2 billion is still missing. JPMorgan was MF Global's largest secured creditor. Corzine either can't or won't explain what happened. He offers neither a theory nor an expert opinion.

Jon Corzine was a huge fundraiser, a "bundler" accumulating contributions from other people for campaigns for the Democratic Party. The Center for Responsive Politics reported that Corzine and his first and second wives contributed a combined $917,000 to Democratic committees and candidates over a 20-year period. Since April 2011, Corzine bundled in excess of $500,000 for President Obama's re-election campaign.

On December 24, 2011, it was announced that President Obama returned direct contributions of $70,000 from Corzine and his wife, Sharon Elghanayan. They had each given the maximum allowable amount of $30,800 to the Democratic National Committee (DNC) and $5,000 to President Obama's campaign.

Of course the DNC and President Obama can't distance themselves fast enough from Jon Corzine now. But if this is to be more than a political stunt, they should toss back the $500,000 that Corzine raised from his friends on Wall Street.

A Few Good Men and Women

A few members of Congress fight for the rights of taxpayers and for the system of justice we used to expect in the United States before special interest groups bought much of Congress.

Representative Marcy Kaptur is a fierce fighter for justice not only for her constituents but for all Americans. She's not alone. The MF Global hearings revealed that a mix of Democrats and Republicans stand up for what is right, but there are members of Congress on both sides of the aisle that don't.

Representative Hayworth: "Goldman Sachs former partners... respect you greatly."

Financial firms like Goldman Sachs spread their money around and contribute to the campaigns of both Democrats and Republicans.

During the hearings of the House Financial Services Committee hearing on December 15, 2011, Representative Nan Hayworth (R., New York) treated Corzine like a royal that had misplaced his crown instead of the CEO of a bankrupt company with hundreds of millions or more of customer money missing under suspicious circumstances:

> Governor Corzine, Mr. Abelow [former COO of MF Global]... I know Goldman Sachs former partners who know both of you and respect you greatly... I hope... you will employ your talents and your minds to enlightening us as to how we can prevent... this from ever happening again.[209]

Later she referred to Corzine's career as "rather stellar... to say the least." If she had spoken to customers of MF Global that found money missing from their "segregated" accounts, she would have heard a different point of view.

In the two previous Congressional hearings both Corzine and Abelow had stonewalled and dodged. These aren't the guys to ask about prevention, unless Representative Hayworth wants their advice on how not to run a financial firm. Corzine was chairman, CEO, and initiator of an enormous risky trade, a net "off-balance-sheet" position of $6.3 billion in sovereign debt disclosed in MF Global's March 2011 annual report. He was in a position to overrule any risk manager. He got rid of one risk manager critical of his trades and installed another. Corzine is the poster child for worst practices in controls and corporate governance.

Representative Huizenga: "Thousands feel cheated"

In the December 15 hearings, Representative Bill Huizenga (R. Michigan) pressed Corzine and got him to admit he was a detail guy "in markets and client activities." Corzine said that in areas of his expertise he is "very hands on."

Huizenga pointed out that the commingling of customer funds is serious. People lose law licenses and real estate brokerage licenses over it. "That's why you're seeing such anger and hostility over this." He challenged Corzine's claiming that he didn't recall details and said it "doesn't ring true."

Huizenga continued: "This certainly doesn't feel or look like you were caring for those other people's money in the way that you should have or certainly were expected to." None of Corzine's money was at risk in these accounts. The representative summed up: "You've got thousands of hard working people around this country that feel cheated."

Are the Congressmen From New Jersey Going Easy on Corzine?

The three Congressional hearings investigating the MF Global bankruptcy have so far had no teeth. During the Senate Agriculture Committee hearings on Tuesday, December 13, 2011, Senator Mike Johanns (R. Nebraska) expressed his disbelief at the representations made by officers of MF Global. The officers had claimed ignorance of the circumstances of the missing money.

Senator Johanns responded: "There must have been many many [sic] people who knew that money was being drained out of client accounts... do you realize how incredible [your claim of ignorance] sounds to this committee?"

Yet Senator Robert Menendez (D., New Jersey) later said: "After three hearings, I don't know what more we'll learn that we don't know today."[210] Menendez is on the Senate banking committee, which hasn't held any hearings. This is strange, because the Senate banking committee is the only one that oversees MF Global's regulators. The senator took the seat vacated by Jon Corzine when he became governor of New Jersey. Menendez is a good politician, since he didn't rule out a Senate banking committee hearing if new facts come up. But it is the purpose of investigations and robust hearings to uncover the facts in the first place.

When it comes to fraud, if you don't look for it, you don't find it, because when it comes to fraud, there is always a cover-up.

Representative Kaptur on MF Global: "I believe most of us would call that theft."

Representative Marcy Kaptur is not on any of the aforementioned committees, but she has been following the hearings in both the House of Representatives and the Senate. She read her special order into the Congressional Record:

> The fact that "customer accounts were not intact," as [CFTC] Commissioner Sommers described it, means that someone took other people's money. I believe most of us would call that theft. Even if some of the money is recovered by the bankruptcy process, that does not alter the fact that the process by which customer accounts were violated broke the law.[211]

A Rigged Financial System and Another Former Goldman Sachs CEO

Representative Kaptur has experience debunking Wall Street's spin. Bank of America's officers withheld material information from shareholders concerning losses and bonus payments related to its takeover of Merrill Lynch during the 2008 financial crisis. Bank of America wildly overpaid for the acquisition and taxpayer bailouts were needed as the extent of losses became apparent. Bonus payments of $3.6 billion were given to Merrill Lynch executives as the firm imploded and was sold to Bank of America. Merrill lost $27 billion in 2008.

> Bank of America agreed to pay a $33 million fine to the SEC but—you guessed it—admit no wrongdoing. A heroic U.S. district judge, Jed Rakoff, refused to rubber-stamp the deal, which he called a breach of "justice and morality" that "suggests a rather cynical relationship between the parties."[212]

The SEC and Bank of America then cooked up a $150 million settlement. This is a classic negotiation ploy among the captured "regulators" at the SEC whose next job is often a lucrative position dependent on Wall Street for revenues. It's called lowballing. You set the expectations so low that you can increase your initial offer by multiples and it will still be a bad-faith joke on the party with whom you settle. Judge Rakoff reluctantly accepted the new settlement of only $150 million, since he felt bound by judicial restraint.

Congresswoman Marcy Kaptur (D., Ohio) took on this issue and more when she grilled then Secretary of the Treasury Henry ("Hank") Paulson and former CEO of Goldman Sachs:

> Your orchestration yielded... an unprecedented dumping of private sector losses on the U.S. taxpayer. History will show that the U.S. government and you knew about Wall Street's growing losses long before the Bank of America / Merrill merger. In fact, Bank of America's purchase of Countrywide in January 2008 was but another positioning of private sector interests in preparation for what I call the greatest Hail Mary pass of all time in taking those Wall Street losses and placing them on the next three generations. What interests me is who you helped and who you didn't.

Goldman Sachs was a major beneficiary of bailouts and continued to pay its employees high bonuses. Warren Buffett got a sweetheart deal for injecting $5 billion into Goldman Sachs. Taxpayers injected $10 billion into Goldman Sachs—among other extremely lucrative ongoing benefits—and got a vastly inferior deal with timing of the unwind controlled by the borrower, Paulson's former firm, Goldman Sachs.

CHAPTER 15 Banana Republic

Anchored Under Water

June 26, 2009

I recently spoke with a senior member of Congress who feels the American consumer needs to gust wind in the sails of the economy. He insisted the Americans with jobs should be spending more: "We want people to save 10% [he may have meant to say 5%], but they don't need to save more. Why aren't people spending money?"

I'll get to that answer in a minute, but first the Americans who are out of work deserve a mention. More than 9.4% of Americans are out of work, and there are others who aren't reporting. Some unofficial estimates put the unemployment rate as high as 15%. Perhaps more banks should have held onto their TARP money, because we have been using both hook and crook to prop up our mortgage loan numbers. Now the credit card charge-offs are kicking in. *Forbes* points out that credit charge offs are at record highs of 10.4%.[213] The charge-offs are right on schedule as beleaguered consumers walk away from credit card debt with the highest interest rate charges, and these are the charge-offs that will have the largest impact on banks' profit margins.[214]

What about the rest of Americans? They can often get good deals in our (temporarily) deflationary environment, and since we are anticipating high inflation to come, one might think this would be a good time to buy. Yet, the average consumer is not spending nearly enough to stimulate the economy, and many appear to be saving more than ever. Even consumers that are free of fear for their economic futures are anchored to their past notion of their former net worth.

The economy is still deleveraging a high average consumer debt load. This creates continued downward pressure on the housing market. Even fiscally responsible Americans have already seen the values of their homes decline, the value of their pensions deteriorate, and the value of their personal investment portfolios plummet. Portfolios are under water compared to past higher values anchored in the minds of investors. The negative wealth effect has had a huge psychological impact.

Those with jobs are trying to save their way back to their former notion of a higher net worth. The old number is stuck in their minds like a barnacle. We have a long wait before American consumers again say "Anchors Aweigh!"

Stranguflation: Deflation and Inflation Where It Hurts America Most

August 3, 2010

The U.S. is suffering from high unemployment combined with too much consumer debt in a weak economy. Current stock market exuberance reflects earnings increases at selective companies that benefited from sputtering stimulus programs. In late 2007 through the fall of 2008, our economy had an appendix attack, and Congress issued potent addictive painkillers instead of fixing our problems.

Meanwhile, the financial system has strangled U.S. growth by parasitically growing from 3% of GDP in 1965 to 7.5% of GDP currently. As Jeremy Grantham pointed out in his quarterly letter to investors, financial services were sufficient for the economy when they were 3% of GDP, but that sector grew by strangling GDP growth elsewhere. The nation's GDP growth slowed from 3.5% in 1965 to 2.4% between 1980 and 2007, and the slowdown occurred before our current crisis.

In other words, our bloated financial sector has been sucking the life-blood out of the U.S. economy for years, and recent decisions ensure it will continue to feed off taxpayers, while the host economy struggles for life.

Jobless "Recovery"

Unemployment exceeds 10%, counting the underemployed it is closer to 20%, and the figures soar beyond that when one counts our unemployed youth. The recovery is being strangled in its crib by low job creation, high consumer debt, high local government debt, high federal government debt, and falling tax revenues.

[Update August 6, 2010: Official figures for overall unemployment as of July, announced August 6, held at 9.5%.]

Since the first meltdown, we've had rising—and still very high—consumer loan defaults. The Fed tried to monetize bad loans, which is just another way of saying the U.S. taxpayer is paying for bad lending decisions by Too Big To Fail financial institutions.

Nominal income is falling. Selected prices have fallen more rapidly than income, but we've had a negative wealth effect. Housing prices and investment assets fell in value. Consumer loan payments of debt-loaded consumers have to come from falling nominal income.

If we didn't have too much borrowing (leverage) in our system, the Fed's rapid pumping of money into the economy might have worked. Unfortunately, consumers and many financial institutions are still overleveraged and many of them will default or fail. This continues to be a drag on the economy and on consumer demand.

Deflation Plus "Staple" Inflation

The economic picture is distorted by both deflation and inflation. Interest rates are low for now, but consumer demand also remains too low. Banks are unwilling to lend to all but those who don't need money in the first place. The negative wealth effect of reduced home prices, a weak housing market, and reduced value of investment accounts and retirement accounts is combined with "staple" inflation on items like school tuition, utilities, certain food items, and even mundane items like printer paper. Many prudent investors and consumers are unwilling to borrow, even at low interest rates.

Moreover, consumers are worried about potential local tax rises and federal tax rises, since many local governments are broke, and our national debt is $13 trillion.

If deflationary pressures combined with rising prices on many consumer items weren't bad enough, many investors are carefully watching long-term U.S. treasury interest rates in case demand for U.S. debt falls and inflation takes off.

The economy's stranguflation is the result of wealth destruction and the quadruple threat of the weak economy, high government debt load, asset deflation with price inflation of essentials, and the fear of future overall inflation.

How to Thwart the Assassins of the American Dream

August 15, 2010

Arianna Huffington's new book, *Third World America: How Our Politicians are Abandoning the Middle Class and Betraying the American Dream*, paints a grim picture of the State of the Union:

> Every day, Americans, faced with layoffs and tough economic times, are forced to use their credit cards to pay for essentials such as food, housing, and medical care—the costs of which continue to escalate. But, as their debt rises, they find it harder to keep up with their payments. When they don't, banks, trying to offset losses in other areas, turn around, hike interest rates, and impose all manner of fees and penalties... (P. 77)

Our mediocre grammar school and high school educational system continues its downward slide. The Great Recession is squeezing school budgets. We are failing our children, our most important resource of all.

In 2009, the American Society of Civil Engineers gave the nation's infrastructure a near failing D rating:

> Flip on a light switch, and you are tapping into a seriously overtaxed electrical grid. Go to the sink, and your tap water may be coming to you through pipes built during the Civil War. Take a drive, and pass over pothole-filled roads and cross-if-you-dare

bridges. The evidence of decay is all around us. (P. 95)

The over-hyped American Recovery and Reinvestment Act of 2009 earmarked only $72 billion of the $787 billion appropriation of taxpayer dollars to projects to improve the country's infrastructure.

Meanwhile, multi-national corporations avoid taxes, sheltering $700 billion in foreign earnings to end up with a measly $16 billion (2.3%) tax bill. GM is among those companies, yet it took almost a half billion dollars in bailout loans. Boeing and KBR Halliburton are among the defense contractors that avoid taxes, while enjoying government contracts worth tens of billions.

Banks (not Fannie and Freddie) Crippled the Housing Market

Fannie and Freddie do not make loans. They purchase mortgage loans and earn fees for guaranteeing payments on the loans. According to the Mortgage Bankers Association, in 2006, Fannie and Freddie accounted for 33% of total mortgage backed securities issuance. In the first half of 2010, they accounted for around 64% of new issuance. They were forced to pick up the slack and buy more when Wall Street's private label securitization Ponzi scheme blew up.

Fannie and Freddie are Wall Street's dumping ground. They would have had problems on their own, but their problems would not have been close to their current scale, and they did not create the housing bubble.

Congress twisted arms to make Fannie and Freddie buy more than $300 billion of phony "AAA" rated mortgage-backed securities from banks, not counting loans that didn't meet their stated requirements. Today Fannie and Freddie want banks to repurchase tens of billions of these loans, since they fail to meet representations and warranties, and the banks are fighting this obligation.

Top subprime lenders included Wells Fargo; Countrywide, purchased by Bank of America; Washington Mutual, now part of JPMorgan Chase; CitiMortgage, part of Citigroup; First Franklin (now closed), purchased by Merrill Lynch, which was purchased by Bank of America; Chase Home Finance, JPMorgan Chase; Ownit, partly owned by Merrill Lynch, which was later purchased by Bank of America; and EMC, part of Bear Stearns, which was purchased by JPMorgan Chase. Most of the rest depended on massive loans from Wall Street. Many of these lenders were sued by states for fraud and paid billions in settlements.

According to *Inside Mortgage Finance*, the top mortgage backed securities underwriters during 2005-2006, only two of the subprime abuse years, included now defunct Lehman Brothers ($106 billion); RBS Greenwich Capital ($99 billion); Countrywide Securities, which is now part of Bank of America ($74 billion); Morgan Stanley ($74 billion); Credit Suisse First Boston ($73 billion); Merrill Lynch ($67 billion); Bear Stearns, which is now part of JPMorgan Chase ($61 billion); and Goldman Sachs ($53 billion).

The above doesn't even include the credit derivatives, collateralized debt obligations (CDOs), and structured investment vehicles (SIVs) that amplified losses. Yet, Arianna notes how America imploded while bankers soared:

> Someone like [Robert] Rubin is able to wreak destruction, collect an ungodly profit, then go along his merry way, pontificating about how 'markets have an inherent and inevitable tendency—probably rooted in human nature—to go to excess, both on the upside and the downside.' This from the man who, as Bill Clinton's Treasury secretary, was vociferous in opposing the regulation of derivatives—a key factor in the current economic crisis—and who lobbied the Treasury during the Bush years to prevent the downgrading of the credit rating of Enron—a debtor of Citigroup. (P. 150)

Robert Rubin operated an economic wrecking-ball from prestigious positions of influence including former co-chairman of Goldman Sachs, director of the National Economic Council, former Treasury Secretary under President Bill Clinton, board member and senior "risk wizard" counselor at Citigroup, member of the President's Advisory Committee for Trade Negotiations, member of the SEC's Oversight and Financial Services Advisory Committee, unofficial economic adviser to President Obama, and co-chairman of the Council on Foreign Relations.

Rubin is just one example of the many bankers, who helped destroy the economy while creating a connected financial oligarchy.

Hide Billions of Losses, Take Bailouts, Collect Billions, Skip Jail

Instead of apologizing for screwing up, the banks demanded the Great Bailout. At the start of the meltdown, the IMF and the U.S. administration estimated losses of $2 to $2.5 trillion. Unemployment and the losses are now shockingly worse. What was merely a recession escalated into the Great Recession.

How big are the actual losses? No one knows.

After destroying the value of major banks, culprits used their enormous political influence—funded with taxpayer dollars—to get Congress to force the accounting board to change accounting rules (as of April 2009) so banks don't have to recognize losses until they sell the assets.

According to former regulator William K. Black, after the much tinier S&L crisis, there were over 1,000 successful felony prosecutions, several thousand successful enforcement actions, and roughly 1,000 successful civil actions.

This time Congress gave us the Great Cover-up. Bank officers dodged jail time and collected billions in bonuses. As one of my South American friends observes, he's witnessed this third-world corruption before, and this time it's in English.

Banks Stall the Recovery and Prolong the Great Recession

Unemployment marched upward, delinquencies soared, and banks stalled foreclosures. The longer banks delay foreclosures and sales, the longer they can avoid acknowledging losses. Phony accounting and zero cost funding from taxpayers created an illusion of recovery.

Stalling helps banks while they pressure Congress to bail out failed mortgages with taxpayer dollars. Instead of working out mortgages with homeowners, they can wait for a government program to buyout or subsidize their failing loans. The markets aren't recovering, because banks own colossal chunks of mystery-meat assets.

It's a black hole of debt. If banks were forced to price these assets at market values and sell them, the market would clear, and the market would make a faster recovery. When Japan did this (Japan failed to make banks mark assets at market value. - Clarifying note added August 22), it stalled its economy for twenty years, and it still hasn't recovered.

Voters Must Demand the Solution

Voters must demand that Congress uncovers and publicizes facts and prosecutes the financial system's massive multi-year frauds. This will mean thousands of felony prosecutions, enforcement actions, and civil actions.

Congress completely failed in genuine regulation and enforcement. It must start over on financial reform, regulate derivatives, commodities trading, update Glass-Steagall, and more. It will have to break-up the Too Big to Fail financial institutions.

CEOs of our Systemically Dangerous Institutions (SDI's) fail to manage them, because no one is capable of doing it. Like a morbidly obese junk food addict, banks won't even get on a scale. Our banks refuse to properly measure (account for) the problem.

Third World America elegantly summarizes the way forward. Arianna Huffington names the culprits and gives a roadmap for solutions. The rest is up to us. We deserve better than a third world economy divided by ultra-rich on one side and debt-ridden middle class and dirt poor citizens on the other. Citizens must demand a clean-up of corruption and a foundation for healthy growth.

Third World America: "Fast Tracking to Anarchy"

August 25, 2010

Among the future consequences of not fixing our national fiscal problems will likely be an increase in social unrest and an increase in crime. A look at Chicago's problems may serve as a call to action for America's middle class. Chicago's city budget is in dire straits. That's also true of the state of Illinois, California, New York and other areas. In Chicago, the same mismanagement that deepened our fiscal crisis has caused a crisis in essential city services.

The police department provides just one example. Sunday's *Chicago Tribune* reported that in 31 days, there were 303 shot and 33 dead: "Crime has been holding steady in Chicago in recent years. Through July, there have been 1,089 shootings in the city, a 2.4 percent decrease over last year."

According to the newspaper, it's a "typical" July. Yet there is nothing typical about it when you look beyond the numbers. The first problem is that the numbers are flat-out unacceptable in any year in any city in the U.S. It is inexplicable that citizens of Chicago have tolerated this situation in poorer neighborhoods for decades. The second problem is a new problem. Years of complacency by Chicago's middle and upper classes have brought the crisis to their doorstep.

In recent years, incompetent and ill-qualified people have been promoted to "leadership" positions. Hiring and exam giving has declined, and the police department is undermanned and demoralized. Even worse is the fragging officers take from politicians, unqualified people in police "administration," and from the local media.

Spiraling Out of Control: Open Season on Cops

The title of this post comes from "A City at War With Itself," a commentary written by Lt. John Andrews, a 25-year veteran of the Chicago Police Department:

> Most horrific for Chicago is that in less than 60 days, Chicago has lost 3 of its police officers, killed by gunfire as victims of robberies. It seems no one is safe in our city anymore.
>
> Chicago's homicide rate this year currently stands toe-to-toe with the total number of military forces killed in both Afghanistan and Iraq.
>
> Thugs, gangs and renegade groups run the streets and neighborhoods, intimidating and victimizing the decent citizens of this city. They go mostly

> unchallenged and unchecked by a totally demoralized police force that is dangerously understaffed and still out-gunned on the streets.

Lt. Andrews describes in detail a police department demoralized by scandals and corruption. He names those who received promotions based on political pull rather than merit or suitability for responsibility. Moreover, police fear reprisals from political special interest groups when using necessary force:

> When asked, most will freely tell you that they do not want to place themselves, their families and livelihoods at risk from a perceived Machiavellian police superintendent or other incompetent "bosses" that could lead them into legal trouble that would risk their liberty and freedom (jail).

(Lt. Andrews later faced backlash for bringing these matters to light.)

Even during televised speeches at the recent funerals of police officers, public officials speak out of both sides of their mouths. On the one hand, they decry the apparent targeted shootings of police officers—one of whom, Michael Bailey, was wearing his uniform after just coming off duty from a night of guarding the mayor's house—and on the other hand, they say that of course, police must follow proper procedures and work within the law (and often pause for effect).

Of course, everyone agrees the police must follow proper procedures, but the subtext of the message delivered at an officer's funeral is repellant. These thinly-disguised campaign speeches suggest the police force needs to be careful not to bring these tragedies upon themselves. Perhaps they think police should round up suspects and put them in Monty Python's comfy chair.

If the goal is to help police officers follow proper procedures at all times, then politicians and the police superintendent have to staff the force with well-qualified recruits (this means creating a reasonable qualification exam), remove corrupt "leaders" by reversing ridiculous promotions, and promote qualified officers based on merit. The police force desperately needs manpower and both physical and leadership back-up. Officers confident that their authority is respected, their judgment is trusted, and their tools are equal to a dangerous and difficult job will produce better results than people who have been left hanging out to dry, while their colleagues are massacred.

Media Strafing

Local media has lost the plot. A couple of days ago, an off-duty police officer shot and killed an armed home invader who had kicked in his door. The officer reportedly lives on a block with five or six other police officers. The intruder allegedly has a history of wrongdoing and invaded a suburban home with another man. He posed as a cable worker and bound and gagged his victims. Yet, some news reports described the intruder as a "victim" and said the off-duty officer was not charged, as if charges should have even been an issue. According to comments posted at *Second City Cop*,[215] *WGN*'s televised news unwisely showed the police officer's home, identified his neighborhood, and zoomed in on his home address.

Mug Mile

Formerly "safe" and "upscale" neighborhoods have become the targets of "wildings." James Carlini, an editor for *Wisconsin Technology News*, gave an eyewitness account of his experience of Chicago's "land sharks" at the premier shopping district known as the Magnificent Mile, or Mag Mile:

> Coming back to the John Hancock to pick up my car at around 9PM, I noticed several little bands of four to five juveniles walking around sizing up people as they walked down the streets. Luckily we were already in our car, but I could sense that these "gangsta wannabes" were up to no good.
>
> There were some arrests made that night but very suspicious that there was no mention in the mainstream media. There have been incidences like this before but never a mention or a caution. Why?

> Afraid to report on the truth or were you told not to report on the truth?

One of Carlini's readers noted that Mayor Richard Daley seems to live in a bubble:

> I think [Mayor Daley] should go out in the evening without his hit squad protecting him with the firearms he professes to hate so much. That would be six more highly-paid police officers who could patrol the downtown streets that you and I walk down—unarmed.

Buy Back America

If nothing else good comes out of our crisis, perhaps it will serve as a wake-up call for the entire nation. It's time to put our shoulders to the wheel to solve our problems.

Doing nothing is not an option for America. Much of poor America, especially in our major cities, has been Third World America for decades. Soon the urban middle classes and even upper classes will become better acquainted with that world.

Washington's political corruption and mismanagement has the same roots as Chicago's. As Arianna points out, on a national level, we need "the mother of all reforms:"

> That is why the first step toward stopping our relentless transformation into Third World America has to be breaking the choke hold that special interest money has on our politicians. (Third World America, 172)

On a local level, Chicago will have to fix its own problems by breaking the choke hold of special interest groups. On a national level, it will take a Constitutional amendment requiring full public financing for political campaigns (for starters). Our politicians have shown us how willing they are to be owned by special interest groups that will buy votes, buy a campaign, or just buy them off. As Arianna explains: "If someone's going to own the politicians, it might as well be the American people."

Endnote: I chose James Carlini's report, because I thought it might interest city officials to know that tourists are feeling intimidated; it's bad for business. It turns out he lives in Illinois (not Wisconsin) and grew up in Chicago. Contrary to some commenters' assumptions, he is not intimidated by Chicago. I could have chosen from several unprecedented incidents (some occurred on Mag Mile) among my neighbors and friends, but Mr. Carlini is a writer and there was a link to his internet article. Likewise, I didn't have a link to the story about multiple shots fired into WGN's window on Mag Mile, since it was underreported, but the eyesore of a board that replaced it made the Tribune Tower less attractive for tourists and shoppers. (The board was up for several weeks, and the window has since been replaced.)

Incidents on Mag Mile are underreported by the media, unless an incident happens to a reporter. On July 14, Chicago Tribune reporter John Thomas was mugged "on the (not so) Mag Mile." Here's an excerpt of his account:[216]

> I was mugged Monday on the Mag Mile. Right in front of the glitzy Coach store. In broad daylight. Surrounded by literally hundreds of people.
>
> The sidewalk was packed with tourists and shoppers, but I felt a strange energy when a kid, probably about 14, sat down close to me on my left while the guy he walked up with stood on my right. It just felt wrong.
>
> Then, literally in a flash, the kid on my left grabbed my iPhone and tried to bolt. I had heard all of the warnings about people snatching iPhones and iPods, but because the street was so crowded I never thought it could happen there and then. Click here to read the rest.

Endnote: I never mentioned race in this commentary, but a few commenters brought up race and made unwarranted assumptions. Some commenters assumed "wildings" only involve black youths.

Chicago is a city with a lot of diversity and gangs of every race. I mentioned a separate incident of an armed intruder being shot and killed by an off duty police officer; the armed intruder was not African American. I also mentioned three police officers were shot and killed within the past 60 days. Two were African American, one was not.

In Third World America, You Can't Buy a Ream of Paper on Minimum Wage

December 18, 2010

In 2010, every one of my work-related conversations turned to personal wealth management. The money-class wants to preserve and increase their considerable wealth, and they are terrified of losing it. Elsewhere in America, those that don't have money are terrified of the rising cost of necessities like food and energy not captured in the [core] consumer price index calculation.

As of July 24, 2009, minimum wage in the United States was $7.25/hour (before taxes). At the beginning of 2010, minimum wage barely bought you a pre-tax $6.79 ream (500 sheets) of paper at Office Depot. By the end of 2010, that cost had skyrocketed to $9.49 per ream, nearly a 40% increase. But printer paper isn't a necessity for those who need to feed and clothe their families. Official unemployment is at 9.8%, and many "new" jobs are part-time jobs that replaced former full-time jobs. Counting underemployment, the misery soars above 20%.

Arianna Huffington's latest book, *Third World America*, explains how those with the least power and money have been getting squeezed for decades:

> The median middle class in September 1979 was earning (in constant, inflation-adjusted dollars) $25,896 a year. In September 1995, that same man or woman was earning $24,700 a year—a 5 percent cut in salary over the intervening decade and a half. (P. 54)

Meanwhile, the financial system has strangled U.S. growth by parasitically growing from 3% of GDP in 1965 to 7.5% of GDP currently. Money was diverted from capital investment, the most important stimulus generator for our economy, to save corrupt financial institutions. Financial services now account for 35-40% of all corporate profits in the U.S. That number should be less than 5% in an honest economy. CEOs of bailed-out banks earn more than they did before the bailout.

Sanders: The U.S. Is a Banana Republic

Senator Bernie Sanders (I. Vermont) explained to the Senate during his tax cut filibuster on December 10 that the gap between the wealthiest Americans and the poorest is the greatest it has been in U.S. history. The bottom 50% of Americans own just 2% of the wealth. The top 1/10th of 1% takes home 12 cents of every dollar earned in America. The top 1% earned 23.5% of all income, more than the combined income of the bottom 50%.

Yet, the lust for money and power by the financial elite knows no limits. Over 10 years, the top 2% of the wealthy in this country will get $700 billion in tax cuts. Meanwhile, the country chokes on a $13.7 trillion national debt.

Deflation and Inflation: Where It Hurts You Most

The disappearing middle class is dying of stranguflation. Nominal income is falling; yet debt-loaded consumers have to meet usurious consumer loan payments, while prices for staples like energy, school tuition, and food rise. Despite a rising stock market, most Americans still feel a negative wealth effect, particularly due to depressed housing prices.

The coming year will be worse for too many Americans. They face the quadruple threat of the weak recovery, the astronomical government debt load, price inflation for necessities, and the fear of future overall inflation.

Congress has blocked meaningful financial reform. It approved the Great Bailout, followed by the Great Cover-Up and the Great Recession. If Congress continues its sham investigations, culprits will never be brought to justice.

As the economy struggles in 2011, expect most of Congress to again protect its cronies in the financial elite, instead of the interests of the average voter. It is a bi-partisan betrayal of the nation's economic health. If Americans don't pay attention and vote out corrupt members of Congress, we'll sink further into a banana republic, and this time it's in English.

Third World America 2011: Forget "Fast Tracking to Anarchy" We've Arrived

June 8, 2011

All hell has broken loose in downtown Chicago. Years of under-hiring have resulted in a police force that is unprepared for wildings and gang violence. Moreover, concealed carry in Chicago is illegal, unless one follows the Constitution.

Tourists and residents have been attacked by mobs of youths on buses, on beaches, on bicycle paths, near the shops of the Magnificent Mile, and outside their homes. Mobs of shoplifters plagued "Mug Mile" stores.

The irony is that these disenfranchised youths are turning to crime—and if justice is done, prison sentences—against innocent targets. Their focus is misdirected. Participating in a peaceful five million man march—a true show of force and power—against elected culprits in Washington would get them better results for lasting change.

The Spring of Anarchy: "A City At War With Itself"

It is still technically spring in Chicago, and wildings have made Chicago and its beaches unsafe. Poorer neighborhoods have long been war zones. The murder rate and gang violence in Chicago has been unacceptable for years.

Yet the police force was gutted, handcuffed, and muzzled.[217] Police officers—some off duty and still in uniform—have been gunned down in the streets. Their crime-fighting abilities are severely hampered by years of irrational policies and genuflecting to politically power hungry special interest groups.

Of course, we want police officers to follow proper procedures at all times, but we also want them to make fast decisions in violent chaotic circumstances, defend themselves, and get home safely to their families and friends. Local media hounds come out in force against police work. It's time they came out in favor of superior training and hiring.

Mayor Rahm Emanuel, with less than a month in office, has called for the arrest of all the youths involved in last weekend's mob attack that included an attack on a shopper and on two middle-aged doctors—in separate incidents—visiting for an oncology convention. Yet there have been ongoing incidents of wildings that didn't make the front page of local papers as did this last attack on tourists.

The woefully undermanned police force plans to recruit and train 300 new officers when some estimates indicated it needed more than 3,000 new officers before the outbreak of the new-pattern crime wave.

Police Superintendent has to Stop Lying to Citizens*

Mainstream media has finally started to report crime in the more fashionable parts of town, but only because it has spun out of control into anarchy. The most reliable source of crime-wave information has been Second City Cop, a blog started by a member of the Chicago police force.

Based on my conversations with friends and neighbors, citizens of Chicago feel lied-to by Police Superintendent Garry McCarthy.* On Memorial Day, North Avenue beach, in one of Chicago's more affluent areas, was closed after gang violence. This is unprecedented. McCarthy repeatedly told the media it was due to people succumbing to the hot weather. Not true. Violence was out of control as beach-goers were harassed by mobs and cyclists were pulled off their bikes and beaten.

Mainstream media now contradicts McCarthy's feeble spin. One police officer told the media that 500 youths exited public transportation for the lakefront and while they were there, citizens were harassed.

CBS reported wilding incidents at this beach earlier in May, and police patrols had already been stepped-up. Two bike riders on the North Avenue Beach path had been mobbed by about 100 teens. They were knocked off their bikes and then thrown into Lake Michigan. Yet Near North District commander Kenneth

Angarone said police responding at the scene did not find a "bona fide incident."[218]

Mobs have swarmed local businesses, shoplifted and intimidated shoppers at high-end stores, attacked bus riders, attacked shoppers near Michigan Avenue, attacked tourists and more. Shortly after Mayor Rahm Emanuel said he would round up perpetrators of last week's mob attack, NBC reported that a mob of 15 to 20 youths beat and robbed two people in Chicago's downtown shopping area.[219]

Memorial Day Mobs: Boston, Nashville, Long Island, Miami, Rochester, and Charlotte

Wildings occurred in other cities on Memorial Day weekend in what may have been coordinated flash wildings. Gangs swarmed beaches in Boston, Nashville, Long Island, Miami, Rochester, and Charlotte in what some believe was a social media coordinated effort.

And Stop Lying to My Friends

In response to the weekend violence, my network of friends emailed around news articles. Mary McCarthy (no relation to Police Superintendent McCarthy), a friend of a friend, emailed local papers about a mob pulling people from cars and taxis right outside her upscale apartment building. When the police arrived 15 minutes later, the crowd had scattered. Here's an excerpt:

> At about 11pm last Friday night, June 3rd, I heard shouting, screaming, horns blaring and tires screeching from my apartment...When I looked out my window to the street below I saw a crowd of about 20 young people...directly across the street from the entrance to my building. They were leaning on parked cars and clogging the street. They were screaming at people walking and driving by. I watched them stop vehicles, including taxi cabs, and

> pull people from the vehicles...It was a frightening scene and I was sure someone was going to be hurt.

The *Sun-Times* wrote of Mary McCarthy's report and Police Near North District commander Kenneth Angarone said that police responded but did not find a "bona fide incident." I believe Ms. McCarthy.

It's Not a Race War; It's a Class War

It's much too easy to let politicians divide the nation, make this about race, and ignore the underlying causes. It's true that many of the mobs in downtown Chicago are comprised of African Americans. Mary McCarthy didn't get a close up look at the mob outside her window, but they appeared white—definitely not African American.[220]

Last year, I never mentioned race in my post about Chicago violence, but a few commenters brought up race and made unwarranted assumptions. Some commenters assumed "wildings" only involve black youths. Chicago is a city with a lot of diversity I thinand gangs of every race. I mentioned a separate incident of an armed intruder being shot and killed by an off duty police officer; the armed intruder was not African American. I also mentioned three police officers were shot and killed within a two month period. Two were African American, one was not.

U.S. Downward Mobility

The destruction of the middle class has accelerated. Housing values have plummeted, and investors earn negative real rates of inflation adjusted returns on "safe" investments like money market funds. Food, fuel, and medical costs have skyrocketed. Essential civil services are underfunded while taxes escalate. The middle class is sinking fast as saved wealth is destroyed and its standard of living erodes.

After being subjected to a national financial crime wave with no meaningful consequences for white collar criminals, the middle class, the core of many cities and communities, is being subjected to a physical crime wave.

The U.S. escalated its debt to fund the ongoing bailout of the banking system. TARP was a small part of it. The Fed now owns over a trillion in suspect assets it bought from banks, and it daily provides them with almost zero cost money so high spreads help them earn their way out of the financial hole in their balance sheets. No one went to jail, and bankers reward themselves with billions in bonuses.

Banks broke their TARP agreement to lend to small and medium sized businesses. They lent to large businesses that outsource a lot of labor. The iPads stolen by Chicago gangs are mostly made in Asia. Banks and their enablers in Washington starved the U.S. of the biggest source of sustainable job growth: capital investment in the United States.

Elected Citizen-on-Taxpayer Financial Crime

Illinois and Chicago are ground zero for the consequences of our local and national fiscal folly. Pension funds are woefully underfunded. Last minute sweetheart deals to crony-connected retirees have contributed to the problem along with bad investment decisions. In general, though, civil servants are blameless. Some are being asked to increase contributions from 8 percent of pay to 12 percent of pay. The State of Illinois is behind on many of its bills. Chicago's city budget is in dire straits.

The suburb of Bellwood provides an example of how graft and corruption have contributed to municipal project debt. A train station project was hijacked by local officials who paid millions above appraisals for properties, and in at least one instance dealt with a mob-linked company. According to the *Chicago Tribune*, taxpayers of the small suburb have a $40 million hole and investigations revealed "questionable players," with laughable financial analysis.[221]

Chicago's unemployment rate and mortgage delinquency rates are among the highest in the country, and home prices have slumped to 10-year lows. The S&P Case -Shiller index shows that Chicago area housing prices have fallen to April 2001 levels. From the housing bubble's November 2006 peak, prices are off 34 percent.

Illinois state income taxes rose this year from 3 percent to 5 percent, a 66.7 percent increase. That is in addition to sales taxes, utility taxes, phone taxes, various automobile taxes.

Chicago is not alone. Cities throughout the country recently experienced wildings, and it will get worse for them as it did for Chicago. Illinois may have the most severe budget crisis in the country, but states like California, New York, New Jersey and more are troubled.

*****

Ongoing Mugging by Wall Street Banks

After the largest bank bailout in world history, we now have a national epidemic of foreclosure fraud. In March, Judge Moshe Jacobius stayed 1,700 foreclosures due to altered documents in Illinois' Cook County.

A complaint of alleged fraud on the part of Goldman Sachs detailed its close relationships with Countrywide, New Century, and Fremont. The complaint showed Goldman knew of "an accelerating meltdown for subprime lenders such as New Century and Fremont."[222] Despite known serious loan problems, Goldman continued to securitize the loans and sell them in packages of residential mortgage backed securities. Goldman Sachs Alternative Mortgage Products (GSAMP) was "garbage sold at mythical prices."

The complaint alleged that Countrywide employees in a Chicago office inflated incomes on 90 percent of reduced documentation loans, also known as "liars' loans." One of Countrywide's mortgage brokerage arms "routinely doubled the amount of the potential borrower's income... so that borrowers could qualify for loans they could not afford." The complaint alleged that brokers, not borrowers, engaged in massive fraud to push loans through the system and earn commissions. Illinois Attorney General Lisa Madigan told *First Business Morning News*: "Countrywide broke the law, homeowners did not."

Arianna Huffington explained that our elected officials allowed banks to thwart usury laws:

> Every day, Americans, faced with layoffs and tough economic times, are forced to use their credit cards

> to pay for essentials such as food, housing, and medical care—the costs of which continue to escalate. But, as their debt rises, they find it harder to keep up with their payments. When they don't, banks, trying to offset losses in other areas, turn around, hike interest rates, and impose all manner of fees and penalties. Third World America, P. 77.

Even when banks initiated foreclosure fraud, they refuse to bear the costs of delays and bad deals of their own making. After pumping up appraisals and falsifying borrowers' income on applications, banks are walking away from abandoned homes and sticking taxpayers with the bill to clean up the mess they left behind.

Banks claim that it is mortgage lenders or mortgage servicers who are guilty, but these are bank affiliates and business partners funded by the banks.

Banks supplied the money (via private label phony securitizations) that fueled this problem. Banks engaged in widespread massive mortgage securitization fraud. As underwriters, banks were responsible for doing adequate due diligence on the underlying loans. Banks were responsible for making sure the representations about risk in their financial products were accurate. Instead, the representations were materially misleading.

According to a local study by the Woodstock Institute, the mortgage servicers and trustees most often associated with abandoned properties are Bank of America, Wells Fargo, U.S. Bank, Deutsche Bank, and JPMorgan Chase.[223]

We Need the Mother of All Reforms

Doing nothing ensures a relentless downward slide into financial and social chaos for great swaths of the country. Washington's political corruption and mismanagement has the same roots as Chicago's. As Arianna points out, on a national level, we need "the mother of all reforms:

> That is why the first step toward stopping our relentless transformation into Third World America

> has to be breaking the choke hold that special interest money has on our politicians. (Third World America, 172)

Money isn't the only way to sway politicians. One can take away the power politicians try to buy with that money. Among voters, a show of numbers is as effective as money. The middle class needs to make its voice heard in the media and in direct contact with their local and national elected officials.

On a national level, we need a Constitutional amendment requiring full public financing for political campaigns (for starters). Too many politicians are owned by special interest groups that buy votes, finance campaigns, employ their relatives, or just buy them off. As Arianna explained: "If someone's going to own the politicians, it might as well be the American people.

Endnote: I use "wilding," since that is the term used by our local mainstream media news articles, including articles at NBC and the *Sun-Times*.[224] This is the definition given by the free online dictionary: "Slang: The act or practice of going about in a group threatening, robbing, or attacking others."

***Update June 8:** Garry McCarthy was approved by the full City Council and named Superintendent of the Chicago Police Department on Wednesday, June 8, 2011.

Update June 9: Two days after the new Superintendent said his men on trains and platforms would break up mobs before they formed and said several arrests proved there were enough police officers downtown to prevent attacks before they occur, Jesse Andersen, 35, brother of Billy Corgan, lead singer of Smashing Pumpkins, was attacked by a group of young people while riding the train on his way to work. Andersen was not seriously hurt.[225] Corgan tweeted about it and told the *SunTimes*:

> He was just sitting there on the train, listening to his iPod. They obviously set [my brother] up to rob him.

Even the *Wall Street Journal* reported this story. Mr. Andersen was much luckier than a victim the previous day, who was robbed of cash and an iPhone and sent to Northwestern Hospital in serious condition.[226]

The Middle Class is Drowning in Debt and Choking on Lies

June 24, 2011

If a drunk driver crashed his speeding rental car into your house and killed your spouse, you would be outraged if law enforcers took bribes and refused to give the driver a blood test. If the judge then gave the killer a small fine and ordered you to pay the fine and pay for all the damages, you'd be outraged. If the government then handed the drunk-driver keys to a bigger faster rental car, handed the drunk driver an even bigger bottle of whiskey, and then gave you the rental bill; you'd storm Washington, blizzard elected officials with protests and organize friends and associates to vote these malefactors, the elected officials that betrayed your trust, out of office.

Yet, we've remained largely silent in the face of the same sort of behavior by Wall Street and Washington. Bonus-seeking bankers crashed into Main Street's economy and ran control frauds within banks that would have failed without taxpayer bailouts. Bureaucrats and elected officials bailed them out without demanding consequences. Bankers are revving their engines again in credit derivatives, currency derivatives, and commodities trades. "Financial reform" addresses none of the latter problems.

Arianna Huffington's *Third World America* explains that the $787 billion American Recovery and Reinvestment Act, the bank bailout package also known as TARP, allotted only $72 billion to infrastructure projects. Another feature of the bill was to have banks agree to lend money to medium and small sized businesses to stimulate the economy. That didn't happen and official unemployment numbers remain above 9%, while unofficial figures for underemployed Americans soar above 20%.

The number one stimulus for any economy is not consumer spending, although that is a powerful secondary effect. The number one stimulus is capital spending, investment in the production of real goods and consumables. Huffington explains: "There were three flaws with the old economy that has crashed. It favored consumption over production, debt over small savings, and environmental damage over environmental renewal."

Our ongoing bank bailouts included the mispricing of around $4 trillion of toxic assets that the banks cannot afford to honestly price, since bank capital would be wiped out sparking another global financial meltdown. We continue to provide cheap taxpayer funding through the Fed. New accounting rules allow banks to cover-up the low price of impaired assets, and government debt guarantees provide ongoing subsidies to banks that have a value of trillions of dollars.

Ground Zero for America's Debt Crisis

Beyond the banks, we have fiscal mismanagement and corruption that plagues middle class taxpayers. I happen to live in Illinois, the best example of this in the nation. Cook County encompasses Chicago and some of its surrounding suburbs. This week, the Cook County Treasurer discovered "stunning" debt. This debt isn't new, but apparently our officials are now properly terrified. Our total debt for the municipality, education, county, sanitary, park, fire, township, library and special services is now $108 billion. That means the debt per person in Cook County exceeds $23,700 (corrected assuming 2.67 average per household) or more than $63,500 per household, and that is just local debt.

The other problem is that the Illinois economy isn't growing. Many of those households have no income coming in other than government subsidies, and some have no income at all. Unofficial unemployment numbers top 20%. State of Illinois taxes increased from 3% to 5%, an increase of around 67%. Taxes on real estate, utilities, sales, and more are expected to skyrocket. Businesses like the Chicago Mercantile Exchange are being courted by low income tax states (at least the income taxes are currently low) like Florida.

We're not doing better on a national level. Americans owe almost $122,500 (corrected assuming 2.69 average per household) per household or around $46,000 per person (Greek citizens owe $44,000 per person). That's on top of our local debt.

David Walker, the former U.S. comptroller general, says it's even worse than that. When he takes into account future obligations for Medicare, Social Security, Federal debt, Military retirement, Civil servant retirement, and more, we owe $546,663 per household. That doesn't even include your local debt—it may not be as bad as if you lived in Illinois, but it's substantial nonetheless—and personal debt including mortgages and consumer debt that average more than $120,000 per household.[227]

We're told we are a great country and we can "grow our way out of it." Exactly how does that occur, when jobs are going overseas, taxes for the wealthiest in our country are uncollectible after exploiting tax breaks, and programs for investment in infrastructure and production are virtually nonexistent?

America's biggest problem by far is that capital spending in new production facilities that create jobs and real products never occurred, not even after trillions of dollars were thrown at banks in the global financial system.

Chicago Police Superintendent McCarthy's Cheap Shot: "Government Sponsored Racism"

One would think that our fiscal problems and corruption by local and national officials would unite citizens in a common cause. I've been very vocal about predatory lending that targeted vulnerable minorities. A practice called "reverse red lining" targeted people of color and those in minority neighborhoods to get them to sign mortgages that had complicated documentation that hid risks. Yes, there was some fraud by borrowers, but the overwhelming problem in the Chicago area, was fraud on borrowers.

I've also been vocal about shootings, mob wildings, and muggings in Chicago and the fact that our officials are lying to our population about the causes. It's true that most of shootings are black-on-black or brown-on-brown and that violence in our poorer neighborhoods is branching out into middle class neighborhoods. In instances where perpetrators are black or brown and the victims are white, it is tempting to say it is all about race, but as I pointed out, this is much bigger than our racial issue; it's a class war. It's much too easy to let politicians divide the nation, make this about race, and ignore the underlying causes.

More disturbing were remarks made by Police Superintendent Garry McCarthy to Father Pfleger's congregation on Sunday June 5, 2011 at St. Sabina's Catholic Church. I provide the entire transcript along with this video, which has already been pulled from the web once, and was retrieved from the Google cache by a concerned citizen.[228] [229]

The last part of the speech is wrong on many levels. I'm happy to speak up about injustices such as predatory lending and how this practice victimized many neighborhoods in Chicago. In fact, I co-authored an Op-ed for the *New York Times* with the Reverend Jesse Jackson on that topic; it wasn't published, however, but we gave it a shot.

When it comes to the type of violent crime referred to by the Superintendent, he has his cause and effects all wrong, and he made it all about racism. He equated gun laws to "government sponsored racism."

If criminals didn't have guns, they would use knives. The killings in our African American communities have nothing to do with racism. These are black-on-black crimes perpetrated by criminals with no respect for authority and no self-respect. They victimize and terrorize decent members of the black community struggling to survive a devastating economic crisis. The Chicago Police Superintendent's pandering and misinformation doesn't make it easy for anyone to respect authority.

Gun control is "government sponsored racism?" Superintendent McCarthy is wrong on many levels. He mentions segregation, Jim Crow and the Black Code. The latter denied African Americans the right to own guns and that left them open to victimization by armed racists. Now they are victimized by armed criminals in their own communities. Only law-abiding citizens aren't allowed to have guns in Chicago, which seems to be a violation of U.S. citizens' Second Amendment rights. The chief challenger of this prohibition in Illinois is an African American man who wants to own a gun so he can defend himself. Moreover, Superintendent McCarthy didn't mention the understaffed and underequipped police officers, many of whom are men and women of color, who have been shot and killed, wounded, or have had guns pointed at them by criminals. How is any of this racism?

Father Pfleger has something to answer for as well. What happened to separation of Church and State? Why does the Catholic Church deserve tax-exempt status if it allows a priest to use the Church pulpit for political rallies?

Politicians divide the nation and try to make these issues about race, and ignore the underlying causes.

Endnote: Transcript of Chicago Police Superintendent Garry McCarthy addressing the Congregation at St. Sabina's Church in Chicago, Illinois on June 5, 2011 (from above video):

> I feel so inadequate after Father Pfleger speaking, but I would never turn down an opportunity to share a couple of words with the community.
>
> Because there's only 24 hours in the day, I'm trying to fit that 25th hour in and get out everywhere and talk to everybody all the time. I've spent an awful lot of time over the last... tomorrow's my three week anniversary. And I'm also up for confirmation tomorrow, so speak to your alderman; that would be very helpful.
>
> But I've spent an awful lot of time speaking to police officers over the last few weeks and I cannot help but be impressed by the sense of pride that they all take in this great agency called the Chicago Police Department. And Father, I've gotta...You know what? I'm there.
>
> I'm going to take one second if you'll forgive me for this. Um, You know I cannot echo or speak as articulate as you did laying out the challenges that we face as a society, but I'm here to tell you one or two quick things. There are no accidents. There are no accidents in this universe and I believe deep down in my soul, I've never made a decision in my police career but God has brought me to this place. I've never made a decision in my police career, and I jokingly tell people that I lead a Forrest Gump type existence, floating along and ending up where I go.
>
> But I did 20 years in the NYPD, and I was there on 911, so I have my own personal opinions about Osama Bin Laden. Please forgive me for that Father. But I was also there to see a change, a big change in the NYPD and the way we do business. And I want to

give you a couple of numbers. In 1990 in NYC, there were 2, 245 people murdered. I'm going to say that again. 2,245 people murdered, and the headlines on the daily news were "Do something, Dave," talking to David Dinkins, the Mayor at the time. Well we changed the way we did business, and the NYPD has been very successful to the point where last year they reduced that number to 450.

Now that's certainly progress, but it's not good enough. Do you realize we're talking about a 75% reduction, which is a big deal, but we had 450 people murdered. That's not okay, that's not okay. And again Father forgive me, I looked at my Blackberry in church, but while we were sitting here, there was another murder in the City of Chicago. It's not okay, and I'm not willing to accept that it's okay. And I'm setting the bar higher than anybody ever sets the bar for me. I set it higher than anybody sets it.

And I had a conversation with Father Pfleger, and I told him my vision, and he basically articulated it. But I want to tell you, we used to react to crime, then we used to prevent crime. That's what we're doing now; that's how we reduce crime. Nobody's ever cured crime. Nobody's ever cured it. The police cannot arrest their way out of crime. It's got to be done on a different level. It's got to be done in recognition of the moral authority of the community to change the behavior of criminals.

Wow, there must be something about this pulpit here, 'cause I'm feelin' strong. I usually, I, I, [sic] should never mix politics and faith, but since, since the Father mentioned it, I want to talk just one thing, and then I promise you I'm giving up the microphone. It's, it's the last time I get invited to speak.

You know I'm going to take a risk here, and I'm gonna give you somethin'. This is definitely the right audience. Father Pfleger talked about gun control, and I wanna, I wanna give a little test here. And this is sensitive. You know, because everybody's afraid of race. Have you noticed that? Everybody's afraid of race.

I'm not afraid of race. I was born and raised in the Bronx, NY, and when I was growin' up, the three biggest problems were gangs, guns, and drugs. Does that sound familiar?

So how, how much have we failed as a society to address this?

I'm 52 years old. I'm 52 years old, and today in 2011, we're talking about gangs and guns and drugs and what we're going to do to fix it. Okay? A big component of this has to do with race.

Everybody's afraid of race. I'm not afraid of race. So here's what I want to tell you. See, let's see if we can make a connection here. Slavery. Segregation. Black codes. Jim Crow. What, what did they all have in common? Anybody getting' scared?

Government sponsored racism. [Long pause.]

I told ya I wasn't afraid. I told ya I wasn't afraid.

Now I want you to connect one more dot on that chain of the African American history in this country, and tell me if I'm crazy.

Federal gun laws that facilitate the flow of illegal firearms, into our urban centers across this country, that are killing our black and brown children. [Long pause.]

The NRA does not like me, and I'm okay with that. We've got to get the gun debate back to center, and it's got to come with the recognition of who's paying the price for the gun manufacturers being rich and living in gated communities.

I, on December 23 in Newark, I was coming from a Christmas Party when we had two back-to-back events. We had five kids who were shot, two of 'em succumbed to their wounds, and then we had two more men who were shot back-to-back within five minutes of each other. I was on my way to one, when I went to the other, and I was walking through shell casings, bullets, spent bullets in the street. They were gettin' stuck in my shoes and I said "You know what? Sumpin's wrong. Somethin's wrong, and I went from one scene to the next, and by the time I got home, probably about 10:30, 11:00 that night, snapped on the TV to relax for a few minutes, and what was on TV? Sarah Palin's Alaska. And she was caribou hunting, and talking about the right to bear arms.

Why wasn't she at the crime scene with me?

I'm gonna need some help. Because people don't want to hear this. Okay? And this is what I'm talking about changing the face of the way we do police in this country starting right here in Chicago. It's with the recognition of what is going on, and a plan to address it.

I couldn't be happier. I feel like I'm in a perfect place, the perfect time, with the right people around me.

Thank you very much everybody. This is gonna be great experience.

Why Some Housing Prices Are Still Falling and Subprime Loans Are Still Sliding

June 27, 2011

In October 2007, CNBC's Diana Olick called me about Countrywide's so-called plan to modify mortgage loans scheduled to reset to higher rates. Subprime borrowers with a strong payment history would be able to refinance and possibly get prime FHA loans. Current paying borrowers with credit issues would be offered Fannie Mae or Freddie Mac loans under a new expanded program.

Mortgage Loans with Less than Zero Value

Mortgage modification programs, including HAMP, were abysmal failures. At the time I told Olick that mortgage servicers were selling loans for 3-6 cents on the dollar and they were happy to dump them:

> They work 13-hour days trying to salvage what they can, doing anything to avoid reporting a delinquency or foreclosure. They disclosed disturbing information unavailable even on trustee reports. The servicer asserted the rating agencies are incorrect in their optimism; recovery rates of 60% are unattainable. My average recovery rate assumption of 30% is also currently unattainable.

If loans couldn't be sold to a sucker, banks and their servicers walked away. Mortgage securitization complicated matters, and often homes are left vacant and not foreclosed upon. Looters strip vacant properties of pipes, fixtures, and anything of salvage value. The loans within the securitizations are worthless.

Why do banks and trustees pretend the loans have value? If banks and lenders foreclosed, it would be revealed that the cost to maintain the property before resale and the legal costs relative to the value of the property meant that they had negative equity.

At first this was a problem for loans with low loan balances, but as property values dropped, even loans with higher balances had the same problem. The problem spread, and it hasn't yet stopped spreading.

Triple Tragedy: Meltdown, Spreading Contagion, and Crime

This tragedy is echoed by similar problems in Ohio, Michigan and other subprime targets on the West Coast, Nevada, and in the South. Although some examples aren't as stark or depressing, the general idea of plummeting property values and vacant properties infecting a neighborhood and its surrounding areas still stands. Affected states have to carry the burden of these paralyzed limbs, and banks and their cronies that perpetrated this mess just walk away.[230]

Since 2007, Chicago's Englewood and West Englewood areas slid into a sinkhole. Homes that once housed lower middle class and middle class families stand empty. Those with the means to move have fled. Those without the means have stayed while the prairie reclaims a large part of the south side of Chicago. More and more homes have been boarded up. Grass has grown so high in some formerly residential areas it obscures all but the tallest humans. Crime soared. Property values in surrounding neighborhoods are plummeting as the wasteland spreads to their doorsteps.

"Countrywide Broke the Law"

It would be easy to turn away from this and blame the borrowers. Some of the borrowers were absentee landlords who knew what they were doing. Some borrowers overreached. But in many cases, people were victimized by predatory lenders. For example, a complaint of alleged fraud against Goldman Sachs includes allegations of fraudulent practices by Countrywide, now owned by Bank of America. A former Countrywide employee stated that approximately 90% of all "liars' loans", loans that allowed reduced documentation about borrowers' income and assets, sold out of a Chicago office had inflated incomes.

The borrowers weren't inflating the income. Countrywide routinely doubled the amount of the potential borrower's income to qualify borrowers for loans they couldn't afford so that Countrywide and its mortgage brokers could continue to earn fees and commissions. Prior to a settlement in which Countrywide paid a paltry $8.68 billion—the damage done is much greater—to eleven states, Illinois Attorney General Lisa Madigan stated: "Countrywide broke the law, homeowners did not."

Fed's August 2007 Back Door Bail Out of Countrywide

In August 2007, investors shunned Countrywide's asset backed commercial paper (ABCP) backed by its mortgage loans and demanded much higher interest rates. In the ensuing panic, Countrywide wanted to borrow around $11.5 billion from banks on its credit card-like revolving credit lines, but the banks balked. The banks asked the Fed for concessions, and the Fed agreed.

The Fed deal appeared to have been leaked. On Thursday, August 16, 2007, the Dow fell more than 340 points when it appeared Countrywide was about to go under, but rebounded to close down only 15 points. The next morning the Fed announced its new bank lending concessions.

The Fed bailed out Countrywide and its affiliated banks through its back door. The Fed agreed to let banks borrow against private label mortgage loans with phony "AAA" ratings, cut the banks' discount rate from 6.25% to 5.75%, and extended "overnight" borrowings to 30 days.

BofA, Wells Fargo, U.S. Bank, Deutsche Bank, and JPMorgan Cut and Run

Banks that supplied money—and in some cases now own—suspect mortgage lenders also packaged up and sold those loans to investors. They own or owned mortgage "servicers" that cannot recover foreclosure costs combined with the costs of maintaining and reselling the house. After pumping up appraisals and falsifying borrowers' income on applications, banks are walking away and sticking taxpayers with the bill.

According to the Woodstock Institute, the mortgage servicers and trustees linked to abandoned properties in Chicago are Bank of America, Wells Fargo, U.S. Bank, Deutsche Bank, and JPMorgan Chase.

Despite evidence of widespread interconnected mortgage lending, securitization, and foreclosure wrong-doing and fraud, there are no meaningful felony indictments of senior executives at mortgage lenders or of senior executives of banks bailed out by taxpayers.

Investing: Bad News, Good News, and What's Next

August 22, 2011

The manic depressive market wildly swings up and down on each new news story: The Fed is meeting at Jackson Hole on August 27 possibly to discuss QE3 (or not), and that news may pump up the stock market. But China's banks seem to be using Enron's accounting manual, Europe's banks need liquidity and are loaded with bad debt, and U.S. banks only temporarily TARPed over trouble. Gaddafi's regime in Libya appears over, but Libya's oil output may not fully recover for years. Venezuela wants banks to open their vaults and send back its gold, but Wells Fargo says gold is a bubble. Pundits say gold is a barbarous relic, but exchanges and banks are now using gold as money. The U.S. is headed for hyperinflation with skyrocketing stock prices, but on the other hand, we seem to be deflating like Japan and doomed to a deflating stock market for another decade. Whom do you trust and what should you do?

No one knows where the stock market or U.S. Treasury bonds are headed tomorrow, but in my opinion, here are some fundamentals to consider.

The Bad News Isn't Going Away

Until we have real global financial reform and restrain the banks, we won't have sustained growth. The stock market hasn't hit bottom. There's a crisis of confidence in banks and all currencies. We haven't taken effective steps to tackle the U.S. deficit through productivity. We haven't examined spending to eliminate fraud and waste, and we haven't addressed our need for more tax revenues by eliminating the Bush tax cuts (for starters).

Savers are punished by "stranguflation:" negative real returns on "safe" assets, declining housing prices, and rising costs of food, energy and health care. The Fed touts the falling cost of iPads, but how often do you buy one of those, and how often do you eat?

Good News (for Now)

The USD is still the world's reserve currency. Even though we devalued the USD, there has been a global flight to U.S. Treasuries pushing down our borrowing costs (yields). No one in the global financial community feels the U.S. has done its best to correct our problems, but severe problems in Europe, China's inflation, and Middle East unrest has money running to the U.S. Since we've devalued the dollar, we appear to be a bargain for foreign investors, even though they are terrified by our money printing presses and the potential for inflating commodity prices in the long run.

How did I play this? My own portfolio is currently more than 20% gold with some silver, and I bought out-of-the-money call options on the VIX when it was in the teens with maturities of 4-6 months. This is "short" stock market strategy, one could have also done well buying puts on the S&P a few months ago. In the first big stock market downdraft in August, I sold the options when the VIX hit the high 30's, and I'll buy more options again if the VIX falls again. Many investors are not comfortable with options, and this strategy isn't appropriate for everyone. The rest of my portfolio is chiefly in cash or deep value opportunities.

What Happens Next?

No one knows for sure, and anyone who tells you he or she does is selling snake oil. The situation is fluid. We tried to reflate our deflating economy. Our massive dollar devaluation may encourage investment, because it's protectionist. It reduces our cost of labor, among a few other "benefits." The problem is that the Fed has printed money, and we haven't done anything to position the U.S. for greater productivity. We're trying to inflate our way out of a problem without investing in productivity. This is a very dangerous way of attacking this problem. Even more "stimulus" would just be an attempt to inflate our way out of our long-standing deep recession. That's the foolish and unsuccessful strategy we've adopted so far. That could lead to runaway budget deficits (our deficit already looks intractable) and bring us to double-digit inflation. Even the European flight to US Treasuries may not save us from a deeper recession in that scenario.

If we don't overreact—and we may have already overreacted—our dollar devaluation results in our foreign trade situation first getting worse (as it has now) before it gets better. Now is the time (actually, we should have started years ago) to spend capital to increase U.S. productivity. The dollar's plunge relative to other currencies will eventually make us more competitive. This will be good for blue chip companies, in particular those that own real assets and manufacture items. The Fed and Washington may do anything, however, so one must watch the news.

What does this mean for the U.S. stock market? In my opinion, it is currently not good value and feels like the 1970s when we experienced a recession followed by inflation. One should consider staying mostly in cash and expect stocks to become cheaper. One might miss an interim rally, especially if the Fed announces QE3 (more "stimulus" and money printing) or more bank bailouts, but that is like using Kleenex laced with sneezing powder. We will see stock prices even lower than they are today. The old paradigm dictated that stocks were a buy when P/E ratios were 13 or less (and many are well above that), dividends at 4%, and book values at 1.3 or less. (This excludes oil companies, which tend to trade at lower P/E ratios in general.) I believe we'll see much better deals in coming months. In 1978/79 P/E ratios sank below 7 for blue chip companies.

Should one buy U.S. Treasuries with long maturities? The long end of the bond market doesn't reward investors due to the potential of rising interest rates. If interest rates spike to double digits, then one can reassess the situation.

Long term investors should consider buying commodities or companies that own physical commodities. We're running out of key commodities especially related to agriculture and fertilizer. Washington's brand of the latter isn't the type we need.

"It's not like I'm anti-China. I just think it's ridiculous that we allow them to do what they're doing to this country, with the manipulation of the currency."

—President Donald J. Trump

CHAPTER 16 China: Our Debt, Her Debt

China Defaults, Currency Basket Threatens Dollar

October 6, 2009

Robert Fisk exposed revived discussions by the Gulf States, China, France, Japan, Brazil, and Russia to replace the dollar as the benchmark oil trading currency with a basket of currencies including gold within 10 years.[231] This proposal is not new and discussions have been ongoing for decades. But other extraordinary moves in the capital markets suggest we should take this threat to the dollar's position very seriously. For example, China has $2.3 trillion in currency reserves (about 70% in dollars), and China knows how to get its way.

In November 2008, Chinese banks said they would no longer play by our rules. Top tier banks (Bank of China and Industrial and Commercial Bank of China) reneged on derivatives contracts. They failed to come up with billions in collateral on dollar/yen FX trades, which were out of the money after the yen's October appreciation. This should have been headline news in every financial newspaper, but it wasn't.

Chinese banks defaulted. They may have been partially motivated by U.S. malfeasance in the capital markets that caused losses in Asia. The U.S. squandered its credibility and our cover-ups have done nothing to restore it.

Most credit support annex agreements would say that closing out these trades would be an event of default, and then the cross default on all the trades would kick in with the same counterparty. But the credit of the Chinese banks was better than many of their counterparties. Everyone was forced to renegotiate contracts with the Chinese banks.

From the perspective of the derivatives markets, this is earth shattering. What would have happened if AIG had done the same thing? (Hey, Goldman, UBS, and others…you want your collateral? Well…Stuff It!)

At the end of August 2009, China signaled that state owned oil consumers: Air China, COSCO, and China Eastern could default on money-losing commodities derivatives contracts.[232]

The U.S. should have done everything in its power to correct our mistakes, clean up the mess in our financial system—instead of sweeping it under the carpet—and turned our efforts to maintaining the credibility of the capital markets and the credibility of the dollar.

Clear and Present Danger

October 31, 2011

The United States is the largest debtor nation in the history of the world, and our borrowing is increasing. In 1950 spending for social programs was only six percent of the total Federal Budget (Note: corrected from one percent in the original version. This represents spending for health and welfare.), and pensions were 4% of the budget. As the economy grew, social programs expanded to include Social Security, Medicare, Medicaid, Food Stamps, Unemployment Compensation, Supplemental Security for the Disabled, and education programs. In 1983 as the United States pulled out of an ugly recession and brought inflation under control, social programs consumed an estimated 26% of the budget, and pensions were over 23% of the budget. In fiscal year 2010, health and welfare ate up 38% of the budget, and pensions another 22%. [233]

The original idea was that if everyone agreed to chip in a small percentage of ever growing income, the percentage of social spending would never have to change even if the programs grew. The percentage for social programs could stay constant because if income doubled every twelve years or so, the amounts available for welfare would also double. Military budgets soared, the U.S. waged unfunded wars, the banking system was bailed out of the consequences of unwise lending more than once, and government bureaucracy grew rapaciously. All of this would likewise be covered by taxes assessed on growing income, or so the theory went. Like many academic economic theories, it was a convenient but misguided story. No country has ever managed to create a perpetual growth machine for its economy.

Time and again U.S. growth was brought to a standstill by (among other things) oil shocks of the kind the U.S. experienced in 1973 and 1979, monetary shocks of the kind the U.S. experienced in 1981, and systemic financial crises of the kind the U.S. experienced in 2008 and will likely experience again in the not too distant future.

Growth in the U.S. has been hobbled by moving many of our smokestack industries and soft manufacturing industries offshore. Traditionally weakening the dollar relative to stronger currencies like the Chinese yuan (the renminbi) stimulated growth as relative labor costs sank in the U.S. Today, much of the benefit of this strategy leaks to offshore manufacturing facilities.

Periods of anemic growth meant the U.S. had to raise taxes, but there is a limit to how much the economic engine and the population will tolerate. Hiking tax rates invites inflation, and artificially low interest rates are a hidden tax that punishes savers while food, energy, and medical care costs have soared. The U.S. can impose consumption taxes on liquor and other discretionary items, impose higher taxes on the rich, and possibly impose a confiscatory wealth tax, but eventually the U.S. will reach a point where this will be counterproductive.

U.S. debt now approaches 100% of GDP. In the long run the U.S. will have to cut social programs and increase taxes, but in the short run the U.S. cannot adjust quickly enough. If the U.S. has to pay its debts and it can't tax more, then it must borrow more. In fact, we are borrowing more, and how we borrow matters.

High rates of debt to GDP are the chief danger to any country's economic future, and any method of borrowing holds its special brand of danger. There are only three ways to fund a government deficit: foreign borrowing, domestic borrowing with monetary expansion, and domestic borrowing without monetary expansion. The U.S. has chosen a combination of the first two. Of the three, the way to get into big trouble very fast is to become dependent upon foreign borrowing. Treasury note and T-bill issuance as of second quarter 2011 was around $14.4 trillion, and the total bond market size estimate by SIFMA (less intergovernmental debt held by the Federal Reserve and Social Security Trust) was around $9.2 trillion. Total foreign holdings of $4.5 trillion represented around 31% of total Treasury issuance or around 48% of SIFMA's estimated government bond market. China's and Japan's combined holdings represent around 14% of total issuance or around 22% of SIFMA's estimated traded government bond market. As of June 2011, Japan held $911 billion or around 20% of foreign holdings of U.S. Treasuries, and China held around $1.16 trillion or approximately 26% of foreign U.S. Treasury holdings.[234]

Why are foreign borrowings such a huge risk for the United States? The funds are currently kept in dollars a lot of which is with American banks. That money is yankable and that can cause a run on the dollar. Military leadership addresses the threat of attacks, and administrative leadership must address the clear and present danger of financial withdrawals. The dollar is still the world's reserve currency, but that advantage doesn't make the dollar bullet proof. U.S. dollars can be converted to yen or to euros. On October 17, China took a key step to internationalizing the yuan and making it an alternative to petrodollars if not an alternative reserve currency; Hong Kong's Chinese Gold & Silver Exchange Society now offers gold quoted in yuan.

This might have been worth the risk if foreign borrowing had been invested for roads, high speed railroads, new industries, cheap energy, airports, and to fund scientific research. The debt would self-liquidate. Instead, some of the debt has been used for transfer payments to fuel current consumption or for items like farm subsidies. It's as if you mortgaged your house to buy groceries. Eventually you'll have no house and no food either. Moreover, a very large chunk of the debt has been monetized through Federal Reserve Bank purchases and used to fill gaping holes in bank balance sheets. Unrepentant banks resist reform and dilute attempts at regulation while soaking up ongoing subsidies. All of this is dead-end financing at the expense of citizens that saved their money and pay taxes.

Greece's distress is an extreme example of what happens when debt service is high but investment in the economy is insufficient. According the *Wall Street Journal*, "Parliament member Panagiotis Kouroumplis...supported the first bailout, but, he says, 'every single euro we got went for debt. We haven't spent a single euro on development.'"[235] The U.S. has a bigger and broader economy, but our bailouts—and the financial malfeasance that preceded and follow them—have nonetheless given our producing economy a body blow while chiefly benefiting fee-seeking dead-end financiers that eat up an outsized percentage of the nation's GDP.

In 1978, we averted a near-crash of our financial system after Kuwait refused to renew a more than $1 billion deposit with J.P. Morgan (then Morgan Guaranty). The Federal Reserve intervened to stabilize the dollar and averted a "19th Century financial panic" that would have triggered a "genuine depression."[236] In 1979 as tensions escalated with Iran, the U.S. sequestered Iranian assets to prevent a repeat of the near-crash in 1978. In the first years after these events, the U.S. seemed to have learned its lesson and reduced foreign borrowings—including borrowings from the Saudis and Kuwait—to around 7% of total borrowings. Decades of bad policies, unfunded wars, and uncontrolled chaos in the financial system ballooned our debts and our foreign borrowings. Today's foreign borrowings are 31% of total issuance or 48% of the estimated government bond market. The U.S. is in hock to foreigners again, particularly to Asia.

How does the U.S. try to counter the danger represented by foreign borrowings? After exporting our profligate spending to China with no intention of reform, we wield the implied threat that if China doesn't continue to lend to us, it will go down with us. The Chinese may not see it that way as they feel the pinch of inflation, experience inevitable cyclical growth slowdowns, and develop new trading partners.

Foreign borrowings of the United States represent a clear and present danger to the U.S. dollar and to the U.S. financial system. Potential dumping of U.S. dollars would start a run on the currency and a financial panic that would tip our already precarious economy into a deep depression. No matter how much currency central banks use to try to manipulate exchange rates, the market always has more. The U.S. needs contingency plans against a large scale withdrawal of funds from the U.S. and from U.S. financial institutions. In the gravest extreme to avoid a run on the U.S. currency and a collapse of the U.S. economy, the U.S. requires a standby plan to sequester a foreign nation's funds, just as we have done in the past.

*****

Chanos Crash: Timing China's Financial Meltdown

December 6, 2011

At an October seminar of the Chicago Council on Global Affairs (CCGA), carnival economist Niall Ferguson promoted his new book, *Civilization: The West and the Rest*. He revealed the blindingly obvious as if it were a divine revelation: the U.S. has serious problems. He preached that the U.S. corrupted its six Ferguson-defined "killer apps": competition, science, rule of law, medicine, the consumer society, and a strong work ethic.

Ferguson claims India and China have downloaded these killer apps and compares the West with a virus infected PC and the East with a fast Mac. Never mind that competition, science, medicine, trade, and industrious workers have been in evidence in India and China for centuries. The West didn't invent these ideas, so perhaps there's more to the story than Ferguson's pat explanation. As for rule of law, that killer app seems as corrupted in the East as it is in the West. Ferguson's crowd-pleasing presentation didn't mention other "killer" apps that are prevalent in China: fraud, high debt levels, and privatizing gains while socializing risks and losses.

Ferguson claims that in 1978 citizens of the U.S. were on average 20 times richer than the citizens of China. Today, U.S. citizens are only five times richer. He apparently defines wealth as acquisition of material goods. That is important, to be sure, and the West should pay careful attention to the material economy. But Ferguson's China supremacy presentation didn't mention the negative human wealth effects of China's one-child policy on the shortage of female mates, the general disregard of public safety, and shortage of essentials like agricultural water and arable land.

Ferguson projects that China will have closed the material goods gap by 2016. This fits right in with popular group-think that China is an unstoppable growth machine. But it is this type of group-think that warned no one about the pending financial crisis in the U.S. in 2008 and now ignores serious potential problems in China.

*****

Bailouts, Railroading, Cover-ups, and the Chinese "Miracle"

China is becoming a version of the U.S., but it's the version that builds lots of Penn Centrals in record time to connect slapped together empty cities before going bankrupt.

When Ferguson claimed China downloaded killer apps from the West, he left out one that is literally a killer in the form of reckless disregard for public safety. China's Ministry of Railroads, an entity with rapidly growing debt of 2.1 trillion yuan ($330 billion), was bailed out when the National Development and Reform Commission announced it had "government support."[237]

The bigger problem is the shoddy construction of China's high speed railroad system, and cover-ups by railroad management. It turns out that railway bridges were constructed by untrained unskilled migrant workers and rocks and gravel were tossed into pier foundations instead of concrete. Unqualified workers also built tunnels. When tunnel problems manifest themselves, they usually involve suffocation of passengers. If you ever wondered how the Chinese can slap together an infrastructure so fast, here's your answer. It literally slaps it together. Fixing the construction problem may ultimately be more costly than having done it properly in the first place. But the social issues are an even bigger disaster for Chinese government.

In July 2011, two bullet trains on the Wenzhou Line crashed. Officials claimed a lightning strike caused the accident, and tried to suppress reports.

After officials claimed everyone was removed from the carriages, bulldozers buried the rubble and onlookers screamed as bodies fell out of the windows of the about-to-be-buried carriages. Then after it was formally announced that all of the bodies in the carriages had been removed, a four-year-old girl was found alive in the wreckage. A spokesman for China's Railway ministry told the reporters shouting at him that it was a "miracle."

Tens of Millions of Mate-less Men

China's population comprises more than 1.3 billion people. According to *Unnatural Selection*, China has 121 male births for every 100 females, whereas the highest natural ratio is around 106 males per every 100 females. Wikipedia's 2008 figures show that in the under 15 age group, there were already 113 males for every 100 females. I'm sure young men and women have given this ratio at least a passing thought, and it's getting much worse.[238]

Putting aside the issues of selective abortion of female fetuses, female infanticide, and the implications of household formation, this means a growth in the tens of millions of frustrated men dispersed throughout China.

The apparent euphoria of western pundits like Ferguson when discussing China makes me wonder if they downloaded an app for a peculiar kind of dementia. Everything we want or need in life comes to us through our relationships with other people. The quality of our relationships, or human wealth, defines the quality of our lives. Ignoring this is a socio-economic hand job. China is fundamentally impoverished in a way that is irreparable in the short run.

China's Housing Price Crash

There's a myth that low leverage makes a housing price crash immaterial. Many Chinese home buyers pay cash, but others make high down payments. Some reported down payments are as low as 30%; high by U.S. "standards," but still painful when housing prices drop 30%. Some investors have bought multiple properties. Even if one pays upfront in full, a housing price decline has a huge impact on how wealthy investors feel.

Here's the most benign case. Suppose a buyer pays cash for an empty investment property. The buyer still has to maintain the property. If housing prices remain stagnant (or go down), and food prices and other prices escalate (as they have), will that buyer feel richer or poorer? Will he have a higher appetite for liquidity or a lower one? Will other potential investors observe this and want to buy real estate so they can enjoy the same delightful experience?

The critical problem is that home prices in China are sliding fast. Some analysts say the "tipping point" started in September and they expect it to get much worse. Chinese newspapers reported riots in Shanghai after developers slashed prices to dump inventory. Contracted home buyers saw prices cut 25%.[239] Some property developments in Beijing have had price cuts of 20-30 percent. China's empty "ghost cities" are seeing price discounts of 30 percent for upfront cash payments. Mainstream U.S. financial media is now reporting possible housing price declines of 20-30 percent for major Chinese cities next year.

China's Debt and Coming Hard Landing

Nothing creates a hard landing better than a housing collapse. Property construction accounts for more than 13% of China's GDP up from around 3% of GDP in 1999 according to the China National Bureau of Statistics.

Local Chinese governments have mounting debt to fund infrastructure projects of 10.7 trillion yuan ($1.7 trillion) and depend on land sales to fund payments. According to investment management company GMO debt in Local Government Funding Vehicles amounts to around 1/3 of China's GDP. The projected slowdown in land sales will pose a huge problem, no matter whose numbers one uses.[240]

A huge problem in analyzing China's debt problems are off-balance sheet obligations. No one knows the size of local government debt obscured by off-balance sheet vehicles. Hidden national government debt includes "support" such as for the railroad and a variety of other guarantees have ballooned China's real debt.

Then there are the obvious problems with undercapitalized banks. When most people think of "Jim" and "China" they think of China advocate Jim Rogers or China skeptic Jim Chanos. Many people haven't heard of Jim Antos, an analyst at Mizuho Securities in Asia. According to Antos, loan growth has slowed to 15% from 30%, but the unsustainable current level of bank loans stands at $6,500 per capita in 2010. Gross domestic product per capita is $4,400. [The CIA estimates 2010 GDP per capita at $7,600 adjusted for purchasing power parity.] On a scale of one to ten, he rates China's debt problem an eight and Greece's debt problem a ten.

GMO reports that Fitch estimates that 35% of bank loans are directly or indirectly tied to the Chinese property market, and UBS estimates it at 40-50% of outstanding loans. No matter which is correct, a pullback will be brutal. ("Between Errors of Optimism and Pessimism," by Edward Chancellor, GMO, September 2011, and "China Real Estate—Final Destination," UBS, August 25, 2011.)

These loans don't count active private lending frauds that fleece entire towns and enrich local bureaucrats, accomplices of "property developers" turned con artists.[241]

Swindles have become so commonplace that James Grant, of the *Grant's Interest Rate Observer,* calls China "The People's Republic of Madoff." Research firm Muddy Waters gives foreign investors ample reasons to be wary. It's been documenting suspicious numbers reported by a plethora of small cap Chinese reverse merger companies listed on foreign exchanges. Muddy Waters' skepticism about a larger company, Sino Forest, caused its stock price to plummet.

If that weren't enough to make investors nervous, Jim Chanos, President and founder of Kynikos, told *Bloomberg* that many large cap shareholders don't realize that all they have is an operating agreement with mainland companies, not control of hard assets.

China has loaded itself up with debt. Unfortunately for Chinese citizens, China also down-loaded the "killer app" of socializing credit risk. Bank deposits are low yielding and the borrowing rate is either very low or negative which encourages explosive loan growth, also known as a debt bubble. ("China Financial Markets: Time to relax credit?" by Michael Pettis, Guanghua School of Management, Peking University, October 31, 2011.)

As for China's official growth figures, one has to be suspicious of government numbers when ministers have already shown they will try to bulldoze over horrific facts. Discovery of the truth takes a miracle.

When Will Strain Lead to a Crash?

China is on track for making as much of a muddle of its economy as many countries in the West have done. While being a fast-growing creditor country helps mitigate the consequences of its folly, the consequences are catching up with China. Are these problems overstated? That's impossible to tell without reliable numbers. The question to answer is how quickly and to what degree will China's problems affect its economy? After all, one wants to be able to get in a good short trade just before it all falls apart, if that is where this is headed.

Dylan Grice points out that anecdotal evidence can be misleading and China may "keep the plates spinning for a few more years." ("Popular Delusions: On China's swindles: how big is the bezzle [sic]?" by Dylan Grice, Societe Generale Cross Asset Research, November 4, 2011.)

It would be useful to come up with a measurement that indicates when things are just about to fall apart. Based on my own anecdotal experience in Iran, one cannot predict the timing of a collapse with certainty, but a good leading indicator is when rats start leaving the sinking ship in droves.

Chanos ("China Chaos") Derivatives

Grice provides a clue for the timing of China's collapse. Since 1990 around 18,000 officials have fled taking an average of around $7 million per flight. Special purpose credit derivatives (perhaps you prefer the term "discredited" derivatives) are a leading indicator for China's hard landing. I call these "China chaos" derivatives, or "Chanos" derivatives.

If the rate of change of public officials fleeing the country, $df/dt > x$, where x is yet to be defined, *or* the acceleration in fleers, $d^2f/dt^2 > y$, where y has yet to be defined, *or* the rate of change of the average amount of loot $dl/dt > z$, where z is yet to be defined, then conditions of the Chanos Equilibrium have been violated and destabilization will occur.

Stated differently, when you see the absolute amount of embezzled wealth fleeing the country suddenly increase, or when you see a sudden increase in the absolute number of Chinese officials leaving the country on "holiday," or when you see an acceleration in the number of officials leaving the country in a stealthier way, you'll know China is sinking.

China 2012: The Year of the Bull (Rogers) or the Bear (Chanos)?

January 9, 2012

When I think of a China bull and a China bear, I think of the legendary dueling Jims: Jim Rogers[242] and Jim Chanos.[243] In response to investors bearish on China, Jim Rogers famously said: "I find it interesting that people who couldn't spell China 10 years ago are now experts." Jim Chanos famously said that China's real estate market is "Dubai times 1,000—or worse."[244] He's been saying that for over two years. Chanos points to a credit bubble, and says he's early and sticking with his short positions. Rogers insists "China is not in a [credit] bubble," rather it's been in a price bubble in urban, coastal real estate, and to compare China to Dubai is a false analogy. Jim Rogers is bullish on China's long term prospects: "China is going to have *many serious* problems along the way as it rises, but 'Dubai 1000 times over'?!"

Jim Rogers: China Bull

James B. Rogers made his fortune as a hedge fund trader and then took off to see the world. If you have a business degree and you've never read his books *Adventure Capitalist, Hot Commodities*, and *A Bull in China*, then you've had an incomplete education. In his world travels, Rogers exposes bridge-to-nowhere investments by world organizations like the International Monetary Fund and corrupt governments and waste. He also points out areas of potential sound investments and areas to avoid or short.[245] He's been short India for over a year. He does his own research and observes that celebrity economists often lump India and China together. "It shows a profound lack of understanding of both."[246]

China's Big Picture

According to Rogers, China will have many set-backs as it grows, as did the U.K. and the U.S. He notes "the U.S.'s many Depressions in the 19th century, a devastating civil war, periodic massacres in the streets, and little rule of law, few human rights, and several military governments. As recently as 1907 the whole system collapsed just as the U.S. was on the verge of becoming the greatest success of the 20th century. Yet the U.S. did a good job for a long time."

What are China's true growth figures? Rogers doesn't trust any government's numbers. He assumes they're all lying. Yet China's growth is faster than that of developed countries. A pullback in the West will affect China, but China will be hurt less. The CIA estimates 2010 exports at only 16% of China's 10 trillion dollar GDP with growth of 10.3% (adjusting the fiat exchange rate for purchasing power parity).

China's high household savings rate relative to the U.S. and reserves give it more of a buffer in a downturn. China is feeling the effects of the developed world's problems and is experiencing inflation, but Rogers says it will suffer less than the developed world. China is a creditor nation and the United States is a debtor nation.[247]

A global slowdown will affect China along with the countries with which it does business. Rogers views the global economy in both absolute and relative terms: "Saying 'I was right on China' when the rest of the world is suffering *more* is embarrassing at least to me. The rest of the world is repeatedly knocking on China's door to help, since China continues to do better than others."

Trouble is Opportunity

Rogers won't live in any of his favorite cities in Mainland China, because pollution levels make them unsafe for his family's health. Some estimates say that by U.S. standards, only 20% of Chinese cities have satisfactory air quality. But Chinese officials say 80% of the cities are satisfactory and improving versus last year. That's hard to believe. The U.S. Embassy called Beijing's pollution "crazy bad."[248] In December, 2011, cancer-causing fine particulate pollution caused a shutdown of the busiest airport in Asia, Beijing's Capital Airport. Rogers sees money making opportunities for companies that can clean up and control pollution.[249]

Rogers acknowledged before Jim Chanos that there are localized real estate bubbles in China. In 2009, he warned about the urban, coastal real estate bubble. The government took action to quell speculation. Rogers believes China's real estate problem is a price bubble more than a credit bubble due to lower leverage in the system.

Chinese borrowers had to have good credit, make a substantial down payment on even a first home—many paid 100% in cash—and make an even larger down payment on a second home. Leverage through toxic securitizations never took off in China. Chinese real estate developers in some cities will collapse, but strong Chinese economic growth comes from various sources. In the U.S., many borrowers bought houses with no deposit and no job and sometimes more than one. Bankers leveraged bad loans many times over. The scale of the U.S. credit bubble was much bigger.

The Chinese economy is much more than just real estate. Even as some of the real estate market collapses, other parts of China are doing well and will continue to do well. If Shanghai real estate speculators lose their shirts, other Chinese will profit in investments in solving China's water problems, air pollution treatment, agriculture, raw materials, and energy.

Long Term Outlook: Speaking the Language

Rogers moved his family from New York to Singapore, where the government is committed to making Mandarin the city-state's mother tongue within two generations. He's committed to making it happen now for his daughters.

In 2009, his daughters participated in a promotional video for Singapore's "Speak Mandarin Campaign." (Official languages include English, Malay, Mandarin and Tamil.) His older daughter, Happy, spoke fluent Mandarin as she instructed Baby Bee, her responsive then one-year old sister sitting on Paige Parker's (Jim's wife and the mother of his children) lap, to clap, clasp her hands in a Chinese New Year ritual, and then point to a light. Rogers' latest book is *A Gift to My Children*.

Explosive Demand

China will experience speed-bumps and pullbacks, but even in a slowing economy market share for specific items can continue to grow. China is experiencing what looks like explosive durable consumer demand, and there is both immediate and long term profit potential.

McDonald's started in China 15 years ago, and it took 10 years to breakeven. McDonald's foreign franchise sales were up 7% in 2011. McDonald's won't release the numbers for China but says sales in China—its fastest global growth area—are up much more in 2011 versus 2010. McDonald's is over the moon about finally catching on in China. McDonald's announced it would increase from 1,300 franchises to 2,000 by 2013, its largest expansion so far in China. In 2011, McDonald's was a top performing large cap stock partly due to the earnings boost from its franchises in China.

According to *Bloomberg*, Yum! Brands, Inc. is thrilled with its KFC restaurant chains' success in China. Its success swamps that of McDonalds. In 2011, revenues from China outstripped earnings from Yum's various restaurant chains in the U.S. for the first time.

Rogers' Bull Trades

Rogers' bullishness is justified in his areas of focus.[250] He has studied China's issues with food production and consumption and its long term needs for raw materials based on global supply and demand for commodities. He favors all commodities over the rest of the decade, but especially suggests looking at the ones still depressed on a historic basis.

The central banks of the world seem determined to print their way out of their problems and destroy the value of their currencies through inflation. That should boost the prices of real assets. Rogers is generally short global equities and owns real assets and producing agricultural land.

Jim Chanos: China Bear

James S. Chanos, President and founder of Kynikos Associates, L.P., made his reputation with a series of notable short calls spanning three decades including the bankruptcies of Baldwin United in the 1980s and Enron at the beginning of this century.

The trenchant critic of fraud and hypocrisy is president of the board of trustees at the Browning School, a trustee of The Nightingale Bamford School, and a trustee of The New-York (sic) Historical Society. Chanos is a visiting lecturer of a well-received course at Yale: "Financial Fraud throughout History: A Forensic Approach."

The churlish bear's most famous current shorts are related to the Chinese real estate market. He's never been to China—his retort to critics is that he never worked at Enron—but his analysts have. His data points to localized housing bubbles. Chanos is short suppliers of materials such as iron ore, cement, steel and coal. His disclosed longs (a hedge) include Macau gambling establishments. According to Chanos, he's "long corruption, short property."

The thing about corruption is that one can never trust where it ends. As "corruption" goes, gambling is legal in Macau. Money laundering,[251] drug-trafficking, prostitution, and cooking the books are another story. Casinos are usually profitable because they enjoy the house odds. Yet I wonder if the books can be trusted to be any more accurate than Chinese reverse merger companies. The shares of Macau casinos may get killed for reasons that make the trade ineffective as the long leg of his hedge...or not.[252][253] When it comes to being long corruption, Chanos may have done his due diligence.

Debt and China's Housing Price Crash

A housing price crash causes distress even to unleveraged homeowners. To the individual homeowner and individual property developer, it matters very much. Many Chinese home buyers pay cash, but others make high down payments. Some first time home-buyers put down as little as 30%; high by U.S. "standards," but still painful when housing prices drop 30%. Second homes require at least 50% down, and third homes (where allowed) require all cash. Some investors have bought multiple properties. Even if a borrower pays upfront in full, a housing price decline has a huge impact on how wealthy investors feel.

Home prices in some areas of China are sliding fast. Some analysts say the "tipping point" started in September and expect it to get much worse. Chinese newspapers reported riots in Shanghai after developers slashed prices to dump inventory. Contracted home buyers saw prices cut 25%. Some property developments in Beijing have had price cuts of 20-30 percent. China's empty "ghost cities" are seeing price discounts of 30 percent for upfront cash payments. Mainstream U.S. financial media is now reporting possible housing price declines of 20-30 percent for major Chinese cities next year.

Nothing creates a hard landing—at least locally—better than a housing collapse. Property construction accounts for more than 13% of China's GDP up from around 3% of GDP in 1999 according to the China National Bureau of Statistics. Local Chinese governments have mounting debt to fund infrastructure projects of 10.7 trillion Yuan ($1.7 trillion) and depend on land sales to fund payments. According to investment management company GMO, debt in Local Government Funding Vehicles amounts to around 1/3 of China's GDP. The projected slowdown in land sales will pose a huge problem, no matter whose numbers one uses.

No one knows the size of local government debt obscured by off-balance sheet vehicles. Hidden national government debt includes "support" such as the stated support for the $330 billion and rising debt of the railroad. A variety of other guarantees have ballooned China's real debt.

Then there are the obvious problems with undercapitalized banks. According to Jim Antos, an analyst at Mizuho Securities in Asia, loan growth has slowed to 15% from 30%. Antos believes there's a credit bubble. He asserts debt is "unsustainable" as the current level of bank loans stands at $6,500 per capita in 2010. Gross domestic product per capita is $4,400, according to Antos. (The CIA estimates 2010 adjusted GDP per capita at $7,600 on a purchasing power adjusted basis.)

On a scale of one to ten, Antos rates China's debt problem an eight and Greece's debt problem a ten. Chanos told me: "China should be thanking Greece," for deflecting attention from China's debts. Critics say the Yuan isn't yet a freely convertible currency, but it's made progress in that direction. China's growth in areas unrelated to real estate, and the high household savings rate, and reserves suggest a very different economic outcome for China.

GMO reports that Fitch estimates that 35% of bank loans are directly or indirectly tied to the Chinese property market, and UBS estimates it at 40-50% of outstanding loans. No matter which is correct, a pullback will be brutal. ("Between Errors of Optimism and Pessimism," by Edward Chancellor, GMO, September 2011, and "China Real Estate—Final Destination," UBS, August 25, 2011.) "Dubai times 1,000—or worse," however, sounds like Chanos talking his book.

The Wukan Rebellion

Slowing property development in selected areas will mean less local revenue from land sales, and that will translate to more non-performing loans. Yet, even if the government eases, and property developers quickly recover; local citizens may be unwilling to sell arable land, because food prices are soaring.

Odd things happen when people feel they're not getting the straight story, and local government officials are stealing their land

and money. In 2011, Wukan's 20,000 citizens drove party officials out of town. Residents of the large fishing village balked when officials tried to illegally sell valuable land to property developers. Inflating food prices meant that people wanted the land to grow more food.

Armed police were unable to retake Wukan. The provincial governor flew in and negotiated an agreement that included ousting corrupt local officials.[254]

The Wukan problem wasn't one of policy or indifference to mass suffering; it was a rebellion against theft of public land by corrupt and greedy officials. This sort of theft has been happening in many areas of China. Now that food price inflation has made arable land more valuable, more citizens may wake up and fight corruption.

Mainstream media spin centers around dealing with outraged townspeople instead of exposing and ousting corrupt officials.[255] In that way, China's politicians are like U.S. politicians, and mainstream media protects the politicians and their cronies.

In other words, nothing has been settled, and it will be interesting to see if China becomes more unsettled in 2012.

Slowdowns, Growth, and Savings

As mentioned previously, China has taken steps to cool its overheated economy and property market. A slowing means fewer local land sales. Some local governments have already begun deferring interest payments on loans. While the Fed holds rates near zero, China's central bank holds rates at over 6.5%.[256] Many economists are calling for easing, a reduction in rates to stimulate China's economy through more lending. The problem with easing is that China is already in the grips of inflation. ("China Financial Markets: Time to relax credit?" by Michael Pettis, Guanghua School of Management, Peking University, October 31, 2011.)

China has loaded itself up with debt, but it is a global creditor nation. High household savings is a buffer as is its relatively faster growth than developed nations. While being a fast-growing creditor country helps mitigate the consequences of folly, the consequences are catching up with China.

Dylan Grice points out that anecdotal evidence can be misleading and China may "keep the plates spinning for a few more years." ("Popular Delusions: On China's swindles: how big is the bezzle?" by Dylan Grice, Societe Generale Cross Asset Research, November 4, 2011.) Localized real estate bubbles, dodgy lending, and outright fraud are specific problems, and supplier slowdowns and price declines are already in evidence. Do the previous anecdotes overstate the problem? That's impossible to tell without reliable numbers. One also has to be skeptical of government growth statistics, yet many U.S. corporations have reported growth spurts that far surpass business in developed countries.

A Bull and a Bear in the China Shop

The question is how quickly and to what degree will China's problems affect its economy?

It seems to me Jim Rogers and Jim Chanos are each answering this question in his own way. Jim Rogers invests in durable demand growth for selected commodities—especially the supply constrained ones that are still depressed on a historic basis. He's bullish on water and air pollution treatment, agriculture, raw materials, and energy. Jim Chanos is shorting specific banks, property developers, and suppliers of construction materials such as iron ore, cement, steel and coal.

It looks as if 2012 isn't the year of the bull or the bear. It's the year of the Jims.

APPENDICES

APPENDIX I

The title of the document is "Comments on SEC Proposed Rules and Oversight of NRSROs," February 13, 2007, by Janet Tavakoli, Tavakoli Structured Finance This letter is still posted on the SEC's web site at this URL:

https://www.sec.gov/comments/s7-04-07/s70407-1.pdf

Appended to the letter is an article about synthetic CDOs and the flaws of correlation models, "The Elusive Income of Synthetic CDOs," by Janet Tavakoli, *Journal of Structured Finance*, Winter 2006 Volume 11, Number 4.

APPENDIX II.

Residential Mortgage Backed Securities (RMBS)

Mortgage lender(s) work with mortgage brokers to originate mortgage loans for investment bank warehouses. Investment banks provide credit lines to the mortgage lenders, and also purchase and warehouse the loans in preparation for structuring an RMBS.

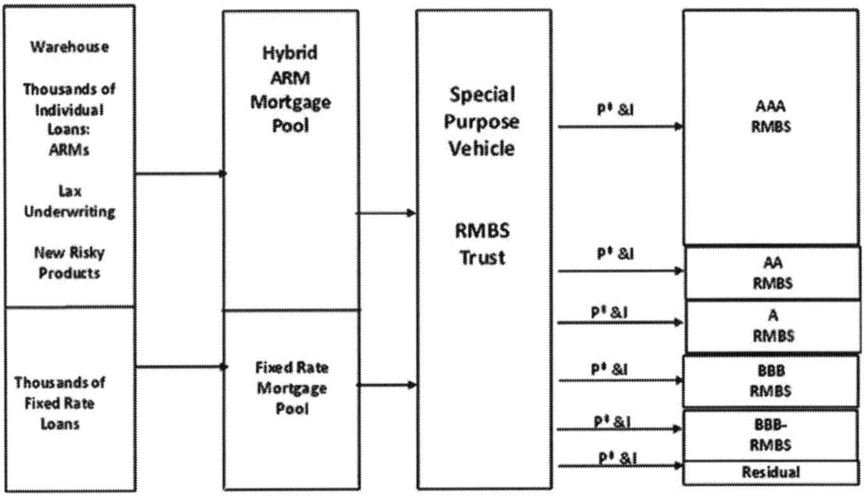

‡ Structures vary. Principal and interest payments are usually allocated to each tranche in sequence. Excess interest is used to reimburse collateral shortfalls.

Source: *Structured Finance & Collateralized Debt Obligations*, by Janet Tavakoli (Wiley 2003, 2008)

APPENDIX III.

Largest Ponzi Scheme in Capital Markets' History

New Investors Fund Old Investors

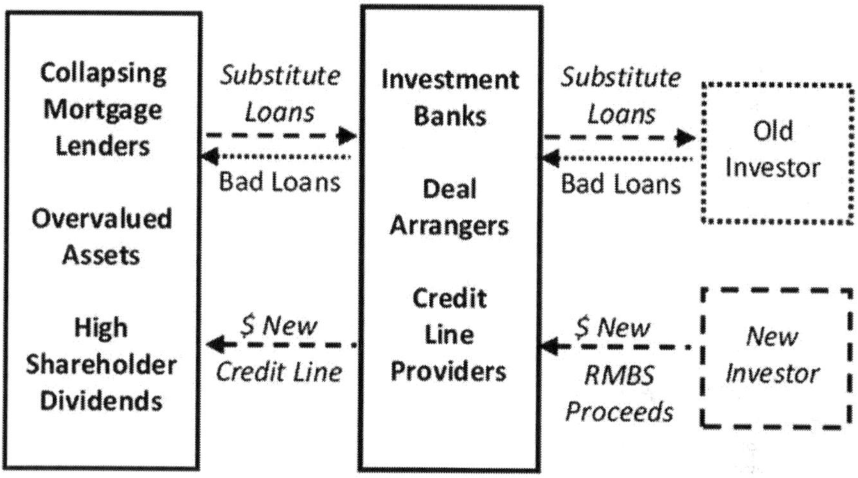

Source: *Structured Finance & Collateralized Debt Obligations*, by Janet Tavakoli (Wiley, 2008)

APPENDIX IV.

Basic CDO Structure

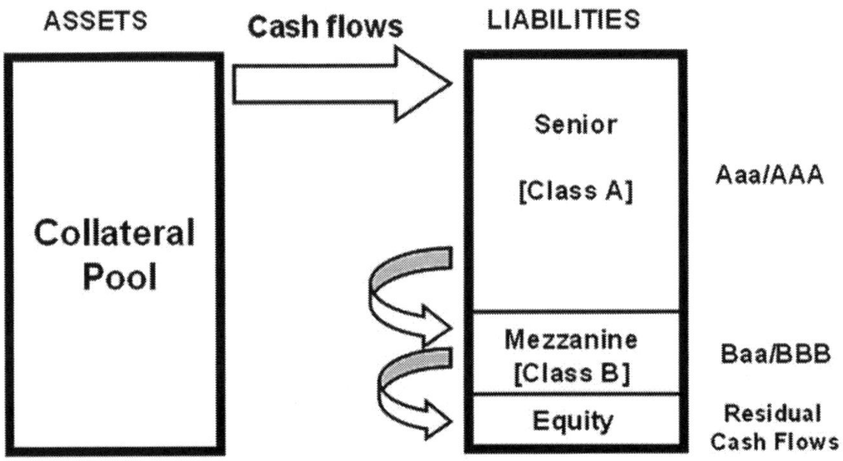

Source: *Structured Finance & Collateralized Debt Obligations*, by Janet Tavakoli (Wiley, 2008)

APPENDIX V.

CDO Backed By Subprime, Alt-A, Risky Prime Backed RMBSs

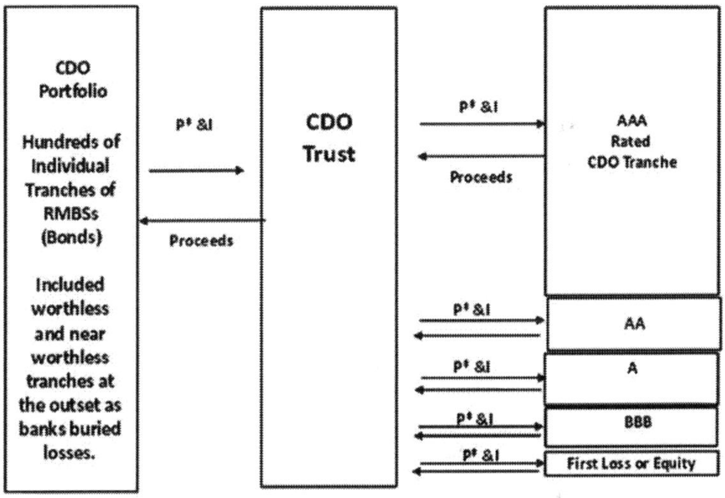

*Structures vary; deal terms vary. Principal and interest payments are allocated to each tranche in sequence. Excess interest is used to reimburse collateral shortfalls, but cash flows may be diverted, if allowed.

Source: *Structured Finance & Collateralized Debt Obligations*, by Janet Tavakoli (Wiley, 2008)

APPENDIX VI.

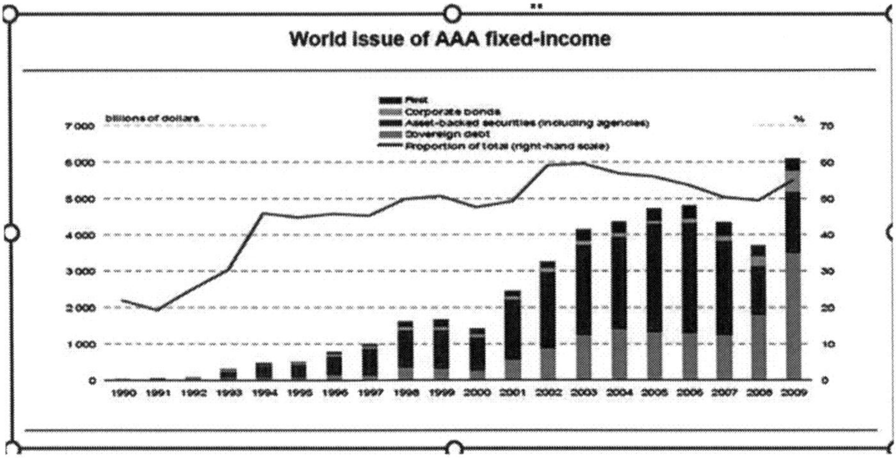

Source: Basel Committee on Banking Supervision. The Joint Forum "Report on Asset Securitisation Incentives," July 2011, Bank for International Settlements. P. 6 Figure 3. The implications of this chart did not escape the notice of mainstream financial media. Tracy Alloway at *FT Alphaville* highlighted this chart on July 15, 2011 in a commentary: "The AAA bubble."

The report noted that from 1990 to 2006, the peak year for ABS issuance, "AAA" rated assets ballooned from 20 percent of rated fixed-income issuance to almost 55 percent. Many of these came at the tail end of this period when the "AAA" ratings were unwarranted, in fact many warranted a junk rating, but BIS didn't mention it. In the first half of 2007, virtually every "AAA" of ABS CDOs warranted junk ratings, but the report did not mention that, either.

The BIS notes that as of 2009, "AAA" issuance from Sovereigns that still have that rating ballooned to outstrip the "AAA" ABS issuance of 2006. This is no surprise. For example, in the U.S. securitized assets were dumped on the balance sheets of the Fed, special purpose entities administered by the Fed, Fannie Mae, and Freddie Mac. Government guarantees allowed for new issuance of

ABS CDOs that otherwise would have no buyers, since the rating agencies are universally mistrusted.

Government bailouts to recapitalize the banks meant that new sovereign debt had to be issued. Capital spending, the biggest driver of economic growth was starved as funds were diverted to banks. The phony "AAA" ratings awarded to ABS CDS and other structured financial products helped weaken the economies of formerly "AAA" rated countries while increasing ostensibly "AAA" rated debt issuance.

APPENDIX VII.

Long-Term Credit Ratings		
Moody's	**S&P**	**Fitch**
Aaa	AAA	AAA
Aa1	AA+	AA+
Aa2	AA	AA
Aa3	AA–	AA–
A1	A+	A+
A2	A	A
A3	A–	A–
Baa1	BBB+	BBB+
Baa2	BBB	BBB
Baa3	BBB–	BBB–
Ba1	BB+	BB+
Ba2	BB	BB
Ba3	BB–	BB–
B1	B+	B+
B2	B	B
B3	B–	B–
Caa1	CCC+	CCC+
Caa2	CCC	CCC
Caa3	CCC–	CCC–
Ca	CC	CC
C	C	C
	D	D

On the Moody's scale, Baa3 and above is considered investment grade, and anything below that is considered speculative grade. For Standard and Poor's and Fitch, anything above BBB– is considered investment grade and anything below is considered speculative grade.

"Super Senior" is not shown on this scale. "Super Seniors" perverted the meaning of "AAA." So-called "AAA" tranches became the "first loss" tranche for the so-called Super Senior. (See also Section III. A. and APPENDIX VIII.)

APPENDIX VIII.

The "Super Senior" Effect

"Super senior" tranches not only further perverted the meaning of "AAA," they didn't live up to their billing as super-safe. Investors in super senior tranches of late vintage CDOs often lost almost their entire investment. The example below shows what happens to the "AAA," when only 20% of the underlying portfolio of assets is lost for two comparable structures. In late vintage CDOs, much more than 20% of the underlying portfolio value was lost.

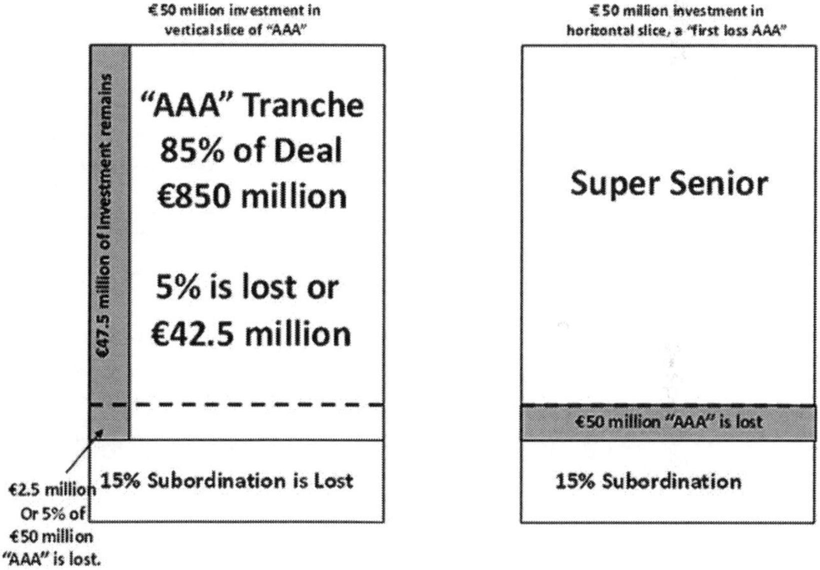

Effect of 20% Losses On "AAAs" For Two CDOs Backed By a €1 billion Portfolio of Assets

APPENDIX IX.

Typical Multi-Sector CDO Backed By Subprime RMBSs

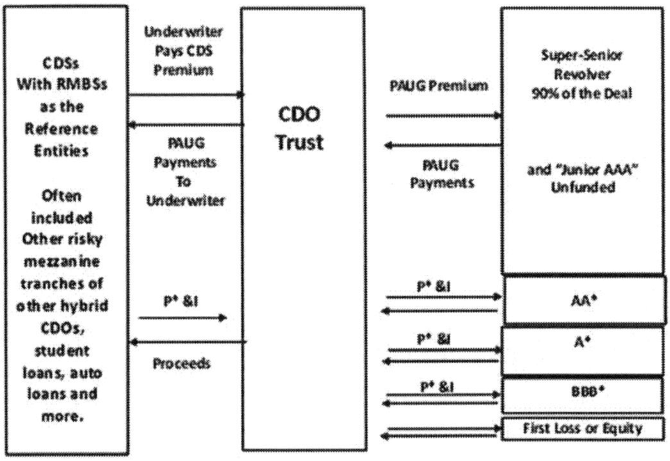

*Not to scale. These are usually funded notes, but the first loss tranche and some junior tranches may be unfunded. PAUG stands for "Pay As You Go," a type of Credit Default Swap (CDS) contract.

Source: *Structured Finance & Collateralized Debt Obligations*, by Janet Tavakoli (Wiley, 2008)

APPENDIX X.

ABS CDOs Underwritten by Merrill Lynch in 2007

Source: Tavakoli Structured Finance - June 10, 2008

ABS CDOs Underwritten by Merrill Lynch in 2007				
Estd Closing	**Deal Name**	**Manager**	**Appx. Size ($MM)***	**Status June 10, 2008**
1/11/2007	Lexington Cap Fundg III	Harding Advsy	1,212.00	Toast**
1/24/2007	Port Jackson CDO 2007-1	Basis Capital	350.00	Toast**
1/25/2007	Highridge ABS CDO I	ZS Structured Credit Cap Mgt	1,500.00	Acceleration**
2/21/2007	Maxim High Grade CDO I	Maxim Capital Mgt	2,000.00	EOD**
2/27/2007	Broderick CDO 3	SCM Advisors	1,500.00	Acceleration**
2/27/2007	Kleros Real Estate CDO IV	Strategos Capital Mgt	1,000.00	Undeclared EOD
3/1/2007	Norma CDO I	NIR Capital Mgt	1,500.00	Acceleration**
3/8/2007	Maxim High Grade CDO II	Maxim Capital Mgmt	2,000.00	EOD**
3/8/2007	Newbury Street CDO Ltd.	Mass. Fincl Svcs. Inv.	2,000.41	EOD
3/9/2007	South Coast Funding IX	TCW Asset Mgmt	540.00	Toast**
3/27/2007	Euler ABS CDO I	Babcock and Brown	675.00	Toast**
3/27/2007	GLACIER-V	Terwin Money Mgmt	498.50	Toast**
3/29/2007	Lexington Capital Funding V	Harding Advisory	615.00	Toast**
3/29/2007	Libertas Preferred Funding IV	Strategos Capital Mgt	500.00	Toast**
3/29/2007	Silver Marlin	Sailfish Structured Inv	1,250.50	EOD
4/3/2007	Kleros Preferred Funding VII	Strategos Capital Mgt	1,498.00	EOD**
4/5/2007	NEO CDO 2007-1	Harding	300.00	Liquidation**
4/11/2007	Forge ABS High Grade CDO I	Forge ABS LLC	1,503.50	EOD**
4/12/2007	IMAC CDO 2007-2	Ivy Asset Mgmt	500.00	Liquidation**
4/18/2007	Mars CDO I	Chotin Group	618.50	Acceleration**
4/26/2007	Brookville CDO I	Petra Capital	499.00	EOD**
4/26/2007	Fourth Street Funding Ltd	N.I.R. Capital Mgmt	500.50	Acceleration**
4/26/2007	Western Springs CDO	Deerfield Capital Mgt.	495.60	Acceleration**
5/3/2007	Jupiter High Grade CDO VI	Harding Advisory	1,501.10	Toast**
5/10/2007	Tazlina Funding - II	Winter Group	1,500.00	EOD**
5/25/2007	West Trade Funding CDO III	N.I.R. Capital Mgmt	2,500.00	Toast**
6/1/2007	Robeco HG CDO-I	Robeco Investment Mgt	1,100.55	Toast**
6/7/2007	Durant CDO 2007-1	SCM Advisors	400.00	Liquidation**
7/26/2007	Biltmore CDO 2007-1	ING Clarion Capital	1,000.00	EOD**
8/28/2007	Bernoulli High Grade CDO-II	Babcock and Brown	1,500.00	Acceleration**

*** Total Notional Amount is approximately $32.6 billion**

**** Means the original topmost "triple-A" tranche has been downgraded to below investment grade, i.e., junk by one or more rating agencies. Note that *all CDOs* shown above have one or more originally "triple-A" tranches downgraded below investment grade by one or more rating agencies.**

An event of default (EOD) usually means failure of an overcollateralization test usually related to a par "haircut" as defined in the prospectus. Senior noteholders and/or other parties to the transaction may choose acceleration (making the principal and interest immediately due and payable), or liquidation (selling the underlying portfolio collateral). Acceleration may be followed by liquidation. Liquidated portfolios have had poor recovery value. "Toast" means the originally "triple-A" tranches have all been downgraded to "junk" by one or more rating agencies that rated the deal, and there is an undeclared EOD. Undeclared EOD means that one or more originally "triple-A" tranches is downgraded below junk status, yet there is an undeclared EOD. The undeclared EOD may be due to no provision in the documents or the declaration is pending.

APPENDIX XI.

Merrill's Durant CDO-Squared circa January 2008

Issuer	Par Amount	Deal Type	Orig Moody's	Moody's	Orig S&P	S&P	Orig Fitch	Fitch	Min Rating	Vintage
Sagittarius CDO	10,000,000	CDO	A2	Ca	A	A-	-	-	A	2007H1
TABS CDO	5,000,000	CDO	Baa3	Ca	BBB-	BBB	-	-	BBB	2006H2
Auriga CDO	3,927,669	CDO	Baa2	Ca	BBB	BBB-	-	-	BBB	2006H2
Longridge ABS CDO	1,300,000	CDO	A2	Ca	A	A-	-	-	A	2006H2
Longridge ABS CDO	7,932,845	CDO	Baa2	Ca	BBB	BBB-	-	-	BBB	2006H2
TABS CDO	5,000,000	CDO	Baa1	Ca	BBB+	BBB	-	-	BBB	2006H2
BFC CDO	9,841,440	CDO	A2	Baa1	A	A-	-	-	A	2006H1
Camber	10,000,000	CDO	A3	A3	A-	A-	-	-	A	2005H2
West Trade Funding CDO	9,998,991	CDO	A2	Baa1	A	A	-	-	A	2007H1
Camber	10,000,000	CDO	A2	Ba1	A	A	-	-	A	2006H1
Camber	7,044,240	CDO	A2	Ba2	A	A	-	-	A	2007H1
Cairn Mezz ABS CDO	10,175,056	CDO	A2	Ba2	A	A	-	-	A	2006H2
Cairn Mezz ABS CDO	10,000,000	CDO	A3	Ba2	A-	A-	-	-	A	2007H1
Corona Borealis	6,000,000	CDO	A2	Ba3	A	A	-	-	A	2007H1
GSC ABS CDO	10,000,000	CDO	A2	Baa1	A	A-	A	-	A	2006H1
Libra CDO	7,000,000	CDO	A2	Ba2	A	A-	-	-	A	2006H2
Libertas Preferred Funding	10,000,000	CDO	A2	Baa1	A	A	A	-	A	2006H1
Montauk Point CDO	10,000,000	CDO	A2	Ba1	A	A	-	-	A	2006H1
Octans CDO	10,000,000	CDO	A2	Ba2	A	A-	-	-	A	2006H2
Shasta CLO	10,000,000	CDO	Baa2	Baa2	BBB	BBB	-	-	BBB	2007H1
Topanga CDO	10,124,485	CDO	A2	B1	A	A	-	-	A	2006H2
Tallships Funding	9,936,581	CDO	A2	Ba2	A	A	A	-	A	2006H2
Vertical CDO	10,000,000	CDO	A2	Ba1	A	A	A	-	A	2006H1
Vertical CDO	10,000,000	CDO	A2	Ba1	A	A	A	-	A	2006H1
Vertical Virgo	10,000,000	CDO	A2	Ba3	A	A	-	-	A	2006H2
West Trade Funding CDO	9,803,887	CDO	A2	Baa1	A	A-	A	-	A	2006H1
Burr Ridge CLO	7,000,000	CDO	A2	A2	A	A	-	-	A	2006H2
Camber	2,898,075	CDO	Baa2	B3	BBB	BBB	-	-	BBB	2007H1
ColumbusNova CLO 2006-II	8,000,000	CDO	A2	A2	A	A	-	-	A	2006H2
Cairn Mezz ABS CDO	6,548,000	CDO	Aaa	Aa1	AAA	AAA	-	-	AAA	2006H2
Fourth Street Funding	10,000,000	CDO	A2	Ba2	A	A-	A	-	A	2007H1
Istana High Grade ABS CD(	2,494,274	CDO	Baa2	B1	BBB	BBB-	-	-	BBB	2006H2
Kleros Preferred Funding	4,550,000	CDO	A2	Ba3	A	A	-	-	A	2006H2
Kleros Preferred Funding	2,000,000	CDO	Baa2	Caa1	BBB	BBB	-	-	BBB	2006H2
Kleros Preferred Funding	4,000,000	CDO	A2	Ba3	A	A	-	-	A	2006H2
Kleros Preferred Funding	10,000,000	CDO	A2	Baa3	A	A	-	-	A	2007H1
Landmark IX CDO	10,000,000	CDO	A2	A2	A	A	-	-	A	2007H1
Libra CDO	2,887,500	CDO	Baa2	B3	BBB	BBB-	-	-	BBB	2006H2
Libertas Preferred Funding	5,000,000	CDO	A2	Ba3	A	A-	-	-	A	2007H1
Libertas Preferred Funding	4,892,221	CDO	Baa2	B2	BBB	BBB-	-	-	BBB	2007H1
Lexington Capital	5,000,000	CDO	A3	B3	A-	BBB+	A-	-	A	2007H1
Lexington Capital	10,000,000	CDO	A2	B1	A	A-	-	-	A	2007H1
Maxim High Grade CDO	9,996,754	CDO	A2	B1	A	A-	A	-	A	2007H1
Norma CDO	4,904,472	CDO	Baa2	Caa3	BBB	BBB-	BBB	-	BBB	2007H1
Octans CDO	8,000,000	CDO	A2	Caa3	A	A-	-	-	A	2006H2
One Wall Street CLO	8,000,000	CDO	A2	A2	A	A	-	-	A	2007H1
Rockvile CDO	1,685,192	CDO	Baa2	B3	BBB	BBB-	-	-	BBB	2006H2
Springdale CDO	6,300,000	CDO	A2	B2	A	A-	-	-	A	2006H2
Stoney Lane Funding	5,000,000	CDO	A2	A2	A	A	-	-	A	2007H1
MKP Vela CBO	7,500,000	CDO	A2	B2	A	A	-	-	A	2006H2
Veritas CLO II	8,000,000	CDO	A2	A2	A	A	-	-	A	2006H1
Whitehorse	8,000,000	CDO	A2	A2	A	A	-	-	A	2007H1
Atrium V	8,000,000	CDO	A2	A2	A	A	-	-	A	2006H2
ING Investment Managemen	8,000,000	CDO	A2	A2	A	A	-	-	A	2006H2
Morgan Stanley ABS	2,000,000	1ome Equit	Aa2	Aa2	AA	AA	-	-	AA	2007H2
RASC	1,100,000	1ome Equit	A1	A1	AA	AA	-	-	A	2005H2

APPENDIX XII.

MBIA's and Ambac's ABS CDO RISKS

MBIA - per Tavakoli Structured Finance, Inc. as of February 20, 2008

Deal Name	Closing Date*	Underwriter*	Manager*	Closing Amt ($)	Insured Amt ($)	Status**
Broderick 2 CDO	8/25/2006	Merrill	Seneca Cap. Mgt	1,600,000,000	1,118,000,000	Acceleration
ART CDO 2006-1	8/2/2006	UBS	Allianz	1,000,000,000	828,000,000	EOD
Wadsworth CDO	9/28/2006	Morgan Stanley	Hartford Inv. Adv	1,200,000,000	601,000,000	Acceleration
Harp 1 CDO	6/26/2006	Credit Suisse	F.I. Adv	1,000,000,000	723,000,000	some slippage
Jupitor V (20% AP)	3/28/2007	Credit Suisse	Harding	1,500,000,000	1,190,000,000	Acceleration
Broderick 3 CDO (20% AP)	2/8/2007	Merrill	Seneca Cap. Mgt	1,500,000,000	1,203,000,000	Acceleration
Newbury Street	2/13/2007	Merrill	Mass Fin	2,000,400,000	1,684,000,000	EOD
Highridge ABS CDO I	1/25/2007	Merrill	ZS Stcd Cred	1,500,000,000	1,177,000,000	Acceleration
Faxtor HG 2007-1	5/25/2007	Lloyds/RW Presp	Faxtor	1,250,000,000	950,000,000	Acceleration
Longshore 2007-III	4/26/2007	TBD	Std Asst Inv.	1,300,000,000	896,000,000	EOD
Bernoulli II (62% AP)	6/20/2007	Merrill	Babcock & Brown	1,500,000,000	563,000,000	Acceleration
Silver Marlin I (62% AP)	2/26/2007	Merrill	Sailfish Stcd Inv	1,250,500,000	469,000,000	EOD
Forge ABS High Grade CDO (70% AP)	3/2/2007	Merrill	Forge ABS LLC	1,503,500,000	450,000,000	EOD
West Trade III (59% AP)	4/25/2007	Merrill	N.I.R. Cap Mgt	2,500,000,000	1,015,000,000	Bad
Tazlina II (62% AP)	4/12/2007	Merrill	Winter Group	1,500,000,000	563,000,000	EOD
Robeco High Grade I (62% AP)	5/24/2007	Merrill	Robeco Inv. Mgt	1,100,550,000	413,000,000	Not Good
Biltmore 2007-1 (62.5% AP)	6/16/2007	Merrill	ING Clarion	1,000,000,000	375,000,000	EOD
Sagittarius I	3/15/2007	Wachovia	Std. Asst. Inv	1,000,000,000	473,000,000	Acceleration
Logan II	5/4/2006	RBC	RBC	1,500,000,000	1,115,000,000	Not Good
Menton III	11/9/2006	RBC	RBC	1,500,000,000	1,077,000,000	Toast
Logan III	2007	RBC	RBC	TBD	990,000,000	Bad
Menton IV	8/24/2007	RBC	RBC	2,500,000,000	2,175,000,000	Bad
* Source: Tavakoli Structured Finance (TSF)					20,048,000,000	

**Source: Rating Agency Reports and TSF interpretation

"Not Good" means downgrades have begun and/or negative outlook per TSF. "TBD" means to be determined.

An *event of default (EOD)* usually means failure of an overcollateralization test usually related to a par "haircut" as defined in the prospectus. Senior noteholders and/or other parties to the transaction may choose *acceleration* (making the principal and interest immediately due and payable), or *liquidation* (selling the underlying portfolio collateral). Acceleration may be followed by liquidation. Liquidated portfolios have recently recovered an estimated one-quarter of original value.

Ambac - per Tavakoli Structured Finance, Inc.
As of February 28, 2008

Deal Name	Closing Date*	Underwriter*	Manager*	Appx.Closing Amt	Insured Amt ($)	Status**
Diversey Harbor ABS CDO	6/1/2006	Citigroup	Vanderbilt Cap Adv	2,500,000,000	1,875,000,000	Acceleration
Belle Haven ABS CDO 2006-1	5/24/2006	Leh / NIBC Bnk	NIBC	1,996,000,000	1,676,000,000	EOD
Ridgeway Court Funding I	7/26/2006	Citi	CSAC	2,000,000,000	1,570,000,000	Acceleration
Duke Funding High Grade IV (includes CDS CDOs)	1/5/2006	Wach / SocGen	Duke	1,501,100,001	1,313,000,000	TSF - Neg
Duke Funding High Grade V	7/6/2006	Wach / SocGen	Duke	1,500,000,000	1,250,000,000	TSF - BAD
McKinley Funding III	11/30/2006	TBD	Vertical Capital	1,509,617,729	1,187,000,000	EOD
Millerton II High Grade ABS CDO (RMBS, CDOs)	2/28/2006	Credit Suisse	Hyperion	1,300,000,000	1,118,000,000	Not Good
Lancer Funding (I or II?)	TBD	UBS	ACA Mgt	TBD	950,000,000	NG or Liquidation
Cairn High Grade ABS CDO II	9/14/2006	RBS Greenwich	Cairn	896,000,000	820,000,000	EOD
ESP Funding I (RMBS plus CDOs)	9/7/2006	Citigroup	Elliott Std Prod	1,000,000,000	657,000,000	EOD
Longshore CDO Funding 2006-1	1/27/2006	TBD (WS?)	Structd Asst Inv	750,000,000	614,000,000	Not Good
Kleros Preferred Funding VI	3/23/2007	UBS	Strategos (Cohen)	3,000,000,000	2,400,000,000	EOD
RidgeWay Court Funding II	6/27/2007	Citi	CSAC	3,007,000,000	1,950,000,000	EOD
Citation High Grade ABS CDO I	1/11/2007	TBD	Highland	1,100,000,000	941,000,000	EOD
Fiorente Funding Limited (CDS ABS, PAUG)	12/21/2006	RBS	VERO Cap	850,000,000	723,000,000	EOD
Adams Square II	6/27/2007	Citi	CSAC	1,000,000,000	510,000,000	EOD
Class V Funding IV (Moody's only rating	TBD	Citi	TBD	TBD	1,400,000,000	Neg Watch
888 Tactical Funding	3/15/2007	Citi	Harding	1,042,700,000	500,000,000	EOD
Class V Funding III	2/28/2007	Citi	CSAC	1,000,000,000	500,000,000	EOD
* Source: Tavakoli Structured Finance (TSF)					21,954,000,000	

**Source: Rating Agency Reports and TSF interpretation

"Not Good" means downgrades have begun and/or negative outlook per TSF. "TBD" means to be determined.

An *event of default (EOD)* usually means failure of an overcollateralization test usually related to a par "haircut" as defined in the prospectus. Senior noteholders and/or other parties to the transaction may choose *acceleration* (making the principal and interest immediately due and payable), or *liquidation* (selling the underlying portfolio collateral). Acceleration may be followed by liquidation. Liquidated portfolios have recently recovered an estimated one-quarter of original value.

About the Author

Janet Tavakoli, founder and president of Tavakoli Structured Finance LLC (2003), is one of the world's foremost experts in credit derivatives, complex derivatives, collateralized debt obligations, and securitizations. Over four decades, she has held senior positions trading, structuring, analyzing, and marketing structured financial products for global financial institutions in New York and London. These include Executive Director and Head of Financial Engineering at Westdeutsche Landesbank in London, senior positions at Merrill Lynch, Bank of America, and Bank One, and roles at Goldman Sachs and Bear Stearns. Today she advises financial institutions, insurance companies, and law firms, and has a perfect record of successful outcomes as an expert witness in high-profile civil suits.

Ms. Tavakoli, a former adjunct associate professor of derivatives at the University of Chicago Booth School of Business, warned years in advance that flawed structured products combined with leverage would cause a financial crisis. *BusinessWeek* profiled her as "The Cassandra of Credit Derivatives." The *University of Chicago Magazine* featured her "Structured Success." *Research Magazine* profiled her work in its cover story, "Finding the Culprits of the Crisis." The International Monetary Fund, the Federal Reserve Bank, the Office of the Comptroller of the Currency, the Federal Housing Finance Agency, and the Securities and Exchange Commission have benefited from her expertise.

She has appeared on CBS's *60 Minutes*, *CBS Evening News*, CNBC, CNN, Bloomberg TV, the BBC, and other networks. She is frequently quoted in the *Wall Street Journal*, the *Financial Times*, the *New York Times*, *The Economist*, and Bloomberg News.

Her books include *Structured Finance and Collateralized Debt Obligations*, *Credit Derivatives and Synthetic Structures*, and *Dear Mr. Buffett*. She holds an MBA from the University of Chicago Booth School of Business and a BS in chemical engineering from the Illinois Institute of Technology.

See also: www.tavakolistructuredfinance.com

ENDNOTES

[1] Tavakoli, Janet. "An alternative to the Paulson plan—one that does not violate the spirit of democracy," *The Financial Times*, September 29, 2008. http://www.tavakolistructuredfinance.com/2008/09/paulson-plan-alternative/

[2] Section 8 was formerly a type of discharge issued by the U.S. military that meant one was mentally unsuited for service. The spirit of Hank Paulson's Section 8 continues to dominate the U.S. financial system.

[3] Liu, Betty and Tavakoli, Janet. "Bailout Plans [Paulson & Frank]," *Bloomberg Television*, September 23, 2008.

[4] Efrati, Amir, Lauricella, Tom, and Searcey, Dionne. "Top Broker Accused of $50 Billion Fraud," *Wall Street Journal*, December 12, 2008. http://www.wsj.com/articles/SB122903010173099377

[5] Yoon, Al. "Business Books: Losing trust in credit markets," *Reuters*, March 12, 2009.

[6] Herbert, Bob. "The Worst of the Pain," The New York Times, February 8, 2010.
http://www.nytimes.com/2010/02/09/opinion/09herbert.html?scp=2&sq=bob%20herbert&st=cse

[7] Tavakoli, Janet. "Wall Street's Fraud and Solutions for Systemic Peril: Summary of presentation to the International Monetary Fund in Washington D.C.," *TSF*, September 21, 2009.
http://www.tavakolistructuredfinance.com/wall-street-fraud-solutions/

[8] Gross, Daniel. "Economy" The Bank Subsidy You May Not Have Heard Of," *Newsweek*, January 12, 2010.

[9] Tavakoli, Janet. "Washington's Bipartisan Betrayal: The 2015 Global Financial Crisis," *The Huffington Post*, May 25, 2011.
http://www.huffingtonpost.com/janet-tavakoli/washingtons-bipartisan-be_b_408308.html

[10] Salas, Caroline, Torres, Craig and Harrington, Shannon D. "Fed Made Taxpayers Unwitting Junk-Bond Buyers, *Bloomberg*, July 1, 2010.
http://www.sanders.senate.gov/newsroom/must-read/fed-made-taxpayers-unwitting-junk-bond-buyers

[11] I gave Reilly an example of an aggregate position of AIG's credit default swaps (CDS) amounting to more than $19 billion. It was backed by BBB-rated tranches of residential mortgage backed securities (including some subprime loans) and other BBB-rated asset backed securities (auto loans, student loans, and more). Mark-to-market means one shows the market price, or if no market prices are available, one records a price based on a model that calculates a price at which one would expect to trade in the market. Given then market conditions, AIG's assertions were not plausible.

[12] Reilly, David. "In Subprime, AIG Sees Small Risk; Others See More," *Wall Street Journal*, August 13, 2007. http://www.wsj.com/articles/SB118696377289895543

[13] Tavakoli. *Dear Mr. Buffett*. Ch. 10

[14] Tavakoli, Janet. *Dear Mr. Buffett: What an Investor Learns 1,269 Miles from Wall Street*, Hoboken, New Jersey: Wiley 2009. Pp. 164-165, 246)

[15] Tavakoli, Janet. "Goldman's Undisclosed Role in AIG's Distress," *Tavakoli Structured Finance* (TSF), November 10, 2009. http://www.tavakolistructuredfinance.com/goldman-aig-bailout/

[16] Sloan, Allan. "Once upon a time in Mortgage Land," *The Washington Post*, November 28, 2009. http://www.washingtonpost.com/wp-dyn/content/article/2009/11/27/AR2009112703059.html

[17] "SIGTARP: Office of the Special Inspector General for the Troubled Asset Relief Program, "Factors Affecting Efforts to Limit Payments to AIG Counterparties, November 17, 2009. www.tavakolistructuredfinance.com/SIGTARP.pdf

[18] Tavakoli, Janet. "Treasury Cover-Up of Goldman's Role in AIG Crisis?" *TSF*, March 18, 2010. http://www.tavakolistructuredfinance.com/2010/03/treasury-cover-up-of-goldmans-role-in-aig-crisis/

[19] Teitelbaum, Richard, and Son, Hugh. "New York Fed's Secret Choice to Pay for Swaps Hits Taxpayers," *Bloomberg News*," October 27, 2009. http://www.washingtonexaminer.com/new-york-feds-secret-choice-to-pay-for-swaps-hits-taxpayers/article/21467

[20] Goldstein, Matthew. "Redacted AIG filing might have spotted worst deals," *Reuters*, January 12, 2010. http://www.reuters.com/article/us-aig-redacted-analysis-idUSTRE60B4K720100112

[21] See redactions on the last four pages of the March 2009 SEC filing: www.tavakolistructuredfinance.com/AIGSEC.pdf

[22] Ng, Serena. "Goldman Confirms $6 Billion AIG Bets," *The Wall Street Journal*, March 21, 2009. http://www.wsj.com/articles/SB123756518992096521#printMode

[23] Jenkins Jr., Holman W. "The Bank Everyone Loves to Hate," *The Wall Street Journal*, October 10, 2009. http://www.wsj.com/articles/SB10001424052748703746604574460971679111660

[24] Quinones, John, Netter, Sarah and Goldman, Russel. "Joran Van Der Sloot Confession: 'The Girl Intruded on My Private Life," ABC News, June 8, 2010. http://abcnews.go.com/GMA/Media/joran-van-der-sloot-confession-girl-intruded-private/story?id=10853209&page=1%20

[25] Bedard, Maurice. "Foreclosures Causing Homeowners to Commit Suicide," *Loansafe*, March 25, 2010. http://www.loansafe.org/foreclosure-causing-homeowners-to-commit-suicide

[26] Starkman, Dean. "Conspicuous Assumption," Columbia Journalism Review, February 5, 2008. http://www.cjr.org/the_audit/conspicuous_assumption.php

[27] Ng. "Goldman confirms…" *WSJ*.

[28] Sloan, Allan. "Goldman Sachs' House of Junk," *Fortune*, April 12, 2016. http://fortune.com/2016/04/12/goldman-sachs-house-of-junk-mortgage-bonds/

[29] Karnitschnig, Matthew, and Pleven, Liam. "Benmosche in No Hurry to Sell Off AIG's Assets," *Wall Street Journal*, August 28, 2009. http://www.wsj.com/articles/SB125141103149364939

[30] Tavakoli, Janet. "I ~~apologize to David Viniar and Goldman's Lawyers and~~ Call For More Regulation of Goldman Sachs," TSF, November 5, 2009. http://www.tavakolistructuredfinance.com/goldman-aig-bailout/apology/

[31] Ng, Serena, and Mollenkamp, Carrick. "Goldman Fueled AIG's Gambles*," Wall Street Journal December 12, 2009. http://www.wsj.com/articles/SB10001424052748704201404574590453176996032*

[32] Zuill, Lilla. "Ambac capital exceeds required minimum," *Reuters*, November 18, 2000. http://in.reuters.com/article/us-ambac-capital-idINTRE5AH3VD20091118

[33] Tavakoli, Janet. "Warren Buffett's Wall Street War," *TSF*, October 20, 2009. http://www.tavakolistructuredfinance.com/2009/10/buffett-wall-street/

[34] Tavakoli, Janet. "Bank of America's Shareholders Should Reject Bonus Plan," *TSF,* May 25, 2011. http://www.tavakolistructuredfinance.com/bofa-merrill-fraud/

[35] Teitelbaum, Richard and Son, Hugh. "New York Fed's Secret Choice to Pay for Swaps Hits Taxpayers," *Bloomberg News*, October 27, 2009. http://www.washingtonexaminer.com/new-york-feds-secret-choice-to-pay-for-swaps-hits-taxpayers/article/21467

[36] Viniar, David. Goldman Sachs's September 16, 2008 Q3 2008 Earnings Call. https://www.scribd.com/document/21702083/GS-Transcript

[37] Sorkin, Andrew Ross. *Too Big To Fail*, New York: Viking, October 20, 2009. [TBTF]

[38] TBTF P. 175

[39] TBTF P. 382.

[40] SIGTARP, November 17, 2009.

[41] Mollenkamp, Carrick, and Ng, Serena. "Report Rebuts Goldman's Claim on AIG," *Wall Street Journal*, November 17, 2009. http://www.wsj.com/articles/SB10001424052748704538404574542192562568738

[42] Drawbaugh, Kevin. "Friedman's Goldman shares a 'conflict': report," *Reuters*, January 27, 2010. http://www.reuters.com/article/us-aig-towns-idUSTRE60Q6WF20100127

[43]*Dear Mr. Buffett*. P. 133.

[44] Goldstein, Matthew. "The 'blame Goldman defense," *Reuters*, August 5, 2009. http://blogs.reuters.com/commentaries/2009/08/05/the-blame-goldman-defense/

[45] Karnitshnig, Matthew, Solomon, Deborah, Pleven, Liam, and Hilsenrath, Jon E. "U.S. to Take Over AIG in $85 Billion Bailout; Central Banks Inject Cash as Credit Dries Up," *Wall Street Journal,* September 16, 2008. http://www.wsj.com/articles/SB122156561931242905

[46] Ng, Serena, Mollenkamp, Carrick, and Siconolfi, Michael. "AIG Faces $10 Billion in Losses on Bad Bets," *Wall Street Journal*, December 10, 2008. http://www.wsj.com/articles/SB122887203792493481

[47]AIG's Nov 2007 report showed Goldman's positions at $23 billion, but something may have happened before Sept 2008 to reduce that amount. AIG was required to price these credit derivatives using market prices, and if applicable, AIG had to provide collateral if the prices moved against it. Terms varied, but after the downgrade, AIG owed collateral for the full mark-to-market value to several counterparties. This is the difference between the original value and the price that Goldman and others put on the credit default swaps. www.cbsnews.com/htdocs/pdf/collateral_b.pdf

[48] SocGen's total margin calls were not available in the November 2007 memo. It is possible that like Calyon—and like troubled Citigroup—SocGen provided a liquidity put on commercial paper (CP) distributed by Wall Street firms to a variety of investors. Calyon agreed to buy the CDO's commercial paper (short term debt backed by the longer term tranches of the CDOs) if demand in the market dried up when it came time to roll the CP. Calyon hedged the risk of the liquidity puts by purchasing credit default protection from AIG.
http://archive.fortune.com/2007/11/09/news/newsmakers/merrill_rubin.fortune/index.htm

[49] Rappaport, Liz. "Lewis Testifies U.S. Urged Silence on Deal," *Wall Street Journal*, April 23, 2009.

[50] Morgenson, Gretchen. "Revisiting a Fed Waltz With A.I.G.," *The New York Times*, November 21, 2009.
http://www.nytimes.com/2009/11/22/business/22gret.html

[51] vanPraag, Lucas. Memo from a Goldman Sachs spokesman: "Goldman's Response to Questions about A.I.G.," *The New York Times*, November 21, 2009.
http://www.nytimes.com/2009/11/22/business/22gretside.html?ref=business

[52] Bowley, Graham. "$500 Million and Apology From Goldman*," The New York Times*, November 17, 2009.
http://www.nytimes.com/2009/11/18/business/18goldman.html?_r=1&

[53] Goldstein, Matthew. "AIG Filing Casts Doubt on 'Limited Exposure' Claim," *Reuters*, February 24, 2010). http://www.reuters.com/article/us-aig-cassano-analysis-idUSTRE60S69O20100129

[54] Wong, Kristina. "Recession Is Over, White House Adviser Says," *ABC News*, December 13, 2009. http://abcnews.go.com/Politics/larry-summers-white-house-economic-adviser-predicts-jobs/story?id=9325851

[55] Rich, Frank. "The Other Plot to Wreck America," *The New York Times*, January 9, 2010.

[56] Chan, Sewell, and Story, Louise. "Goldman Pays $550 Million to Settle Fraud Case," *The New York Times*, July 15, 2010. http://www.nytimes.com/2010/07/16/business/16goldman.html

[57] Goldstein, Matthew, "Abacus might have had other benefits for Goldman," *Reuters*, April 24, 2010. http://www.reuters.com/article/us-goldman-circular-exclusive-idUSTRE63M4U820100424

[58] Ng, Serena and Mollenkamp, Carrick. "Goldman Fueled AIG's Gambles," by Serena Ng and Carrick Mollenkamp, *Wall Street Journal*, December 12, 2009.
http://www.wsj.com/articles/SB10001424052748704201404574590453176996032

[59] Teitlebaum, Richard. "AIG Probe May Lead to Criminal Cover-up Charges, Barofsky Says," *Bloomberg News*, April 28, 2010.

[60] Mollenkamp, Carrick, and Ng, Serena. "Senate's Goldman Probe Shows Toxic Magnification," *Wall Street Journal*, May 2, 2010.
http://www.wsj.com/articles/SB10001424052748703969204575220300651236446

[61] Dealbook, "Blankfein Says He's Just Doing 'God's Work,'" *The New York Times*, November 9, 2009.
https://dealbook.nytimes.com/2009/11/09/goldman-chief-says-he-is-just-doing-gods-work/

[62] http://jessescrossroadscafe.blogspot.com/

[63] Fitzpatrick, Dan, Solomon, Deborah, and Craig, Susanne. "BofA's Latest Hit," *Wall Street Journal*, January 16, 2009.

[64] See also: Tavakoli, Janet

[65] Rappaport, Liz, and Fitzpatrick, Dan. "Cuomo Urges Probe of BofA Deal Pressure," *Wall Street Journal*, April 24, 2009.
http://www.wsj.com/articles/SB124050588176348711#mod=testMod

[66] "Top 25 Subprime Lender List," *ML Implode*. http://ml-implode.com/top25-Q206.html

[67] Bajaj, Vikas, and Haughney, Christine. "Tremors at the Door," *The New York Times*, January 26, 2007.
http://www.nytimes.com/2007/01/26/business/26mortgage.html?_r=1&pagewanted=all%20

[68] Norris, Floyd. "Color-Blind Merrill in a Sea of Red Flags," *The New York Times*, May 16, 2008.

[69] Tavakoli, Janet. "Dead Calm: No One Trusts You," *TSF*, July 30, 2008. http://www.tavakolistructuredfinance.com/merrill-cdo-fraud/

[70] Dealbook, "S.E.C. Seeks New Charge Against Bank of America," *The New York Times*, January 11, 2010. https://dealbook.nytimes.com/2010/01/11/sec-seeks-to-add-new-charge-against-bofa/?_r=0

[71] DeCambre, Mark. "JPMorgan coal hole," *New York Post*, June 8, 2010. http://nypost.com/2010/06/08/jpmorgan-coal-hole/

[72] Kopecki, Dawn. "Blythe Masters Says 'Don't Panic' as Commodities Slip," *Business Week's* (*Bloomberg News*), August 3, 2010. All words in this article in quotation marks are from this major scoop after the leak to Kopecki of a tape of an internal JPMorgan July 22 conference call:

[73] Lowrey, Annie. "Too Big to Fail Rears its Head Again," *Washington Independent*, October 14, 2010.

[74] Cordray, Richard. "Attorney General's Foreclosure Fight," *CNBC*, October 15, 2010. http://video.cnbc.com/gallery/?play=1&video=1616345642

[75] Arrington, Michael. "Facebook Is Secretly Building a Phone," *Techcrunch*, September 19, 2010. https://techcrunch.com/2010/09/19/facebook-is-secretly-building-a-phone/

[76] Teitelbaum, Richard. "Blankfein Flunks Asset Management as Clark Vows No More Goldman," *Bloomberg News*, January 24, 2011.

[77] McCraney, Lacy. "Groupon Singled Out in Lawsuit: Man Claims Chicago-based Website Offers Illegal Gift Certificates," *NBC Chicago*, March 2, 2011. http://www.nbcchicago.com/news/local/Groupon-Singled-Out-in-Lawsuit-117230603.html

[78] Maysh, Jeff. "The female Mark Zuckerberg: How 21-year-old created a social network because she didn't like her school yearbook photo…and is now worth $20m," *DailyMail.com*, March 1, 2011. http://www.dailymail.co.uk/news/article-1361740/Female-Mark-Zuckerberg-How-Catherine-Cook-created-myyearbook-com.html

[79] Kirpalani, Reshma. "New Jersey Siblings Net $200 Million for myYearbook Sale," *ABC News*, July 22, 2011. http://abcnews.go.com/Technology/teens-start-company-sells-100-million/story?id=14127273

[80] Raice, Shayndi. "Is Facebook Worth $100 Billion?" *Wall Street Journal*, July 14, 2011. http://www.wsj.com/articles/SB10001424052702304584404576442950773361780

[81] [Hat tip to Hilary Till, co-founder of Premia Capital.] This is an excerpt from the announcement:

http://www.marketswiki.com/mwiki/Hilary_Till

www.cmegroup.com/tools-information/lookups/advisories/clearing/files/Chadv09-452.pdf

[82] Sloan, Allan. "Wall Street's role in Greek crisis should be no surprise," *Washington Post*, March 10, 2010. http://www.washingtonpost.com/wp-dyn/content/article/2010/03/09/AR2010030904243_pf.html

[83] The Hunt Brothers used a similar earlier strategy in an attempt to corner the silver market in 1979-80 as recounted by Stephen Fay in *The Great Silver Bubble* (Coronet, 1982).

[84] Cui Carolyn, and Hoyle, Rhiannon. "J.P.Morgan Will Accept Gold as Type of Collateral," Wall Street Journal, February 8, 2011. http://www.wsj.com/articles/SB10001424052748704422204576130192457252596

[85] Efrati, Amir, Lauricella, Tom, and Searcey, Dionne. "Top Broker Accused of $50 Billion Fraud," *Wall Street Journal*, December 12, 2008. http://www.wsj.com/articles/SB122903010173099377

[86] Zuckerman, Gregory. "Fees, Even Returns and Auditor All Raised Flags," *Wall Street Journal*, December 13, 2008.

[87] Pittman, Mark. "Fed Refuses to Disclose Recipients of $2 Trillion," *Bloomberg News*, December 12, 2008. http://www.gata.org/node/6987

[88] Parloff, Roger. "Wall Street: It's Payback Time," Fortune, January 6, 2009.

[89] IMF's April 2007 Global Financial Stability Report. http://www.imf.org/External/Pubs/FT/GFSR/2007/01/index.htm

[90] IMF's April 2008 Report. www.imf.org/External/Pubs/FT/GFSR/2008/01/pdf/text.pdf

[91] Tavakoli, Janet. "Greater Global Risk Now Than At Time of LTCM," *The Financial Times*, May 7, 2007. http://www.tavakolistructuredfinance.com/2007/05/global-systemic-financial-risk/

[92] Geithner, Timothy F. "Risk Management Challenges in the U.S. Financial System," Federal Reserve Bank of New York, February 28, 2006. https://www.newyorkfed.org/newsevents/speeches/2006/gei060228.html

[93] Patterson, Scott, and Lauricella, Tom. "Did a Big Bet Help Trigger 'Black San' Stock Swoon?" *Wall Street Journal*, May 10, 2010.

[94] Furmans, Vanessa. "Former IKB Chief Convicted of Market Manipulation," *Wall Street Journal*, July 15, 2010. http://www.wsj.com/articles/SB10001424052748703792704575366561218672260

[95] Spence, John. "Oppenheimer downgrades Lehman shares to perform," *Market Watch*, March 24, 2008. http://www.marketwatch.com/story/oppenheimer-downgrades-lehman-shares-to-perform

[96] Gaffen, David. "Analyst Boxscore: Citigroup," *Wall Street Journal*, November 1, 2007. http://blogs.wsj.com/marketbeat/2007/11/01/analyst-boxscore-citigroup/

[97] Dash, Eric. "Analyst Raises Doubts About Citigroup Dividend," *The New York Times* November 1, 2007. http://www.nytimes.com/2007/11/01/business/01citi-web.html?ref=business

[98] Reilly, David. "In Subprime, AIG Sees Small Risk; Others See More," *Wall Street Journal*, August 13, 2007.

[99] Self, Will. "The Thinker," *GQ* UK edition, May 2009. First page, second column, 7th full paragraph. Taleb's web site home page showed this article as one of two "most representative overall profiles." After my [May 19] query, Taleb added a qualifier next to the link to the article: "(with typo on the 'billions')." [with no further clarification at that time]

[100] On June 3, 2009 I sent this to Taleb to give him a chance to respond to my commentaries if he chose to do so: "[I]f you look at the following linked commentaries, I am happy to issue appropriate corrections, revisions, updates, or more if it is in order." Taleb did not respond.

[101] Salmon, Felix. "Understanding Taleb," *Reuters*, June 1, 2009. http://blogs.reuters.com/felix-salmon/2009/06/01/understanding-taleb/

[102] The only mention of Empirica on Taleb's web site was as follows: "Owned **Empirica LLC** a trading/hedging/protection operation (currently the business became the Black Swan Protection Protocol managed by the traders at **Universa** –I am an advisor). Note that EMPIRICA WAS NEVER

CLOSED. **Current Corporate Boards**: a few hedge funds. A prophetic novel by Viken Berberian about Empiricus Kapital." There was no mention of Empirica Kurtosis Limited (Empirica Kurtosis), a fund, or of its returns even though it seems it may have been part of this operation at one time. The fund's returns are not mentioned in Taleb's *Wikipedia* profile (as of this writing). The returns for Empirica Kurtosis Limited are mentioned in Mark Spitznagel's *Wikipedia* profile, but in an incomplete way. Spitznagel was a partner with Taleb in this venture: "Empirica was reported to have made a 60% return in 2000 and lower (though unconfirmed) returns from 2001 to 2004."

[103] Staff. "Transcript: Bin Laden determined to strike in US [August 6, 2001]" *CNN*, April 10, 2004. http://www.cnn.com/2004/ALLPOLITICS/04/10/august6.memo/

[104] Gapper, John. "A pugnacious pundit Wall Street can't ignore," *Financial Times*, July 17, 2009.

[105] Gasparino, Charles. "Banking On Goldman," CNBC, July 14, 2009. http://video.cnbc.com/gallery/?video=1182513260&play=1

[106] Yarow, Jay. "Gasparino Drops F-Bomb On Air (Clip)," *Business Insider*, January f29, 2009. http://www.businessinsider.com/2009/1/gasparino-drops-an-f-bomb-on-air-clip

[107] Staff. "This Message Brought To You By Goldman Sachs' Noble Liquidity Provisioning Team," *ZeroHedge*, July 20, 2009. http://zerohedge.blogspot.com/2009/07/this-message-brought-to-you-by-goldman.html

[108] Tavakoli, Janet. "Commentary: What Wall Street Owes You," *CNN*, July 15, 2009. http://www.cnn.com/2009/POLITICS/07/15/tavakoli.goldman.earnings/index.html

[109] VIDEO: Inside Merrill Lynch, *CNBC,* October 24, 2007

[110] VIDEO: The Bigger Problem for Bonds, *CNBC*, January 25, 2008. http://video.cnbc.com/gallery/?video=628168183&play=1

[111] Mockenhaupt, Brian. "The Stolen-Valor Detective," *The Atlantic*, December 2016.

[112] Staff. "CIBC analyst got death threats on Citigroup – report*," Reuters*, November 4, 2007. http://in.reuters.com/article/businessNews/idINIndia-30326420071104

[113] Birger, Jon. "The woman who called Wall Street's meltdown," *Fortune*, August 6, 2008.
http://archive.fortune.com/2008/08/04/magazines/fortune/whitney_feature.fortune/index.htm

[114] Goldstein, Matthew. "Bear Stearns' Subprime IPO," *Business Week*, May 11, 2007. https://www.bloomberg.com/news/articles/2007-05-11/bear-stearns-subprime-ipobusinessweek-business-news-stock-market-and-financial-advice

[115] Wenzel, Robert. "Janet Tavakoli versus Meredith Whitney," *Economic Policy Journal*, March 24, 2009.
http://www.economicpolicyjournal.com/2009/03/janet-tavakoli-versus-meredith-whitney.html

[116] Helmore, Edward. "The new sage of Wall Street," *The Guardian*, September 27, 2008.
https://www.theguardian.com/books/2008/sep/28/businessandfinance.philosophy

[117] Berenson, Alex. "Fannie Mae's Loss Risk Is Larger, Computer Models Show," *New York Times*, August 7, 2003.
http://www.nytimes.com/2003/08/07/business/fannie-mae-s-loss-risk-is-larger-computer-models-show.html

[118] Weisenthal, Joe. "Nassim 'Black Swan' Taleb Busted For Exaggerating Returns," *Business Insider*, June 1, 2009.
http://www.businessinsider.com/wait-before-you-invest-in-nassim-talebs-new-fund-2009-6

[119] Wenzel, Robert. "Nassim Nicholas Taleb Fires Back," *Economic Policy Journal*, June 30, 2009.
http://www.economicpolicyjournal.com/2009/06/nassim-nicholas-taleb-fires-back.html

[120] Solomon, Deborah. "Crash Course," *The New York Times Magazine*, May 14, 2009. http://www.nytimes.com/2009/05/17/magazine/17wwln-q4-t.html

[121] Staff. "Charlie Lets Zero Intelligence Have It," *ZeroHedge*, July 22, 2009. http://www.zerohedge.com/article/charlie-lets-zero-intelligence-have-it

[122] Lewis, Michael. "Davos is for Wimps, Ninnies, Pointless Skeptics," *Bloomberg News*, January 30, 2007.

[123] Henriques, Diana B., and Bergman, Lowell. "MORTAGED LIVES: A special report.; Profiting From Fine Print With Wall Street's Help," *New*

York Times, March 15, 2000.
http://www.nytimes.com/2000/03/15/business/mortgaged-lives-special-report-profiting-fine-print-with-wall-street-s-help.html

[124] Staff. "Wachovia reaches settlement with ex-analyst," *Charlotte Business Journal*, January 11, 2006. Arturo Cifuentes, Ph.D., had years of experience at investment banks and early in his career, as a Sr. V.P. at Moody's, he developed early CDO technology (where his ratings had meaning) from 1996-1999. Upon my recommendation, Dr. Cifuentes testified before the Senate Committee on Banking, Housing and Urban Affairs in April 2008 about subsequent unsound practices and the role of the credit rating agencies in the global financial turmoil.
http://www.bizjournals.com/charlotte/stories/2006/01/09/daily20.html

[125] Staff. "Questions lie behind CPDO hype," *The Financial Times*, November 13, 2006.

[126] Staff. "Michael Lewis: Wall Street Collapse A Story of 'Mass Delusion' (VIDEO)*,"* *Huffington Post*, May 14, 2010.
http://www.huffingtonpost.com/2010/03/14/michael-lewis-wall-street_n_498690.html

[127] Dash, Eric. "Fed Helped Bank Raise Cash Quickly," The New York Times, March 12, 2010.
http://www.nytimes.com/2010/03/13/business/13freedom.html?_r=0

[128] Staff. "Janet Tavakoli: Wall Street Mortgage-Derivatives Trading Was 'A Massive Ponzi Scheme,'" *Huffington Post*, April 17, 2010.
http://www.huffingtonpost.com/2010/02/15/janet-tavakoli-wall-stree_n_462791.html

[129] Lamb, Brian, and Tavakoli, Janet. "Q&A," *C-SPAN*, April 20, 2009. (VIDEO)
https://www.youtube.com/watch?feature=player_embedded&v=WA20Am0pwtA

[130] Kouwe, Zackery, "Hedge Fund Manager Strikes Back at Obama," *The New York Times Dealbook*, May 5, 2009.
https://dealbook.nytimes.com/2009/05/05/a-hedge-fund-manager-strikes-back-at-obama/?_r=0

[131] Smith, Randall, and Pulliam, Susan. "As Funds Leverage Up, Fears of Reckoning Rise," *Wall Street Journal*, April 30, 2007.
http://www.wsj.com/articles/SB117789801972686591

[132] Hagerty, James R., and Holzer, Jessica. "U.S. Move to Cover Fannie, Freddie Losses Stirs Controversy," *Wall Street Journal,* December 28, 2009. http://www.wsj.com/articles/SB117789801972686591

[133] Beckel, Michael. "Campaign Cash From Wall Street Favored Representatives Who Opposed Financial Reform Bill," *OpenSecrets.org*, December 12, 2009. http://www.opensecrets.org/news/2009/12/campaign-cash-from-wall-street/

[134] Richard, Christine. *Confidence Game: How a Hedge Fund Manager Called Wall Street's Bluff*, Hoboken, New Jersey: Wiley, 2010. P. 6.

[135] *Confidence Game,* P. 137.

[136] The full text of this commentary including all Appendices is available in the "News" section of my website or via this link: "Tavakoli Structured Finance Revokes the Credit Rating Agencies' NRSRO Designation," July 26, 2011. http://www.tavakolistructuredfinance.com/tavakoli-revokes-cra-nrsro/

[137] The full text of this commentary including all Appendices is available in the "News" section of my website or via this link: "Tavakoli Structured Finance Revokes the Credit Rating Agencies' NRSRO Designation," July 26, 2011. http://www.tavakolistructuredfinance.com/tavakoli-revokes-cra-nrsro/

[138] Huffington, Arianna. *Third World America*, New York: Crown, 2010. P. 153

[139] Simon, Ruth, and Timiraos, Nick. "What Did Fannie and Freddie Know?" Wall Street Journal, September 6, 2011. http://www.wsj.com/articles/SB10001424053111903648204576553011839747054

[140] Morgenson, Gretchen. "Raters Ignored Proof of Unsafe Loans, Panel is Told," *The New York Times,* September 26, 2010. http://www.nytimes.com/2010/09/27/business/27ratings.html

[141] *Third World America.* Pp. 77 & 78.

[142] Black, William K., and Wray, L. Randall. "Foreclose on the Foreclosure Fraudsters, Part 1: Put Bank of America in Receivership," Huffington Post, October 22, 2010. http://www.huffingtonpost.com/william-k-black/foreclose-on-the-foreclos_b_772434.html

[143] Tavakoli, Janet. "Repairing the Damage of Fraud as a Business Model: Address of Janet Tavakoli, president of Tavakoli Structured Finance to the Federal Housing Finance Agency's Supervision Summit on December 8, 2010. http://www.tavakolistructuredfinance.com/fhfa-bank-fraud/

[144] Davis, Evan, and Buffett, Warren. "Evan Davis talks to Warren Buffett – Part 1," BBC, October 25, 2009. https://www.youtube.com/watch?v=22hWInng3gA

[145] Buffett bought $5 billion in Goldman Sachs's preferred stock paying a 10% annual dividend with warrants to buy $5 billion in common stock at a price of $115 any time before October 1, 2013.

[146] Tavakoli, Janet. "Warren Buffett's Wall Street War," TSF, October 20, 2009. http://www.tavakolistructuredfinance.com/2009/10/buffett-wall-street/

[147] Story, Louise. "Executives Kept Wealth as Firms Failed, Study Says," *The New York Times,* November 22, 2009. http://www.nytimes.com/2009/11/23/business/23pay.html?_r=1

[148]Davis, Evan, and Buffett, Warren. *BBC*'s mp3 podcast of Oct 26, 2009 @7:15 minutes. http://www.tavakolistructuredfinance.com/bbc.mp3

[149] Afonso, Gara, Kovner, Anna, Schoar, Antoinette. "What happened to US interbank lending in the financial crisis? " *VOX*, April 26, 2010. http://voxeu.org/article/what-happened-us-interbank-lending-financial-crisis

[150] Staff. "Munger Tells 25 Million Americans To 'Suck It In', And To 'Thank God for Bank Bailouts' As BRK Benefits From $95 Billion Of TARP Funding," *ZeroHedge*, September 20, 2010. http://www.zerohedge.com/article/munger-tells-25-million-americans-suck-it-and-thank-god-bank-bailouts-brk-benefits-95-billio

[151] Scism, Leslie, Holm, Erik, and Eaglesham, Jean. "Buffett's Policies Went Unheeded," *Wall Street Journal*, April 6, 2011.

[152] Chon, Gina, and Ng, Serena. "Mixed Signals Marked Sokol Meeting," *The Wall Street Journal*, April 2, 2011. http://www.wsj.com/articles/SB10001424052748704530204576237170960624878

[153] Press Release. "Warren E. Buffett, CEO of Berkshire Hathaway, Announces the Resignation of David L. Sokol," *Business Wire*, March 30, 2011. http://www.businesswire.com/news/home/20110330006798/en/Warren-E.-Buffett-CEO-Berkshire-Hathaway-Announces

[154] Baer, Justin, and Lemer, Jeremy. "Munger defends Sokol share deal," *Financial Times*, April 5, 2011.

[155] Goldstein, Matthew. "Special Report: OMG! Dan Loeb said what?" *Reuters*, March 11, 2011. http://www.reuters.com/article/us-hedgefunds-fairfax-loeb-idUSTRE72A4NH20110311

[156] Main, Andrew. "General Re reinsurance scandal still haunts Warren Buffett," *The Weekend Australian*, January 25, 2010. http://www.theaustralian.com.au/business/opinion/general-re-reinsurance-scandal-still-haunts-buffett/news-story/325f5e750c96f100f4a4e4d93a7d7380

[157] U.S. Securities and Exchange Commission Litigation Release No. 21612 / August 4, 2010. https://www.sec.gov/litigation/litreleases/2010/lr21612.htm

[158] Ng, Serena, and Ovide, Shira. "Buffett Scrambles to Limit Damage," T*he Wall Street Journal,* May 1, 2011. http://www.wsj.com/articles/SB10001424052748704436004576297392368003436

[159] Fabrikant, Geraldine. "Sokol's Ways Questioned in Past Suits," *The New York Times*, April 5, 2011. http://www.nytimes.com/2011/04/05/business/05sokol.html

[160] Staff. "Participants in the Future of Finance Initiative," *Wall Street Journal,* December 14, 2009. http://www.wsj.com/articles/SB10001424052748704193004574587943895484618

[161] Starr. "Fixing the Global Financial System," *Wall Street Journal.* http://www.wsj.com/public/page/future-of-finance-121409.html

[162] WSJ London, "Volcker Praises the ATM, Blasts Finance Execs, Experts," *Wall Street Journal*, December 8, 2009. http://www.wsj.com/articles/SB10001424052748704240504574585882066474634

[163] Tavakoli presentation to the IMF, 2009. http://www.tavakolistructuredfinance.com/wall-street-fraud-solutions/

[164] Staff. "Regulatory Frontier," Wall Street Journal, December 14, 2009. http://www.wsj.com/articles/SB10001424052748704825504574586262807292416

[165] Staff. "Don't Kill the Big Banks: Robert E. Diamond Jr. of Barclays on the benefits of size," *Wall Street Journal*, December 14, 2009. http://www.wsj.com/articles/SB10001424052748704240504574585882066474634

[166] Zuilli, Lilla. "Ambac capital exceeds required minimum." *Reuters,* November 18, 2009. http://www.reuters.com/article/us-ambac-capital-idUSTRE5AH5MH20091118

[167] Asset list for Abacus 2006-2 circa January 2008. www.tavakolistructuredfinance.com/AIGGS.pdf

[168] Kolhatkar, Sheelah and Bhaktavaatsalam, Sree Vidya. "The Colossus of Wall Street." Bloomberg News December 9, 2010. https://www.bloomberg.com/news/articles/2010-12-09/the-colossus-of-wall-street

[169] Letter from Representative Darrell E. Issa to William C. Dudley, President of the Federal Reserve Bank of New York, October 30, 2009. www.tavakolistructuredfinance.com/Issa.pdf

[170] Staff. "Paul Volcker: Think More Boldly," *Wall Street Journal*, December 14, 2009. http://www.wsj.com/articles/SB10001424052748704825504574586330960597134

[171] Unredacted pages of the March 2009 SEC filing pertaining to the AIG bailout. It shows counterparties, deals and shortfalls. static.reuters.com/resources/media/editorial/20100127/Schedule%20A.pdf

[172] Goldstein, Matthew. "AIG filing casts doubt on "limited exposure" claim," *Reuters*, January 29, 2010. http://www.reuters.com/article/us-aig-cassano-analysis-idUSTRE60S69O20100129

[173] Offering Circular for Octonion I CDO, Ltc. Octonion I CDO Corp., March 16, 2007. Most of Everquest's assets were priced as of December 31, 2006, but there were some 2007 additions to the portfolio. For example, it owned some of the "first loss" equity risk of a CDO named Octonion I CDO (Octonion), a deal underwritten by Citigroup in March 2007. If the IPO came to market, some of the proceeds from Everquest would pay down Citigroup's $200 million credit line. Octonion's prospectus disclosed an inexperienced CDO manager with conflicts of interest with the CDO investors. It used 95% credit default swaps referencing BBB rated asset backed securities including subprime assets. This CDO appeared to be a very risky investment for investors in the AAA or AA rated tranches. The equity, 48% of which was owned by Everquest, may have been entitled to the residual cash flow of the deal, even if they did not, the tranches looked high risk, undeserving of an investment grade rating. Time proved my concerns warranted, since Octonion triggered an event of default in February 2008, at which time even the original senior-most AAA tranche was downgraded to CCC by S&P (it

was still AAA by Moody's). By the summer of 2008, the senior-most "AAA" had been downgraded to Caa3 by Moody's and CCC- by S&P.

[174] Statement by William K. Black, Associate Professor of Economics and Law, University of Missouri - Kansas City before the Committee on Financial Services, United States House of Representatives regarding "Public Policy Issues Raised by the Report of the Lehman Bankruptcy Examiner." April 20, 2010. William K. Black is also the author of *The Best Way to Rob a Bank is to Own One: How Corporate Executives and Politicians Looted the S&L Industry* (University of Texas Press, 2005).

[175]Richard, Christine, *Confidence Game: How a Hedge Fund Manager Called Wall Street's Bluff*, Hoboken: Wiley, 2010. P. 295.

[176] Froomkin, Dan. "William Black Warns That Financial Reform Bill Won't Stop the Wall Street Crime Wave," *Huffington Post*, April 21, 2010. http://www.huffingtonpost.com/2010/04/21/william-black-warns-that_n_546806.html

[177] SEC v. Goldman Sachs & Co. and Fabrice Toure. www.sec.gov/litigation/complaints/2010/comp21489.pdf

[178] When banks sell short, it is often to hedge their risks. Sometimes hedges result in a net loss, and sometimes they result in a profit. Some hedge funds ethically sold short shares in companies with sham-based-accounting earnings. Short sellers were often the only people sounding the alarm as Pershing Square head Bill Ackman did with bond insurer MBIA. Christine Richard's just released book, *Confidence Game* (Wiley, 2010) is the gripping account of how he tried in vain for years to get regulators to listen. Meanwhile MBIA, at first an apparently healthy company, was a financial mirage and within a few years the "AAA" rated company sank like a stone. Short sellers were not responsible for the death of Lehman Brothers. My book on the meltdown, *Dear Mr. Buffett* (Wiley, 2009) is exculpatory evidence for anyone who shorted the stock or bought puts on the shares of Bear Stearns, Lehman, Merrill Lynch, Citigroup (and more) prior to the financial crisis. This type of short selling is very different from shorting a healthy company and spreading false rumors. It is also different from selling short while withholding damaging information.

[179] Eisinger, Jesse, and Bernstein, Jake. “The Magnetar Trade: How One Hedge Fund Helped Keep the Bubble Going,” *ProPublica*, April 10, 2010. https://www.propublica.org/article/all-the-magnetar-trade-how-one-hedge-fund-helped-keep-the-housing-bubble

[180] Nocera, Joe. "A Wall Street Invention Let the Crisis Mutate," *The New York Times*, April 16, 2010. http://www.nytimes.com/2010/04/17/business/17nocera.html?src=busln

[181] The *Wall Street Journal's* Serena Ng and Carrick Mollenkamp wrote a front page about Merrill, Magnetar, and others involved in a CDO called Norma. "Wall Street Wizardry Amplified Credit Crisis," December 27, 2007. http://www.wsj.com/articles/SB119871820846351717 This was a PAGE ONE article. On January 14, 2008 the *Wall Street Journal's* Serena Ng and Carrick Mollenkamp explained Magnetar's strategy, "A Fund Behind Astronomical Losses." http://www.wsj.com/articles/SB120027155742887331

The *Wall Street Journal's* Aaron Lucchetti wrote about the complexity of the final payouts for a value-destroying synthetic CDO called Sagittarius (MBIA (LaCrosse Financial Products), Deutsche, Wachovia, UBS ended up in a dispute over the cash): "CDO Battles: Royal Pain Over Who Gets What" December 17, 2007. http://www.wsj.com/articles/SB119785147303432641 This article appeared on the front page of the Markets (C1) section.

Susan Pulliam, Randall Smith, and Michael Siconolfi wrote a PAGE ONE article on serious CDO pricing issues including shenanigans such as trades with various hedge funds to inflate marks and gimmicks to temporarily disguise the risk (I was quoted in the article). This was before Lehman's famous gimmick of REPO 105. "Investors Face an Age of Murky Pricing," *Wall Street Journal*, October 11, 2007.

[182] CBS, "State Budgets: Day of Reckoning," *60 Minutes*, CBS, December 19, 2010. http://www.cbsnews.com/news/state-budgets-the-day-of-reckoning/

[183] Abelson, Max, and McDonald, Michael. "Whitney Municipal-Bond Apocalypse Short on Specifics," *Bloomberg News*, Feb 1, 2011. https://www.bloomberg.com/news/articles/2011-02-03/whitneys-muni-forecast-is-short-on-specifics

[184] Mysak, Joe. "Meredith Whitney Trips Over Her Muni Default Tale," *Bloomberg*, May 19, 2011.

[185] Braun, Martin Z. "Whitney's Armageddon Belied by '11 Returns," *Bloomberg News*, December 16, 2011.

[186] Applebaum, Binyamin, and Stolberg, Sheryl Gay. "At I.M.F., Men on Prowl and Women on Guard," *The New York Times*, May 19, 2011. http://www.nytimes.com/2011/05/20/business/20fund.html

[187] "At I.M.F…." *NYTimes*.

[188] Staff. "Greek Sovereign Debt Q&A," *ISDA*, October 27, 2011. www2.isda.org/uploaded_files/tinymce/Update%20on%20Greek%20Q%20and%20A%2027%2010%2011.pdf

[189] Form 10-K, MF Global Holdings LTD. for the year ending March 31, 2011
https://www.sec.gov/Archives/edgar/data/1401106/000119312511145663/d10k.htm

[190] Staff. "Rogue futures trader accused of $141.4M loss," *Associated Press*, February 28, 2008. http://www.nbcnews.com/id/23388778/ns/business-us_business/t/rogue-futures-trader-accused-m-loss/

[191] Stempel, Jonathan. "UPDATE 2-MF Global in $90 million accord over rogue trader," Reuters, August 11, 2011.
http://www.reuters.com/article/mfglobal-idUSN1E77A21820110811

[192] Coleman, Murray. "MF Global Admits To Mixing Money Between Customer Accounts," *Barron's*, November 1, 2011.
http://blogs.barrons.com/focusonfunds/2011/11/01/mf-global-admits-to-mixing-money-between-customer-accounts/?mod=BOLBlog

[193] Brush, Silia, and Leising, Matthew. "MF Global Probe May Involve Hundreds of Millions in Funds," *Bloomberg News*, November 1, 2011.
http://www.fa-mag.com/news/mf-global-probe-may-involve-hundreds-of-millions-in-funds-8799.html

[194] Barrett, Devlin, Patterson, Scott and Spector, Mike. "MF Global's Collapse Draws FBI Interest," *Wall Street Journal*, November 2, 2011.
http://www.wsj.com/articles/SB10001424052970204394804577012061970129588

[195] Staff. "UPDATE 5-MF Global trustee doubles estimates of shortfall," *Reuters*, November 21, 2011. http://www.reuters.com/article/mfglobal-idUSN1E7AK0RJ20111121

[196] Morgenson, Gretchen. "Sad Proof of Europe's Fallout," *The New York Times*, November 5, 2011. http://www.nytimes.com/2011/11/06/business/in-mf-global-sad-proof-of-europes-fallout.html?_r=3

[197] Protess, Ben, and Roose, Kevin. "Corzine Resigns From MF Global," The New York Times Dealbook, November 4, 2011.
https://dealbook.nytimes.com/2011/11/04/corzine-resigns-from-mf-global/?_r=0

[198] Singer, Bill. "Did Someone At FINRA Do Corzine A Favor And Waive His Registration Requirements?" *Forbes*, November 4, 2011.

[199] Zeng, Min. "MF Global's Downfall Raises Question on Fed's Primary Dealer Pick," *The Wall Street Journal*, November 1, 2011. http://blogs.wsj.com/deals/2011/11/01/mf-globals-downfall-raises-question-on-feds-primary-dealer-pick/?mod=google_news_blog

[200] Goldstein, Matthew. "MF Global and the rubber check," *Reuters*, November 5, 2011. http://blogs.reuters.com/unstructuredfinance/2011/11/05/mf-global-and-the-rubber-check/

[201] Prezioso, Jeanine. "INSIGHT-Clients who fled MF Global face clawback risk," *Reuters*, November 10, 2011. http://www.reuters.com/article/mfglobal-clawback-idUSN1E7A717U20111110

[202] Hilzenrath, David S. "Republican commissioner will direct CFTC probe of MF Global," *The Washington Post*, November 10, 2011. https://www.washingtonpost.com/business/economy/gensler-recuses-himself-from-cftcs-probe-of-mf-global/2011/11/10/gIQApqIz9M_story.html?utm_term=.f8061d009842

[203] Grynbaum, Michael M. "Paulson Urges Americans to Be Patient on Economy," *The New York Times,* July 23, 2009. http://www.nytimes.com/2008/07/23/business/economy/23econ.html

[204] Quigley, Mike, U.S. Representative for Illinois' 5th District. "Paulson's Actions Raise Serious Ethical Questions," *The Huffington Post*, February 5, 2012. http://www.huffingtonpost.com/mike-quigley/paulsons-actions-raise-se_b_1131556.html

[205] U.S. Department of Treasury, "Duties & Funcsions of the U.S. Department of the Treasury." https://www.treasury.gov/about/role-of-treasury/Pages/default.aspx

[206] Sommers, Jill E., Commissioner. "Testimony before the U.S. House of Representatives, Committee on Agriculture, Washington, DC," U.S. Commodity Futures Trading Commission, December 8, 2011. http://www.cftc.gov/PressRoom/SpeechesTestimony/opasommers-18

[207] Barrett, Devlin, Patterson, Scott and Spector, Mike. "MF Global's Collapse Draws FBI Interest," *Wall Street Journal*, November 2, 2011. http://www.wsj.com/articles/SB10001424052970204394804577012061970129588

[208] Bennett, David. "MF Global Revelations, Allegations and Amnesia," *NationalHogFarmer,* December 15, 2011. http://www.nationalhogfarmer.com/business/mf-global-revelations-allegations-and-amnesia

[209] "MF Global Bankruptcy Investigation, Panel 1 Part 1," *C-SPAN*, December 15, 2011. https://www.c-span.org/video/?303205-1/mf-global-bankruptcy-investigation-panel-1-part-1

[210] The Auditor, "N.J. Sen. Robert Menendez note keen to question Jon Corzine on MF Global scandal on Senate banking committee," *NJ.com,* December 25, 2011. https://www.c-span.org/video/?303205-1/mf-global-bankruptcy-investigation-panel-1-part-1

[211] Excerpt from Representative Marcy Kaptur's Special Order on MF Global December 14, 2011. http://www.tavakolistructuredfinance.com/kaptur-special-order/

[212] *Third World America.* P. 154.

[213] Craft, Matthew. "New Highs for Credit Card Charge-Offs," *Forbes*, June 24, 2009.

[214] See Transcript: Janet Tavakoli, *Forbes*, April 27, 2009.

[215] Second City Cop is a blogspot run by a contributing retired officer and a current officer of the Chicago Police Department. http://secondcitycop.blogspot.com/

[216] Thomas, John D. "Mugged on the (not so) Mag Mile," *Chicago Tribune,* July 14, 2010. http://articles.chicagotribune.com/2010-07-14/opinion/ct-oped-0714-mugged-20100714_1_mag-mile-flower-shirt

[217] Tavakoli, Janet. "Third World America: 'Fast-Tracking to Anarchy,'" *The Huffington Post*, August 25, 2010. http://www.huffingtonpost.com/janet-tavakoli/third-world-america-fastt_b_694903.html

[218] Staff. "Police Step Up Patrols After Lakefront, Downtown Mob Attacks," *CBS Chicago*, May 11, 2011.

[219] Lutz, BJ, and Perez, Alex. "Mob Attacks Two People Downtown," *NBC Chicago 5*, June 7, 2011. http://www.nbcchicago.com/news/local/chicago-wabash-mob-123423719.html

[220] Byrne, Dennis. "Disclose the race of flash mob victims and attackers," *Chicago Now*, June 8, 2011. http://www.chicagonow.com/dennis-byrnes-barbershop/2011/06/disclose-the-race-of-flash-mob-victims-and-attackers/

[221] Ryan, Joseph. "Bellwood digs $40 million hole for taxpayers, has no new Metra station to show for it," Chicago Tribune, April 4, 2011. http://articles.chicagotribune.com/2011-04-04/news/ct-met-bellwood-metra-station-20110404_1_mayor-frank-pasquale-bellwood-officials-metra

[222] Landesbank Baden-Wuerttemberg v. Goldman, Sachs & Co. And TCW Asset Management Company, October 4, 2010. www.tavakolistructuredfinance.com/LBBW.pdf

[223] Podmolik, Mary Ellen. "More banks walking away from homes, adding to housing crisis," *Chicago Tribune*, January 13, 2011. http://articles.chicagotribune.com/2011-01-13/news/ct-biz-0113-walkaway—20110113_1_foreclosure-process-foreclosure-filing-servicers

[224] Staff. "'Wilding' Victim Speaks Out: 'I was just trying to get away while fighting them back,'" NBC Chicago 5, June 6, 2011. http://www.nbcchicago.com/news/local/Wilding-Victim-Speaks-Out.html

[225] Baichwal, Ravi. "Billy Corgan's Brother Attacked On CTA Red Line," *ABC 7 Eyewitness News*, June 9, 2011. http://abc7chicago.com/archive/8181402/

[226] Jargon, Julie, and Brat, Ilan. "Chicago Police Brace for 'Flash Mob' Attacks," *Wall Street Journal*, June 9, 2011. http://www.wsj.com/articles/SB10001424052702304778304576375661383528354

[227] Cauchon, Dennis. "Leap in U.S. debt hits taxpayers with 12% more red ink," *USA Today*, May 29, 2009.

[228] Lutz, BJ. "Top Cop: Gun Laws Akin to 'Racism,'" *NBC Chicago 5*, June 23, 2011. http://www.nbcchicago.com/blogs/ward-room/emanuel-mccarthy-sabina-124439094.html

[229] Remarks by Chicago Police Superintendent McCarthy: http://youtu.be/xIX4j2sormY

[230] Glanton, Dahleen, Olivo, Antonio, and Mullen, William. "Abandoned homes multiply in Englewood, and crime follows," *Chicago Tribune*, June 23, 2011. http://articles.chicagotribune.com/2011-06-23/news/ct-met-englewood-empty-houses-20110623_1_foreclosure-crisis-englewood-and-west-englewood-vacant-properties

[231] Fisk, Robert. "The demise of the dollar," *Independent*, October 5, 2009. http://www.independent.co.uk/news/business/news/the-demise-of-the-dollar-1798175.html

[232] Reporting by Eadie Chen and Chen Aizhu in Beijing, Alfred Cang in Shanghai, George Chen and Michael Flaherty in Hong Kong; Editing by Jonathan Leff. "UPDATE1-Beijing's derivative default stance rattles banks," *Reuters*, August 331, 2009. http://www.reuters.com/article/china-derivatives-idUSSP47327420090831

[233] Source of the numbers for 1950 and 2010 is www.usgovernmentspending.com, and 1983 estimate is via TSF.

[234] Major Foreign Holders of Treasury Securities via treasury.gov http://ticdata.treasury.gov/Publish/mfh.txt

[235] Forelle, Charles. "For Ordinary Greeks, Big Bailout Adds Up to Years of Hardship*," Wall Street Journal,* October 29, 2011. http://www.wsj.com/articles/SB10001424052970203554104577003892831820960

[236] Janssen, Richard F., and Levine, Richard J. "A Threat to Economy Was Factor in Pressing U.S. to Defend Dollar," *Wall Street Journal* (Front Page), November 6, 1978.

[237] Chang, Gordon G. "Chinese Ministry Saved from Default," *Forbes*, October 23, 2011.

[238] Hvistendahl, Mara. *Unnatural Selection: Choosing Boys Over Girls, and the Consequences of a World Full of Men,* New York: Public Affairs, June 7, 2011.

[239] Fung, Esther. "Shanghai Homeowners Smash Showroom in Protest Over Falling Prices," *Wall Street Journal*, October 25, 2011. http://blogs.wsj.com/chinarealtime/2011/10/25/shanghai-homeowners-smash-showroom-in-protest-over-falling-prices/

[240] Hornby, Luch, and Chiang, Langi. "China's Ordos property bust offers warning sign," *Reuters*, December 2, 2011. http://www.reuters.com/article/us-china-property-bubble-idUSTRE7B10XA20111202

[241] Moore, Malcolm. "'BMW town' crashes in pyramid fraud," *The Telegraph*, September 23, 2011. http://www.telegraph.co.uk/news/worldnews/asia/china/8783588/BMW-town-crashes-in-pyramid-fraud.html

[242] Jim Rogers and I have been professional admirers for several years, and his blurbs appear on the dust jackets of two of my books: *Structured Finance*, and *Dear Mr. Buffett.*

[243] I attended the New-York [*sic*] Historical Society 2011 History Makers Awards honoring Henry Kissinger and James Chanos as one of Chanos' several guests. The theme was "China: An Evening with the Experts."

[244] Barboza, David. "Contrarian Investor Sees Economic Crash in China," *The New York Times*, January 7, 2010. http://www.nytimes.com/2010/01/08/business/global/08chanos.html

[245] Srinivasan, S. "Why is Jim Rogers Sceptical of India's Future?" *Forbes India*, March 11, 2010.

[246] Rogers, Jim. "India" http://www.jimrogers.com/content/stories/articles/india.html

[247] Chamon, Marcos, Liu, Kai, and Prasad, Eswar. "The puzzle of China's rising household savings rate," *VOX*, January 18, 2011. http://voxeu.org/article/puzzle-china-s-rising-household-saving-rate

[248] West, James. "Just How Bad Is Beijing's Pollution? Hint: Crazy Bad." *Mother Jones*, December 7, 2011. http://www.motherjones.com/blue-marble/2011/12/beijing-pollution-problem-press

[249] Watts, Jonathan. "Twitter gaffe: US embassy announces 'crazy bad' Beijing air *pollution," The Guardian*, November 19, 2010. https://www.theguardian.com/environment/blog/2010/nov/19/crazy-bad-beijing-air-pollution

[250] Fitz-Gerald, Keith. "Why China's 'Blindside' Could Be A Great Buying Opportunity*," Money Morning*, January 6, 2012

[251] Staff. "A Window on China, " *The Economist*, December 10, 2011. http://www.economist.com/node/21541417

[252] Zarathurstra. "Where Chanos is wrong on China," *MacroBusiness*, October 4, 2011. http://www.macrobusiness.com.au/2011/10/where-chanos-is-wrong-on-china/

[253] O'Keefe, Kate. "Macau Gambling Revenue Rose 42% Last Year," *Wall Street Journal*, January 3, 2012. http://www.wsj.com/articles/SB10001424052970203550304577138030085916546

[254] Cohen, David. "What Wukan Really Meant," *The Diplomat*, January 1, 2012. http://thediplomat.com/2012/01/what-wukan-really-meant/

[255] Moses, Russell Leigh. "Will Wukan Be the New Normal?" *Wall Street Journal*, December 28, 2011.

http://blogs.wsj.com/chinarealtime/2011/12/28/will-wukan-be-the-new-normal/

[256] Sanderson, Henry, and Forsythe, Michael. "Provincial borrowers defer loan payments," *ChinaDaily.com,* December 26, 2011. http://www.chinadaily.com.cn/bizchina/2011-12/26/content_14326726.htm

INDEX

A

AAA ratings, 121, 138, 158, 187, 206, 223, 277, 306
  "mezzanine AAA" tranches, 160, 162–163, 174
  sovereign, 38, 62, 143, 155–156, 164, 166, 169–174, 211, 336–337
  structured products and, 51, 63, 66–67, 99, 102–103, 132, 136, 141–143, 145–150, 155–157, 159–160, 162–165, 167–168, 174–175, 186, 211, 214, 336–339
  See also rating agencies; super senior tranches
Abacus CDOs. *See* Goldman Sachs: Abacus CDOs of
ABS CDOs. *See* collateralized debt obligations
ACA Financial Guaranty, 31, 66
accounting, 24–25, 27, 30, 33–35, 40, 55, 67, 75, 82, 96–97, 100, 104, 161–162, 218, 224, 230, 243, 264, 266, 296, 307
  phony, 22, 56, 83, 121, 123, 135, 137, 165–166, 170, 279
  See also mark-to-market accounting
Ackman, Bill, 231
  MBIA and, 136–139
  Pershing Square Capital Management, 136, 138
African Americans, 285, 291, 299, 302
AIG (American International Group), 21, 31, 66, 206, 243, 249
  bailout of, 17, 22, 29–30, 35–37, 40–41, 44–48, 50–54, 56–58, 72, 80, 105–106, 118, 130, 138, 161–162, 211–216, 219, 221–222, 226, 228–229
  bonuses at, 29–30, 40, 109, 214, 216, 221–222
  collateral calls on, 33–37, 41, 43–50, 52, 55, 57, 80, 109, 216, 219, 221, 248, 311
  counterparties paid in full, 36, 42, 44, 48, 52, 56–57, 72, 105–106, 212, 214–215, 219
  credit default swaps written by, 22, 33–34, 41, 44–45, 47–55, 57–58, 72, 80, 105–106, 109, 130, 161–162, 212–213, 215–216, 219–220, 248
  Financial Products unit of, 40, 50, 109, 220
  Goldman Sachs and, 17, 22, 33, 35–37, 41, 43–59, 65, 72, 105–106, 161–162, 211–216, 219, 221, 226, 228–229, 311
  Maiden Lane III and, 44, 50, 52, 54, 216
  mark-to-market losses of, 33–34, 37, 40, 42–43, 47–50, 52, 109, 118, 161–162, 212–213, 219–220, 228–229
  redacted filings of, 54
  Societe Generale and, 35–36, 50–51, 212–213, 220
  warnings about, 17, 33–35, 107, 118, 214–215, 219, 232
Ally Bank. *See* GMAC (Ally Bank)
Ambac, 31, 44, 46, 72–73, 138–139, 166–167, 212, 215, 343
  See also monoline insurers
American International Group. *See* AIG
Angelides, Phil, 222–225
Antos, Jim, 319, 327
AQR Capital Management, 129

arbitrage, 25, 91, 175, 242
Argentina, 82, 239, 241
Asness, Clifford, 129–131
asset-backed commercial paper (ABCP), 99, 132, 160, 167, 305
auditors, 31, 34–35, 48, 52, 66, 77, 84, 86, 98, 150, 153, 162, 164, 177–178, 206, 264

B

bailouts, 21, 23–25, 31, 35–38, 41, 45–48, 50–51, 57, 63, 71–72, 80, 83, 87, 106, 131, 140, 143, 162, 168, 171–172, 200, 202, 212, 215–216, 219, 229, 231, 236–237, 258, 277, 286–287, 293, 309, 312, 317, 337
  backdoor, 52–53, 305–306
  banks' bonuses and, 30, 40, 214, 221–222, 270–271, 291, 296
  of Europe, 103, 235, 314
  restructuring as alternative to, 134
  taxpayer cost of, 17, 27, 29–30, 53, 95, 100, 129–130, 133, 138–139, 170, 198, 201, 213–214, 221–222, 262, 270–272, 279, 296, 306
  See also AIG: bailout of; Troubled Asset Relief Program
Banana Republic, U.S. as, 195, 273, 287
bank capital, 102, 134, 142–143, 148–149, 166, 169, 319, 327, 337
Bank for International Settlements (BIS), 142, 145, 149, 175, 336
Bank of America, 71, 181, 193, 209, 239, 251
  bonus plans of, 64–65, 270–271
  Countrywide acquisition by, 65, 192, 271, 277–278, 305
  foreclosures and, 277–278, 294, 306
  Merrill Lynch acquisition by, 47, 51, 61, 64–65, 67, 130, 159, 192, 270–271, 277–278
bankruptcy
  of Lehman Brothers, 159, 200
  of MF Global, 18, 124, 244–245, 247–248, 250, 252–254, 262, 267, 269
  of Oakwood Homes, 195–196
  of Ownit, 66, 164
Barclays, 83, 192, 210
Bartmann, Bill, 151, 154
Bear Stearns, 31, 45, 65, 83, 101, 107, 116, 159, 196, 227, 252, 263, 277–278
  hedge funds of (BSAM), 67, 117, 130, 210, 217–218, 222, 224–225, 228
Bear Stearns Asset Management (BSAM). *See* Bear Stearns: hedge funds of
Benmosche, Robert, 42
Berkshire Hathaway, 34, 45, 63, 185, 195, 197, 199–200, 202–204, 206–207
  See also Buffett, Warren
Bernanke, Ben, 25, 31, 100, 197, 216–218, 229, 231
black swan, 26, 104, 110–115, 118, 158
  See also Taleb, Nassim Nicholas
Black Swan, The (Taleb), 104
Black, William K., 192–193, 198, 224, 231, 258, 279
BlackRock, 213–215, 220–221
Blagojevich, Rod, 124, 256
Blankfein, Lloyd, 37, 41, 43, 48, 50, 53, 55, 59, 186, 213, 219, 225
Bloomberg, 22, 24, 47, 49, 73–74, 79, 101, 171, 201, 206, 222, 225, 228, 233, 254–256, 320, 325
Blum, Michael, 66, 164
bonuses, bankers', 27–28, 55, 96, 99–100, 102, 123, 132, 138, 161, 170, 180, 193, 228, 279, 291, 296
  at AIG, 29–30, 40, 109, 214, 216, 221–222
  at Bank of America, 64–65, 270–271
  at Goldman Sachs, 37, 65, 213–214, 216, 221–222, 271–272
  at Merrill Lynch, 65, 67, 270–271

Bove, Richard, 108
broker-dealers, 264
BSAM. *See* Bear Stearns: hedge funds of
Buffett, Warren, 35, 39, 75, 124, 199, 228, 231
AIG warning to, 17, 33–34, 107, 219
Berkshire Hathaway and, 34, 63, 185, 195, 197, 200, 203–204, 206–207
class war and, 200
credit derivatives and, 107, 135, 195
financial press and, 17, 203, 206–207, 222
Goldman Sachs investment of, 17, 33, 196–198, 200, 219, 271–272
mark-to-market accounting and, 22–23
Moody's and, 185, 206
Oakwood Homes and, 195
Sokol affair and, 203–204, 206–207
See also Berkshire Hathaway; *Dear Mr. Buffett*
Buffettgate. *See* Sokol, David

C

Calyon, 35, 44, 50–51, 212, 229
campaign contributions, 17–18, 102, 134, 261, 267
capitalism, 131, 197, 322
crony, 21, 42, 57, 186, 191, 238, 254–255, 257
Carlini, James, 283–285
Cassano, Joseph, 50, 220
Cayne, Jimmy, 116
CBS, 57, 289
CDOs. *See* collateralized debt obligations
CDS. *See* credit default swaps
CFTC. *See* Commodity Futures Trading Commission
Chancellor, Edward, 319, 327
Chanos, Jim, 319–320, 323, 326–327, 329
China bear thesis of, 316, 321–322, 325
Chicago, 36, 57, 83, 103, 112, 123–125, 149, 251, 256, 293–294, 301, 306
crime and violence in, 280–281, 283–285, 288–292, 298–299, 305
Magnificent Mile ("Mug Mile") of, 283–285, 289–290
police in, 280–281, 285, 288–289, 291, 295, 299–300, 303
public finances of, 126, 231–232, 239, 280, 292, 297–298
Chicago Council on Global Affairs (CCGA), 123–126, 316
Chicago Mercantile Exchange (CME), 81, 88, 90, 123, 247, 264, 297
China, 38, 84, 87, 180, 204, 315–316
banking system of, 45, 61–62, 83, 198, 307, 311, 314, 317, 319–324, 327–328
currency basket and, 61, 198, 307, 310–311, 313–314, 317, 319, 322, 326–327
derivatives default stance of, 45, 61–62, 198, 311–312, 321
gender imbalance in, 317–318
housing bubble in, 318–319, 321–329
local government debt in, 319, 326–328
pollution in, 323–324
savings rate in, 323, 327–328
U.S. debt held by, 307, 313–314
Wukan rebellion in, 328
See also Chanos, Jim; Rogers, Jim
Chinese wall, 180
Cioffi, Ralph, 49
Citigroup, 44, 65, 159, 192, 203, 232, 239, 277
bailout of, 72, 130
CDOs and "super senior" exposure of, 46, 72, 109, 117, 222–223, 225, 228

FCIC hearing and, 222–225, 228
Rubin and, 72–73, 222, 225, 278
short sellers of, 107–108, 117, 225–226
Clark, Jim, 74
class warfare, 56, 123, 125, 127, 200, 291, 298
Clayton Holdings, 163, 177, 192
Clews, Henry, 20
CNBC, 63, 71, 104, 115–116, 119–120, 204, 234, 303
Cohn, Gary, 48
Colbert, Stephen, 113–115
collateral, 17–18, 22, 25, 33–37, 41, 43, 46–49, 57, 61, 99, 132, 135, 137, 141, 144, 146–147, 152–153, 159–160, 163, 167, 177, 187, 196, 214, 216, 219, 221, 229, 247–248, 259–260, 278, 311
calls for, 44–45, 50, 52, 55, 88–89, 109, 266
gold as, 80–81, 85–89, 172
collateralized debt obligations (CDOs), 25–26, 46, 53, 55, 95, 130, 139, 195, 213, 278
ABS CDOs, 135, 142–143, 165, 229, 336–337, 341, 343
CDO-squared, 27, 66, 99, 132, 141, 159–160, 165–167, 342
Goldman Sachs and, 22, 35–36, 43–44, 48–52, 54, 56–58, 72, 105–106, 161–162, 186, 215–216, 219–220, 222, 225, 228–229
Magnetar and, 227–230
Merrill Lynch and, 22, 47, 50–51, 63, 66–67, 164–167, 220, 227, 341–342
ratings of, 18, 27, 30, 34–35, 39, 66–67, 72, 99, 109, 117, 132, 135–136, 138, 141–143, 145–150, 155, 158–168, 175, 178, 183–186, 214, 216, 220–221, 223, 228, 248, 336–337, 339
"super senior" tranches of, 33–34, 47, 51, 63, 66, 142, 145, 148–149, 161, 175, 214, 222, 339
synthetic, 54, 137, 142, 216, 227–229, 331
See also super senior tranches
Comex, 92–93
Commercial Financial Services (CFS), 151–154, 158, 181
commodities, 60, 69, 84, 91–94, 103, 141, 169, 184, 234, 244–247, 252–254, 280, 296, 308–309, 312, 322, 325, 329
speculation in, 68, 89–90, 144, 168
Commodity Futures Trading Commission (CFTC), 270
MF Global and, 94, 243–247, 249–250, 253–254, 260–261, 264–265
precious metals and, 84, 89–91, 94, 244–246, 253–254
conflicts of interest, 47–48, 147, 152, 175, 179–186, 220
Congress, U.S., 18, 23, 27, 29, 39, 55, 58, 69–70, 79, 81, 88, 96, 135, 145, 163, 188, 191, 195, 222, 225, 273–274, 277, 279
AIG investigation by, 54, 57, 59, 107, 219
bailout legislation in, 24, 30, 80, 83, 131–132, 287
financial reform and, 30–31, 38, 59, 80, 83, 104, 131–133, 140, 173, 186–187, 280, 287
lobbying of, 38, 56–57, 59, 102, 134, 261, 268
MF Global hearings in, 124, 258–259, 261–264, 268–270
See also Financial Crisis Inquiry Commission
conservatorship, 17, 192, 201, 255
constant proportion debt obligations (CPDOs), 136, 155–157, 167, 174
control fraud, 30, 165–166, 170, 198, 226, 296
Cordray, Richard, 71, 193
corporate governance, 207, 251, 269
corruption, 17, 21, 70, 124, 127, 136, 138–139, 159, 161, 177, 187, 225, 229, 231, 256, 279–280, 282, 284,

286–287, 292, 294, 297–298, 316, 322, 325–326, 328
Corzine, Jon
congressional testimony of, 124, 258–262, 264, 268–270
customer funds and, 124–125, 258–262, 265, 267–269
Goldman Sachs career of, 18, 124, 244, 246, 248, 250–253, 258, 263, 267–268
Obama and, 18, 261, 267–268
primary dealer status and, 246, 252, 263
risk-taking by, 244, 246, 248, 251, 253, 259–260, 263, 269
Countrywide Financial, 65, 124–126, 162, 192, 220, 271, 277–278, 293, 303, 305–306
CPDOs. *See* constant proportion debt obligations
credit bubble, 17, 191, 322–324, 327
credit default swaps (CDS), 72, 143, 166, 176
AIG and, 33, 41, 44–45, 47, 50–55, 57, 80, 109, 130, 161–162, 215–216, 219, 248
ban proposed on, 21, 44, 50, 58, 79–81, 83, 86, 88, 130, 215–216, 337
gold payoffs demanded for, 79–81, 85–86, 88–89
on Greece, 82, 240
ISDA and, 82, 240–241
sovereign, 80, 82–83, 86, 88, 241, 337
on U.S. debt, 79–81, 85–86, 88
See also credit derivatives
credit derivatives, 22, 25, 60, 66–68, 91, 99, 132, 135–138, 141–142, 144, 158–159, 168–169, 218, 224, 230, 240, 246, 278, 296, 321
AIG and, 30–31, 35, 40–41, 47, 49, 52, 57, 107, 118, 212, 215–216, 228–229, 243, 248–249
ban proposed on, 79–81, 88, 183–184
documentation risk in, 82, 85–86, 160–161, 183–184, 241
Goldman Sachs and, 41, 47, 49, 52, 57, 212, 215–217, 228–229
MF Global and, 94, 243, 245, 248–251
See also credit default swaps
Credit Suisse, 46, 192, 196, 278
criminal prosecution, lack of, 18, 29, 39, 56, 83, 96, 102, 124–125, 134–135, 154, 192, 200, 206, 218, 279–280, 282, 288, 291, 306
Cuomo, Andrew, 64

D

Daley, Richard, 283–284
Dallas, William, 66
Davis Square CDOs. *See* Goldman Sachs: Davis Square CDOs of
Davis, Evan, 198–199
Dear Mr. Buffett (Tavakoli), 17, 39, 63, 124, 135, 197, 200, 222, 228, 231
debt, U.S. national, 275, 287, 297, 313
deflation, 194, 201, 237, 273–276, 287
delta hedging, 105
derivatives
Jefferson County and, 191–192
regulation of, 25, 60, 82, 91, 94, 138, 142–144, 168, 183–184, 186, 191–192, 218, 243, 245, 249–250, 278, 280, 296
See also credit default swaps; credit derivatives
Deutsche Bank, 50, 83, 162, 192, 294, 306
Dimon, Jamie, 33, 35, 70–71, 107, 219
Dodd-Frank Act, 59–60, 68, 89, 143–145, 147, 173, 177, 179, 181, 183–187
Dubai, 83, 322, 327
Dudley, William C., 246, 252, 263
due diligence, 27, 58, 99–100, 135, 138, 144–145, 153, 155, 163, 177–178, 184, 192, 205, 294, 326

Duffy, Terry, 264–265
Durden, Tyler, 120

E

Emanuel, Rahm, 232, 256, 288–289
Emergency Economic Stabilization Act of 2008, 21
Empirica Kurtosis, 112–113, 118
Englewood (Chicago), 305
Enron, 24, 63, 150, 178, 230, 278, 307, 325
euro, 80, 172, 237–238, 240, 314
  See also Europe
Europe, 103, 155–156, 164, 170, 172–175, 177, 179, 183, 185, 210, 235, 243, 249–250, 308, 314
  banks in, 25, 141, 181, 184, 237–240, 307
  credit default swaps and, 80, 82
  See also Greece; Ireland; Italy; Portugal; Spain
European Central Bank (ECB), 237–240
European Union, 80, 103, 238
Eurozone. *See* Europe
exchange-traded funds (ETFs), 84, 86

F

Faber, David, 119
Facebook
  fake user profiles on, 73, 75–78
  Goldman Sachs private offering of, 73–74
  valuation of, 73–78
Fannie Mae and Freddie Mac, 17, 30, 38, 56, 118, 133, 171, 191–192, 255–257, 277, 304, 336
FCIC. *See* Financial Crisis Inquiry Commission
Fed. *See* Federal Reserve
Federal Deposit Insurance Corporation (FDIC), 30, 100, 133, 170–171, 213–214, 218, 239, 254
Federal Housing Finance Agency (FHFA), 192–193
Federal Reserve, 38, 59, 90–91, 96–97, 100, 104, 115, 125–127, 133, 145, 149, 159, 168, 196, 200, 209, 225, 229–230, 251, 256, 275, 307–308, 313, 315, 336
  AIG rescue and, 36, 44, 47–48, 50, 56–57, 72, 211–216, 219–221
  audit of, 31
  cheap funding from, 17, 21, 27–28, 30, 72, 85, 88, 101–103, 122, 132, 170–172, 191, 197, 213, 215, 217–218, 220–221, 252, 263, 291, 296, 305–306, 309, 314, 328
  Countrywide and, 305–306
  primary dealers and, 246, 252, 263–264
  See also Federal Reserve Bank of New York
Federal Reserve Bank of New York (FRBNY), 31, 48, 52–53, 101, 212–215, 219, 252, 263
Ferguson, Niall, 316–318
FGIC, 31, 44, 138, 212, 215
  See also monoline insurers
Financial Crisis Inquiry Commission (FCIC), 59, 192, 222, 225, 228
Financial Times, 21, 150, 156, 336
FINRA, 248, 250–251
First Franklin, 65, 220, 277
Fitch Ratings, 135, 139, 141, 146–151, 154, 180, 319, 327, 338
  See also rating agencies
foreclosures, 218, 279, 304
  fraud in, 70–71, 124, 126, 193, 293, 306
Fortune, 41, 96–97, 117, 162, 233
Fowler, William Worthington, 32
France, 35, 44, 50, 62, 135, 212–213, 220, 238, 311
fraud, 31, 75–76, 115, 123, 137, 150–151, 170, 187, 198, 206, 209, 233, 258–260, 267, 270, 280, 296, 307, 316, 325
  "as a business model", 70–71, 135, 141, 159, 191, 193

foreclosure, 70–71, 124, 126, 193, 293, 306
in mortgage lending, 17–18, 29–30, 56, 71–72, 85, 99–100, 102, 124–126, 132–135, 138, 141, 158–162, 166, 171, 177–178, 192, 224–226, 228, 277, 293–294, 298, 305–306, 320, 329
in securitization, 17–18, 26, 56, 66, 99–103, 105, 124–126, 132, 135, 138–139, 141–142, 153–154, 158–163, 165–167, 177–178, 186, 191, 216, 224–226, 228, 231, 293–294, 306, 328–329
See also control fraud; Ponzi schemes
Freddie Mac. *See* Fannie Mae and Freddie Mac
Friedman, Stephen, 48, 50, 213, 219
futures commission merchants (FCMs), 124, 244–245, 254, 259–260
futures markets, 18, 84, 87, 91, 105, 244, 254, 259, 266

G

Gasparino, Charles, 115–116, 119–120
Geithner, Timothy, 31, 41, 53, 101–102, 197, 214–218
Gensler, Gary, 244–246, 253–254
Germany, 80, 106, 172, 201
Glass-Steagall Act, 100, 102, 134, 170, 218, 280
Glenn, Martin, 247, 262
GMAC (Ally Bank), 71, 192
gold, 84, 90, 307–308, 311, 314
as collateral, 80–81, 85–89, 172
cornering market in, 83, 85, 87
price manipulation and, 79, 85–86, 91
See also silver
Goldman Sachs, 62, 104, 159, 186, 197, 199, 270, 305
Abacus CDOs of, 44, 54, 56, 105–106, 212, 220
AIG and, 17, 22, 33, 35–37, 41, 43–59, 65, 72, 105–106, 161–162, 211–216, 219, 221, 226, 228–229, 311
backdoor bailout of, 23, 35–36, 41, 43–48, 50–53, 56–57, 72, 83, 105–106, 162, 198, 200, 212–216, 219, 221, 229, 271–272
conflicts of interest of, 47–48, 220–221, 244–245
Davis Square CDOs of, 51–52, 57, 212, 220–221
Facebook offering of, 73–74
"God's work" remark and, 33, 59, 191
GSAMP Trust 2006-S3 and, 35, 41, 50, 162, 196, 220, 293
hedges against clients by, 17, 35, 41, 43–48, 50–52, 57, 115, 212–213, 216–218, 222, 225–226, 254–255
MF Global and, 18, 124, 244–246, 248, 250–254, 258, 263, 267–268
Paulson and, 23, 41, 50–51, 55, 64, 162, 213, 219, 230, 254, 271–272
SEC and, 56, 105–106, 191, 196, 225, 278
Senate investigation of, 59, 191, 225–226
Societe Generale and, 35–36, 50–51, 192, 212–213
Timberwolf I and, 49
See also Blankfein, Lloyd; Paulson, Henry (Hank); Viniar, David
Goldstein, Matthew, 49, 54, 222
Grantham, Jeremy, 107, 274
Great Depression, 21
Great Recession, 28, 55, 138, 276, 279, 287
Greece, 80, 169, 235, 237–239, 297, 314, 319, 327
credit default swaps on, 82, 240, 242
Greenspan, Alan, 229

Gresham Investment Management, 91, 265
Grice, Dylan, 320–321, 328–329
Groupon, 73–75, 78
GSAMP Trust 2006-S3. *See* Goldman Sachs: GSAMP Trust 2006-S3 and

H

Hayworth, Nan, 268–269
hedge funds, 18, 26, 30, 63, 67, 82–84, 87, 95, 97–98, 104, 109–110, 112, 115, 117–118, 122, 129–131, 133, 136, 140, 142–143, 160, 187, 204–205, 210, 217–218, 222–225, 227–231, 241, 255–257, 322
Holm, Erik, 47
housing market, 25, 27, 101, 119, 123–124, 132, 151, 158, 177, 192–193, 195, 227, 273, 276, 291, 293
  bubble in, 56, 133, 138, 277, 292, 325
  prices in, 29, 100, 164, 171, 275, 287, 292, 303, 307, 318–319, 326
Huffington Post, 19, 211
Huffington, Arianna, 119, 191–192, 276, 280, 286, 293, 296
Huizenga, Bill, 269
Hunt brothers, 85, 88–90, 266–267
  See also silver

I

Iceland, 169–170, 238
IKB Deutsche Industriebank, 105–106
Illinois, 124, 126, 231–232, 256, 258, 280, 284, 292–293, 297, 299, 305
IMF. *See* International Monetary Fund
India, 76, 170, 204, 316, 322
inflation, 85, 90, 133, 170, 194, 198, 201, 273–276, 286–287, 291, 307–309, 312–313, 315, 323, 325, 328
  See also stranguflation
insider trading, 103, 203, 206
interest rates, 17–18, 60, 68, 85, 88, 118, 141, 169–173, 184, 193, 201, 218, 249, 273, 275–276, 293, 305, 309, 313, 320
International Monetary Fund (IMF), 87, 99, 101–103, 135, 229, 235–237, 241, 279, 322
International Swaps and Derivatives Association (ISDA), 82, 230, 240–242
investment banks, 17–18, 24, 26–27, 31, 39, 43, 55, 61–63, 83, 95–97, 107, 109, 122, 135, 139, 141, 144, 147, 156, 165, 175, 178, 203, 214, 251
Ireland, 169, 235–237, 249–250
ISDA. *See* International Swaps and Derivatives Association
Italy, 169, 210, 235, 237, 249–250

J

Japan, 139, 173, 198, 279, 307, 311, 314
Jarecki, Henry, 91–93, 265–266
Jefferson County, Alabama, 191, 233–234
JPMorgan Chase, 82, 130, 159, 164, 191–192, 210, 217–218, 228, 233, 238–239, 241–242, 277–278, 294, 306, 315
  AIG warning to, 35, 46–47, 64–65, 71, 107, 219
  commodities division of, 68–70
  gold accepted as collateral by, 81, 83, 87–88
  MF Global and, 18, 267
  See also Dimon, Jamie

K

Kaptur, Marcy, 267–268, 270–271
Kernen, Joe, 116

L

Lehman Brothers, 17, 45–47, 83, 107, 117–118, 159, 196, 200, 226, 234, 246, 278

Levin, Carl, 59, 191
Lewis, Ken, 51, 64, 209, 251
Lewis, Kenneth. *See* Lewis, Ken
Lewis, Michael, 53, 121, 123, 231, 244, 253
Liar's Poker, 121, 244, 253
Liddy, Edward, 40
lobbying, 17, 56, 59, 68, 217–218
London, 81, 83, 88, 93, 210
Long-Term Capital Management (LTCM), 101, 122, 168, 230, 243, 248

M

Madigan, Lisa, 126, 293, 305
Madoff, Bernard, 26, 95–96, 205, 320
  See also Ponzi schemes
Magnetar Capital, 227–230
Maiden Lane III, 44, 50, 52, 54, 130, 214, 216
Man Group, 252, 263
mark-to-market accounting, 22–24, 27, 33, 48–50, 61, 109, 161
market manipulation, 37, 69–70, 82, 122, 310, 315
  in gold and silver, 79, 85–86, 90–93, 103, 106
  IKB and, 105–106
Markopolos, Harry, 96
Marshall, Kate, 234
Masters, Blythe, 68–70
Mayo, Michael, 108
MBIA, 31, 44, 66, 136–139, 166–167, 215, 227, 229, 343
  See also monoline insurers
McCarthy, Garry, 289–291, 295, 298–299
McHenry, Patrick, 258
Merkel, Angela, 80
Merrill Lynch, 44, 62, 83, 116, 196, 224
  Bank of America acquisition of, 47, 51, 61, 64–65, 67, 130, 159, 192, 270–271, 277–278
  CDOs underwritten by, 22, 50–51, 63, 66–67, 164–167, 220, 227, 341–342
  control fraud at, 165–166, 226
  Ownit and, 66, 163–164, 277
  Ponzi finance at, 66, 163
MF Global, 19
  bankruptcy of, 18, 124, 244–245, 247–248, 250, 252–254, 262, 267, 269
  CFTC and, 94, 243–246, 249–250, 253–254, 261, 264–265
  CME and, 247, 264
  congressional hearings on, 124, 258–259, 261–264, 267–270
  customer segregated funds diverted by, 18, 124–125, 243, 246, 248, 250, 253, 258–262, 264–265, 267–269
  JPMorgan Chase and, 18, 267
  primary dealer status of, 246, 252, 263–264
  rehypothecation and, 261, 265, 267
  repo-to-maturity trades of, 243, 245, 248–251, 265, 269
  sovereign debt bets of, 243, 249–250, 259, 261, 269
  See also Corzine, Jon
Mizuho Securities, 319, 327
Mocatta Metals, 83, 265–267
monoline insurers, 27, 39, 44, 46, 57, 63, 66, 72, 136, 138, 141, 150, 158, 166–167, 212, 215–216, 229, 231
  See also Ambac; FGIC; MBIA
Moody's, 135, 137–141, 146–149, 151, 154, 158, 162, 164, 173, 180, 185, 188, 206, 211, 221, 338
  CPDO rating methodology of, 136, 155–157, 174
  Iceland rating by, 169–170
  See also rating agencies
moral hazard, 149, 198, 209
Morgan Stanley, 46, 65, 83, 104, 159, 192, 278
Morgenson, Gretchen, 53, 248

mortgage-backed securities, 22, 41, 53–54, 72, 82, 125, 164, 195, 220, 228, 252, 263, 278
  ratings of, 27, 34, 56, 99, 107, 132, 141–142, 158–160, 162–163, 216, 277, 293
mortgages, subprime. *See* subprime mortgages
Moskow, Michael, 125–126
Muddy Waters Research, 320
Munger, Charlie, 200–201, 204
municipal bonds, 25, 27, 66, 72, 136–138, 166, 231–234, 292, 297

N

negative basis trades, 50–52
Nevada, 234, 304
New Century Financial, 162, 220, 230, 293
New Jersey, 18, 124, 246, 251, 258, 267, 269–270, 292
New York Fed. *See* Federal Reserve Bank of New York
New York Times, 56, 111, 118–119, 227, 236, 248, 255–256, 298
NRSRO designation, 99, 135–136, 139–140, 144–145, 163, 180, 183, 188, 211, 331
  See also rating agencies

O

Oakwood Homes, 195–196
Obama, Barack, 30, 129, 131, 224, 278
  Corzine and, 18, 267–268
  financial reform and, 217–218
Occupy Wall Street, 125
Ohio, 71, 193, 271, 304
Olick, Diana, 119, 303–304
oligarchy, financial, 21, 197, 230, 278
Ortseifen, Stefan, 106
Ownit Mortgage Solutions, 66, 163–164, 277

P

Pandit, Vikram, 130
Patrick, Tom, 63
Paulson plan, 21, 23
Paulson, Henry (Hank), 80, 83, 197, 256–257
  bailout plan of, 21, 23–24, 41, 50–51, 162, 213, 219, 255, 258, 271–272
  Goldman Sachs and, 23, 41, 50–51, 55, 64, 162, 213, 219, 230, 254, 271–272
  See also Paulson plan
Peabody, Charles, 108
Pecora Commission, 225–226
Pershing Square Capital Management, 136, 138
Pettis, Michael, 320, 328
Pfleger, Michael, 298–299, 301
Pleven, Liam, 40
police, 27, 125, 217, 232, 282–284, 301, 328
  Chicago, 280–281, 285, 288–291, 295, 298–300, 303
Ponzi schemes, 28–29, 136, 163
  Madoff and, 26, 95–96
  mortgage securitization as, 17, 25–26, 38–39, 56, 66, 95–97, 99–100, 102, 123, 132, 135, 138, 141–142, 159, 161, 195–196, 228, 277
  rating agencies and, 17, 39, 102, 141–142, 161
Portugal, 169, 235, 237, 249–250
PricewaterhouseCoopers (PwC), 35, 48
primary dealers, 246, 252, 263–264
Prince, Chuck, 222, 225
ProPublica, 227

Q

Quigley, Michael, 256–258

R

rating agencies, 30, 39, 54, 67, 133, 137–138, 146, 150, 159–162, 165–166, 168, 171–172, 184, 186–187, 192, 207, 225, 304
- CFS securitizations misrated by, 151–152, 154, 158, 181
- conflicts of interest of, 147, 152, 175, 179, 181–183
- CPDOs and, 136, 155–157, 167, 174
- fees of, 18, 38, 102, 147, 178–179, 182–183, 185
- methodologies of, 141–142, 144–145, 148–149, 152, 157–158, 173, 175–177, 181, 185
- NRSRO designation of, 99, 135–136, 139–140, 144–145, 163, 180, 183, 188, 211, 331
- sovereign ratings by, 140–141, 143, 169, 336–337
- statistical principles ignored by, 135–136, 139–140, 144, 152–153, 155, 178, 188
- *See also* AAA ratings; Fitch Ratings; Moody's; Standard & Poor's

rating agencies, credit. *See* rating agencies
real estate, 54, 62, 98–99, 132, 160, 178, 269, 297, 318–319, 321–325, 327, 329
recession, 28–30, 55, 138, 276, 279, 287, 308–309, 312
- *See also* Great Recession

regulators, 25, 27, 30, 38, 56, 70, 82–83, 91, 93–94, 104, 122, 133–134, 139, 142, 145–146, 148–149, 168, 173–175, 177, 179, 181, 183–188, 191–192, 195, 197, 200, 209–210, 226, 228, 245–246, 248–251, 262, 264–265, 270–271, 279
- failures of, 39, 101–102, 138, 141, 150–151, 159, 180, 224, 243, 256

rehypothecation, 261, 265–267
Reilly, David, 33–35, 214
repo-to-maturity, 243, 245–246, 248–249
Reuters, 26, 49, 117, 204–205
Rich, Frank, 56
Richard, Christine, 47, 136, 231
risk management, 29, 46, 101–102, 113, 122, 166, 209, 219, 244, 250, 253, 263, 269
RMBS. *See* mortgage-backed securities
Rogers, Jim, 107–108, 117, 232
- China bull thesis of, 319, 321–325, 329

Rose, Charlie, 22, 107
Rosenberg, Alan, 91–93
Rubin, Robert, 70
- Citigroup and, 72–73, 222, 225, 278
- FCIC testimony of, 222, 225

S

S&P. *See* Standard & Poor's
Sanders, Bernie, 287
Sarbanes-Oxley Act, 18, 106, 143, 164
savings and loan crisis, 102, 134, 192, 279
Scholes, Myron, 119
Schwartz, Alan, 45
SEC. *See* Securities and Exchange Commission
Securities and Exchange Commission (SEC), 22, 24, 27, 58, 97, 101, 104, 137, 146, 204, 207, 221, 223–224, 243, 250, 271
- AIG filings and, 36, 105–106
- Goldman Sachs and, 56, 105–106, 191, 196, 225, 278
- Madoff and, 96
- rating agencies and, 38, 67, 136, 140, 145, 156–157, 161, 166, 173–174, 187–188, 206, 211, 225, 331

securitization, 44, 72, 86, 96, 130, 133, 139, 171, 212, 221, 304, 323
- CFS and, 151–152, 154, 181

fraud in, 17–18, 26, 56, 66, 102–103, 124–126, 132, 135, 141–142, 160–161, 166, 177, 216, 294, 306
as Ponzi scheme, 17, 25–26, 38–39, 56, 95, 97, 100, 102, 123, 135, 141–142, 161, 195–196, 277
rating agencies and, 18, 27, 38–39, 56, 99–100, 102–103, 117, 121, 132, 140–142, 144–147, 150–152, 154–155, 159–161, 164, 166–170, 177, 181–185, 188, 336
segregated customer accounts, 18, 81, 125, 243, 246, 253, 258–262, 264–265, 268
Shiller, Robert, 123–126, 292
short selling, 68, 82, 84, 86–87, 90, 108, 117, 136, 139, 160, 255, 265, 322, 325, 329
SIGTARP, 36, 44, 48, 51–53, 58–59, 211, 226
silver, 79, 308, 314
certificates, 91–93
Hunt brothers and, 85, 88–90, 266–267
price manipulation and, 90–93, 103
See also gold
60 Minutes, 121, 123–124, 231–234
Sloan, Allan, 41, 82, 162
Societe Generale, 35–36, 50–51, 192, 213, 220, 321, 329
Sokol, David, 203–204, 206–207
See also Buffett, Warren; Berkshire Hathaway
Sommers, Jill E., 260–261, 270
sovereign debt, 82, 88, 143, 169, 172, 198, 238–239, 243, 249, 259–261, 269, 314–315, 337
sovereign ratings, 143, 168–169
Spain, 169, 235, 237, 249–250
Spitzer, Eliot, 137
Standard & Poor's (S&P), 105, 135, 139–141, 146–155, 157–158, 162, 173–174, 180–181, 188, 223, 234, 292, 308
See also rating agencies
Stockman, Michael, 244, 253
stranguflation, 18, 201, 274, 276, 287, 307
stress tests, 25, 27, 166
Structured Finance and Collateralized Debt Obligations (Tavakoli), 18, 137, 146, 229
structured investment vehicles (SIVs), 99, 132, 160, 167, 278
subprime mortgages, 38, 49, 64–65, 106, 151, 158–159, 162–163, 167–168, 215, 220, 222, 225, 227, 277–278, 293, 303–304
losses on, 25, 34, 59, 67, 161, 165–166, 191, 229
Summers, Larry, 55
super senior tranches, 33–34, 47, 51, 54, 63, 65–66, 102–103, 109, 118, 142, 145, 148–149, 161, 174–175, 214, 222, 338–339
systemic risk, 22, 39, 45, 49, 59, 72, 99, 101–102, 133–134, 226, 252, 263, 280, 313

T

Taleb, Nassim Nicholas, 114–115
black swan funds and, 104, 110–113, 118–119
Colbert interview of, 113
Universa trade and, 104
See also black swan
TARP. *See* Troubled Asset Relief Program
Tavakoli Structured Finance, 36, 139, 226, 331
taxpayers, 24–25, 37–38, 62, 69, 95, 131, 192–193, 197, 199, 217, 233, 268, 274, 277, 292, 294, 297
AIG bailout and, 17, 22, 29–30, 53–54, 56–57, 72, 80, 105–106, 130, 138, 211–214, 221–222
bailout costs borne by, 17–18, 21, 27, 29–30, 53, 55, 67, 80, 100, 129–130, 133, 138–139, 170,

198, 201, 211–214, 221–222, 262, 270–272, 279, 296, 306
Fed funding and, 21, 27–28, 30, 56–57, 72, 104, 122–123, 170, 213–214, 218, 275, 296
Teitelbaum, Richard, 73, 254–255, 258
too big to fail, 17, 30, 70, 90, 104, 209, 231, 275, 280
total return swaps, 160, 183–184, 210, 230, 243, 245–246, 248–249
Treasury Secretary. *See* Geithner, Timothy; Paulson, Henry (Hank)
Treasury, U.S. Department of the, 21, 80, 83, 96, 101, 171, 217, 231, 239, 255–257, 313–314
AIG and, 40–42, 45–46, 50–51, 55, 161–162, 211, 214–215, 219
Goldman Sachs and, 23, 41, 45–46, 50–51, 53, 55, 72, 115, 162, 211, 214, 219, 222, 225, 271, 278
See also Geithner, Timothy; Paulson, Henry (Hank)
Troubled Asset Relief Program (TARP), 17, 21, 36, 38, 44, 48, 51–53, 58–59, 65, 67, 71, 80, 83, 118, 130, 211, 215–216, 226, 258, 273, 291, 296, 307

U

UBS, 46, 50, 83, 227, 311, 319, 327
unemployment, 28, 55, 173, 193, 198, 273–275, 279, 286, 292, 296–297, 312
United Kingdom, 29, 85, 101–102, 168, 200, 216, 322
Universa Investments, 104–105

V

van der Sloot, Joran, 37, 235
Vernon Capital, 63
Viniar, David, 43, 46–47, 49
Volcker, Paul, 90, 102, 209, 218
Hunt brothers and, 85, 88
reform proposals of, 29, 85, 88–89, 217

W

Wachovia, 50, 52, 65, 227
Wall Street Journal, 26, 33–35, 37, 40–43, 59, 64, 76, 95, 104–107, 112, 161, 165, 191–192, 202–203, 209, 211, 227–229, 295, 314
Warren, Elizabeth, 38, 122, 126, 198, 201
Washington Mutual, 64, 277
Weil, Jonathan, 206–207
Wells Fargo, 64–65, 200, 277, 294, 306–307
Whitney, Meredith
AIG and, 107, 118, 232
Citigroup call of, 107–108, 117, 232
death threats and, 117–118
municipal bond predictions of, 232–234
Winkelried, Jon, 48

Z

ZeroHedge, 120, 201
Ziman, Kenneth, 247, 262
Zuckerberg, Mark, 75, 77

Made in United States
Orlando, FL
11 November 2026

90609402R00210